John M Browning

John M. Browning, 1855-1926

JOHN M. BROWNING

◆ AMERICAN GUNMAKER ◆

An Illustrated Biography

of the Man and His Guns

by John Browning and Curt Gentry

with Postscript by Col. W.R. Betz

CONTENTS

Illustrations   v

Preface   vii

Part One: The Father   1

Part Two: The Son   23

Part Three: The Man   73

Part Four: The Guns   223

Notes   305

Bibliography   311

Index   313

Postscript   325

Postscript Illustrations   327

Postscript Bibliography   391

ILLUSTRATIONS

John M. Browning, 1855-1926, *frontispiece*

Jonathan Browning's home and the first Browning gunsmith shop, *page 7*

Jonathan Browning's slide gun, *page 10*

John Moses Browning's Superposed Shotgun, *page 11*

Jonathan Browning's home in Nauvoo, Illinois, *page 16*

Jonathan Browning's early repeating rifles, *page 19*

Map of the Mormon exodus, *page 21*

Jonathan Browning, gunmaker, Mormon pioneer, and sire of twenty-two children, *page 28*

Jonathan Browning's lathe, *page 42*

John M. Browning at eighteen, *page 55*

Patent-application model for John M. Browning's single-shot rifle, *page 6*

John M. Browning's experimental single-shot rifle, *page 61*

Rachel Teresa Child at eighteen, before becoming the wife of John M. Browning, *page 63*

John M. Browning's first firearm patent, *pages 64-66*

The Browning Bros. Factory, Ogden, Utah Territory, *page 87*

T. G. Bennett, Winchester Repeating Arms Company, *page 98*

John M. Browning at about thirty, *page 105*

Matt Browning in his mid-twenties, *page 106*

Production model of Winchester 1886 Lever Action Repeating Rifle, *page 108*

Ogden newspaper advertisement, *page 109*

Original and production models of Browning arms, *pages 113-116*

The Four B's, Utah's premier live-bird team, *page 119*

"The most popular hunting rifle ever built—bar none!", *page 125*

The Winchester 1895 Lever Action Repeating Rifle, *page 132*

Browning's machine-gun-belt loading device, *page 135*

Artist's sketch of John M. Browning's first gas-operated experimental model, *page 146*

Letter from Browning to Colt, *page 149*

Original model of John M. Browning's first gas-operated machine gun, c. 1890-91, *page 152*

John M. Browning with his Colt 1895 "Peacemaker," first automatic machine gun purchased by the government, *page 161*

Two of the world's best-known military arms: the Browning Automatic Rifle and the Government .45 Caliber Automatic Pistol; World War II production models, *page 166*

Formal portrait of John M. Browning with 1917 .30 Caliber Water Cooled Machine Gun, *page 168*

Browning Automatic Machine Guns, an essential part of United States military power since World War I, *pages 173-175*

John M. Browning testing his .50-caliber machine gun in Hartford, *page 177*

Skilled artisan in Liege, Belgium, engraving receiver of one of the Browning arms, *page 182*

Fabrique Nationale d'Armes de Guerre, Liége, *page 187*

The Browning shop in Ogden shortly after the turn of the century, *page 188*

John M. Browning's workbench, *page 189*

John M. Browning's revolutionary automatic shotgun, *page 191*

Decorations awarded to John M. Browning, *page 200*

John M. Browning with Belgian Government and Fabrique Nationale officials *page 201*

John M. Browning with his automatic shotgun, *page 204*

Testing the 37-mm. cannon outside Ogden, March 1921, *page 209*

Preparation for official government tests of the cannon, *page 210*

John M. Browning at Aberdeen Proving Ground, *page 211*

John and Rachel Browning in 1926, *page 213*

John and Matt Browning on a big-game trip, *page 215*

The great gunmaker had laid down his tools, *page 221*

The Browning guns, *pages 225-302*

PREFACE

A bronze plaque hangs in the Fabrique Nationale d'Armes de Guerre factory in Liége, Belgium. On it is the likeness of a man: neither young nor old but balding, with a medium-full mustache, an intent, serious look, and, in the eyes and the lines of the mouth, just a hint of inner amusement. The wording on the plaque is in French. In English translation it reads:

TO THE MEMORY OF JOHN M. BROWNING 1855-1926. This is the place where, thirty years previously, he came from Ogden to have his first automatic pistol manufactured and where, on the twenty-sixth of November, 1926, while he was busily engaged at work death overtook the greatest firearms inventor the world has ever known.

"The greatest firearms inventor the world has ever known." Firearms experts don't dispute this statement; some have put it even more emphatically. And yet today, as in the inventor's own lifetime, many a hunter, a favorite Browning-designed gun in hand, might ask: Who was *John M. Browning?*

In relation to his genius, surprisingly little has been written about this remarkable man. Philip B. Sharpe, in his authoritative book *The Rifle in America,* gives one reason: "Browning was a peculiar sort of individual. He did not seem to be tremendously enthused over popularizing the name Browning . . . If his name appeared on the inventions of his manufacture the name of John M. Browning would today be more widely known than that of Henry Ford."

Most people associate the Browning name only with the Browning Automatic Rifle (the B.A.R.), the .30- and .50-caliber machine guns, and the sporting arms of the Browning Arms Company (a company formed a year after the inventor's death). Few are aware that during his lifetime the inventor took out a total of 128 patents, covering more than eighty separate and distinct firearms, and that these included many of the most famous guns produced during the past century—by Winchester, Colt, Remington, Savage, Fabrique Nationale, and others.

Among the forty-four guns Browning sold to Winchester were the Model 85 Single Shot; the Models 86, 92, 94, and 95 lever-action repeating rifles; the Models 87, 93, and 97 repeating shotguns; the Model 90 .22-caliber pump-action repeating rifle; and the Model 1900 bolt-action .22.

Browning's Remington guns included the automatic shotgun, the Model 11, later the Sportsman; the Models 8 and 81 autoloading center fire rifles; the Models 24 and 241 .22-caliber autoloading rifles; and the Model 17 20-gauge pump gun.

His Colt guns included not only the many models of his .30- and .50-caliber machine guns, and his 37-mm. aircraft cannons. All of Colt's automatic pistols, from the first produced in America in 1900 to those currently in production, including the Government .45 Caliber, the Colt Woodsman, and numerous others, are of his basic design.

The list goes on, through the complete lines of sporting arms and pistols produced by Fabrique Nationale and the Browning Arms Company, and includes the .25 Caliber Pocket Pistol, the Automatic-5, the Superposed Shotgun, and many others.

This, then, is the story of "the greatest firearms inventor the world has ever known." It is more than a "gun book," however, for John M. Browning, while often ahead of his times, was also a product of them, and exciting times they were.

Born in 1855, in the small frontier settlement of Ogden, in Utah Territory, John Moses Browning was one of twenty-two children fathered by polygamous Mormon Jonathan Browning, pioneer gunmaker, acquaintance of Abraham Lincoln, and manufacturer of many of the guns and implements used in Brigham Young's trek West. Against the backdrop of the conquest of a vast wilderness was born also the partnership of the Browning Brothers—John, Matt, Ed, Sam, and George—and the building of what has been humorously described as "the largest arms factory between Omaha and the Pacific," a crude gunshop out of which for nearly a half century came gun designs that revolutionized the fields of sporting and military arms.

The authors gratefully acknowledge the aid and assistance given by the following individuals, companies, and organizations in the research and preparation of this book: the many descendants of the Browning

Brothers, who generously gave of their time and recollections; the Browning Arms Company, Ogden, Utah, in particular Val Browning, John Val Browning, Bruce Browning, and Harmon Williams, for their invaluable help and complete co-operation; the Winchester Gun Museum and the Winchester-Western Division of the Olin Mathieson Chemical Corporation, New Haven, Connecticut, in particular Thomas H. Hall and Bill Trimble; Colt's Patent Fire Arms Manufacturing Company, Hartford, Connecticut, in particular Fred A. Roff, Jr., Charles H. Coles, George Perloto, and Ronald H. Wagner; Fabrique Nationale d'Armes de Guerre, Liege, Belgium; The Remington Arms Company, Bridgeport, Connecticut; The National Rifle Association, Washington, D.C., in particular Walter J. Howe, Major General Julian S. Hatcher, M. D. Waite, and L. E. Olson; George M. Chinn, Lieutenant Colonel, USMC, Ret., Frankfort, Kentucky; Clarence Adney, Visalia, California; T. R. Walker, John M. Browning Memorial Museum, Rock Island Arsenal, Rock Island, Illinois; Leo Carten, Pentagon, Washington, D.C.; C. R. Goins, Smithsonian Institution, Washington, D.C.; R. C. Kuhn, Lieutenant Colonel, USAFR, Ret., Chicago, Illinois; S. Gordon Green, Colonel, USA, Ret., Gray, Georgia; the John M. Browning Armory, Ogden, Utah; the Historical Division of the Church of Jesus Christ of Latter-Day Saints, Salt Lake City, Utah; Richard Dillon, Sutro Library, San Francisco, California; and George Goldfine, 6th U. S. Army Reference Library, Presidio of San Francisco, California.

The following authors and publishers generously granted permission to quote from the works indicated: Combat Forces Press, Harold F. Williamson, *Winchester: The Gun That Won the West;* Deseret Books Company, Joseph Fielding Smith, *Essentials in Church History;* Funk and Wagnalls, Philip B. Sharpe, *The Rifle in America;* McGraw-Hill, Levin H. Campbell, Jr., Lieutenant General, *The Industry-ordnance Team;* Military Service Publishing Company, Julian S. Hatcher, Major General, USA, Ret., *Hatcher's Notebook;* Serven Books, James E. Serven, *Colt Firearms;* and Superintendent of Documents, U. S. Government Printing Office, George M. Chinn, Lieutenant Colonel, USMC, *The Machine Gun: History, Evolution and Development of Manual, Automatic and Repeating Weapons, Vol. I.*

JOHN BROWNING AND CURT GENTRY

PART ONE

THE FATHER

GUNSMITHING

The subscriber is prepared to manufacture, to order, improved Fire-arms, viz: revolving rifles and pistols; also slide guns, from 5 to 25 shooters. All on an improved plan, and he thinks not equalled this far East. (Farther west they might be.) The emigrating and sporting community are invited to call and examine Browning's improved fire-arms before purchasing elsewhere. Shop eight miles south of Kanesville on Musquito Creek, half a mile south of TRADING POINT.

JONATHAN BROWNING

Advertisement in the *Frontier Guardian*,
Kanesville, Iowa, September 19, 1849.

1

JONATHAN BROWNING was born October 22, 1805, at Brushy Fork of Bledsoe Creek in Sumner County, Tennessee.

Sumner County lies toward the middle and along the northern boundaries of Tennessee. The topography is varied: level valleys; gently undulating uplands that rise into hills, many of them too steep for cultivation; numerous creeks, each with a historic name, pouring their flood into the beautiful Cumberland River. To the east are the foothills of the far-stretching Cumberland Mountains, and, farther beyond but in clear view, the towering mountains themselves.

Today there are well-cultivated farms, fields of waving grain, orchards producing in abundance most of the fruits that can be grown in a temperate climate, pastures in which well-bred horses and cattle stand knee deep in bluegrass. There is one sizable city in the county, the river port of Gallatin, and Nashville is just one county away.

Bledsoe Creek has its source in the hills of the northern part of the county. It is a moody creek, often slow, almost sleeping in the shade of overhanging trees and vines—suddenly awake, alive, and rushing through the sunlit hills on its way to the great river. Prehistoric Indians built a large community on the creek, at a place later called Bledsoe Lick, not far from the bend known as Brushy Fork. The hills and forests around the creek supplied wildlife in abundance. Countless buffalo, deer, and elk fed on the wild succulent grasses in the valley; bear, wolf, and catamount roamed the dark forests. The creek itself was crystal-clear, a source of good, clean water. Small patches of land were cleared for the raising of corn. Since time out of mind the area had been a favored hunting ground. It is not surprising that the Indians fought so hard to retain it.

When the first white explorers came about 1765 they saw an unbroken wilderness, the home of wild beasts and the haunt of wilder men, and they moved on. But the East was moving West. The first settlers arrived about 1779, few at first but before long in increasingly large numbers. They were mainly from North Carolina and Virginia, with some from Pennsylvania and South Carolina. Most were men of obscure birth, accustomed to poverty, though there were others more prosperous, even a few families with slaves. Nearly all the men were fresh from the battlefields of the Revolution. Few brought extensive provisions, but almost without exception they carried the rifles and muskets with which they had helped to win independence for their country. Most of them cleared and farmed land given them by land warrants for their services in the war. At first the Indians avoided them, but when it became plain that the intruders intended to stay, the tribesmen defended their land. Between 1787 and 1793 eighty-three settlers in the county are known to have been killed by Indians. The number of Indian dead is not recorded.

Edmund Browning, Jonathan's father, was born November 14, 1761, in Culpeper County, Virginia, the descendant of a long line that went back to Captain John Browning, who came to America in 1622 aboard the *Abigail* and established one of the first families of Virginia. Following the war Edmund married and moved to Tennessee with his new bride, cutting out a small farm near Brushy Fork. The seven children of Edmund and Sarah Browning were born here. Edmund was a strong but gentle man, given as much to reflection as to farming. He was also a fine violinist, and the only harshness that Jonathan knew as a child came from the land.

An old Sumner County history notes: "From the beginning the men of the county were in constant peril. They seldom ventured from their homes without arms . . ." Every home by necessity had a gun. Other than providing the bare essentials of living, the farms were not success-ful. However there was much game, and Jonathan probably learned to shoot almost as soon as he was old enough to shoulder a musket.

There was no school, no church, no community as such, only a number of widely scattered farms. Jonathan's early education was self-directed. At the age of thirteen or fourteen he was given an old flintlock rifle for a week's work on a neighbor's farm. He later recalled it was the only enthusiastic farming he ever did. Since the gun did not work and there was no gunsmith closer than Nashville, the farmer had discarded the gun as worthless. It was left hanging in a shed, where Jonathan spied it.

About a mile from the Browning farm was the shop of a good-natured blacksmith. From hanging around the shop and watching the smith at work, Jonathan progressed naturally into lending a hand. The smith wasn't averse to using this "big chunk of a boy" who could use his head as well as his hands.

When the smith saw the old gun, he thought, like the farmer, that his helper had made a poor bargain. But as the results of the boy's tinkering began to appear he gradually changed his mind. When Jonathan sold the gun back to the farmer for four dollars, cash, he was visibly impressed.

Out of the transaction Jonathan got an idea and working capital. He placated his easygoing father by doing his chores on the farm early in the morning and late at night. In the intervening hours he worked with the smith; for remuneration he received the freedom of the shop, a dollar now and then, or a sack of corn. The smith himself was paid more often with produce than with cash. Jonathan expanded the smith's business, along with his own knowledge, by combing the countryside on horseback, gathering repair jobs. There was no competition for miles around. In the shop he learned the fundamentals of hand-forging, welding, brazing, tempering, and soldering, before long becoming a pretty fair blacksmith. He never liked to shoe a horse or ox or shrink on a tire, but he could do it. In later years these knacks, by preventing long delays, were to save lives.

By the time he was nineteen Jonathan considered himself a competent gunsmith. Of course he had never seen a gunsmith, but he had repaired a lot of guns, using tools of his own design.[1] He was also earning his living and saving money. As his increasing skill with tools stimulated his imagination, he began to think of making guns as well as repairing them. The mechanisms did not bother him; they were so simple, he would later say, that all it took was a little figuring. But he did need lessons in the making of barrels. His vague plan took form when he was shown a gun bearing the stamp of Samuel Porter, Nashville. He examined it with unusual care before handing it back to its owner.

A few days later he borrowed one of his father's horses and jogged off to Nashville, some thirty miles away. He did not bother to send notice of his coming. It was easier for him to make the trip than to write a letter. He was sure he could get along with the gunmaker, just as he had with the blacksmith.

Jonathan at nineteen was over six feet tall and well muscled. He prepared himself for the meeting by setting a serious face and forging a calm self-confidence. But the moment he entered Porter's shop he forgot his act, unable to hide his amazement. He could not imagine uses for so many tools! Actually the shop was crude, as were all frontier shops, but by Jonathan's standards it was all a mechanic could ask for on earth.

Perhaps it was his intentness that won Porter's immediate approval. Jonathan stated the purpose of his visit, in his slow manner of speaking; he had repaired a good many guns, and nearly everything else, and proposed to do, as well as he could, whatever Porter might set him to, in exchange for lessons in the making of barrels. If Porter harbored any doubts they were probably dispelled by Jonathan's offer to forego wages. Asking only for an opportunity to observe and in due time to hammer out a barrel or two, he made it clear that he was not seeking a permanent job. His lessons learned, he intended to return home and set up his own shop.

The two shook hands, and Jonathan set to work, with no more ado than taking off his hat and coat and rolling up his sleeves. Within a short while Porter began paying him two dollars a week, which he was able to save, since his employer also gave him his meals and the use of a hayloft.

At the end of three months, Jonathan announced that he was ready to leave. Porter urged him to stay on, promising him a share of the business, arguing that Nashville was a growing town, with possibilities for a young man, while the region of Bledsoe Creek would never be more than a scattering of starving farms.

Jonathan was probably tempted. But he had got what he came for; he could, Sam had to confess, "make a pretty good barrel," and there was, in addition to his parents, a girl back at Brushy Fork.

The two men, friends by then, said good-by reluctantly. Jonathan's earlier savings, plus the money Porter had paid him, had already been converted into tools. In addition, as a parting gift, Sam gave him some boring and rifling tools, plus several mandrels of different calibers, used in the hand-forging of barrels. As Jonathan later told it, he reached the end of his savings and the carrying capacity of his horse about the same time.

Nearing home he stopped and shot a few squirrels, to make sure there would be more than cornpone and sorghum in the house when he arrived.

He was to remember the afternoon of his ride home from Nashville as one of the pleasantest times of his life.

To crease a squirrel, to leave that red line on the skull that is the stamp of the expert; to be nineteen and, he believed, the master of his own fate, returning to a girl he intended to marry and a business he intended to create—these were very real pleasures to be sure. But even more important was the knowledge that he had gone to Nashville a tinkerer and was returning a gunsmith. As proof, the rifle he carried was one to which he had fitted a barrel made entirely with his own hands. On it Sam had slyly stamped JONATHAN BROWNING 1824.

2

JONATHAN SETTLED DOWN to making guns. He acquired a small house to live in, as well as a shed which he used for a shop. On November 9, 1826, a month after he became twenty-one, he married Elizabeth Stalcup. Their first child was born in August of the following year.

Jonathan Browning's home (right) and the first Browning gunsmith shop (left), Brushy Fork, Bledsoe Creek, Sumner County, Tennessee. The young gunsmith lived and worked here from 1824 to 1834.　　JOHN M. BROWNING ARMORY

Jonathan possessed the rare ability to concentrate, coupled with an exceptional mechanical talent. Both gave him an armor against the arrows of circumstance. The new family had little in the way of possessions other than Jonathan's tools. No one in the vicinity had much more. During this period Jonathan threw all his energies into the shop. With scant equipment he made the most of his opportunities. To make and repair guns seemed fulfillment enough.

His working habits and the increase in his family, with attendant responsibilities, might have kept him in Brushy Fork for the rest of his life had not the population of that region begun to move away. Reports, more and more enticing, were singing siren songs of the West; there was land, limitless land, free for the taking. Families, singly or in parties, abandoned their worn-out farms and departed. Jonathan was splashed, then soon drenched, by the swelling stream that passed his shop. At first his business did not diminish but grew: no man set forth on such a venture without a perfect gun, either his old gun repaired or a new gun hammered out with incredible speed. Hammer marks might be left on the rifles he turned out, but the lands and grooves were clean-cut, the locks worked smoothly.[2]

But Jonathan was making plans as well as guns. Self-preservation, if nothing else, forced him to join the exodus. Before long he found himself considering the move with growing excitement. Several of his brothers moved away, then his parents. Jonathan especially felt the loss of one of his younger brothers, a cooper by trade and a mainstay of the early shop; but his brother agreed to keep his eyes open and write Jonathan as soon as he found a likely location for a gunsmith.

In September 1833, Jonathan received word that his father had died in Wayne County, Illinois, at the age of seventy-three. Several months later a happier letter arrived, an enthusiastic message from Quincy, Illinois: a good location had been found.

Jonathan closed the shop, then loaded two wagons with his family and the contents of shop and home. Accompanied by a young cousin, they set out for Quincy.

From Brushy Fork to Quincy was about 400 miles, a good journey for that time. It may be imagined that Jonathan and his family took longer than most to travel the distance, for it is only a slight exaggeration to say that passing through the communities along the way Jonathan heard no new metallic sound without stopping to investigate, that he visited most of the shops he saw, often picking up a new knack, another skill to be developed and used, and probably adding another tool to the weight of the wagons.

He had plenty of time for reflection and thought about the future. It was perhaps best that he could not see too far into it, for waiting there, among other things, were persecution, murder, hardship, repeated exodus, and the taming of a land much harsher than Sumner County. The four hundred miles would be only the start, the first quarter of his eventual wandering. That he would in time be the father of one of the world's greatest gun inventors would probably have seemed more believable to him than the knowledge that this family too was only a start, that while now, at twenty-eight, he had a wife and five children, before his death he would have three wives and twenty-two children, eleven boys and eleven girls, the last child born when Jonathan himself was seventy-one years old.

3

QUINCY, favorably located on the Mississippi, was small but flourishing. The population of the city in 1834, the year of the Browning family's arrival, was 753; that of Adams County, in which Quincy was located, was 7042. Within a few years both figures would double, then triple.

In Quincy, Jonathan had the advice of relatives and friends, but beyond that he needed little help. His savings were ample to provide him with a home as good as the one he had left; his new shop was much better.

Jonathan and his neighbors had advanced a whole generation in their migration from Brushy Fork to the Father of Waters. Placid habits could not survive without the old, shambling rail fences to lean upon. Here everything was new: buildings, plans, ambitions. There was excitement in men's voices; it showed on their faces and spread contagiously. During this period Jonathan invented a repeating rifle, one of the first. The exact year is not remembered.[3]

He was one of many gunsmiths, in many countries, who, stimulated by the novelty and seductive superiority of the percussion cap, were struggling to produce a multi-shot rifle. Jonathan, in his first attempts, simply adapted the cylinder of the cap-and-ball revolver to actions of his own devising, as others were doing. The precision work required to make a cylinder, accurately locate the chambers, and obtain a tight fit against the bore, overtaxed both his shop facilities and his patience. He made a number of these guns, despite the difficulties.

Yet Jonathan was not satisfied. What he really wanted was an efficient repeating rifle that could be hammered out easily and rapidly. It looked like a big order, and it was. His fancy was permitted no soaring flights, but was confined to the narrow confines of the shop, limited by forge, anvil, vise, foot lathe, and the hand tools that littered his bench.

What he finally brought forth is, in all probability, one of the simplest practical repeating rifles ever made. It is doubtful if any other rifle of its kind ever contained so few parts, all of which can be easily made and assembled. Today it is a curio; in its own time it was capable of continuous fire unequaled by any contemporary arm.[4] The rifle brought considerable local fame to its inventor, plus so many orders that he was never able to fill more than half of them. The system, which Jonathan did not bother to patent, would doubtlessly have been widely used had not the metallic cartridge replaced the percussion cap, just as the cap replaced the flintlock.

The magazine of this gun is simply a rectangular bar, chambered for powder and ball, with cut-in nipples integral with the metal, one at the rear end of each chamber. The length of the magazine, and its consequent capacity, is limited by convenience. Jonathan considered five shots about right, although he frequently made magazines of greater capacity to special order. At least one extra magazine was sold with each gun.

The Father: A close-up of Jonathan Browning's slide gun, one of the earliest American repeating rifles, invented by Jonathan while he was residing in Quincy, Illinois, during the period 1834-42. Note the extreme simplicity of the mechanism.   ROCK ISLAND ARSENAL

The receiver is a frame which houses the magazine, and on which the hammer and trigger are hung. Everything is in plain sight. An ingenious small lever, thumb-operated, moves the magazine to successive firing positions, not only locking it but camming it forward to a gastight fit against the bore of the barrel. The receiver is tapped at one end for the barrel; side plates, hand-forged in one piece with the receiver and nicely finished, hold the stock.

Jonathan loved simplicity and despised complexity, attitudes he passed along to his sons and which he brought to concrete expression in this gun. Moving the hammer from its conventional position on top of the receiver he hung it on the bottom, letting it swing upward to fire. The trigger guard he tempered to serve as mainspring.

The Son: The Superposed Shotgun, invented by Jonathan's son, John Moses Browning, in 1925; one of more than eighty firearms designed by the Ogden, Utah, inventor. Wild fowl, not buffalos and Indians, are its targets. Browning Diana grade 20 gauge, current production model.   BROWNING ARMS COMPANY

Jonathan was energetic, and his business thrived. He now entered a period of comfortable prosperity.[5] He was able to build a new home of logs, spacious and comfortable. He invested in land. When he had time to sit, he could sit under his own "vine and fig tree" and talk with men of varied experience. Quincy grew and with it Jonathan's knowledge and outlook on life. At the insistence of his cousin Orville Browning, he ran for and was elected justice of the peace, which office gave him the title of judge and a certain standing in the community. By the time he was thirty-five he had eight children.

Orville H. Browning was one of a number of Brownings residing in the vicinity of Quincy. Jonathan took particular pride in this young cousin from the Kentucky branch of the widely scattered family, who was already well established in politics and the practice of law.[6] He saw Orville often, and through him made the acquaintance of another young lawyer by the name of Lincoln. Orville, whose home was too small to accommodate a guest, twice brought his friend to Jonathan's home for the night.

The first of these occasions stuck very clearly in Jonathan's mind; it was more than a twice-told tale years later, when Jonathan repeated it to his sons. Allowing for the passage of time, which is perhaps too kind to some recollections, we must also note that Jonathan, while he had imagination and a fine sense of humor, was not given to exaggeration. It probably occurred much as his sons remember his telling it.

On this night Jonathan and Abraham had the evening to themselves. With chairs tilted comfortably against opposite walls of the kitchen, they chatted of one thing and another. The two had more in common than their height. Their birthplaces were not far apart— Tennessee and Kentucky; neither had spent a full year in school, and although Mr. Lincoln was more fluent in speech, he used the same easy words. Orville was different. He had a fine education, and it was already apparent to Jonathan that he would make a name for himself. But young Mr. Lincoln . . .

"Judge," he said, one thing leading to another, "somebody told me that a youngster in the neighborhood broke his arm yesterday and you set it. Do you fix anything that breaks—plow, gun, bone?" He smiled broadly.

Jonathan grinned back. "Well, a doctor would have charged a dollar for the job, but I couldn't charge a neighbor for setting a bone any more than for helping him pull his wagon out of a mudhole. Fact is, I nearly turned doctor one time. When I was learning to read, and poking all around the countryside to find a book or two to practice on, I picked up a doctor book. Traded a gun for it that I'd fixed up. Fact is, that's the way I got my first Bible—traded a gun for it."

Mr. Lincoln slapped his leg, and the chair snapped upright. "Now, hold on, judge~ Give me a minute to figure that one out. I want to laugh, but I don't quite see the point. It's tangled up in my mind with the saying about turning swords into plowshares, or is it pruning hooks?"

"Plowshares," Jonathan answered. "Isaiah."

"Well, that's what you did in a way, turned a gun into a Bible. But the other fellow—he canceled you out by turning a Bible into a gun. Looks like the trade left the world just about where it was."

The two men enjoyed a chuckle.

"Well," Jonathan said after a moment, "there was something else funny about that trade. To tell the truth, the mainspring in that old gun was pretty weak, and the stock . . ."

Lincoln interrupted with an upraised hand. "Judge Browning!" he rebuked, in an exaggerated courtroom manner. "You mean that you cheated in a trade for a Bible—a *Bible!*"

"Not exactly," Jonathan replied, his face as sober as Abraham's. "When I got to looking through that Bible at home, I found about half the New Testament was missing."

The mirth of the two frontiersmen, as Jonathan later described it, "near to shook the logs." When they had both stopped laughing, Jonathan rose.

"Mr. Lincoln," he said, "I hate to end a pleasant evening like this, but you'll be wanting some sleep, I reckon. I'll light a candle for you. There's a water bucket and dipper, and your bed is right through this door. I hope you'll find it comfortable."

Mr. Lincoln stepped to the corner and took the dipper from its nail. "I hope your little patient is comfortable tonight."

"He'll be strutting around in a day or two with his arm in a sling. Nice, clean break."

"It's a fine life you're leading here, judge," Lincoln said thoughtfully, "mending anything that breaks. Looks funny at first glimpse to see a man welding a broken gun part for a farmer one day and next day setting a bone for the farmer's son. But the two jobs are somewhat alike."

"No difference," Jonathan smiled, "except that the bonesetting's a lot easier. Nature does most of that welding. But if it's two pieces of iron, you've got to blow up the forge and pound. Nature won't help with that."

Lincoln nodded soberly. "Hammer and hammer," he repeated, swinging the dipper to and fro. "I can't weld, but I've seen it done. Heat and hammer, heat and hammer. Whatever man makes, man breaks. And then somebody must mend. Judge Browning, there's a lot of mending to be done in these United States—a lot of mending."

He swung the dipper like a hammer, striking the palm of his left hand with such force that Jonathan expected the handle to snap. A quick smile of apology crossed his face; then the voice continued, quieter now.

"I've knocked about a good deal—even made a couple trips down the River on a flatboat, clear to New Orleans. And wherever I go, I hear sounds of little things breaking, and I see big things bending danger-ously near to it. You see the signs all around you, hear the sounds. Fact is, I'm so worried that I have nightmares, and not all of them when I'm asleep. I get plain scared to death when I look a few years ahead."

For a long time he seemed to be doing just that, trying to look into the future. Jonathan nodded politely, but he was puzzled and worried too. He wondered if his guest was going into one of those moody spells Orville had mentioned. But with another swing of the dipper the shaggy giant continued.

"Judge Browning, the United States ought to become the greatest country on earth. But what if the hotheads break it in two, right down the middle? That would be a welding job! It would need the fires of the inferno for the forge. And where is the anvil? Where is the hammer? Where is the blacksmith?"

The swinging dipper struck the low ceiling, and again an apologetic smile touched the rugged face. "It was the talk of your bonesetting and welding that started me off, judge; maybe I'm just seeing stumps and gnarled limbs in the dark, and imagining bears. Hope so."

He took a drink of water, accepted the lighted candle, and stepped toward his room.

"Good night, Judge Browning, and many thanks for your hospitality."

"Good night, Mr. Lincoln."

"That's about the way it happened," Jonathan would say, some thirty years later in Utah. "Two frontiersmen yarning. Only I'm just beginning to realize that I was listening to prophecy."

4

IN QUINCY, Jonathan again seemed to have found his place and to be permanently rooted. During his middle thirties, however, he became interested in religion, with more ramifications than he could possibly have foreseen.

He had long been interested in religion as a generality. Had there been a church of any denomination within easy reach of Brushy Fork, it probably would have drawn him into its fold. The same could be said of his father and of his old friend the blacksmith, each of whom read his Bible daily (and not much else), a habit carried over from preceding generations of churchgoers.

In a sense, Jonathan grew up with the Mormon Church, though knowing nothing of it. Jonathan and Joseph Smith had been born in the same year, 1805, Jonathan in Tennessee, Smith in Vermont. Jonathan repaired his first gun at thirteen or fourteen; when he was fifteen, Joseph Smith had the first of the many visions which were to become the foundation for the Church of Jesus Christ of Latter-Day Saints. Except for his trip to Nashville, Jonathan had spent his first twenty-eight years in Brushy Fork, learning to be a gunsmith. By the same age Joseph Smith had resided in a number of states, had founded the fastest-growing church in the United States, and had been set upon by mobs in both Ohio and Missouri.

The main cause of much of the early Mormon persecution was not the Church's religious or matrimonial beliefs. Smith was intent upon founding his own religious community, and such a community, wherever it settled, constituted a formidable voting block. Inevitably it became involved in local politics and disputes over slavery and states' rights.

In 1839 Joseph Smith escaped from the jail at Liberty, Missouri, where he had been imprisoned unjustly, and fled across the Mississippi. Here, on the Illinois side of the river, about halfway down the state, only a few miles from both Missouri and Iowa, the Mormons built a new community, which Smith christened Nauvoo. At first no one begrudged them their presence or the land, which was a dismal swamp. Within a year they had filled in the swamp and turned Nauvoo into a model city, perfectly laid out in large neat squares, with over 250 houses and the cornerstone for a new temple laid and dedicated. Converts began to arrive in large numbers.

Forty-three miles to the south lay Quincy. The Mormons being a proselytizing people, then as now, with missionaries already in England and Europe, Quincy was not long immune to their attention.

Sometime in the year 1840, while the city of Nauvoo was still under construction, a Mormon came into Jonathan's shop with a repair job. Like most of his fellows, he was fired with zeal. Encouraged by Jonathan's interest, he returned the next day with some tracts and a copy of the Book of Mormon, asking Jonathan's permission to call at his home some evening to clarify any points of doctrine that might seem obscure.

Jonathan read, at first idly, soon with concentration; and through his scant and foggy knowledge of dogma and precept, he began to see a light. As continued reading and long discussions with his widening circle of Mormon friends caused that light to grow brighter, he seemed to perceive a clearly marked road to salvation, a map, in effect, to guide a man through the wilderness of life to the gates of heaven. Saul of Tarsus saw a light and followed it. Jonathan Browning also saw a light, which he followed through more than a decade of hardship and danger, and which finally led him across the Great Plains to Utah.

Deserted by necessity, the Nauvoo, Illinois, home that was Jonathan Browning's between 1842 and 1846. The first floor served as the Browning Gun Shop. The mob violence which followed the murder of the Mormon prophet, Joseph Smith, forced the Latter-Day Saints to abandon their homes and flee westward across the Mississippi ice.   JOHN M. BROWNING ARMORY

In 1842, Jonathan again sold his property, loaded his family and belongings into several wagons, and moved to Nauvoo. Again he set up shop—building on Main Street a two-story brick residence, with the first floor serving as his shop—and began the manufacture and repair of guns. But there was little time for inventing new weapons. Though the new temple on which Jonathan frequently worked was well under construction and the city itself the fastest growing in the country, these were not creative times. Each day new converts arrived, bringing, in addition to the endless repair jobs, new tales of hardship. There were repeated attempts on the life of the Prophet, as well as the ever present threat of mob violence. Several times Smith was arrested, tried, and released; the courts were used as a weapon of harassment.

When Jonathan and his family first arrived in Nauvoo, the Prophet would stop and talk to the people he met on the street. Now, even when he addressed the members in church, there were armed men near or around him. When Joseph Smith and his brother Hyrum were arrested on June 25, 1844, and lodged in the jail at Carthage, Illinois, on an unfounded charge of treason against the state of Illinois, most of the Mormons were not particularly fearful; such things had happened before, ending each time with Smith's release. Moreover their fears were lulled by a promise of protection from the governor, Thomas Ford. Late in the afternoon of Friday, June 27, a mob of more than two hundred men, armed with rocks, boards, muskets, revolvers, and bayonets, surrounded the jail. That evening a horseman galloped into Nauvoo, some eighteen miles from Carthage, crying that the Prophet and his brother had been assassinated.

In the days that followed, the Mormons were rescued from panic and possible dispersal by Brigham Young, who, with a rare combination of zeal and common sense, gave himself to the task of restoring faith and confidence. From the very first it was evident to Young that the Mormons could not find peace within the United States. As mob violence continued, the church leaders began making plans for an exodus from Illinois. Jonathan himself did not often speak of this period, but it is not difficult to imagine his activity in the following paragraph from Joseph Fielding Smith's *Essentials in Church History:*

"In the meantime every available building in Nauvoo had been converted into a shop where wagons, harness and other necessary articles could be manufactured for the journey. The timber for the wagons was cut and brought to Nauvoo, where it was prepared and boiled in salt and water or kiln dried. Teams were sent to various parts of the country to procure iron; and blacksmiths, wheelwrights, carpenters and other workmen were kept busy night and day. There was very little sale of property because of the opposition of the citizens of the country, who used their influence to discourage sales by making threats against the new settlers as well as harassing the Saints."[7]

Brigham Young had planned to make the move in the spring of 1846, but attacks by Illinois and Missouri mobs forced the Mormons to leave early that February, fleeing across the Mississippi on the ice, with a bare fraction of their possessions. Jonathan got nothing for his home and shop. Only a few of the Saints were of hardy pioneer stock; a great many of the converts from the eastern states, England, and Wales were city dwellers. For nearly a month they camped at Sugar Creek, on the Iowa side of the river, until threats of renewed persecution forced them to move on. Again according to Smith:

"March 1, 1846, camp was broken and the journey was resumed. The weather was extremely cold and stormy, and a great number of the people were without proper clothing and necessary shelter. Many of the wagons were without covers, and others had covers which would not shed the rain. Several members of the camps died from exposure and lack of proper care. The roads were almost impassable because of the constant storms. At this time there were some four hundred wagons on the road, heavily laden and without sufficient teams to permit of rapid travel. In this condition the exiles continued their toilsome journey over the plains of Iowa."[8]

In June they reached the banks of the Missouri. There was fresh water and some good land, and the Omaha and Pottawattamie Indians proved friendly. The Mormons settled temporarily in the vicinity, Jonathan and his family choosing a spot eight miles south of Kanesville (Council Bluffs) on Mosquito Creek.

Brigham Young was looking for a new Zion, a haven for the Saints outside the borders of the United States. Within these boundaries the church had met little but persecution; over the years the repeated appeals for protection to the state and federal governments had, except on rare occasions, been either ignored or denied. It must have surprised Young, then, when a United States Army officer arrived in July of 1846 with a message from the President of the United States, requesting four or five companies of volunteers for the war against Mexico.

Young reacted with characteristic diplomacy. He called a meeting of the Mormon men at Mosquito Creek, and, addressing the group himself, asked for five hundred volunteers.

Jonathan added himself to the line of men, but Young, directing all activities, surveyed the line; coming to the tall gunsmith, he took him by the arm and led him aside, saying in a low voice, "Brother Jonathan, we need you here."

Jonathan, obedient, but with his heels still itching, watched the Mormon battalion depart—five hundred undrilled men, who were to make one of the longest infantry marches then recorded.

The scene was to be repeated the following spring, when the first companies were formed for the move West. Again Jonathan volunteered to go with the first scouts, and again Young, who seemed to know where every man among his thousands would best fit, told him that it was his

Chosen by Brigham Young to make guns and implements for the Mormon exodus, Jonathan Browning provided the pioneers with his Slide Repeating Rifle (right), an ingenious arm whose magazine was simply a rectangular iron bar with holes to accommodate the hand loads, and his Cylinder Repeating Rifle (left), which operated on the same principle as the single-action revolver. Both arms were simply constructed, easily operated, and quite effective, whether supplying meat or protection. BROWNING ARMS COMPANY mission to remain and lend his specialized knowledge and skill to the labors of preparation.

Young's arguments were convincing. Each wagon train must be equipped not only for survival on the way, but for survival in whatever abiding place the Lord should choose. The brethren must be provided with guns; they would need every gun that could be made or obtained and made serviceable—work for which, Young noted, Jonathan had no equal. Farm implements, sawmills, gristmills, tools of every kind—all would have to be selected, inspected, and carefully packed. The leader followed on down the list to axes to be ground, knives sharpened. And he might have added, had he been less the diplomat, that Jonathan's large family, without him, would become a charge on relatives and friends.

Jonathan was again an onlooker, as the party of pathfinders and homeseekers with their wagons and handcarts creaked off into the vast, mysterious, and beckoning West.

Jonathan again established his business, manufacturing "improved Fire-arms, viz: revolving rifles and pistols; also slide guns, from 5 to 25 shooters. All on an improved plan . . ." as he worded it in the advertisement from the Kanesville *Frontier Guardian* which opens this section.

Business was good. The repeater gave the pioneers much greater protection from Indian invasion and massacre than the slow single shot. Among the most famous tales of the West are those concerning the advent of these guns. The Indians over the years had developed a simple but effective tactic. After surrounding a wagon train, several Indians would stand and charge, making themselves clear targets. The pioneers would invariably shoot their single ball; then, while they were reloading their weapons, the Indians would attack in force. Owners of early repeaters turned this trick to their own advantage. They would fire a single shot, then, when the Indians attacked, continue firing, to the fatal amazement of the red men.

On the twenty-fourth of July 1847, Young led his party of 143 down through the last canyon of the long journey. Out of the mountains, which for weeks had seemed to fill the world, weary and ill with hardship and the weight of responsibility, he alighted from his conveyance on a rough hill dominating the valley and lake of the Great Salt Lake. Leaning on his cane, he stood with uncovered head, staring at the bleak scene below. The wagons were strung out behind him; his counselors clustered around him, silent, waiting. Finally he thrust decisively with his cane and said, "This is the place."

It was not until 1852 that Jonathan was permitted to load his wagons and follow that westward trail, now deeply rutted, for by this time it had been traveled not only by thousands of Mormons, the gold rush to California had been racing over it for four years. Not for a long time, however, would those thousand wild miles be tamed. Many of them are still wild; even today the echoing Rockies give back war whoops for every taunt of whistle as trains roar through gorges speeding toward the valley of the Great Salt Lake.

The Mormon Exodus
FROM NAUVOO, ILLINOIS to SALT LAKE CITY, UTAH
1847

PART TWO

THE SON

John was staring at the Wasatch Mountains, watching the changing tints of a brilliant sunset, when one of his sons asked: "If Jonathan had been a wealthy man, a millionaire cheese manufacturer, for instance, and had made it possible for you to have a roomful of guns, big-game hunts in Africa, Alaska—all that sort of thing—how many guns do you think you would have invented?"

John was taken off guard and, for an instant, looked like a boy caught in a melon patch. Then his expression became serious. It was a bantering question, of course, but it caused a frown of concentration.

"Why," he said, "I wouldn't have made any guns. It wouldn't have occurred to me to try. For I can tell you one sure thing. A man may give his days and nights to his work, enjoy it, take pride in it, but it isn't fun—not like the fun we had catching those trout for supper, not like the fun I had eating them. No, I'd not have made any guns," he said. "And," bursting into laughter he added, "I'd not have made any cheese, either."

1

O GDEN, John Moses Browning's birthplace, had its beginnings as a backwater, fed from the swelling stream of immigration that followed Brigham Young's trail of 1847. Its growth was encouraged by fertile soil and abundant water. In 1850, two years before Jonathan and his family arrived, five years before John was born, the settlement was surveyed, planted, and officially named after Peter Skene Ogden.

Its namesake was a Canadian, son of a lawyer and a man of culture, but spurred by the spirit of adventure to spend years exploring the western mountains for Hudson's Bay Company. Writing in his journal in 1832 Ogden noted: "Here we are at the end of the Great Salt Lake, having this season explored one-half the north side of it, and can safely assert, as the Americans have of the south side, that it is a barren country, destitute of everything."

Twenty years later, when Jonathan first saw the lake and surrounding region, it was, for the most part, just as Peter Ogden had described it.

When Jonathan arrived, in the fall of 1852, there were from a thousand to twelve hundred people in the town, with as many more in outlying settlements. Under the direction of the church leaders, forts or log stockades had been constructed at strategic points in the area, for protection against possible Indian attacks. In general, Brigham Young preached the wisdom of feeding rather than fighting the Indians, but he backed this with an impressive state of preparedness that included, in addition to the forts, the organization of companies of militia. Few clashes resulted in bloodshed. The Indian depredations were small matters compared to the plague of locusts, summer droughts, and bitter winters which in turn threatened the communities with starvation.

Ogden might have been the capital of Brigham Young's remote and singular little empire but for the impassable last few miles of Weber Canyon, which compelled a detour that led into the valley thirty miles to the south, where Salt Lake City was founded. Young could not have failed to be impressed by the natural advantages of this valley. There is an irregular triangle, the mile-high Wasatch Mountains forming one side, the other sides marked by two of the largest rivers in Utah. The Ogden River foams through the craggy splendors of Ogden Canyon, or did until a large dam of comparatively recent construction impounded its water for irrigation and power. Now only in the spring is it free to tear at the retaining walls with its roiled and boiling overflow, in understandable rage against civilization. Leaving the canyon, the Ogden winds through the town, while a few miles to the south the Weber River, draining a wide region of mountains and valleys along its own colorful path, angles erratically to a junction with it, on the west edge of town.

The home builders soon diverted the water from these rivers through a network of ditches and canals to irrigate outlying farms and to spread to many parts of the town. The standard lot was an acre. In addition to a farm not far from the settlement, the pioneer usually had, within his home fence, a bountiful vegetable garden with space for a cow and a team. This practical arrangement, again that of Brigham Young, kept the people in groups for common defense and facilitated aid in case of accident or illness.

Jonathan had enjoyed one of his intermittent periods of prosperity while residing at Kanesville and waiting impatiently for the start of his trek West. Elected captain of his company, in the long wagon train that creaked from Iowa to this mountain and river triangle (an expert marksman, he furnished the train with meat from the large herds of buffalo), he arrived with six loaded wagons, and with nearly six hundred dollars carefully hidden beneath a false bottom in a flour barrel. That made him, comparatively, a man of substance. By trading his surplus oxen for materials, labor, and assorted supplies, he was able to provide food and shelter for his large family before winter whitened the valley.

But he was no longer the placid gunmaker of Quincy, content to watch the days, one much like another, pass, while he hammered and filed. Circumstances had worked him over, and with rough hands. When the Mormons were expelled from Nauvoo, Jonathan went with them, calmly salvaging what little he could from the property he had acquired. Between that violent uprooting and his arrival in Utah, six years intervened, years of uncertainty. It is perhaps not surprising that many industrious habits were left strewn along that trail, as were the material possessions those habits had in quiet intervals accumulated. Or that Jonathan never again applied himself to inventing new guns.

He scattered his energies in too many directions, became proficient at too many things.

The needs of the people were endless and critical; means had to be devised to supply those needs. It soon developed that Jonathan was not only a mechanic, he was a rough-and-ready engineer. Out of remembered observations, with instinct and practical experience as guides, he was called upon and seemed able to achieve, by one makeshift or another, any mechanical objective.

Thus, versatile, generous, never thrifty, obeying more wholeheartedly than most the admonition to "love thy neighbor as thyself" and—let it be admitted—gullible, Jonathan soon saw his shop turned into a community first-aid station for all manner of machinery. He made money, but always, as soon as it came in, there was a new project waiting for it, or the outstretched hand of a borrower. If he had possessed (or retained) a moderate talent for business management he could have become wealthy. As it was, it is doubtful if many men in the community worked harder, accomplished more, and had less to show for it. He lived in confusion and seems to have been only mildly troubled by it.

In those early days the Mormon Church advocated polygamy. Jonathan, a community leader, followed the practice to the extent of taking two more wives. First married in Tennessee at twenty-one, he brought to Ogden a large family; eleven of his twelve children were still living. Two years after his arrival he married Elizabeth Clark, a convert from Virginia, who became the mother of John, Matt, and a daughter who died in infancy. Five years after his second marriage, in 1859, he married Sarah Emmett, who bore him seven more children, for a grand total of twenty-two.

John Moses Browning was born January 23, 1855. Matthew Sandifer Browning was born October 27, 1859. The children of the first family, some of them already married when they reached Utah, were so much older than John and Matt that intimate ties never developed.

It was otherwise in the case of the four boys in the third family. Jonathan Edmund (Ed), the eldest, was born a few months after Matt. Thomas Samuel (Sam) arrived the following year, followed by William Wallace (Will) and George Emmett.[1] While the boys were still young, Jonathan built a home for this family on the corner across the street from Elizabeth's adobe house. Encouraged by proximity and general correspondence in age, the six boys of the second and third families grew up in close association. For the whole of their lives their homes were no more than a block apart.

Jonathan Browning—gunmaker, Mormon pioneer, and sire of twenty-two children, the last born when he was seventy-one years old. He was married first at twenty-one and twice thereafter, and a wifely scolding had long since lost its edge.   JOHN M. BROWNING ARMORY

John's seniority gave him the important rank of big brother while the boys were young, and certain inborn qualities maintained him in that position all his life. Matt, in particular, adopted him as a second father—a first father, it might more accurately be said, for Jonathan's paternal solicitude had to cover a considerable area. Young Matt, affectionate and companionable, with few playmates among the thinly scattered neighbors, attached himself to John's heels as soon as he could walk.

This was the beginning of the partnership of the Browning Brothers, a union that bound John and Matt in close intimacy all their lives.

At the time Jonathan bought the acre for Elizabeth, building the small adobe home in the corner formed by the two streets, he moved his shop into a hastily built structure, best called a shed, only a few yards from the house. He left a much more productive location in what was becoming the business district of the settlement, and it has been suspected that his purpose, at least in part, was to hide the shop from too easy accessibility. Most of his outside jobs required shop work, and random repair jobs irritated him. Whatever the purpose, the shop was at John's door, ready and waiting, when he was born.

It was built of rough, green lumber, cut from the inferior fir of the nearby mountains. The boards were set endwise, the cracks battened with strips of slab to which the bark was left clinging, gradually to weather and shred, finally reminding one, John later remarked, of an old buffalo with tufts of hair on its mangy sides. Jonathan from time to time expressed an intention of replacing it with a more substantial building, but when he died at the age of seventy-four it was still the Browning shop.

That shop has been called, in many articles, the inventor's school; in point of fact, it was almost John's only school. Jonathan went so far as to have his children learn reading, writing, and simple arithmetic. Beyond that, he considered schooling a waste of time. Better uses could be found for children at home. Jonathan feared for the soul of an idle child. College was to him a word of vague meaning. He was separated from colleges by two thousand miles and a world of indifference. He had picked up what he needed in the way of education as the need arose. By that method no time was wasted in accumulating a surplus. John, in the main, followed the same method, the difference being that his needs were much greater than his father's. For instance, making the first of his many trips to Belgium when he was forty-seven, he soon lost patience with the slow process of transacting business through an interpreter and learned French.

The ringing of hammer on anvil was among the first sounds John was to hear; his first steps were toward the gunshop; his toys were tools and gun parts. His mother, telling her grandchildren of those early toddling trips, would often add, "And there's been grease on John's face to this blessed day!"

If it is said that guns fascinated the small boy John, it should also be said that guns still fascinate most boys and many of their fathers. The boy spent hours at a time pawing through the junk pile in the corner of the shop, whereon Jonathan tossed countless odds and ends, never wasting a piece of metal, no matter how bent or seemingly useless. The pile served as a gunmaker's primer, from which John learned the names of gun parts before he learned his letters. His father, usually patient and good-natured, could always glance down from his work long enough to answer the boy's questions. In his middle fifties then, Jonathan could look back a long way. He was probably reminded of questions he had asked in the blacksmith shop in Tennessee, remembering, too, the clumsy flintlocks he had repaired—even admired—before the coming of the cap. What an improvement that was! And now he was even seeing breechloaders, with powder, bullet, and cap all together in a metal case. How fast things had been changing! No telling what kind of guns that child in the corner would live to see.

John's mother was sure that John could not have been more than six when he dragged in a box to serve as workbench, set it beside the junk pile, and started his career. Already Jonathan was using him. Finding need for something he remembered tossing on the pile, he would tell John to dig it out, then if necessary set him to cleaning off the rust with file and buffer. Now and then school interrupted his shop work, but not often. The many canals provided a greater temptation. "Going in swimming was simple," John said. "You just slid out of what happened to be left of shirt and jeans, and dove." Trout, suckers, and chubs strayed from the rivers and were caught on bent pins. John, improving the pin, made fishhooks in the shop, ringed and pointed them, cut beards and tempered, adding to his knowledge and his hoard for trade.

He enjoyed play as much as any boy. A few times, much against his will, he was put to work on one or another of his father's projects outside the shop. But more and more he was occupied within the shop by his own desire and inclination. There were days at a time when the shop was left in charge of Elizabeth and John, while his father was absorbed in an outside enterprise. Often a customer would come in with a repair job, to find the boy alone at his little bench. Elizabeth would come at John's summons, write a tag, and make a guess at the time the job would be finished. Jonathan, trapped by his wife's promises, followed many a busy day with night work, by the light of a kerosene lamp. Frequently it would fall to Elizabeth to collect for the finished work, little windfalls that were important to her domestic economy. It was she who kept the shop precariously alive, until John was able to scribble a name on a tag.

2

WHEN JOHN WAS about seven and beginning to take himself seriously as a gunsmith, he was pressed into service in a tannery which his father built and for a time operated. This employment lasted less than a month, but during this time, despite his age, John learned the processes through which a hide passed on its way to becoming leather, and what he once learned he remembered. He had the best seat in the house from which to view the activities; he rode the horse, old Button, that powered the tannery.

Early of a morning, bareback on Button, father and son rode to the tannery, some blocks from home in the straggling business district. Usually they took lunch with them, stayed late, and rode Button home at night. Through the long day John and Button circled the pit where the bark was ground. Home again evenings, John had his regular chores to do.

"The job," John said, "was interesting for a while, in spite of the smell, but by and by it got so monotonous that now and then I'd go to sleep and fall off the horse. When I fell off, Button stopped, and when Button stopped, the tannery stopped. When the tannery stopped, you could hear the tapping of the two cobblers in their corner, making boots. I don't know why Pappy left the pleasant smells of the shop and the work he did so easily and so well to wear himself out in a tannery—of all places.

"Anyhow, there I was, barefoot in my father's tannery. Big rolls of leather piled here and there, two cobblers at work, and I was barefoot. For that matter, there was not much more between Button and me than the hair on his back. That shows the kind of manager Pappy was. He had fun building the tannery. He had no interest in selling leather and collecting for it. His idea was sound, and the man who bought the tannery from him made money. But Pappy was fifty years old when I was born, and his wanderings after he joined the church had scattered his energies in so many directions that he could not settle down to steady work at the bench. Just repairing guns, the same old jobs over and over, can get pretty monotonous. I got so tired of it myself that I would have tried something else if I hadn't got to figuring on that single-shot. If Pappy had been a young man when the breechloaders began to come along, he probably would have done some more inventing. He had done about as much as could be done with the percussion lock. In his place I'd have been looking for a change myself."

John's sons and daughters, enjoying and encouraging his reminiscences as the family sat together on the porch in the early Ogden evenings, were ever amazed at his remarkable memory. He not only remembered the details of the tannery, he claimed he could still smell it.

"Mother put an end to that job after a few weeks. One evening when I came home too tired to eat supper she said, 'Pappy, we ought to be ashamed of ourselves, letting a little boy work so hard!' Pappy knew the signs. He firmly believed that when the Lord appointed six days for labor, he meant man, woman, and child, all day and hard. He hated idleness—he was even suspicious of the luxury of his own rocking chair— but he also liked peace, and Mother was ruffling up. He pulled his whiskers and said, 'Maybe he is a mite young for that job. You reckon we could spare him in school for two or three months?'

"On the way back to work the next morning, Pappy got to wondering who'd ride the horse, and it struck him that the only times Button stopped were when I fell off. So he tried tying a bag of shavings to the old nag's back, and he plodded around as well as ever. Somebody yelled 'giddup' now and then, or threw a piece of tanbark at him. Thereafter, when Pappy said that one of the boys was not worth a sack of shavings, we all knew exactly what he meant."

John went to school "mostly," his mother Elizabeth said, "to learn to write repair tags. At night he'd cut up all the paper he could find, and make tags. I had to help him print the names of all the people he could think of. He was always like that, centered on something. The other boys went to school because they were sent; John went to learn to fill out repair tags."

John attended school intermittently until he was fifteen. Most of the time, however, he spent in the shop. He liked to have his father away so he could take charge, Elizabeth recalled.

"He might be doing a chore for me, or just playing in the yard, and a block away he'd see a man with a gun. It was funny to see John race to the shop and be ready with a file in his hand, looking busy when the man came in. He'd ask the questions he'd heard Pappy ask so many times, rattling off the names of gun parts as well as Pappy himself.

"One day a man I'd known a long time came to the house, after leaving his gun in the shop with John. He was grinning all over.

'Elizabeth,' he said, 'that's a kind of young gunsmith you got out there, but he seems to know his business. He takes my old gun, squints at it, tries the lock, and tells me the mainspring's busted—which it was. But then he looked up at me and asks me if I'd left a load in it when the spring busted, and darned if I hadn't'."

Elizabeth recalled, too, that frequently a stranger would come into the shop and ask, "Where's the gunsmith, sonny?" John would say, "Pappy's out for a little while, but I'll tag your gun and tell him what you want done." Every time the stranger would be treating John like a man before he left.

Elizabeth's recollections, John's reminiscences, and many of the stories of this period survive only because of the remarkable foresight of Matthew Browning. At some point in his adulthood, probably over a number of years, he found the time to set down incidents regarding John which he found particularly interesting. He also urged his son and those of John to do the same, though they proved less conscientious than he. His notes are undated and sporadic and lack continuity, but much more important, they are lively and informative. Several of the conversations quoted here, and in succeeding chapters, also took place in the presence of co-author John Browning, eldest son of the inventor. No claim is made that these are word-for-word transcriptions, nor has an attempt been made to reproduce the exact idioms the brothers used; often these were more typical of the frontier than of the Mormon surroundings.

3

THE FIRST GUN John made had as its components the smashed barrel of an old flintlock, a stick of wood, a piece of wire, and a scrap of tin. The barrel was probably on the junk pile when John was born; as far back as he could remember he had used it to root through the pile for something Jonathan wanted, or just to be rooting.

John was ten when the inventive urge came. Calling Matt into the shop he started him sawing off a foot or so at the muzzle where the barrel was smashed. John took the first board that came to hand and hacked out a stock with a hatchet; the finished stock was about three feet long, with the front half thinned down to an inch that was partly square and partly round, depending on how the grain ran. There was no time for perfection. Jonathan was supposed to be gone for the day, but the two glanced out the door periodically for confirmation.

After having Matt file a strip through the rust along the top of the barrel, John fastened the barrel to the end of the stock with a tight spiral-wind of wire, dropping on solder here and there to keep the barrel from turning. He then screwed a scrap of tin to the wood, just under the vent, bending it into a rough funnel shape, with the small end against the vent. He knew enough to fix it so the priming wouldn't flash back in his face. There was no hammer or trigger.

Matt was then set to punching a can full of holes and affixing a wire handle while John blew up the forge and brought a dozen small lumps of coke to a glow. Filling the can half full with coke, John showed Matt how to swing it to keep the coals hot. The perforations worked as well as a bellows. Then, with a last look to make sure Jonathan was nowhere in sight, John pilfered enough powder and shot from Jonathan's supposedly hidden hoard to make a load, ramming in a little extra for good measure.

The southern limits of Ogden at that time extended only slightly beyond the Browning acre. The two boys headed south, barefoot and on the run—John carrying the gun, Matt swinging the can—and were in open country in a few minutes. They flushed a few prairie chicken but ignored them, hoping for a pot shot into a big bunch. They couldn't afford to waste their load on a single; John had brought no extra powder or shot; he was worried enough about the one load he had taken.

They finally spotted three birds dusting, two almost touching, the third three or four feet to one side. It wasn't as good as they had hoped for, but it was late, past time for chores, and John decided to try for a double, though he knew his mother would have to make a lot of biscuits and gravy to fill out the meal.

On their way John had split off a long sliver of pine and had instructed Matt in its use. When John gave the command Matt was to poke the stick down into the coals, blow till the end glowed, then ram it into the pan of priming powder.

When they got as close as they dared, about forty or fifty feet from the birds, John knelt and snuggled the stock against his shoulder. He had often fired Jonathan's old gun. Usually when Elizabeth sent him out in the late afternoon to get birds for breakfast, Jonathan took John along to run down the cripples and carry home the game, usually letting him also have a shot or two.

John whispered, "Now," and Matt blew till the end of the stick glowed, then thrust for the powder pan, missing it by several inches, John's ear by less than one, and singeing John's hair on the side. On the next try he functioned perfectly. The gun fired, and, as John told it, "I went down hard on my hunkers."

When John straightened up and could see through the smoke, the single bird was lying right where it had been before John shot and Matt was off after the other two, which were badly crippled. Catching both, Matt began whooping and trying to wring their necks.

How the barrel managed to reach out and nail the single bird was not as mysterious as it might seem. The rough shot had been made in the shop, with a crude apparatus of Jonathan's own devising. A handful of rust had probably gone out with it.

The excitement was momentary. On the way back the two brothers had plenty of time to worry about explanations, especially the use of the ammunition. They settled on the easiest way: tell Elizabeth first. Her laughter was some encouragement, as was her advice to say nothing that evening. "In the morning we'll have prairie chicken and biscuits for breakfast," she suggested. "When Pappy comes in the kitchen to eat, you boys be out in the yard. I'll tell Pappy to start while I call you, and by the time you get to the table he'll already be eating. We'll just leave things in the hands of the Lord from there on."

All went as planned. Jonathan was halfway through a breast when he thought to ask where the birds had come from. John explained. Jonathan didn't reply. He appeared to be pondering the matter seriously as he took another biscuit and a back and went on eating. Then, as he was picking the last bone, he said, "John Mose, let me see that gun." John brought it from the shed, aware that its appearance had changed since he and Matt had started out with it. Jonathan held it, looked at it closely, and shook his head. "John Mose," he said. "You're going on eleven; can't you make a better gun than that?" Putting the gun down he went on out to the shop, leaving the boys to finish breakfast.

John tried to eat, but was unable to swallow. Matt's snickering didn't help. Jonathan had said nothing about the powder and shot, and the sin of stealing. He had gone directly to John's pride.

"It *was* a hell of a gun, I told myself," John recounted later, recalling that he had thought the swear word out of spite. "The thing that hurt worst was knowing I could have made a better gun if I'd taken the time. Once the harm was done, I could see several ways to improve it. But in the meantime I could think of nothing better to do than just face it out, as though the matter was of no importance."

"Taking the gun with me, I followed Pappy to the shop. I got a pair of plyers and unwound the wire from the barrel, whistling soft and low, to show how unconcerned I was. I coiled the wire and hung it on a nail. Putting a foot on the stock I broke it in two, then dropped the pieces on the stack of kindling near the forge. I remember thinking, rebelliously, that for all Pappy might say, the gun had got us three fine birds for breakfast. Then I set to work. Neither of us mentioned it again."

John didn't always get three birds with one shot. Late one afternoon, a year or two later, he walked alone out toward Birch Creek, carrying a single-barrel muzzle-loader he had just finished repairing. The man had asked him to fire two or three shots when the job was done, to make sure everything functioned right, and had given John powder and shot. John didn't want to waste the ammunition firing at a stump.

He was equipped as a hunter by then, having made a powder horn and a buckskin shot pouch. He sneaked through the sunflowers toward an old strawstack, in which vicinity he nearly always found birds, either prairie chicken or quail. Reaching the end of the sunflowers he saw, near the corner of the stack, not twenty-five yards away, at least twenty quail in a close huddle.

It looked like a full meal with one shot, as well as the opportunity of a lifetime, and in loading John poured in an extra large handful of ammunition. Then he crawled the last few yards and wiggled into position for a knee rest.

"I still feel sorry for that youngster," John recalled. "He was never to feel a greater excitement than when he drew bead and pulled that trigger. And he was never to feel keener disappointment than when he ran through the smoke to pick up the family breakfast and saw quail running off in all directions and one lone bird flapping a broken wing.

"I should explain," John digressed from his account, "that if a pot shot like that sounds like an exhibition of poor sportsmanship nowadays, it didn't then. The word *sportsman* hadn't got that far West at that time. The first objective of hunting was to get something to eat. A good hunter brought home meat; it was wasteful to use a whole load on one bird. A man would not brag about a right and left double but about sneaking up on a covey of feeding or dusting birds and getting three or four with one shot. It was especially exciting when the birds were feeding. They'd shift this way and that, several would get nearly in line, then one or two would break rank. I was pretty good at it, that pot shot excepted of course."

Then another memory tickled him. "Maybe the old spirit still twitches when the occasion is just right. Years later, when I was a grown man, Alex Brewer and I were out after quail. We were skirting the edge of some thick scrub oak that covered a hill, looking for a way through, when we found a cattle trail that wound up toward the top and decided to take it. Alex went ahead. Suddenly he put out an arm to stop me, at the same time pushing a branch aside so I could see too. I hadn't thought it could happen twice, but there it was. About twenty yards up the trail at least a dozen quail were in a huddle, just as I'd seen them as a boy. Alex had an excited grin, and he clutched one of my arms and whispered 'My God, John—what a chance for one of us alone!' We both laughed, and, of course, the birds flushed, and in that thick brush neither of us even tried to shoot. Shooting a limit apiece wouldn't have been half as much fun. But, you see, then neither of us had to worry about breakfast."

4

EVEN BEFORE he entered his teens, John was being hailed in passing by a housewife whose scissors were dull, or who had a pan to be soldered, or a skillet with a broken handle. No utensil, in those days, was thrown away while repair was possible. Something was wrong with a sewing machine; would John repair it? John looked and learned. He learned so well that years later, developing his first belt-feed machine gun, he spent hours at his wife's sewing machine, stitching loops in strips of canvas. Nobody else, even under his direction, could have made the belt to suit him. To the wonderment of his watching children, he manipulated the machine as easily as did their mother. It was just one of many knacks, picked up in his youth, stored away in his bag of tricks, that was to provide surprises in his later years.

At the age of twelve John ventured briefly into the art of cobbling. Twice a year, for over a decade, an old Indian came to the Browning acre with mysterious regularity. Asking leave of no one, he dumped his ragged bundle in the barn. Since the lot was half a block long, with the barn at one end, and the house and shop at the other, there was plenty of room. He never spoke, never even nodded; the lot might still have belonged to his people, so calmly did he make himself at home.

Early on the morning after his arrival, the Indian would carry his bundle to an apple tree on the lot, sort out his material and tools, sit down with his back to the trunk, and start making moccasins. Nights he would sleep in the hayloft. At least once each day Elizabeth sent John out with something for him to eat. This gained the condescension of an almost affable grunt, and was probably the reason for his repeated pilgrimages. John, delivering his mother's offering, would watch for a while, boylike, then wander off. One morning the Indian would be at work under the tree, and again the next; the third he would be gone.

One morning, however, John squatted in the weeds under the Indian tree, as it was called, and soon was as absorbed in the work as the redskin. When he returned to his vigil after the noonday meal, he brought an extra-generous donation of food, thereby cementing the peace treaty. He watched for two days, and although there was no exchange of words, there was doubtless a spiritual confabulation between the two creative artists. John was permitted to pick up this or that piece for close examination, to slip a hand into a finished moccasin and trace every seam. Thus he learned to make moccasins.

John and Matt left their children no harrowing tales of hardships endured in their childhood. It is characteristic of them that, instead of nursing bare, bruised feet through the years, they kept alive the story of the moccasins, particularly enjoying the comedy which John plotted, staged, and in which he played a leading part, as a means of acquiring the buckskin for his project.

A shifty-eyed young brave, somewhat older than John, made frequent rounds of the neighborhood, never missing Elizabeth's door, where he could be sure of at least a cold biscuit. Matt was eight and ever ready to follow John's lead. In this case he had the added impetus of the promise of a pair of moccasins and the prospect of some fun. His job was to watch for the Indian. When he saw him, he ran into the shop and told John their victim was approaching.

The boys, as was frequently the case, had the shop to themselves. John and Matt watched the Indian through the window until the distance seemed about right. Then John walked out in a businesslike manner, a bow and a half-dozen arrows in one hand, in the other a board on which he had dabbed a six-inch bull's-eye. Leaning the board against the end of the shop, he stepped off twenty paces and jabbed five of his arrows into the ground. The sixth he nocked and let fly into the mark, apparently not noticing the staring black eyes but not doubting that they were on him. He had no fear of missing his target; he hunted rabbits with bow and arrows. His demonstrations had made the weapon one of the most profitable items in his stock of trade goods. He could get his chores done for a week for a bow and a couple of arrows. And the owner of the bow was sure to be back for more arrows, bringing a squash, some potatoes, eggs, or, once in a while, a nickel. It is not surprising that the combined skills of bow maker and archer drew the redskin nearer and nearer.

John, still pretending to be unaware of his watcher, pulled out the arrow with an exaggerated tug. He had purposely selected a soft board. Studying the point of the arrow, he returned to his firing station, to find his customer waiting. The Indian boy had lost the impassivity of his race. He indicated the bow with clutching fingers and thumped his chest. But John just shook his head carelessly, nocked the arrow, and turned for another shot. Then, seemingly struck by an idea, he faced the boy and asked, "You ketchum buckskin?" His answer was a blank stare.

Matt, his part in the plot memorized, ran into the shop and got a ragged piece of buckskin from which Jonathan cut patches for bullets. Matt, it should be said, had been so thoroughly drilled by John, the producer of the drama, that he never forgot a moment of the scene in all the years that followed; and Elizabeth, from her little porch, had an over-all view of the scenes as they unfolded.

John took an arrow and outlined on the ground an irregular area that contained perhaps five square feet. Then he squatted and went through the motions of stretching the piece of skin to cover the area, casting upward glances for signs of understanding in the Indian's face. He seemed to be getting something of the idea, and John began to talk fast. He used sign language of his own improvisation. He tapped the dark, bare leg, tapped the buckskin, tapped his own chest. He took the bow, smacked it emphatically. You bring me buckskin, I give you bow. The young redskin nodded.

But when? John pointed at the sun, described a wide circle in the air, and held up one finger. One day? The boy shook his head. Two days? Three days? That did it. But as he nodded, the boy eyed the bow. Full of tricks himself, he trusted nobody. But John quickly settled the matter. He scooped up the six arrows and thrust them magnanimously into the Indian's hands. The Indian, without an instant's hesitation, clutched them and ran.

"But," Matt asked, worried, watching the Indian lope away, "what if he just keeps the arrows and never comes back?"

"Never fear," John grinned. "The arrows will do him no good without the bow and they'll make him hurry back all the faster. I'll bet the arrows" *(them there arrers,* he put it) "are prodding him in the t'other end right now. Look at him go!" The Browning Brothers threw back their tousled heads and exploded with laughter—a laughter that was to deepen in tone as their chests broadened, but which never lost the echoing ring of boyhood.

(John, amused by remembered crudities of speech in the young settlement, later remarked "Now, why in the world did we go to the trouble of saying *arrer?* Arrow is a smooth and easy word, while arrer is a jawbreaker. Try it.")

The boy was back the next day with an exceptionally fine piece of buckskin. Just how he came by it was his own business, John figured, or a matter to be settled within the tribe, for it was a piece that would surely be missed. John was not interested in the recent past of the skin, however, so much as in its immediate future. First he made a pair of moccasins for Matt, then a pair for himself.

(In a railway station, many years later, John noticed some Indian handiwork displayed at the newsstand. Picking up a moccasin, he said to his companion, "There are some nice little tricks in making one of these. For instance, look here . . ." And he pointed out those long remembered intricacies.)

John could have gone into business as soon as he and Matt paraded the neighborhood in their new footwear, but he was not attracted to cobbling. A year or two later he did make a pair of leather shoes for one of his half sisters, after staring for several days through the grimy windows of a shoemaker's shop, on his way to and from school. The sister said many times in after years that the shoes were the most comfortable she ever wore. But allowance should be made for the fact that her memory was comparing the comfort of those shoes with the agony of cold, bare feet.

5

ONE DAY, when John was a few months past his thirteenth birthday, a wagon freighter came into the shop with a loud and hearty manner, a strong smell of whiskey, and the wreck of what had once been a better than average single-barrel shotgun percussion lock. A heavy box on his load had slipped and the edge had pinched the middle of the gun, breaking the stock, leaving hardly a metal part without bend or twist. Jonathan, with John taking it all in, explained that the job could be done after a fashion, but would cost more than the original price of the gun and take considerable time.

The stranger was easily convinced, for the evidence was obvious; besides, he was in a hurry and ended the matter by purchasing one of Jonathan's reconditioned guns. He paid with a ten-dollar gold piece that made John stare and Jonathan rich for a day. Then, a gun in each hand, he started for the door, but, noticing John, almost as an afterthought handed him the wreck, grinning broadly and saying, "Hey, younker, want a gun?" With a good-natured guffaw, he departed, leaving John too astonished to say thanks, though he had enough presence of mind to grab the gun.

The man probably never thought of John again, but John never forgot the man. The gun, like the proximity of shop to home, was doubtless a strong directive influence in the inventor's life. The coming of the freighter was what he later characterized as a stroke of particularly good luck, one of those nudges chance gives a mind now and then, pushing it from dozing to awareness.

John already thought of himself as a gunsmith, with more justification than his father accorded him. He had picked up the knacks of the shop so easily and smoothly that Jonathan was unloading more and more responsibility on him without realizing how much the boy was helping. If a part had to be repaired or replaced, John could usually get it out of the gun; and when Jonathan had the part ready, John could reassemble the arm. The percussion-lock gun has never been equaled in simplicity; the components were few and easily reached, and John had known them all by name as far back as he could remember.

He could braze and weld. He could drill out a battered and rust-tight nipple, retap the hole, and from his collection find a nipple to fit, or one that could be rethreaded to fit, or, if necessary, make a new nipple, using the foot lathe. As a gunsmith he was emerging from the embryonic stage. He no longer thought of himself as a boy. But he did not suspect, even in his most manly moods, the full extent of his accumulated knowledge until the freighter's gun, laid on the bench for study, challenged him with its battered, bent, and broken parts. He accepted the challenge with the one attribute of genius he would ever acknowledge: an unyielding tenacity.

Jonathan told him he had better screw out the barrel—fortunately, it had escaped with no greater hurt than a few scratches—and see what other parts were worth saving. John nodded absently and studied the gun. Jonathan decided to save his breath; there was no need to try to

Jonathan Browning's lathe, hauled by ox team across the plains from Council Bluffs to Ogden, Utah Territory, in 1852. For many years powered by a foot pedal, it was later adapted to operate from a small steam engine. On this lathe, John M. Browning made the pilot models of many of the famous firearms produced by Winchester, Colt, Remington, Fabrique Nationale, Savage, and others.   JOHN M. BROWNING ARMORY

convince John that the job was beyond him, the gun would do that. He turned his own attention back to some work for a sawmill he was setting up in partnership with another man, ignoring the youth beside him.

John stood staring at the gun on the bench. At first he wasn't worried about fixing it, only wondering where to begin. He could picture it in his mind just as it had been before the accident, a little beauty, about eighteen or twenty gauge, and lighter than most guns that passed through the shop. In his mind he would get it all fixed up, ready to go hunting, and then something would slip, and he'd have the battered lump in front of him again. His next reaction was instinctive, the natural reaction of every gunsmith who sees a beautiful gun badly damaged— he began getting mad. For a moment he could skip past the knowledge that this was the first man-sized job to come his way, know how it felt to own the best gun in town; then, as suddenly, he was again confronted with the ugly fact. Finally he swore aloud, not knowing that the words were coming until he heard them.

Jonathan stopped his filing. John caught a glimpse of him out of the corner of his eye: tall, broad-shouldered, straight, a ring of gray whiskers around his face and under his chin, a Biblical patriarch in looks and demeanor. "John Mose, don't you know that everything you say and do is recorded?" He gave a couple of jabs upward with the file, in case the recording angel was dozing.

John didn't say a word. Jonathan went back to his filing. If the recording angel had materialized pointing an accusing finger at John at that moment, John would have pointed to the gun and said, "Write that down." He knew Jonathan was feeling a little sorry for him or he would have said considerably more about the swearing. He wanted neither help nor pity, just to be left alone.

As John later told it, "Finally the idea came. A good idea starts a celebration in the mind, and every nerve in the body seems to crowd up to see the fireworks. It *was* a good idea, one of the best I'd ever had, and so simple it made me ashamed of myself. Boylike, I had been trying to do the job all at once with some kind of magic. And magic never made a gun that would work. I decided to take the gun apart, piece by piece, down to the last small screw, even those parts that were mashed and twisted together. And when I did, finally finishing long after supper that night, the pieces all spread out before me on the bench, I examined each piece and discovered that there wasn't one that I couldn't make myself, if I had to."

To John the step-at-a-time method was a revelation. As he put it, "If I had been in school that day, I would have missed a valuable lesson."

He began work the following morning, going through the damaged parts, finding a piece that could be replaced from the junk pile, another that would do with a little fitting and tinkering, another that he could soften in the forge, then straighten and heat-treat. And here and there were pieces he would have to make.

He had the barrel to encourage him. It was brighter than most barrels that got that far West, and fortunately the breech plug had kept it from being flattened by the blow. So the one part he couldn't make was in good shape.

The job took all of his spare time for several weeks. Jonathan doubtless saw the boy make and impatiently correct mistakes from time to time, but wisely withheld advice. When John was finished he had a gun, and the conviction that he was a gunsmith. "Pappy nearly came right out and said so," John chuckled in recollection. "But he was never exuberant in his praise. He could have watched Elijah's contest with the prophets of Baal without cheering. He might have said 'Elijah's miracles are working pretty well today, though one of them hung fire a little.' All the same I knew he was pleased; he let me saw the wood for my stock from his precious plank of walnut."

For both John and Jonathan the gun was an important turning-point, the period itself a fateful one. John sensed that he had made a large step in his transition from boyhood to manhood; Jonathan was startled into awareness that there was another gunsmith in the family.

John had picked up his skills in the shop so easily, had turned his play so smoothly into work, that his father, born mechanic himself, unable to remember when he could not do things with tools, and in nowise vain of his skills, might have occasionally observed to himself, "The boy's got an old head on his shoulders," but probably had let it go at that.

Over the years Jonathan had grown more preoccupied with ventures outside the shop. Politics still tempted him: elected a member of the city council soon after his arrival in Ogden, he later became a justice of the peace, was appointed probate judge of Weber County, and served for a time in the legislature. In the ecclesiastical sphere he was, in turn, bishop's councilor, member of the high council, and president of the high priest's quorum. In addition to starting the tannery and the sawmill, he ventured into real estate, the erection of an iron-roller molasses mill, and the manufacture of plows, mill irons, and nails.

He was often in debt; his indifference to money made him a poor collector. He forgave debt in anyone else; in himself it was a mortal sin. He was sixty-four years old and feeling the weight of his toilsome years. It is likely that he had been looking on John much as a farmer watches a precocious son harness a team, using a box to increase his height. The farmer might enjoy a momentary touch of pride but feel no great surprise. For what is more commonplace on a farm than harnessing a team?

Yet the repair of the gun marked the end of a period. John, having undertaken an apparently hopeless task under the shadow of his father's disapproval, had proven himself. His apprenticeship ended when Jonathan gave him the walnut for his stock. There was no ceremony, but that piece of wood was in the nature of an accolade. A tall towhead was accepted into the ancient order of gunmakers.

When John undertook the repair of the gun, he saw the possibility of owning one of the best shotguns in Ogden. As a matter of fact, since there were not many shotguns in the settlement, John's was unquestionably one of the best. The rifle had been the most useful arm for the trip across the plains, as it was for wild regions generally, because it provided the much needed meat of big game, and served as the best defense against hostile Indians. The pioneers, those first years in Utah, were too busy building homes, digging irrigation ditches, and taming their wild acres to spare time for hunting birds.

But the Brownings were not farmers. Elizabeth's brother, Moses, who lived on the next acre, put in a vegetable garden for her every spring, but there is no record that John ever bent his back pulling weeds. For that matter, even after he was grown and married he never made a shelf for his own home, replaced a washer in a leaky faucet, or nailed a loose picket in place. Driven by exasperation, he now and then got his can of gun oil, always in a drawer of the library table, and ran down a squeaky hinge. He would even oil the sewing machine if his wife complained that it was running hard. And once, hearing her wish with a sigh that a knife-and-scissor sharpener would come around, he gathered all the cutting knives and scissors in the house, rolled them up in a newspaper, took them down to the shop, and sharpened them. His brother Ed offered to do it, adding, "You don't remember how." "The hell I don't!" John replied, then joined in the laughter that ran along the benches. Spreading the cutlery on the kitchen table that evening for his wife's inspection, he said, "See, Mama, I sharpened all these things myself, just to show that I could still earn a living if I had to." He stared down at the array for a moment and added, "I could have done that job as well when I was twelve years old, from which it would appear that there isn't much of a future in knife and scissor grinding."

Now that he owned his own shotgun, John spent more and more of his time hunting. Shopwork took up less time than might be expected; there was not much business; over the years Jonathan, pursuing his outside interests, had let the business slip. Customers tired of visiting the shop only to find it unoccupied. John enjoyed hunting and loved to explore the hills beyond Ogden, but his hunting was in part an escape. Now in his early teens, he was dissatisfied and restless. Though his future as a gunsmith seemed assured, he felt lost, without direction. At times he was impatient with his younger brothers; other days he would play their games with intensity. He was in a no man's land, and disquiet weighed heavily upon him.

John's inventiveness was beginning to make itself apparent, though it was not as yet directed to the creation of new guns. One evening Jonathan and his Bible were in communion. Jonathan occupied his rocking chair; on a table to his right was a kerosene lamp. His eyes were not as keen as they had been, however, and to aid the lamp he held in his left hand a candlestick and lighted candle.

The rocker creaked gently in slow motion under Jonathan's weight; his lips moved as they shaped the words of holy writ; the low-ceilinged room seemed to be entertaining the very spirit of restfulness.

Then came a loud plop. The candle flame vanished, and a familiar smell filled the room. Jonathan sniffed the end of the candle and called his wife.

Elizabeth, coming from the kitchen, stopped in the doorway. "Gunpowderl" she exclaimed. "I smell gunpowder. Where'd that come from?"

"Where's John Mose?" Jonathan asked, holding the candle near the lamp and examining the wick end.

"You can't blame John Mose for this—whatever it is," Elizabeth responded. "He and Tad Pidcock went downtown an hour ago to hear the band concert."

Jonathan considered the candle, chuckling, then explained. "He punched a little hole down to the wick and filled it with powder. Knows I always hold the candle just the same way, though I'd never thought of that before. And, of course, he experimented till he found just the right charge to blow out the candle and hardly splash the melted tallow . . ."

He mused a minute or two silently and admiringly. There was no doubt in his mind that John had been the inventive one. He was almost ready to comment on this when his sterner self returned. "Gone to hear the band, you say?"

"He never misses a concert," Elizabeth replied. "Says he'd like to join the band when he's older. The boys say he can make a tune on any instrument he picks up."

"Huh," Jonathan grunted. "We must try to guide him away from that. You know my father fiddled, spent more time at it than he had cause to. And one of my uncles in Tennessee fiddled too, no account for anything else. Played for all the dances, weddings, everything—even funerals. I must admit he could play right soft and sweet for a funeral, and that was the only place he didn't take his jug. Always that jug was beside his chair when he fiddled. Hope there's none of that blood in John Mose. I've noticed he sings and whistles a lot when he's working. That's far enough to go with music."

6

"ONE OF THE FIRST articles written about the inventor," Matt Browning notes, "contained the statement that when he was in his early teens, John made a gun for each of us out of parts from his father's junk pile, and the story keeps bobbing up from time to time. It didn't quite happen that way. Oh, Pappy had accumulated a big pile of junk, and no mistake. He was the only gunsmith for miles around, and it seems to me, as far back as I can remember, that half the guns brought to the shop were not worth fixing, so the pile kept growing.

"That's not strange when you consider the trip a gun had to make to get to Ogden. A man might come in with an old gun, hoping to raise a little money on it. Pappy would take one look and shake his head. There was nothing more discouraging than Pappy looking solemn and shaking his head. 'That's a dead mule' was one of his favorite expressions. The man may have hoped to get a couple of dollars for the gun but *dead mule* would jolt him down a dollar at least. Finally, Pappy would say, 'Well, maybe I can use the hammer sometime. If you want four bits for it, pitch it on the junk pile yonder.' The words *junk pile* would make the man hurry to grab the four bits, which, after all, would buy a pint of whiskey. Pappy was a good trader. He had about all the qualities needed to make him rich, except the ability to keep money.

"But about that first gun. Actually at one time or another John made me dozens of guns out of wood. I'd lose one or trade it off, then find a likely board and get him to whack me out another. He's been whacking out real guns ever since.

"In making my play-guns, however, he'd rough a board down to width with a hatchet, then screw it in a vise and go at it with a drawknife. Now and then he'd back off and take a squint, and in a jiffy I'd have the start of a gun. He somehow made me think it was fun to stand on a box by the small vise, and file and sandpaper my gun till it could pass his inspection. I was well into my teens, six feet tall and able to do a pretty good job of stocking before it dawned on me what John had been up to. He saw he was going to need an assistant before long, and was making one. He kept stepping up the pace a little, making the work more interesting—and harder. Some of our highest grades we finished in style, even putting on a coat of shellac. For a few of the extra specials, he dug out old trigger guards and hammers. It was part of my job to straighten and polish those extras, and screw them on. You could have held up a stage with some of those guns. Now and then I'd sell one for a nickel, or even trade one for a watermelon."

But wooden guns no longer satisfied Matt, not after John acquired the shotgun. One day when the two brothers were alone in the shop Matt decided to ask John to make him a gun. Embarrassed by the magnitude of his request, and trying to gather courage to broach the subject, he got to fidgeting, hanging by his elbows on the edge of the bench and rolling under and out on a round object his feet had found amid the accumulated odds and ends.

"Matt, if you haven't anything better to do," John suggested, "you can get the broom and sweep out under there."

Matt, seeing an opportunity to put himself in John's good graces, complied. After a minute or two of sweeping, he blurted out his request: "I wish I had a gun that would shoot."

"You ought to have a gun," John answered. "If you can find a barrel in this shop that's worth a tinker's dam, I'll make you one."

That was bringing the gun within reach, then jerking it away; Matt jabbed viciously under the bench with the broom. Something fell with a thump. Bending down Matt picked up a burlap-wrapped object about the length and weight of a rifle barrel, but so covered with dirt, grime, and filings that he could not be sure. In a minute he had stripped off the burlap. John took the object for closer examination.

John doubted that the discovery was worth that "tinker's dam" but withheld judgment. He thought he knew every part in the shop, but he hadn't seen this before. Scratching through the grime with his finger nail he found that it really was a barrel, but so caked he couldn't tell whether it was round or octagonal. He sniffed it and recognized the smell of beeswax. Picking up a wood chisel he shaved across the end, exposing the hole; warming the end a little over the forge, he wiped a portion of it clean. It actually looked new. It was round and seemed to have no marks of wear on it. He guessed it was about a .32 caliber.

John knew that whoever had taken the trouble to dip the barrel in wax must have prized it. If it wasn't Jonathan's, it was someone else's, and whoever owned it might be back for it. For a long time he was silent, thinking. Matt waited impatiently. Finally John came up with a plan.

He would ask Jonathan if he could make Matt a gun, but they would have to make sure Jonathan was in a good humor first. To start, Matt could take the water bucket and fill it at the well. It was a warm day, and there was nothing Jonathan disliked more than flat and tepid water. While he was at it, Matt could fill the bucket for the house, just in case Jonathan stopped there first. Then it might be a good idea to chop up a little wood. Elizabeth needed some, and if Jonathan were to arrive and find Matt working, it wouldn't hurt his case.

Jonathan arrived in due time. Matt watched from the woodpile as he entered the shop, took off his hat, pulled out his big bandanna, mopped the perspiration from his face and neck, and reached for the water bucket. Matt chopped furiously for a few minutes, but his curiosity got the better of him. Slipping around the edge of the building, he crouched under the window.

John was talking about the job at hand. Ordinarily Matt liked to listen to Jonathan and John talking. It wasn't like a man and a boy; it was like two men. But from the casual tone of the conversation Matt was afraid John had forgotten all about his gun. Finally John changed the subject.

"Pappy," he said. "Matt was in here a while ago, and he's growing fast. I've already got him pretty handy with tools, considering his age." Jonathan said he'd noticed, and seemed pleased. "Well," John went on, "he'll be working here with us, I suppose, and the more he learns about guns the better. He can already out shoot most men, and I've been thinking I'd like to make him a gun for his birthday, which is only about four months away. It would take me that long, just working spare time."

Jonathan asked how old Matt would be. When John answered, "Ten come October," Jonathan expressed surprise. For a while the conversation was one-sided, as Jonathan slipped into recollection. But before long he thought to ask, "What would you make the gun out of?"

John reminded him of a box of frames and parts for his slide rifles that he had brought from Council Bluffs but never used. There was even a tap and die for fitting the barrels, John noted, pulling the box down from a shelf. Opening it, Jonathan began recalling his days in Iowa, his unfulfilled intention to make more of the guns when he arrived in Utah. "But what about a barrel? You can't put an old rusty barrel in one of these frames. There's pretty good work in them if I do say it."

John sprang the trap. "Well, Matt was sweeping under the bench, and he knocked down that thing there. I shaved off enough to see that it's a barrel, and the end looks pretty good. It seems to be covered with beeswax."

"Beeswax!" Jonathan said, letting out one of the big guffaws that he saved for something that really amused him. "I'd forgot. Five years ago, I reckon, one of the winters the smallpox was so bad in town, I'd just come in from visiting one of the stricken families, and helping a little with the nursing, when a stranger stomped in out of the snow. He said he'd seen one of my slide rifles downtown and wanted me to make up one for him. He handed me this long lump of beeswax, saying there was a brand-new barrel in it."

Jonathan took time to laugh again. "That's as far as we got. Just then your mother put her head in the door and asked me how the smallpox patients were feeling. I told her I'd just been in to see them and found them breaking out nicely. Well, that man yelled, 'Smallpox,' and reached for his barrel, but jerked back as though it had turned to a snake. He said never mind, he'd take a receipt. And then he said never mind that, either, he'd take my word for it, and out he went, taking the name of the Lord in vain about as bad as I ever heard!

"He never came back," Jonathan added, "and I was just as glad. A man with a new barrel way out here was suspicious. Through the window, I saw him grab some snow off the ground and start to wash his hands, but then he threw that down quick, and wiped his hands on his pants. No mistake, this whole town was contaminated for that man."

Jonathan handled the barrel for a minute, then returned to the box of frames and parts. "That's a fine idea, John Mose; I'd like to see one more slide gun made up."

The gun was finished in time for Matt's birthday. In Matt's own words: "It was a pretty thing for its day. John and I both used it, the same as his shotgun, and with the two guns we brought in a fine assortment of game that fall and winter. Not only prairie chicken and quail. One snow, they say, fattens a brush rabbit, and the same is true of the big white hare. Some of them must have weighed close to five pounds, and Mother fixed them up in different ways. She often   sent us out for meat, just as a boy might be sent out to the butcher. John and I had so much fun that it makes me homesick to think back   on it."

The gun saw another use the following summer, when a freighter passed through carrying a big load of salt to the mines in Idaho and Montana. Matt, who saw him tying up in front of the shop, wandered over. The freighters fascinated the boys. The wagon and load were always something to look at, and there were inevitably tales of where the men had been, with maybe a little Indian fighting thrown in to add a touch of flavor. The men were rough and tough—they had to be, to stand the life.

This man wanted something done to his rifle, and like every stranger who came into the shop and found John there alone, he asked where the gunsmith was. That always irritated John. He didn't let his temper interfere with business, though, and before the freighter knew what was happening, John was turning the screws out of his gun. The stranger looked doubtful; John was tall, but it was plain that he was just a youngster, and it was a good-looking rifle.

John told him the job wouldn't take long. The man decided to wait; the way he watched, it was evident he wanted to see what was going to happen to his gun. In a few minutes he began to relax.

John drove in the last screw and said, "One dollar."

"Ah, see here," the man said. "That didn't take half an hour. Six bits ought to be enough."

John shook his head. "Some gunsmiths might have put in two hours on the job and charged you a dollar and a half."

There wasn't much the freighter could say to that, and he handed over the dollar. John took it and said, "That's a nice rifle you got there, mister." He said it quietly and sincerely; only Matt was aware that John was still mad.

"Best damn rifle west of Omaha," the freighter bragged.

John nodded as though he agreed, then asked, "Pretty good with it, I suppose?"

"Why," the man said, "me and that little gun just quit missing long ago."

"That so?" John smiled. "I'll bet you this dollar against a sack of salt that my younger brother here can beat you!"

That surprised the freighter. John looked so confident that he began getting a little hot under the skin.

"Why, sonny," he said. "I wouldn't like to take money from children."

"You won't," John replied.

"All right. Where do we shoot?"

"We got a target out by the barn," Matt volunteered.

The freighter was obviously disturbed. He was a big man; he had covered a lot of country and seen many places the two brothers had never even heard about. He had done a lot of shooting. Somehow it didn't seem right, coming into an out-of-the-way settlement and being challenged by a youngster with not even a whisker on his face. He had to shoot or back down completely, and he wasn't one to back down. John and Matt readied the target as he went back to his wagon for his ammunition kit.

The freighter fired first, followed by Matt. Matt now owned one sack of salt. The freighter's amazement turned to laughter. He immediately claimed another chance.

John, seeing that he was a good sport, began to take to the man. "Hold on," he said. "Where you're going with it, that salt's worth more than a dollar a sack, I'll bet. We'll change the bet. We'll bet you our sack of salt against a dollar. That will make it all fair and even."

The freighter looked at John a second, then slapped his thigh heartily. He had been so surprised at the challenge that he hadn't thought about the bet itself. John had bettered him even before the first shot was fired. Usually he got five dollars a sack for salt at the end of his haul; the longer the haul, the higher the price. After setting up the targets again, the two fired. Matt won again. The freighter, who was himself a good shot, was now even more amused than the boys. Pulling out a dollar, he handed it to Matt. "You made the bet," he told John, "but the youngster here won it. Now, get that wheelbarrow and come and get your salt." After he had pulled down a sack and fastened the tarps back in place he climbed up into the seat. John and Matt untied for him.

"Boys," he said, "if I meet any folks headed this way who need some gun repairing, I'll tell them where to come." Then, as an afterthought, he added, "But I'll also tell them not to get into any shooting matches."

He popped the long whip, the horses tightened their tugs, and the big wagon creaked away. Matt later said: "It made me feel sort of lonely to see him go. The dollar in my pocket was the first I'd ever had."

John, too, stared long at the departing wagon. "Matt," he said, "that fellow could shoot a damn sight better than I expected."

The year 1869 brought the long awaited completion of the transcontinental railroad. None of the Brownings attended the celebration at Promontory, some fifty miles from Ogden, where the tracks of the Central Pacific and the Union Pacific were joined, but others did, and for days after people in Ogden talked of little else. It was common knowledge that Leland Stanford, who was to drive the last spike, had missed the spike altogether and that an alert telegraph operator had saved the day by flashing the long awaited news to Washington, where, above the Capitol, a magnetic ball fell, touching off a transcontinental celebration.

The following January saw the completion of Brigham Young's Utah Central Line, which connected Salt Lake City to Ogden. This time all of the brothers were in attendance, skipping school, meals, and chores to watch as the tracks approached the city limits, attending the mammoth celebration in the city when the line was completed. John was nearly fifteen, five-ten and still growing; Matt, ten, and Ed, nine, were shorter, though not for long; Sam, eight, Will, seven, and George, four, completed the graduated scale. The event was momentous, but it is doubtful if either John or Jonathan understood just how important it really was. When the Utah Central joined the transcontinental railroad, with Ogden as its terminus, that community ceased to be a small, isolated settlement, a backwater of Mormon immigration; it was now tangibly connected to the Atlantic and the Pacific. Within a few years, this was to have its effect on the fortunes of both Ogden and the Brownings.

7

JOHN WAS GRADUATED from school a few months after he turned fifteen. He was in the sixth reader when, in early spring, the short school year ended. School ended when the frost was out of the ground.

Six classes were seated in one log room, under one teacher, a man. All of John's teachers, judging from his infrequent and casual references to them, were men. With few exceptions, they had scarcely any training; most of them, in fact, had little schooling. During those early years they organized and conducted classes with a scant supply of textbooks and virtually no supervision.

On the last day of school, as John was leaving with the others, the teacher put a hand on his shoulder and drew him aside. "Hold on a jiffy, John," he said. "I don't see any sense in you coming back to school next fall. You know as much as me."

The teacher was, in effect, his own principal and school board; his decision was authoritative. John had started to school with the intention of learning to write repair tags; this had been accomplished long ago, and for some time he had felt he was wasting time, accumulating a surplus of learning that extended beyond his needs.

Jonathan assumed that once John finished his schooling he would spend all his time in the shop. John was less sure. Possessing mechanical talents far beyond his years, he had for a long time been conscripted for all manner of jobs. Most of them had given him practice with tools, but had tended to squander his talent rather than concentrate it. Jonathan had let circumstances make him into a jack-of-all-trades; John was determined that this would never happen to him, yet he seemed headed in that direction.

He kept working in the shop, but for long periods he lived in a state of barely controlled exasperation. At times both the table and his back were so nearly bare that it would have seemed wiser to look for work that paid a wage. But he possessed an attitude that had also been Jonathan's. He couldn't bring himself to ask a man for a job. It was not pride—he admitted that all he knew was shopwork. Nor was it a feeling of inferiority. It was closer to shyness—it seemed to him that making such a request was a presumption on his part. As a result, he never asked. "The fact is, I was lazy," John later told one of his sons. "The only shop work I liked was gun work, and even that had become a great bore. My appetite had to have guns to feed on, but I'd handled muzzleloaders so often they no longer interested me. I don't know what would have happened if the breechloader hadn't come along."

With the arrival of the breechloader John's interest was set aflame. And no one, not even John, could apply the word lazy to the years that followed.

We do not know when the first breechloader reached the Ogden shop, or its make or model. We suspect, however, that John was referring not to the first he saw, which could have been at any time from his childhood on, but to the many he examined and repaired once they began to be manufactured in great numbers.

Cannon that loaded at the breech, the rear end of the barrel, in contrast to muzzle-loaders, which were loaded through the muzzle end, were in use in England during the reign of Henry VIII. In 1776 Major Patrick Ferguson of the British Army invented a breech-loading rifle which saw use in the Carolina campaign of the American Revolution. One of the first American breechloaders, the Hall, invented by Captain John Harris Hall of Maine, was patented in 1811 and saw use in both the Mexican War and the Civil War. Others—the Sharps, the Peabody, the Remington-Rider "Rolling-Block"—had all appeared by 1870. They came with a rush, once the development of a safe metallic cartridge made them practicable.

The cartridge was the important thing, and Tyler Henry is generally credited with its creation. About 1858, while employed as plant superintendent for Oliver Winchester's Volcanic Firearms Company, Henry succeeded in placing a projectile, powder charge, and primer in a single metallic case. The fixed metallic cartridge did away with the dangers of hand-loading ("Just a little more powder for good measure"— the last words of many a hunter) and solved the problem of making the breech gas-tight. The breechloaders followed in great numbers.

John was a youthful witness to that revolutionary change. Just as Jonathan had watched the percussion lock gradually replace the flint-lock, so John now viewed the passing of the percussion lock. "Guns have given me a lot of trouble," he once said. "I'd have escaped all that and probably lived ten years longer, if the breechloader hadn't come along." He said it without regret.

Though John was running the shop, aided by his brothers when the work demanded it, Jonathan still kept his hand in. One day, on returning from an errand, John found that Jonathan had bought a large quantity of charcoal at a bargain price. Always a little suspicious of windfalls, John asked if he had tried a sample on the fire. Jonathan said it wasn't necessary; anyone could see it was first-class charcoal. John shoved a generous heap onto the forge and pumped the bellows.

John M. Browning at eighteen.   JOHN M. BROWNING ARMORY

The charcoal had been rained on and was damp. There was also a hotter bed of coals in the forge than John had realized, hidden under the ash. With the first wheeze of the bellows the charcoal began to explode, flying out to ignite the shavings on the floor and under the bench. Because the soles of the men's shoes were thin and the shavings underfoot were soft, the shop was swept out only once or twice a year. In moments father and son were fighting a dozen separate blazes. Jonathan yelled for Elizabeth and the water bucket. After a few doubtful minutes, the three succeeded in saving the building.

Looking at the mess, John swore. Jonathan, eager to get off the subject of charcoal, began a lecture on John's use of profanity. But Elizabeth quickly interrupted. "It would have been a good thing if this rubbish heap had burned down long ago. Maybe then you'd have built something that wouldn't be a shame to you. What do you reckon people say when they pass here? Even your old gunsmith sign is hanging by one nail, straight up and down, the letters nearly weathered off. *I wouldn't keep pigs in this place!*" She stormed back to the house.

Jonathan had been married first at twenty-one and twice thereafter. A wifely scolding had long since lost its edge. After sending one of the boys to the well for a fresh bucket of water, he sat on the edge of the forge and took a leisurely drink from the dipper. John, observing his lack of concern, also left angrily. After finding a hammer, nail, and ladder he set about straightening the sign. As a gesture of defiance it was next to useless, he realized. The sign was so faded as to be almost illegible, whereas, hanging by one nail it might have attracted some attention.

As John nailed the sign into place his anger grew. His mother had been right; he doubted if any man, seeing the shop in passing, would be encouraged to take his gun in for repair. He decided to go inside and have it out with Jonathan.

The encounter always remained vivid in his memory. Several times he described it to his sons: "I was ready to tackle Goliath, but when I came in and saw Pappy sitting on the anvil, he looked, somehow, like Vulcan himself. I was so used to seeing him that I don't think I had ever really seen him *clearly* before. He was a giant of a man, shaped by a rough and rugged life. Seated on the anvil, one heel hooked on the block, the sledge and hammers and tongs sprawled around him, he made a picture that hasn't faded in all these years. After that, I'd always take a second glance when I saw him in the evenings, sitting in his rocking chair—it seemed strange, a kind of anticlimax."

Jonathan had anticipated him. Before John could start, he said, "John Mose; your Ma's got a pretty sharp tongue when she loses her patience, but maybe she's right this time. The place does look a little run down. You've had some idees now and then about fixing it up?"

The responsibility passed back to John. After some thought, he came up with a plan. Recalling that they were owed lumber by a little mill up the canyon for work done in the shop, John suggested that they get Uncle Mose to haul it down in his wagon; in exchange they'd give him enough for a new fence. The boys could do the work—rip off the old batting strips and cover the building with bright new boards; then John could make up some whitewash, and Matt, or one of the others, could go over the inside.

The shop had been in use since Jonathan built it shortly after his arrival in Utah in 1852. John's "reconditioning" occurred about 1873. It was here, in 1878, that John invented the first of his many famous guns.

8

TWO YEARS BEFORE John's death, one of his sons made an estimate of the monetary returns from each of the Browning arms. It was a rough estimate, though accurate enough for its purpose, which was simply to activate his father's memory. One afternoon on the porch he asked John: "Which of your guns, would you say, was the most profitable?"

As promptly as though the answer had been in his mind a long time, which it probably had, John answered: "Why, the first gun, of course. The Single Shot."

"The Single Shot?" The son expressed surprise. "You only got eight thousand for that."

"But it was such a big eight thousand," John chuckled. "They don't come that big anymore. A check that size wasn't often deposited in the local bank; it made me so rich that I've never worried about money since. It gave me eight thousand dollars worth of certainty that I could invent things for which people would pay large prices."

The idea of inventing a new gun had been in John's mind for a long time. But there were also other questions there, naive, he later admitted, but no less bothersome by virtue of their simplicity. How did a man invent? Did he learn it in college? He would need a fine shop, John decided; nobody could do any inventing in their present shack. The answer seemed to lie back East.

"I could have made a gun at twenty," John said later, "if I'd just thought I could, if it had occurred to me to buckle down and make a gun. I knew enough, I knew all that it was possible to learn in our shop, but I didn't know how to use what I'd learned. Every now and then, in repairing a gun, I'd see what looked like a better way to perform an operation, and even make a rough sketch, still wishing I lived back East where all the inventing was done. Inventing was still far beyond the mountains, mysterious. When some of us walked down to the station now and then to watch the trains, it was always an eastbound train I wanted to be on. Back where guns were made. It doesn't seem possible that I could have been six feet tall and so benighted . . .

"If Pappy had gone on making guns, the way he did back East," John continued, "I'd have got some ideas; but he never made a gun after he came to Utah. We ridiculed some of the guns we fixed, and I damned some of them when Pappy wasn't near, but it never occurred to us to make better ones. He was too old, and I was too young."

Often, when pressed with work, John would say in exasperation, "I still get hot when I think that I could have been making guns three or four years earlier than I did." But then, his anger spent, he would usually add one of his afterthoughts, such as "All in all, though, I was lucky. What if Pappy had been a farmer!"

One day in the early part of the year 1878, shortly after John turned twenty-three, he was repairing a single-shot rifle, the parts spread out before him on the bench. Many of the guns he repaired were remarkably well built, but this one was a freak. He wondered how a man could figure out parts so complicated.

Jonathan was sitting on the anvil, examining a gun, pretending to be busy. He was old and tired and wouldn't admit it. He would come into the shop nearly every morning, even though Elizabeth tried her best to keep him lying down. Sometimes he would do a little job, but mostly he'd sit on the anvil. He liked the sounds and smells of the shop; occasionally John would consult him about the job at hand to keep his interest alive.

John called him over to look at the freak he had spread out on the bench, noting that it was the funniest gun he had ever seen. Jonathan stepped over and leaned on the vise, bending low because his sight was failing. He shook his head in disgust.

"I could make a better gun than that myself," John said. He did not mean it literally; it was just his way of saying the gun was no good.

Jonathan looked up and as matter-of-factly answered, "I know you could, John Mose. And I wish you'd get at it. I'd like to live to see you do it."

John was stunned for a minute, then protested that he had too much repair work piled up. Jonathan paid no attention: "Matthew is pretty handy, especially making stocks, and I can tell him how to do things that would tire me too much. We'll get along. The Lord will provide."

We have no step-by-step account of the making of the model. John could not have given such an account the day the job was finished. For every idea incorporated into the model, several others suggested themselves for consideration. John later said that his greatest difficulty was sorting out the parts that seemed to be going through his head, picking the simplest, for he didn't have the equipment to make anything complicated.

Jonathan gave up his seat on the anvil; lacking a milling machine, John had to use it to hand-forge the larger parts. He would shape them on the anvil, bringing them as near as possible to their final form, in order to spare himself interminable filing and chiseling. With the foot lathe and breast drill, he honeycombed the places in the receiver blank that had to be opened, and cleared out the webbing with broach, chisel, and files.

John brought in a big box for Jonathan to sit on when he got tired. Jonathan would work awhile, mostly bossing Matt; then he would sit and study the templates John made to check the size and movements of the parts. John made many of them. Before long Jonathan also had the mechanism so clearly in mind that they could talk about it, calling orthodox parts by name, inventing names for new ones.

For the first time John was completely absorbed in his work—the sketches, templates, and, eventually, the finished parts.

Matt remembered with particular amusement an occurrence one noontime. At their mother's call, the brothers went in to dinner; as usual John had an excellent appetite, although it was evident that he was not seeing or tasting what he was eating.

"There wasn't much variety," Matt wrote. "Mostly biscuits, but plenty of those. John would split one, jab at the butter, eat the biscuit in two bites, and reach for another. After having finished a good-sized meal he stopped and pulled out a little template, or the beginning of one. It was shaped, but had nothing on it but some lines. He studied it, using his thumb nail as a compass, and seemed to locate the points he wanted. Then he licked his fork and made a couple of dots with a tine. He laid the template on the table and picked up his knife. He saw some butter on the end, split a biscuit, wiped the knife—and ate the biscuit while he stared at the template. Then, using the knife as a ruler and the fork as a scriber, he drew a line between the two dots. He came half awake after that, looking surprised to see where he was. Slipping the template back into his pocket he said 'Ma, I don't seem to have much appetite today.'

"Ma gave me a little wink and said, 'So I notice, John, and it worries me. You ought to at least eat a biscuit or two to stay your stomach until supper.'

" 'All right,' John said, eating several more biscuits.

"Sometimes," Matt concluded, "a genius can be a lot of fun in a house. Sometimes."

We should like to know just how long it took John to design and make the rifle. The job would have been notable enough if he had given two years to it. Few original successful arms have been brought to the test-firing stage in the space of two or three years. Many of the guns that are widely used today were four or five years from inception to pilot model, though, perhaps fortunately, John did not know that. All available evidence indicates that the making of the gun took John less than one year. It was started sometime after his twenty-third birthday, January 23, 1878, and completed sometime prior to his application for a patent on May 12, 1879. The model had to be finished before the time consuming procedure of applying for a patent could be complied with. There was, we know, considerable correspondence with the patent attorney in the East—and there was no air mail. John also had to give some study to the drawings, for he had never seen a blueprint. When the amount of time consumed by these formalities is subtracted from May 12, 1879, it becomes obvious that both the designing and model-making had to be done in the year 1878. The best evidence is the patent model itself, now on display in the Smithsonian Institution, Washington, D.C. Stamped upon its barrel is: J. M. BROWNING OGDEN U.T. 1878.

This is all the more remarkable when we realize that during the same year, 1878, John made another single-shot rifle. This gun differs from the single-shot John patented in that it has a fixed trigger guard and a separate finger lever which drops the breechblock and cocks the hammer. As far as is known, the only surviving model of this gun—now owned by Ed's son, Frank Browning—was the only one made. This rifle bears the same markings as the patent model of John's other single-

Patent-application model for John M. Browning's Single Shot Rifle. From this prototype came the Browning Brothers Single Shot and the first of Browning's Winchester guns, the Model 1885. The model is on display in the Smithsonian Institution, Washington, D.C. The markings read: J. M. BROWNING OGDEN U.T. 1878. THE SMITHSONIAN INSTITUTION

During 1878, the twenty-three-year-old fledgling inventor designed two single-shot rifles. This was the second, an experimental model with a fixed trigger guard and a separate finger lever which drops the breechblock and cocks the hammer. This model, now in the collection of Frank Browning, Ed Browning's son, is believed to be the only one of this design made.
FRANK BROWNING AND GERALD KEOGH

shot.

The patenting perplexed the inexperienced young inventor. How did one go about getting a patent for a gun? No one in Ogden seemed to know. Finally, after several long discussions among the brothers, John came up with a solution. He had a catalogue from Schoverling, Daly and Gales, a jobbing house in New York. They had already purchased about fifty dollars' worth of shop supplies from this firm. John figured that constituted as good an introduction as any. There were several order blanks in the catalogue, and John used one for the letter. It was short and to the point: "Please tell me how to patent a gun, and oblige."

After several weeks the jobber sent them the name of a patent attorney. The brothers wrote him an identical letter, which in turn brought a letter explaining patent procedure and even a copy of a patent application.

By studying that, John got the form for describing what he had that was "new and novel," after which he and Jonathan drew up a list of claims and sent them to the attorney to put in proper legal form. John always suspected that the arrival of the letter produced loud laughter in the attorney's office. 'We dropped a capital letter, or a punctuation mark, here or there, just because we'd seen them in books. We had no dictionary, and probably more than half the words were misspelled. Anyhow," he would add, "we got a patent, and it was good enough to suit the Winchester Company when they bought it."

9

THE APPLICATION for the patent was made on May 12, 1879. A month earlier John had taken another momentous step. On April 10, 1879, John Moses Browning married Rachel Teresa Child.

Rachel's father, Warren G. Child, merchant and landowner, had passed the Browning shop too many times to be entirely pleased with his daughter's choice. Still, he had to admit that John was a good-looking young man, a practicing Mormon who did not smoke or drink. He gave the couple his blessing, together with a cook stove, bedroom set, cottage organ, and a cow. Delivery on all these items had to be delayed until their new house was finished; the Browning adobe was already crowded, and the cow, which would not "come in fresh" for some months, was comfortable on a farm that Mr. Child owned. Rachel had to wait about a year for her house, as nearly as we can estimate.

By the time the house was finished, John was building his new shop downtown and was so pressed for money that he could add to father Child's contributions only a few essentials: kitchen table and chairs, a few dishes and utensils, and two indispensables, a rocking chair and a cradle. It has become a Browning family legend that after Rachel had arranged and rearranged, making as brave a showing as possible with the little she had to work with, John looked through the house, frowned thoughtfully and said, "It seems a little crowded, Rachel, but I believe there is still room for the cow."

Jonathan's health was failing rapidly. One of the greatest pleasures of his life occurred when John handed him the finished single-shot rifle

Rachel Teresa Child at eighteen, shortly before she became the wife of John M. Browning.   JOHN M. BROWNING ARMORY

to test-fire. "He stood as straight as he had at the turkey shoots in Tennessee," John remarked, "loaded, closed the action, fired, snapped out the empty and asked for another cartridge." Gunmaker himself, Jonathan was devoutly proud in the knowledge that he had sired a greater gunmaker, and had helped to give direction to his talent.

Jonathan died on June 21, 1879, in his seventy-fourth year. "Died of weariness," John said. "He had worked so hard that, finally tired out, he went to sleep and didn't wake up." He had turned the shop over to John

J. M. BROWNING.
Breech-Loading Fire-Arm.

No. 220,271.   **Patented Oct. 7, 1879.**

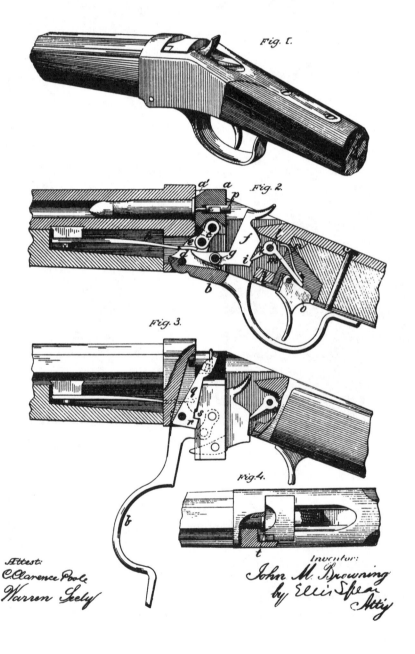

Fig. 1.

Fig. 2.

Fig. 3.

Fig. 4.

Attest:
C. Clarence Poole
Warren Seely

Inventor:
John M. Browning
by Ellis Spear
Atty

UNITED STATES PATENT OFFICE

JOHN M. BROWNING, OF OGDEN CITY, UTAH TERRITORY.

IMPROVEMENT IN BREECH-LOADING FIRE-ARMS.

Specification forming part of Letters Patent No. **220,271,** dated October 7, 1879; application filed May 12, 1879.

To all whom it may concern:

Be it known that I, JOHN M. BROWNING, of Ogden City, Utah Territory, have invented an Improvement in Breech-Loading Fire-Arms, of which the following is a specification.

My invention relates to breech-loading fire-arms, and consists in certain details of construction, hereinafter fully described and particularly indicated in the claims, whereby the operating parts are greatly simplified and rendered more durable and certain in their operation.

In the drawings, Figure 1 represents a perspective view of the breech and a part of the stock of my improved gun. Fig. 2 represents a longitudinal vertical section of Fig. 1, some of the parts being shown in side elevation. Fig. 3 is a side elevation, the case being partly broken away to show the interior mechanism. Fig. 4 is a top view, some of the parts being broken away to show the position of the cartridge in place and the retractor.

My invention relates particularly to that class of breech-loading fire-arms in which the breech is closed by a vertically-sliding block operated by the guard-lever, and carrying the hammer with it in its motion up and down.

The breech-block *a* slides vertically within the breech-piece, to which it fits closely, and against which it bears both in front and rear, so that when it is raised it effectually and securely closes the breech of the gun. This breech-piece is moved by the guard lever *b*, to which it is connected by the link *c*, within the slot in the interior of the block. The guard-lever *b* is pivoted to the breech-frame at *d*, slightly in front of the breech-block. The guard is also formed with lugs *e e*, adapted to fit into the slotted breech-block and to receive between them the link *c*, to which they are connected by a pin at a point within the slot when the guard is brought into a position for firing. The guard-lever is also so constructed that when it is brought into the position last specified it effectually closes the opening through which the block and the hammer move when the lever is depressed, as in opening the breech.

The hammer *f* is pivoted to the block at *g*, within the slot of said block. The tail of the hammer extends through the slot and rests, when the block is raised, under the end of the spring *h*, which is secured to the barrel, as shown in Figs. 2 and 3.

The breech-piece is slotted to the rear sufficiently to give space for the hammer when at full-cock. The hammer is constructed with an offset at *i*, against which the dog *k* bears, when the breech-block is raised, to close the breech. This dog is pivoted at *l*, and is provided with an arm, *m*, and spring *n*, the latter bearing against the shell in the breech-frame, so as to keep the arm *m* pressed down against the trigger *o*. The pressure of the spring *n* keeps the end of the dog *k* against the rear edge of the hammer, whether the breech-block be raised, as shown in Fig. 2, or lowered, as shown in Fig. 3. When the guard *b* is depressed for the purpose of opening the breech of the gun, by means of the links *b* it draws down the breech-block, carrying with it the hammer *f*, the hammer being thrown forward in its passage, and the tail of it dropping from contact with the spring *h*. When the lever is elevated its return movement lifts the breech-block, and with it the hammer; but as the dog *k* comes in contact with the offset *i* the rear part of the hammer is arrested in its movement and held in place while the forward part continues to rise, being carried upward by the continued movement of the lever *b*, so that the hammer is thrown back by the completion of the movement and held at full-cock, resting over the point and on the breech-piece, while in the latter part of the movement the tail of the hammer has come in contact with the spring *h*, and lifted it sufficiently to bring the strain of the spring upon the tail of the hammer, so as to give a suitable blow upon the firing-pin.

The breech-block is supported when the guard-lever is closed by means of the links and lugs *e e*, the pivot-pin which connects the said link and lugs being carried into line with the other link-pin and pivot of the guard-lever, or slightly past the dead-point, so as to securely lock the block in closed position.

The firing-pin is of the ordinary construction, and is represented at *p*. The retractor is shown at *q*. It is pivoted at the lower left-

2   **220,271**

hand corner in a slot in the breech-piece, and rests in a recess cut in one side of the breech-block. The shape of the retractor is shown in Fig. 3. At the lower end it has an offset, r, which projects into a groove in the lower part of the breech-block. A projection, s, on the breech-block extending across the upper end of this lower slot strikes the offset r upon the lower end of the retractor when the block is near the limit of its downward motion, and throws the upper end of the retractor back, thus ejecting the empty shell. A stud projecting inwardly upon the retractor, as shown at t, Fig. 4, rests beneath the flange of the shell, so as to obtain a suitable hold and allow the retractor in its motion to throw out the shell. The retractor extends upward through its recess in the breech-piece, and the upper end of it is flush with the surface of the latter. This effectually closes the slot in the breech-block against the admission of dirt or anything which might clog the block. The breech-block is beveled at a', in order to push home the cartridge in case it should happen not to be sufficiently pushed forward into its place when the block rises.

I am aware that a breech-block carrying a hammer pivoted upon the block and cocked by upward motion of the said block, in connection with the trigger, is not new.

What I claim as my invention, and desire to secure by Letters Patent of the United States, is—

1. In a breech-loading fire-arm, the combination of the slotted breech-block and the hammer pivoted within the slot with the spring in front of the block, projecting between the lugs e e of the guard-lever and bearing upon the tail of the hammer, and with the link c, connecting the block and guard-lever, as set forth.

2. The combination of the slotted breech-block, the lugs e e, the link c, and the hammer f, pivoted at g, and extending between the lugs c, to bear against the spring h, as and for the purposes set forth.

3. The dog k, provided with the arm m, resting on the trigger, and with the spring n, operating in connection with the rear of the hammer and the offset i, and with the breech-block and spring h, as and for the purpose set forth.

In testimony whereof I have signed my name to this specification in the presence of two subscribing witnesses.

JOHN M. BROWNING.

Witnesses:
JONATHAN BROWNING,
C. F. MIDDLETON.

a year before his death, saying, "You've earned it ten times over, John Mose, and anyhow, it's not much of a gift. Maybe if you run it your way, you can make something of it."

The first of John M. Browning's many firearms patents, covering the Single Shot Rifle. The application was filed May 12, 1879, and U. S. Patent No. 220,271 was granted October 7, 1879. The writing of the patent application seemed to the brothers more complicated than the inventing of the gun.

JOHN M. BROWNING ARMORY

John became nominal head of the brothers of the second two families by right of age; he had never assumed authority over them, although they always looked up to him. The responsibilities Jonathan had handed over to him in increasing volume, year by year, as the elder one's strength failed, had matured John. He did not, as might be expected, immediately try to modernize the shop. Instead he set in motion a few simple plans for stimulating business. His schemes cost little or nothing; he simply made use of already existing opportunities.

General conditions helped him. The town was growing rapidly, enjoying its first boom as a result of the coming of the railroad. Ogden was now the most important railroad center between Omaha and the west coast, a supply point for regions as far away as Montana. The wheels of the freight wagons cut ruts which served as guides for the railroads' expanding network of branch lines.

John arranged with a few reliable freighters to pick up repair jobs along their routes and bring them into his shop. He worked out a scheme whereby a freighter would bring in a job, pay John's charges when he picked it up, then collect the repair charges plus his own transportation charges when he delivered the gun. There were many men in remote places glad to avail themselves of this service. A broken gun, far from a gunsmith, was a calamity. In such cases, the question was how soon rather than how much.

Jonathan's prices, usually fixed by impulse, and always too low, were now revised upward. John felt that the only way to make money repairing guns was to work fast and charge as much as a slow gunsmith. "Don't try to make an old gun look new," John told his brothers. "Just make it work. The owner is used to the way it looks."

Other stimulants for business were two signs John set up at strategic points. A branch of the Overland Trail ran straight through the middle of Ogden, north and south. As much of the trail as lay within the city limits was named Main Street, and that well-traveled highway passed just a block from the shop. Down on Uncle Davy Jenkins' corner, its little log house long a landmark, John erected a sign, neatly lettered in red, which offered expert gun repairing one block east.

Two blocks north of that sign, on the same highway, the Douglas Blacksmith Shop did a thriving business, its prominent location drawing to it the greater share of the "through travel." John was well acquainted with the owner and his helpers, and was permitted to nail his second sign near the wide front door. It simply announced, EXPERT GUN REPAIRING. INQUIRE WITHIN. All inquiries were directed two blocks south and one block east, to the shop. The spirit of neighbor-help-neighbor was very much alive in the settlement, as it was in all the Mormon communities, and Mr. Douglas took a genuine interest in finding work for the boys.

John was astonished at the amount of business sent to the shop by those signs and at the number of jobs brought in by the freighters. The lean days seemed to be over. By the end of 1879, he and Matt were so swamped with work that he got Ed to give up his job in the railroad freight yard and turn his hand to gunsmithing. This was entirely to Ed's liking. He had helped with the shopwork from time to time and had spent many evenings watching John when nightwork had to be done. At such times, John usually gave him something to do. Within a year he was a first-class gunsmith. Eventually he became John's model-maker, and the two tall half brothers worked together side by side until John's death.

John was looking beyond the immediate needs of the shop when he cleared a place on the littered bench and bought a new vise for Ed. Even before he made the model of the single-shot, when it looked as though he was to be a gunsmith all his life, he had decided that he would build a new shop downtown, where he was sure he could double his business. By the time his model was finished, he was considering a still larger shop, a small factory, no less, and that would mean employing more mechanics.

For a time he had avoided facing his most bothersome problem: what does a man do with a gun once he has made it? He had little experience to guide him. He knew that most of the breechloaders bore the names of men, presumably the inventors. It looked as though, in each case, a man had invented a gun and then manufactured it himself, maybe beginning in a shop and building up from there. Jonathan had made guns of his own design in Illinois and Iowa, a good many. They were muzzleloaders, to be sure, their parts easier to make than those of the breechloaders; still, it might be managed.

He had considered the advisability of trying to sell his patent and had drafted a letter to the patent attorney, asking for suggestions as to procedure; but the harder John concentrated on the subject, the less he liked it. He tore up the letter. There was no question that selling the patent was the sensible thing, the simple thing, to do. He was a greenhorn and knew it. He could see himself going East and trying to peddle his gun. That was what it seemed to him—peddling. Suppose he managed to get an interview with the head of a big factory, and asked a couple thousand dollars for the rifle. He would be asking a favor even in seeking permission to show the model. He was damned if he would ask a favor of anybody, especially if there was a good chance of his being laughed at. There was no likelihood that a buyer would come way out into the wilds to him. He was left finally with no alternative but to make the rifle himself.

He was not completely unprepared. He had his motive power and a large pile of brick. For two years, snugly housed in a small lean-to nailed against one end of the shop, regularly oiled against attacks of rust, a five-horse upright steam engine had been waiting. It came to that comfortable berth in this wise. Ed, working in the railroad freight yard, casually mentioned to John that a boxcar, being switched, had got a bump and a pretty little upright engine had been damaged. It was not much hurt, in Ed's opinion, but the consignee had refused to accept it. Ed figured a fellow could buy it for a song, and fix it up without much trouble. John said he would sing a couple of songs for a little engine; if he ever built a new shop it would come in handy. The brothers examined it and saw that they could make the repairs easily enough. They could also, at the same time, have some fun learning about steam engines. The price John paid is not recorded, but we can be sure that anything John bought in those days did not cost much. The little engine chugged for years in the Browning shop, turning miller and lathe for many of John's models. Three of the oldest of Jonathan's grandsons remember staring at it in fascination, feeling the heat on their faces, wondering if it would explode.

The pile of brick that waited not far from the engine shed was a memento of one of Jonathan's ventures. He had undertaken the making of brick as a means of saving his sons from the sin of idleness. The sons were so sure of his motive that they never quite forgave him. Happily for the boys, the project proved unprofitable, and Jonathan abandoned it in less than a year—by gradual face-saving degrees and with considerable relief, as he was getting too old for such heavy labor. At first John was assigned to work in the yard during the forenoons; before long he was back in the shop full time. His replacement, Ed, was then offered a job handling freight for the railroad, a job he had quietly but diligently solicited. Jonathan thereupon developed a pain in his back and shut down the yard.

When Jonathan gave the shop to John, he included the odds and ends of brick that had been scattered about the yard. He said they were defectives and bats that nobody would buy but suggested that if John should build a new shop he might use them for the rear end, where they wouldn't show much, and buy new brick for the front, near the street. When the time came, they went into the factory walls, at the rear end, as Jonathan had suggested, furnishing nearly half the needed supply.

John gave a good deal of time to looking before he leaped. First, he drew a rough but adequate plan of the building and had a local jack-of-all-trades figure an approximate cost. The cost is another lost item, but again we can safely say, not much. The same can be said of the pieces of used equipment he purchased, mostly in Salt Lake City.

Before he spent a cent on the new enterprise, John had a fairly accurate estimate of the outlay that would be required. It looked as though his savings would more than suffice for the milling machine, lathe, shafting, pulleys, and belts he had picked out. There were a good many things in the old shop he could use. He had a good anvil, three vises of different sizes, an emery wheel, and the foot lathe, which he could hook up to the power and use for small work. And there was the forge, with its bellows. A new brick foundation for the forge and a little paint on the bellows and they wouldn't look so bad. All of his hand-tools were serviceable. He had made many of them himself.

For the building site, John selected a thirty-foot piece of property, on the edge of the business district but not in it. He probably got it for not more than two hundred dollars. There were only two buildings on the lot; one, the Douglas Blacksmith Shop, whose proximity had influenced his choice of location, was less than two hundred feet away. The location was also less than three blocks from home, making an easy walk, with not much time lost coming and going. This was a consideration of importance in the winter and spring, when the sidewalks were deep snow, slush, or mud.

John thought he could pay for the building out of current shop earnings, by purchasing materials in small lots, just enough to keep ahead of the workmen. If he found himself getting behind, he would simply halt the job until he could accumulate more money. That way there would be no debts.

On January 22, 1880, the day before John's twenty-fifth birthday, his wife Rachel gave birth to a son. A blizzard was roaring furiously down from the mountains. That east wind, happily infrequent, had on occasion flattened fences, uprooted stout trees, and even unroofed houses in Ogden. John, roused from sleep, dressed hurriedly, yelled to his mother to start a fire, and ran across the street to the home of Sister Sarah Pidcock, midwife.

Returning, and forcing the door closed against the wind, John found his mother with a hatchet and an upturned kitchen chair. During the evening she had twice reminded John that the wood was low, but he had forgotten. Now she was preparing to split up the chair.

John took the hatchet and looked around the room, his usual self-composure blown away by the blizzard. Suddenly he spied a gunstock, finished and shellacked the previous evening, which had been brought in to dry by the kitchen stove. Kicking a brick out from under the stove, where several were kept for foot warmers, and using it for a block, he split the stock into kindling before his mother's wide eyes. "It was the only time," Matt later said, "that we know John completely lost his head."

John's first-born, a son, who was named John, arrived without further complications. The checkered stock was not quickly forgotten, however. It became a source of boisterous conjecture for the brothers in the shop. Why had John passed up the chair—which was old, loose-jointed, and replaceable for a dollar—in favor of a four-dollar finished stock? The boys, familiar with their Bible, decided that John had wanted to make a burnt offering and had laid his fattest calf on the altar. It was fortunate, they decided, that the model of the Single Shot had been left in the shop.

PART THREE

THE MAN

In his maturity, John was offered an honorary degree by a university but refused it with the brief explanation that he made it a hard and fast rule never to accept anything he had not earned.

He did not deviate from this rule when, during the First World War, some of his friends in Army Ordnance tried to persuade him to accept a colonelcy, arguing that the title would enhance his authority, especially in his almost daily contacts and conferences with members of the armed services.

"Gentlemen," John said, beginning one of his longest public speeches. "I appreciate this very much, and I might even adjust myself to being called Colonel around the factories and proving grounds. But I'd never dare take the title West."

1

THE BUILDING and operation of John's arms factory may well be
unique in the annals of industry. It even taxed John's credulity,
when he looked back from middle age and retraced the entire episode
from the budding idea of the rifle to its manufacture and sale.

He undertook to build his factory with under a thousand dollars in
the bank. He had never operated a power-driven machine; he had not
seen very many in operation. He proposed to use Ed, Sam, and George
as masons and carpenters in the construction, and as mechanics thereafter, though all three lacked experience in both fields.

He planned to keep Matt and Ed in the shop whenever there was
sufficient work; when a dull half day came along, one or both could trot
down and lay brick. Sam was working at the freight yard but was
lonesome there with no Brownings around and was glad to get back to
the clan. George, still a boy, was studying to be a bookkeeper, but he
arranged for his teacher to give him night lessons and joined his
brothers during the day. Though Sam and George lacked actual training with tools, they were sons of Jonathan and, as such, had been
drafted for many tasks in their father's varied enterprises.

John did not go so far as to leave the boys to struggle alone. He hired
the jack-of-all-trades who had helped him figure costs on the building to
make masons and carpenters out of them. The boys were not totally
lacking in qualifications. They were tall and muscular, with thick,
serviceable calluses on their hands. They did not tire easily.

The whole operation attracted a great deal of amused attention. The
Brownings knew and were known by everyone in the town, and few
passersby failed to stop long enough to flip a jibe at the toiling crew.
They quickly dubbed the enterprise "the Browning Brothers Factory,"
little realizing that this was exactly what John had in mind, to build a
factory in Ogden. Skepticism soon gave way to wonder.

The boys, as carpenters and masons, did a rough job, as may be imagined, but a rapid one. John was more concerned with speed than smoothness of walls. Protruding corners of brick bothered him not at all. He was a little disturbed one day to find Sam knocking a row of loose brick from the wall and scraping off the mortar. After John reminded him that he was supposed to be putting up a building, instead of tearing it down, Sam sadly explained. A pretty girl had walked past, and the course of brick had followed her nearly all the way to the corner.

In retrospect it would appear that John had been planning the factory all his life. From boyhood, he had made the acquaintance of almost every piece of machinery that came to town. The railroad shops, growing rapidly, drew him often and taught him much. He seemed to have no difficulty in edging up to a machine and talking with its operator. Perhaps the grease on his own hands was a kind of pass; also, his questions were so sensible that they received answers. It seems that genius possesses, among its more amazing characteristics, an abnormal acquisitive instinct, gathering knowledge and knacks far beyond foreseeable needs. As far back as anecdote and reminiscence give us glimpses into John's youth, we find his interests wide-awake, exploring, gathering.

Yet, as John later admitted to one of his sons, the whole plan looked like a fool's venture. "Every once in a while," he said, "alone in the old shop, trying to scratch out enough for the payroll and the bills for materials, I'd get a sudden odd feeling about the future. It didn't look like days and weeks I was heading into. It looked like an avalanche I'd started and that was rolling down on me. Sometimes I felt like running for it—jumping right over the anvil, which was between me and the door. But I was too busy to do much worrying."

He expressed his feelings even more concisely when he once said, "There were times I'd go a week without a good laugh."

Before long, however, John's planning began to pay off. Jonathan's old shop was paying fabulous dividends, better than 100 per cent a month on the original investment, John estimated. He was now able to meet his wage obligations every Saturday night and to pay his bills for materials with reasonable promptness. Wages in all occupations were low, and the members of John's crew, with the exception of the foreman, were hardly more than boys, two of them being still under twenty. John himself was just twenty-five, and there is good reason to guess that he and Rachel were living on not more than a dollar a day. There was no lack of food, however. Rachel took pride in her cooking. As soon as the cow began to produce, Rachel made her own butter and traded the surplus at one of the stores for staples.

There was not only the day's work, and keeping an eye on the building; John had to plan, or try to plan, ways to make the guns when the new shop was ready. And he had to give the boys lessons, especially the youngest ones, Sam and George. Now and then he would have them all come to the shop after supper and study the model. Each would have a turn at taking the rifle apart and putting it together. He soon had a fine assembly line—minus the parts to assemble.

The receiver, of course, was the big job, and they went over it again and again, studying how they would make the cuts in a miller. John learned as much as his brothers. As the lessons went on, he made numerous small changes. Occasionally he would see a short cut—for example, a change in the shape of a part that permitted one operation to do the work of two. These little simplifications eventually saved money in manufacture. When John made the first model, he left enough metal on the end of the lever to make a curve that would fit the thumb for ejection. It would also look pretty, he decided. But when he started to shape that end, he realized that sticking out as it did, it would have to be stamped carefully and given a nice smooth finish, else it would be conspicuous and ugly. And that would take more time than it was worth. So he just whacked off the end, leaving half an inch that he shaped to lie flat on the lower tang. When Winchester brought out the rifle, they used the curve, but they had the facilities to make it without much expense, whereas it would have cost the Brownings three or four hours' work. There were many such small economies.

In his plans John tried to anticipate every need, knowing that one overlooked essential might delay production indefinitely. High on his list of requirements were barrels and forgings. Again he wrote to Schoverling, Daly and Gales for help. That firm sent him the names of two manufacturers who would supply barrels to his specifications. As for forgings, the firm itself could furnish them through a connection and would obtain prices for him if he would send samples of the parts desired. He made wooden blanks to serve as samples. In writing to the jobber, he baited the letter with the statement that he and his brothers were planning to add a complete stock of sporting goods as soon as possible after completion of the new shop. The sporting goods store was Matt's idea, enthusiastically seconded by George, and approved, with some reservations, by John.

The prices for the barrels and forgings are not known, but that they must have been absurdly low by present standards is made evident by the fact that standard grades of the rifle, after it became known as the Winchester Single Shot, retailed as late as 1900 for $14.50, with generous discounts to jobber and retailer. We know, moreover, that the price had to be very low to come within John's budget.

The completed structure was substantial and weather-tight, not at all imposing in a frontier community where expediency was the architect. It was twenty-five by fifty feet, allowing space for additional equipment when it could be afforded. Economy prescribed a low ceiling; it effected a saving in brick and labor and simplified the problem of heating in winter. Shafting and pulleys were just high enough to give ample head-clearance to the tall brothers.

There could be no basement, for there was no drainage system in town. The street in front of the shop and the square block across from it were a bog in spring, when the melting snows sent their rivulets down from the hills. It was not uncommon for a heavy freight wagon to drop a wheel in a chuckhole out front, and stick there, despite some of the finest swearing in the territory, until townsmen waded out to help.

2

WITH THE ARRIVAL of the first load of materials, John set up a sign at the edge of the sidewalk, bearing the announcement NEW BROWNING GUN SHOP. The fact that he had made and patented a rifle was well known in the town. To many people, the gun was less impressive than the patent. John had been working with guns as far back as anybody could remember him; there was little surprise in his making a gun. But a patent was mysterious and, as such, important. It excited curiosity and gave the factory a good deal of advance advertising. The boys, working on the main street, exposed to the public, received many inquiries relative to price and delivery date. John gave instructions to take the name and address of every man who seemed interested and to tell him that he would be among the first to be notified as soon as guns were ready. The price would be reasonable. These instructions were not qualified by ifs. John did not propose to go into the manufacturing business with a nervous and doubting crew; whatever doubts he may have had himself he kept hidden. His brothers seem to have ridden on his confidence as upon a flying carpet.

The boys were young, healthy, and full of pranks. There were times when John, who carried most of the responsibility for the enterprise, felt that they were not seriously considering the job ahead. He was looking for a good lead into a sermon when Split Barlow came in.

His full name, as far as the brothers ever knew, was "Split Nose" Barlow. At some moment in the dim past his nose had been split so that it looked like not one but two noses. Plenty of people could tell how it had happened, but each version differed, since Split never gave the same explanation twice. Now and then Split got happily drunk. Usually at such times he would tell one of his outlandish yarns: bear fight, Indians, whatever the subject, it always ended with, "And that's how I come to get my nose split." By one account, when Split was a young man his family moved from one community to another. In loading the wagon his father's quarter-can of gunpowder was chucked into the oven of the stove, to save space. Upon arrival at their destination that evening, they assembled the stove first thing and built a fire in preparation for supper. "Blowed off both oven doors," Split said, "killed the cat under the stove, and thumped all four lids against the ceiling." At this point, by habit, Split would pause in his narrative, take out a plug of tobacco and a jackknife, cut off and take a chew, then finish grandly with, "Well, I looked up too late to dodge. And that's how I come to get my nose split."

Split did a little farming, but he made his living principally by hunting and trapping, in partnership with another man. His shack was located high up in one of the mountain valleys. John was always glad to see him. If it was the season for anything to be caught or shot, Split usually brought it—trout, blue grouse, or a roast of venison—along with his sense of humor.

Split's partner, a man named Sprague, once told John about one of their hunting trips. There were a few grizzlies in the mountains in those days; one day the two men found one. They were going down a game trail through thick brush, when all at once the trail opened into a glade covered with clumps of service berry bushes. Not over thirty feet ahead, a grizzly was standing straight up, ten feet high, feeding. He would wrap his arms around a big clump, hug it close, and bite off the berries. Fortunately for the men, his back was toward them. Throwing up his old Sharps, Split took aim. Sprague had better sense. Grabbing Split's arm he whispered, "Too much b'ar, Split! Too much b'ar!" Sprague claimed he didn't draw a breath until he'd pulled Split a hundred yards up the trail.

When Split came into the shop he was carrying his old Sharps. John had repaired it more times than he had any other gun. It was a good rifle, but Split led it a rough life. John had already put on two or three stocks, and it seemed to him that he had replaced every part at least twice. He took down the box of Sharps parts automatically. On this day Split needed a new mainspring.

Split was a little tipsy, some of his front teeth were gone, and he had a big wad of tobacco in his mouth. As usual, he talked fast. He peered into the box. "John," he said, "that spring's jul-uk a mool shoo." "It's what?" John asked. "Jul-uk a mool shoo," Split repeated. And for the first time John noticed that the Sharps mainspring did look just like a mule shoe.

As John was putting in the spring Split noticed a model of the Single Shot, leaning against the wall, in a little rack John had made. Matt had drawfiled and polished all the parts that showed, and had made a stock and fore end that were a big improvement over the first model, which John had whacked out in a hurry. John had casehardened the parts and put on a shiny barrel.

It looked pretty good to Split. He operated the lever, and was tickled to see the hammer cock as he closed the action. His praise was spontaneous; he immediately wanted to know when he could get one and for how much. John told him what he had been telling everyone; he could not make any definite promises but would let him know. Split pulled out his poke and shook out a ten-dollar gold piece. John knew he didn't have ten dollars often, and there appeared to be nothing else in his poke, but he slapped the coin down on the bench like a millionaire and said it was advance payment on the first gun. As much as he needed it, John couldn't take the money, but he weakened to the extent of promising Split the first gun.

That evening the brothers assembled in the shop and excitedly told John that they had taken four orders that day.

John inquired as to how much actual money they had been offered, then let them stutter a minute. Then he gave his lecture. One of the brothers later recalled, "John had heard a lot of preaching. He knew when to talk loud, and when to talk low; when to point a finger, when to thump something. But no preacher ever painted a darker picture of the times ahead."

Then John let up a little, recalling that the new shop was finished, throwing in a little praise. But he also told them that all the orders they had talked about were up in the clouds. Some of them might come down within reach, but most of them would probably drift away. As far as he knew, only one order had been backed by anything more substantial than wind.

Then he told them about Split. Matt said: "When he took that imaginary gold piece off the bench and held it up between his thumb and forefinger, we saw it, and when he smacked it down on his left palm, we flinched, afraid he'd drop it. He'd made it plain that we had a big job ahead. But when he finished, the factory came down from the clouds and landed kerplunk on its foundations. We could almost hear the windows rattle."

3

IT IS NATURAL to suppose that John felt sharp pangs on the day of the move, as the brothers backed Uncle Mose's wagon up to the door of the old shop for loading. From the deeply rooted contents they selected first those items which would permit gun repairing to be resumed in the new shop with minimum interruption. The heavy anvil, the lathe, the forge and bellows, the vises; all those reminders of Jonathan, hauled by him across the plains, had so long occupied their places that they were like works of nature, akin to the mountains. To disturb their long and steadfast vigil might well have seemed like desecration to John, inheritor and custodian. According to Rachel, however, John was particularly gay. Had he not kept telling the boys to get a move on, that they had to be ready for work the next morning or they'd not get paid Saturday night, he might have appeared to have been loading the wagon for a big-game hunt.

Some writers have made a shrine of the old shop. But there was nothing of this attitude in John's feeling for it in those years of struggle. He had sweated in the shack when the summer sun scorched and wrinkled the boards; he had shivered in it when winter winds whistled through the cracks of summer's warping. Time and again, he had interrupted a job in hand to make a needed tool. He had ground a keen edge on a cold chisel and with it sharpened a file worn smooth. The big bellows had wheezed and groaned under his weight and impatience; its companion, the forge, had in retaliation smoked and singed him until his mother complained that he smelled like an Injun. He had swung the sledge, while Jonathan or Matt held the tongs, turning a glowing lump this way or that at his bidding.

John did not pat the side of the shop affectionately, and apostrophize it for the historian, nor did he sigh a fond farewell. He acted toward it as he would with a completed gun in later years; he was finished with it and he immediately put it out of mind. After everything had been hauled to the new quarters, or sold to Pierce's foundry, he told Uncle Mose, "If you can use the boards in the old shop for a chicken coop or a cow shed, tell Little Mosey to come and get them." The year was 1880.

The new shop could not be made to run smoothly in a day. Once the contents of the old shop had been moved, there was still the miller, lathe, and other items of equipment shipped from Salt Lake City, to be hauled up from the freight yard in Uncle Mose's wagon. By the beginning of the afternoon of the second day all was moved. But the machinery and accessories lay scattered in disarray around the floor, each item where it had happened to land when skidded in from the wagon. Nothing was new; the signs of wear and tear and the tangled heaps of belting made a scene more suggestive of the catastrophic collapse of an old factory than the beginning of a new one.

John's luck remained with him; as he stood staring at the disorder, unsure where to begin, it materialized in the form of a short, sturdy Englishman. Frank Rushton, gunsmith, who had recently joined the Mormon Church in England and had come for a look at the New World, strolled in through the door, hands in pockets, stiff hat tilted back, mustache jauntily twisted. Rushton had seen the sign outside and had thought that a shop way out in the wilds, especially a new one, might be in need of some expert help.

He seemed to size up what was going on with a single glance, and he stepped among the components of the factory-to-be as among old acquaintances, making frequent comments, more to himself than to the others. The others were speechless, even John. The brothers—untraveled, untaught—stared at the little man. They were all six feet, mostly over. He was scarcely more than five feet, yet he came with a giant's assurance. He summed up the results of his brief inspection by announcing, "It will take a bit of doing, but I think we can 'ave 'er 'umming in a few days." As a casual afterthought, while the brothers still stared, he mentioned that he had worked in some of the best shops and factories in England.

He addressed John, obviously the oldest of the group, and presumably the leader. Names, handshakes, and bits of information were exchanged; at the conclusion of the ceremony, John, his composure regained, said, "All right, Frank, throw your hat and coat on the bench over there and we'll find a gunny sack that will do for an apron. If we both like the idea at six o'clock we'll talk wages. Suit you?"

"Suits me," Rushton replied.

The alliance thus begun lasted only a short time, the few years until Rushton's untimely death, but it was of great importance to the success of the new shop. Rushton was soon one of the family and was always remembered with affection and admiration by the brothers. John later confessed, "When Frank walked in, all cockney and cocky, I was pretending a confidence I was far from feeling."

John had realized that it would take time to get the machinery set up and operating profitably. It was up to him to learn all the tricks of the milling machine, teaching Ed as he learned. Then he had to figure out the fixtures, so that it would not be necessary to make a separate painstaking setup for every cut on every part. He would have to show the boys how to file and finish and assemble the parts. And there was the repair work, which had to finance them; John was the only one able to do some of the complicated jobs. Rushton was the answer to an unspoken prayer.

"I'm not so sure I could have pulled us through without Frank Rushton," John said. "I can see him yet, as he swelled his chest. For the first hour I was a little irritated by his strutting, but he was just compensating for his size I suppose. We were a hulking lot of overgrown youngsters, yet Frank could see in no time that he knew more about setting up that machinery than all of us put together. Pretty soon, he didn't look so short to me. He looked more like one of the angels Pappy thought might drop in any time. When we got well enough acquainted to joke about such things, we agreed that Frank was just what we needed to bring our average down so we could walk through the doorway without bumping our heads. I learned more from Frank than from any other man I ever knew, except Pappy."

According to Ed, John gave Frank a free hand with the installation. "He didn't say much," Ed chuckled. "He knew that if he wasn't careful, he'd say the wrong thing, and give himself away. He didn't mind so much us boys knowing, but he didn't want Frank to find out how green he was. If Frank knew, he forgot it. By the time we were actually turning out parts, Frank was consulting John about everything of importance. I didn't realize how smart John was, until I saw him overtake and pass Frank in three months—and Frank ten years older, and with a world of experience in gunmaking. The difference was, Frank had his set ways of doing things, ways he'd been taught. John figured out new ways, short cuts, that made Frank blink."

John's first production schedule called for twenty-five rifles but fixed no time limit. Twenty-five guns would enable him to establish the most efficient routine; he would be able to determine the special aptitudes of each of the boys and to distribute the work accordingly; parts that got to running ahead could be slowed down, and their momentum diverted to parts that lagged. Then, too, twenty-five new rifles, displayed in the gun rack in the front end of the shop, would be impressive, visible proof that the Browning Gun Factory was in production. John had the list of names that had accumulated while the building was going up, and it seemed safe to assume that a fair proportion of the men would still be sufficiently interested to drop in, if notified a stock of guns was on exhibition.

Ed did most of the milling-machine work. Matt made all the stocks. Frank Rushton made patterns which enabled both Sam and George to tap centers for all pin and screw holes and to drill those holes on the lathe. The foot lathe was belted to the power, and served for light work. Sam and George also did much of the preliminary filing of parts later to be finished by John and Frank. Frank mounted the barrels and sights, operations that needed his high-order skill and painstaking care. John had to do most of the trigger-sear-hammer assembly, with their springs, until Sam and George were able to help. And the repair work had to continue to pay the wages every Saturday evening until the assembly of guns could begin.

A breast-high partition cut off about twenty feet of the front of the room from the shop proper. This space was to be the sporting-goods store, a project that was waiting only for necessary capital. A gun rack, shelves, and a counter were already in place along the south wall, and Matt and George had studied Schoverling's catalogue more assiduously than they ever had a schoolbook; but, for the present, the display was limited to finished repair jobs, a few assorted boxes of cartridges, and a small supply of loose ammunition. Matt and George had an initial order made up and had planned just how the stock was to be arranged.

John kept his doubts to himself. Matt, however, assuming more and more responsibility, was not so calm. His only recorded reminiscence of this period was, appropriately, one of comic relief. The incident occurred just a few weeks before they began to assemble the rifles in the midst of the watermelon season.

Aware of their close financial situation, Matt had wanted to borrow two or three hundred dollars from the bank, using the new building as security. John had vetoed the plan, noting that Pappy had worried enough about debt to do the whole Browning family for three generations. Matt argued that they were cutting it too close.

One day, shortly after their conversation, a farmer from a nearby settlement arrived in town with a load of watermelons. He raised the best melons the boys had ever tasted and was always sure of a sale at the shop. On this day he came in, leaned on the partition, and called out, "Boys—how about some melons?"

"Big ones?" John called back.

"Damn near as long as a Browning and dead ripe," the farmer yelled above the noise of the machinery.

"Bully!" John answered. "Matt, help him lug in about four—and pick the biggest."

Matt knew what was in the till—sixty cents. Trying to sound casual, he asked the price of the melons. They were twenty cents apiece. Telling the farmer to wait a minute, he went back along the bench to John. Speaking in a low voice so the others couldn't hear, he told John he had paid out a C.O.D. an hour ago; there was only sixty cents in the till, the melons would be eighty, and he didn't have a cent of his own.

To Matt, then only twenty-one and tired from overwork and worry, the situation seemed catastrophic. John just threw back his head and laughed, fishing out a couple of dimes from his pocket.

"There you are, Matt. As Pappy always said, 'The Lord will provide.' Now go help lug in those melons."

A halt was called in production. There was a big box out back where they cut the melons. Using a long butcher knife that had seen similar use in the old shop, John, by custom, presided at the cutting. Always he sliced lengthwise; he felt it was a sacrilege to cut a large melon in rings, and a small melon was just an exasperation. Given a good slice of melon John didn't appear to have a care in the world.

Matt pulled the box into the doorway and straddled it, so as to keep an eye on the shop in case of customers. And a man did come in.

"Tell him to come back and have some melon," John suggested. But the man was in a hurry and couldn't join them; he had just stopped by to pay three dollars for a stock they had made for him.

As Matt came back, all he could think of were the words, "The Lord will provide." John noticed his strange expression and asked, "Who was it? What did he want?"

"Oh," Matt said, "it was just the Lord. He's around providing today."

The others hadn't heard the earlier conversation and didn't know what he meant. But John knew.

"How much?" he asked.

"Three dollars," Matt answered.

"Well, well," John said. "I wish I could have cut Him a slice of melon."

In three months, the twenty-five rifles were in the rack, all except number one, which was laid away for Split Barlow. John had personally stamped the figure "1" on that rifle. On the evening before the grand opening, the brothers came back to the shop after supper and went over every gun with rags and wiping sticks. John put a dummy through each gun several times, making sure that the opening and closing movements were smooth, the trigger-pull clean, the ejection snappy. He had already done this time and again, as each gun was assembled; he had, in fact, examined every part before assembly, now and then giving a gentle stroke with a file, passing it through the delicate gauges of thumbs and fingers: *the feather touch,* as one old mechanic of John's acquaintance called it.

The rifles made a pretty sight, lined up with straight-edge precision against the new unpainted pine. There had been no time or money for painting the rack. It was hard for John to leave the glittering row. He had made his big bet on these guns. His pockets were empty. The next few days were to determine whether he was to win or lose. It is seldom that a man confronts the future with the odds so definite. No chances could be taken, and when the rifles were locked up for the night, Matt was left as guard, to sleep on a cot near the display.[1]

4

At THE END of a week, rack and shelves were bare, and John had several hundred dollars in the bank. The rifle sold for $25.00, but with the indispensable extras—the reloading outfit, powder, lead, and primers; the canvas covers, wiping sticks, and other odds and ends— most sales totaled over $30.00.

John gave each of his crew a five-dollar gold piece as a bonus, and took one home to Rachel, telling her to spend it all on herself. She

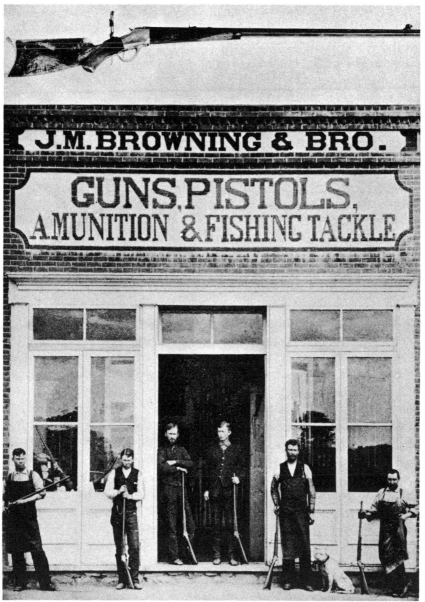

The Browning Brothers Single Shot Rifle and the staff of "The Largest Arms Factory Between Omaha and the Pacific"—the Browning Brothers Factory, Ogden, Utah Territory, about 1882. (Left to right), Sam Browning, George Browning, John M. Browning, Matthew S. Browning, Ed Browning, and Frank Rushton. The rifle is a deluxe grade trimmed up by Matt for his own use. Note John's spelling of the word ammunition.   JOHN M. BROWNING ARMORY bought—and remembered—a hat, shoes, material for a dress, some fancy buttons, and colored ribbons. And there was enough left over for a roast of beef. Around this time John began taking home a can of Booth's Canned Oysters for supper every Saturday night.

He had reason to feel flush. When he began planning the manufacture of the rifle, he had a little over a thousand dollars, the savings that he had accumulated after several years of hard work and frugal living. The steam engine and Jonathan's gift of brickbats could be counted as additional cash. Now, with a suddenness that dazed him, John saw over five hundred dollars pour in, with no bills of importance outstanding. All his charge accounts were as good as cash; his brothers had strict orders never to charge a gun, or repair job, without consulting him. He had worked too hard making the rifles and remembered Jonathan's example too well to let any of them be carried away on doubtful promises. He whistled and sang at his work, and his laughter frequently rang above the whirring of pulleys and the flapping of belts.

He had started with materials for one hundred guns, thinking he would be doing well to make and sell that many in a year. He had guessed that number would permit him to feel his way and acquire much needed experience, without chancing heavy loss. He was surprised and delighted to see the rack emptied in a matter of days, with a nest egg of several orders in Matt's order book. But he was not excited. It was his opinion that the local accumulated demand had been taken care of in the first week and ways would now have to be devised to advertise the gun throughout the territory. There was enough material left for seventy-five rifles, and he let Matt order barrels and forgings for an additional hundred. No purpose would be served in ordering more. His sources of supply had assured him that repeat orders would be filled promptly. If production began to fall very far behind orders, which he doubted, he could buy another miller and lathe, and take on another man or two.

Now that two or three hundred dollars could be spared, he gave his approval to the plan of putting in a small stock of sporting goods. Today, it would be a small stock indeed that two or three hundred dollars would purchase, but in 1881 the Winchester Repeater, Model 1873, retailed for $25.00, and the 1876 for $27.00, with dealer discounts of 25 and 10 per cent. (Both rifles, by the way, were soon to be superseded by arms invented by John.) A box of fifty .22 shorts retailed for 15 cents. Most of the best makes of revolvers were under $15.00 retail.

The sporting-goods store seemed made to order. There was no competition nearer than Salt Lake City. The town was growing rapidly;

fish and game were abundant. The store and the shop were closely related. A customer for one was a possible customer for the other. Every man who came either to the shop or the store would see the rifle on display. John had only one objection. The store would take a good deal of somebody's time, and the shop might suffer. Matt, however, was sure that he could make more stocks than needed, and still have time to wait on customers in the store.

The stock was ordered, mainly from Schoverling, and in due time was received and arranged. The record established by the opening sale of rifles was broken. The twenty-five rifles were sold in a week; most of the stock of sporting goods disappeared in a night. The boys came to work one morning and found rack and shelves stripped of everything of value. A window in the rear had been broken, and fresh wheel tracks indicated that the loot had been hauled away. John made the best of it, consoling himself with the good he found mixed with the evil. In the few days of its activity the store had taken most of Matt's time and a good deal of George's. Much of the time, he observed, had been spent in unprofitable talk. It is probable that the proportion of conversation to sales runs higher in a sporting-goods store than in any other retail business.

John vetoed all proposals to send in a second order. Contrary to his expectations, rifle sales remained steady. They were behind with their orders, and he put the boys back to work making guns. When they could keep ahead of orders he would talk sporting goods again. (Matt bided his time—within a year they put in a new stock.) Doubtlessly John was blazing mad for a time because of the loss of his model, which went with the loot. Perhaps he blamed the store for that loss. We can be sure, however, that the time he spent fretting over the model would not have totaled a full day. Already he was learning to go within himself, to use his work as a protective shield for his feelings. His family knew how deeply sensitive he was; few others did. He was, when the occasion demanded, a gifted actor, and he developed an iron self-control. He did not brood over his disappointments. He looked into the past to pick out from his experiences something that might be useful for the job at hand or to recall for a few minutes an incident his sense of humor had immortalized; but he visited no graves.

Shortly after production in the new factory began, two men moved into Ogden who were to help considerably in broadening John's horizons. Dr. A. L. Ulrich was a German physician, zealous in both the practice of medicine and the study and use of target rifles. Professor H. W. Ring came to Ogden to take charge of an extensive educational program undertaken by the Congregational Church. Like the doctor, he divided his zeal between his professional duties and his rifles.

In explaining Professor Ring's presence, it should be noted that Ogden now differed considerably from many of the other communities in Utah. The arrival of the railroad brought to the city people from all walks of life, including people of many different religions. Prior to this time Utah had been almost wholly Mormon. Irving Stone, in his monumental history *Men to Match My Mountains,* notes: "Many of the smaller communities were so solidly Mormon that the inhabitants never laid eyes on a gentile." This was no longer true of Ogden, and the arrival of men such as the doctor and the professor had its effect on John's outlook and attitudes.

With the sure instinct of enthusiasts, the two men found the Browning store and each other before either had been in town many days. When they made their first visit to the store, by chance happening in one behind the other, only seconds apart, Matt came to the counter from his vise to wait on them. He explained briefly the nature of the Browning business—gun repairing and gun manufacturing. To illustrate the second activity, of which he was pardonably proud, he took a finished rifle down from the rack and explained the operation to the astonished men. When one of them asked, "But where did you get the rifle? Who designed it?" Matt jerked a thumb over his shoulder and replied, "Oh, my brother John invented it—down there at the third vise."

Not long after that a notice appeared in the local newspaper, inviting interested persons to attend an evening meeting in the Browning store, at which time plans for organizing a rifle club would be considered.

Thus the Ogden Rifle Club came into being. As the most important railroad junction between Omaha and the Pacific, Ogden was increasing rapidly in population and broadening in civic outlook. Every town of any size in Utah had a baseball club, and Ogden had one of the best. There was also the Ogden Brass Band that strutted from time to time in uniform, led by its drum major, Charley Lane, six and a half feet tall, his magnificence completed by a two-foot white shako. It was a propitious time for the doctor and the professor to propose a rifle club.

A range was laid out west of town, along the Weber River, cut out with ax and scythe by club members, and weekly shoots were held. John and his brothers attended whenever they could spare time from work.

It was at one of these weekly shoots, on this range, that John literally picked out of the air the idea which led to his first experiments with automatic arms. This range held its popularity until the advent of trapshooting. There were not many men among the shooters who had the time or money to indulge in both sports, and trapshooting proved to hold the stronger attraction.

Both the doctor and the professor bought a Single Shot. We know that they were exceptionally attractive jobs, since they were copies of a rifle Matt had trimmed up for his own use, now owned by his son. The metal parts were nicely polished and blued, the stocks were of rich and glossy walnut curls, the rear stock with cheekpiece and Schuetzen butt plate. Peep and globe sights completed a fine example of gunmaking.

John needed the association of such men as the doctor and the professor, although it was something he would never have sought deliberately as a basis for self-improvement. When the two came to him with an enthusiastic and intelligent knowledge of target rifles, however, he let himself be drawn into a pleasant intimacy. If they found him rich in knowledge of guns and ballistic eccentricities, he found them equally rich in knowledge of the world beyond the mountains. Admiring the smooth flow of their speech, he became more and more aware of uncouth frontier idioms in his own conversation and in that of most of the people around him. He had never had time to give his English more than a coarse-file finish; as a matter of fact, he did not learn the parts of speech until he took up French, when he was well into his forties. But clarity of thought seemed to lead him to an instinctive choice of the right word, and brevity of speech lessened his chances of error.

5

IT CAN HARDLY be said that the Browning Gun Factory flourished. It got along. Lacking capital for expansion and markets for its products, it could not grow much beyond its gunshop heritage. It was nearly a thousand miles from any large centers of population (excepting Salt Lake City), surviving precariously in a thinly settled area that was still being held in defiance of a vast wilderness. Two of the brothers were not out of their teens; John himself was only halfway through his twenties. Not one of them had had experience in merchandising. Laughing at the impossible and helped by John's miracles, they made rifles, set each one as it was finished into the short rack at the front end of the building, and, after the grand opening, never managed to accumulate more than a dozen guns at one time. When the shop was photographed, with the factory's entire staff lined up in front, each of the six holding a rifle, only two of those rifles were finished and ready to be set in the rack.

Once in a great while production reached three rifles a day, but not often. Each man was so important to the total operation that a bad cold or a cut finger would slow production. When production reached two guns a day and was maintained at that level for a month, John raised salaries a dollar a week. On that occasion Sam is said to have struck an oratorical pose and declaimed, "The days of bread and sorghum are over!"

About this time, Ed Ensign, a young man of twenty, was added to the force. Ensign had worked a year in a blacksmith shop. With that experience and his unusual mechanical talent, he soon became one of John's most versatile helpers. He worked more than forty years in the Browning shop, to within a few days of his death, much of that time as foreman. Toward the end of his first year he took in a job that still occupies a high place among the haloed absurdities of the shop.

It happened one noon hour. By common consent, the men took turns staying through the lunch break; the shop had to be kept open in order that no sale or repair job be lost. At noontime John would ask, "Well, who wants to stay today?" The question would be settled around the washbowl; whoever was left would go on working until one o'clock. John's turn somehow never came round, principally, it is thought, because he so disliked meeting strangers and talking repair jobs and prices. Such things had been an onerous necessity in the first little shop; now there were helpers to relieve him.

On this particular day Ed Ensign was elected to take the shift. After the others had gone a man came in whom Ed recognized as the owner of a large gambling house. A good Mormon, Ed had been taught, and believed, that gambling was a major sin, and he probably felt a vague fear that he might be contaminated in the presence of one of the devil's right-hand men. Instead of horns and the smell of sulphur, however, here was an amiable person with a surprisingly honest-looking face.

The gambler unwrapped a faro box, the first Ed had ever seen. Before the unsophisticated youngster knew what was happening, he was being hypnotized by the gambler's description of an ingenious scheme he had devised for rigging the box. The scheme was in itself a confession of crookedness, of course, but explained to Ed as to an understanding friend, it was made to seem not cheating so much as a good joke on some of the boys.

The idea was so clever that the mechanic in Ed was fascinated; before long he was nodding again and again to the rhythm of the suave voice, saying, "Yes, I see. Pretty slick—darned if it isn't." The gambler's question, "Can you do it?" touched Ed's pride, and he answered, "Sure, sure I can." He could have it ready in a day or two. Following the formula for repair jobs, he explained that he could not tell the price until the job was finished and passed on by the boss. But the gambler interrupted him with a pat on the shoulder and said, "Never mind that, my boy. You know what I want the box to do. Just make it do it and there'll be no argument about price."

Ed was perched on the counter, toying with the box, studying how best to start the job, when his fellow workers began to string back from dinner. It was only then that he began to wonder how the others would feel about accepting work from a gambler. If the box had just needed a drop of solder, say, or any legitimate repair, nobody could object. But to rig it for deliberate cheating . . . Ed was beginning to feel the stirring of compunctions, for his moral code was as rigid as any in the shop. But the charm of the gambler, plus the fascination of the trick he had contrived, had so weakened his resistance that he had promised to do the job without second thought.

Some playing cards had been left in the box for Ed's experiments, and the brothers, clustering around, guessed that it was a gambling device, even though some of them did not know its name. Questions from the group soon brought out the obvious fact that the purpose of the work to be done on the box was sinful gain, downright cheating. Sam and George, the most militant of the brothers in matters of religious conviction, and the youngest in age, were all for throwing the contraption into the street, appropriately muddy at the time. Ed refused; he had promised to do the job, and he had never broken a promise. Against every argument hurled against him by Sam and George, he argued, "We're a repair shop, and open to the public," or, "A promise is a promise."

John and Matt had said nothing, except for a few words of inquiry while Ed was explaining the manipulations of the box. Now and then they exchanged winks and sly grins. The hard-pressed Ed, sensing that the older men were not taking the matter seriously, turned suddenly, said, "Here, John, you're the boss," and handed over the box.

It was an excellent tactical move. Each of them, whatever his thoughts and feelings, followed an ingrained habit and stiffened to attention, waiting for John's opinion.

"Now, Ed, let's see," John said, studying the box, "he wants it fixed like this." And he went over the description as Ed had given it.

"That's it."

"Slick little trick."

"You bet!" Ed agreed. "The man said he started out to be a watch-maker."

John nodded. "How long will it take you to do the job?"

"Couple of hours, I figure."

"I'd figure about two hours," John agreed. "And how much can you get for it?"

Ed decided to make a bold bluff. There was no doubt now that John was leaning his way. He thought fast. He had considered asking as much as two dollars, but remembering the gambler's words and the pat on the shoulder, he calmly announced, "I think I can get ten dollars."

There was an audible gasp and a shuffling of feet but not a word until John, after a moment, cleared his throat. "H-m-m," he said. "That's more than we make on a rifle. Sometimes, when we don't sell a rifle, the whole shebang doesn't make that much in a day. Get at it, Ed. And lay yourself out on the job. Make it shine. He may bring over some more boxes."

As John broke up the conference by slipping off his coat and starting toward the row of nails that served as a clothes rack, he laughed. "Two hours. Ten dollars. Boys, let's stop calling that gambler a crook."

During the second year of the factory's operation, John made Matt a full partner. After the others had finished work each evening, the two brothers would stay late and count the money. Sitting on the counter, they would tear off a piece of wrapping paper, total the cash and charge accounts, and in a few minutes figure out, within a dollar or two, the day's profits. Some days they made as much as twenty dollars.

The partnership was nothing new. The two brothers had been partners all their lives, sharing their hoarded stores of ammunition as boys, sharing also the biscuits on a plate when either could have eaten all of them. The first sign on the front of the factory said J.M. BROWNING & BRO. A little later John decided that BROWNING BROS. would look better; so he had a new sign painted and hung but without removing the earlier one. A third sign read: GUNS, PISTOLS, AMUNITION & FISHING TACKLE.

One day John's former schoolteacher came in and leaned on the counter. "John," he called down the long bench, "you never were worth a damn in spelling, but there are two words I'd expect you to know how to spell by this time—*gun* and *ammunition*." Then, as an afterthought he added, "I suppose you can spell *gun?*"

"What's that?" John asked, looking up from his work, irritated at the interruption. "What's a spelling gun?"

The man led him outside, and production halted as the brothers followed. "There you are," the man pointed. "Only one *m* in ammunition."

"Looks all right to me," John protested. "Any of you boys ever notice anything wrong with that word?" They admitted they hadn't. Matt ran back into the store and brought back a box of cartridges. Marking the word with his finger, he showed the box to John. "He's right, two m's."

"Boys," John said, "this is bad. I'm so ashamed I don't know what to do. Why, everybody'll think we're ignorant."

"Oh, don't worry about that," the teacher laughed. "That news got out years ago—back when you were going to school."

"Hold on!" John said. "When I finished the sixth reader, didn't you tell me that I needn't come back—that I knew as much as you?"

"But since then I've learned how to spell ammunition," the teacher parried.

"So have I," John grinned, "and that makes us even. As for the missing m, just keep mum about it, and nobody will ever notice."

The factory work settled into an established routine, and, as the brothers began to assume responsibility for the factory's operation, John began to think of making other guns.

In March of 1882, he applied for a patent on a tubular magazine repeating rifle, and the patent was issued in July of that year. The designing and modelmaking must have proceeded slowly, with many interruptions. There was an interval of about two years between the setting up of the factory and the filing of the patent application, but during the first year John probably had little time for inventing. How he managed to make a repeater of some complexity and draw up a patent application by March 1882 is a mystery. It is certain that he did the job in fragments of time stolen from busy days, obviously an unsatisfactory method of doing creative work.

The gun embodied several ingenious features, but John apparently lost interest in it once he made it work, for he soon laid it aside to start on another repeating rifle. Application for the patent on the first repeater was filed March 20,1882; on September 13, 1882, he filed a patent on the second gun. In other words, he made a repeating rifle of completely original design in six months or less, amid the confusion of factory and repair work.

This was a tubular-magazine, lever-action type, and its simplicity causes one to suspect that the young inventor was trying to make a repeater of so few parts that it could go into production with the Single Shot, given an additional machine or two and a couple of men. It is unlikely that many repeating rifles have been made with so few parts. If we omit from the count those conventional parts—hammer, trigger, magazine spring and follower, etc.—we have left only three pieces that can properly be called working parts, as John noted in his patent application. These are a lever and block in one piece, a carrier, and an extractor. There was no sear; one spring served both hammer and trigger. Though unconventional, none of the parts were of eccentric design, none would have presented manufacturing difficulties. But John was not satisfied, and his second repeater went up on the shelf alongside the first.

The making of these arms served to acquaint John with the tricks of repeating rifles, gave him confidence, and fixed the direction in which he was to travel through life. As instructive experiments, they were well worth the labor they cost. John seems to have realized this, shelving both guns as indifferently as one puts away schoolbooks at year's end.

But there was another reason John put them aside, the most important one. He had another, better idea, the concept of a repeating rifle that made him class his previous efforts with the wooden guns he had whacked out for Matt. And he was impatient to work on it. According to Ed, at no other time in his life was John so short-tempered as during the winter of 1882-83. He was in the anomalous position of hating to see the business boom, because it forced his attention away from what interested him most, the mechanism of the new gun. John knew it would be a good rifle, if he ever got it finished. But he couldn't then foresee either its completion or just how good it would prove to be. The concept would become the Model 86 Winchester, one of the greatest forward strides in the industry since the advent of fixed ammunition. It would not only prove immediately popular, it would long outlive its inventor, remaining in the Winchester line for seventy-one years. John's impatience is understandable. He was twenty-seven years old.

For a time it looked as though John's luck had deserted him, leaving only two choices, each disagreeable. He could close the factory, which would be hard on his brothers and his two other helpers, and which would also hurt his pride, since it would have the appearance of failure. Or he could continue his inventing in such hours as could be spared from factory and repairs, a course which he knew he could not follow very long. As people usually do when one direction is as uninviting as another, he temporized. He kept the Single Shots coming through, inspecting each one as it was finished, meanwhile accumulating drawings and templates to check every operation of the new rifle that was beginning to work so smoothly in his mind.

6

H IS LUCK HAD not deserted him.

Sometime early in the year 1883 Andrew McAusland, a salesman for the Winchester Repeating Arms Company, in the course of his travels came across a single-shot rifle that was new to him. Stamped on the barrel were the words: BROWNING BROS. OGDEN, UTAH U.S.A. On the lower face of the receiver was stamped the number 463. McAusland seems to have been a man of acumen and initiative. He bought the rifle, which showed signs of hard usage, but which still worked smoothly, and sent it to the Winchester factory, with a letter in which he stated that he hoped the management would find the arm sufficiently interesting to justify the fifteen dollars he had paid for it.

It was found so interesting that, within the week, Mr. T. G. Bennett, Winchester vice-president and general manager, was on his way to Ogden, authorized by his board of directors to buy the rifle.

Bennett was a puzzled man, he admitted to John in later years. He had heard the name Ogden and associated it vaguely with the railroad on which he was riding westward. But the name Browning Bros. had no meaning for him. And yet there it was, stamped on the barrel of the best single-shot rifle he had ever seen. Moreover, the rifle bore the serial number 463, not a large number, to be sure, but a good many guns, and the threat of competition from a new quarter. He had enough of that in the East.

It grew increasingly clear to Bennett as he pondered his problem that he had to have the Browning. The Winchester line of arms was limited to repeaters, successful with the .44/40, for instance, but not

T. G. Bennett, vice-president and general manager of the Winchester Repeating Arms Company. New Haven came to Ogden.   WINCHESTER GUN MUSEUM

adaptable to the .45/70/405, the standard government cartridge, the .45/90, several .50 calibers, and so on through the rapidly growing list of "punkin slingers," as they were sometimes called. These cartridges, interesting now only to collectors, appeared in endless modifications. The Browning sent in by McAusland was a .45/70, and Bennett was sure the rifle would handle any cartridge made. He was a graduate in mechanical engineering of the Yale Sheffield Scientific School, with administrative experience as general manager of the Winchester Company; few men were as competent to judge the merits of firearms. So far, he had not been able to develop within his factory, or to buy, a repeating or single-shot rifle that would fill the dangerous gap in his line.

This experienced man was not unmindful of the fact that he was weakening his trading position by going West as a buyer, thereby making obvious a more than ordinary interest in the rifle. The trip itself—five or six days, according to the connections one made—was evidence of a well-considered intention to try to buy the gun. Bennett could have had one of his salesmen drop in and make a casual approach to the subject of the rifle. But he was a man who always handled important matters himself, and this business was very important. Remington or Marlin or one of the others might get at the Brownings any day.

It is not difficult to imagine the state of mind of the large, heavily bearded man who entered the Browning store that day in the early spring of 1883. He stopped by the breast-high partition, stared down through the shop, taking in the miller, lathe, emery wheel, and the earnest little upright engine in the far end of the room. So this was an arms factory! (Had he been told that it was, at the time, the largest such between Omaha and the Pacific, he would have been no more nonplussed.) The seven men he counted, intent on their work, looked for the most part to be boys. Had he found the right place? He soon found out, for one of the youngsters, Matt, as it happened, came toward him, wiping his hands on his pants.

"Am I in the Browning Factory, where the Single Shot rifle is being made?"

"Yes, sir," Matt replied, remembering his manners in the presence of a man of such dignity.

"I'd like to speak with the Browning Brothers, if I may," said Mr. Bennett.

"I'm one of them," said Matt.

Something was wrong. This youngster had only fuzz on his chin. As a matter of fact, Matt's beard was late sprouting and gave him considerable concern in that bearded age. John now sported both a mustache and a short beard. Matt didn't look over eighteen, although he was twenty-three.

"Do you have an older brother?" Bennett asked.

"That's him," Matt pointed. "Third vise."

"I wonder if you could both spare me a few minutes?"

"Sure—oh, John, there's a man up here wants to see you."[2]

Thus began an alliance that was to last nineteen years and change the course of firearms development. New Haven had come to Ogden.

Within a few years Winchester would become the largest producer of sporting arms in the United States, and almost all of the Winchester arms would be Browning inventions.

The negotiations in the Browning store were concluded in short order. Bennett wanted to buy, and John wanted to sell, and neither wanted an argument. John could not fail to see the advantage of his position; nevertheless he showed token reluctance, explaining that he and his brothers and two other men were making a good living and that they all liked the work. Still, he admitted, he would rather be inventing than manufacturing. Just now, for example, he had a rifle pretty well worked out in his mind, a repeater that would handle the big cartridges, something no other repeater could do. It was the fattest worm in John's bait can. Bennett asked a few tactful questions, such as John could answer without divulging secrets respecting the mechanism, and quite frankly admitted that he would be interested in a rifle of that type.

Coming back to the Single Shot, John, as Matt told the tale, got a faraway look in his eyes and began to speculate on how he could handle things. He thought that by enlarging the store, places could be made for three of his brothers. Ed could help with the modelmaking and lend a hand with the repairs when Ed Ensign and Frank Rushton got behind. There would be the expense of remodeling the store. The boys could do most of the work, but they would have to be paid, and nothing much would be coming in for a while. Then there would be the big outlay for merchandise. He was thinking aloud. Abruptly he arrived at his total and turned to Bennett. "Ten thousand," he said.

Bennett would probably have gone to twenty thousand. His experience and acumen told him that he was in the presence of an unusual young man, one who should be tied to the Winchester Company. John's mention of a high-power repeater was the best trading bait he could have dangled, and he knew it, for he was aware that the time was exactly right for the appearance of such a rifle. That awareness had started his search for a way to make one. But John had not been a hundred miles from his shop, and ten thousand was about as high as he could think in terms of money.

Bennett was compelled by habit to dicker. He proposed the sum of eight thousand dollars, in addition to which he would place the Brownings on the Winchester jobbing list, provided the business was expanded. That would compel other manufacturers to do the same. These jobbing grants, he pointed out, would be worth many times the two thousand he was deducting from John's price. He made the offer contingent upon the assurance that the forthcoming repeater be shown to him first.[3] He would give the Brownings a check for one thousand dollars now, the balance to be paid in thirty days, if investigation showed that the patent gave adequate protection. In any event, the Brownings would keep the one thousand.

"How about it, Matt?" John asked, turning to his brother, who had remained a silent listener. "Think you and Sam and George can run a big store?"

"We've been running a pretty good little store right here," Matt replied, with a sweeping gesture that took in the well-stocked shelves.

"It won't be the same thing," John said prophetically, "but I guess you can all make a living out of it." And then to Bennett, "Shall we fix up some kind of agreement?"

"I'll write you a letter, now, stating the terms, if you'll give me pen, ink, and paper, and you can write one, accepting those terms. Is that satisfactory?"

The two short notes, scratched off on the counter, concluded the business and set an example that was followed in all subsequent negotiations between Winchester and the Brownings. No contract was ever drawn for them by a lawyer. The matter of the Single Shot was settled in a few hours; Mr. Bennett entered the store early in the afternoon and was able to take a train out of Ogden the same day.

All concerned were happy. Bennett had come West, determined to buy the Single Shot, and he had bought it, at a figure probably less than he was prepared to pay. John, once he saw an opening, was just as determined to sell and get out from under the burden of the factory. Matt, Sam, and George were enthusiastic about giving full time to the sporting-goods business, and Ed Ensign and Frank Rushton were content with the repair work. Ed Browning was getting into stride in the work he did so well and so long—model-maker extraordinary.

As for John, he was on his way. He had made what he considered a false start, false certainly in that the management of a factory was something his temperament could not long abide. He had had the luck to get out with a good little shop and enough to live on for quite a while. And the experience.

It is curious that the rifle escaped the notice of all the arms manufacturers in the East for upwards of three years, during which time nearly six hundred were made and sold in Ogden, a large proportion to travelers, freighters, nomadic hunters, trappers, and the like, through whom it must have gained fairly wide distribution. Most in the major American arms collections show signs of heavy use, yet the .40/70s still look as ready for deer, the .45/70s for bear and elk, as when they stood gleaming new in the rack in the front of the factory-store.

Winchester brought out the rifle in 1885, advertising it widely, stressing the simplicity of its mechanism and its ability to withstand the pressures of the most powerful cartridges. Many modifications of that original model followed. It was made in four different weights, with high sidewalls for heavy cartridges, and low walls to facilitate loading with small cartridges, down even to the .22 short. In its long lifetime, this product of the Rocky Mountains became the best-known and most widely used single-shot rifle on the market. The safety of its locking system was proverbial. It was subjected experimentally to pressures as high as could be obtained with shells of standard make, overloaded to capacity, and though barrels were swelled, the breechblock never budged. One by one, competitive single-shots gave up the race, and the rifle went on alone, until the rising popularity of repeaters caused the Winchester Company to discontinue it in 1920.

In his book, *The Rifle in America,* Philip B. Sharpe notes: "The Winchester Single Shot was one of the most famous in the entire line. This gun, designed by John M. Browning, was first manufactured in 1885 and in a tremendous variety of styles for a large range of cartridges, running from the .22 short up to the .50/95 Winchester Express. Practically any of the cartridges of yesterday were adapted to this gun . . ." After mentioning that a number of these guns were used for buffalo hunting, and that one modification, the Winder Musket, was used for training troops in the early part of World War I, Mr. Sharpe concludes by saying: "Had not Winchester disposed of all dies and jigs for the manufacture of this old-time model, this author believes it would have been revived in recent years, as the demand for the action has been growing, particularly among those shooters who desire a super-accurate single-shot rifle for small game hunting and vermin shooting, as well as a target gun."[4]

7

BENNETT'S STIPULATION that he should be allowed thirty days in which to have the rifle patent examined by his attorneys cast a shadow of doubt on the validity of the instrument, as Bennett had more than likely intended, good trader that he was. John deliberately magnified the danger, as a means of restraining Matt, Sam, and George, who were all for starting to remodel the store. John was never one to leave a modest certainty for an extravagant promise, and he told the boys that he was not going to tear things up and close out a profitable business until he had the full eight thousand dollars. Moreover, he pointed out, there remained forgings and barrels for quite a number of guns, a total loss if not used. The thing to do was to speed production to the limit and use the parts on hand, even if it took three or four months.

That is the plan they followed, with considerable embarrassment to John. The check for seven thousand dollars, balance, came through in due time, and with it the grant of jobbing privileges. The deal was closed. But the forgings and barrels had not been used up, and a large number of back orders had accumulated. Led by John, who was furiously impatient to get at his new repeater, but reluctant to see good parts wasted and orders cancelled, the boys continued to make guns at a faster pace than ever before. The work continued until stopped by a letter from Bennett. The Brownings had escaped his attention for a long time, but he seemed to be keeping an eye on them now.[5]

Years later John could laugh about it, but not then. "That letter from Bennett was probably the most embarrassing thing that ever happened to me," he admitted. "I knew, of course, that I'd sold Bennett the right to make the rifle, but I don't remember even thinking that I no longer had the right to make it myself. It doesn't seem possible that a man could get to be twenty-seven or -eight and remain such a greenhorn. The letter itself made me hot. Bennett wrote as though he was trying to explain something to a bunch of kids—and that's about what it amounted to. All we knew was making guns. Then, too, the letter showed me up before all the boys, and that made me hotter still. It always strained me some to laugh at a joke on myself," John confessed. "But," he noted, "by the time the letter came, we had used up practically all the forgings and barrels, had no unfilled orders, and not more than a half dozen rifles in the rack. And somehow they got sold when I wasn't looking."

An even greater absurdity lay in the fact that while John was driving his brothers and himself in order to save a few hundred dollars' worth of forgings, he was carrying in his head one of the most valuable arms ever invented. Sharpe says of this rifle, "The Winchester Model 1886 action is probably the smoothest job ever developed in a lever action gun. This functioned practically without effort and in operation cannot be compared with any other lever gun ever produced with the possible exception of the Model 71, its successor in revised form."[6]

Made first for the .45/70, then the official United States Army cartridge, it was later adapted to the .50/110, probably the most powerful of the black powder cartridges, and still later to the .40/82, the .45/90, and numerous other calibers. Designed for those heavy cartridges, so popular until made obsolete by smokeless powder, it led its field by a wide margin. While the booming echoes of black powder lasted, the rifle was alone in its class. Moreover, it was able to handle the highest pressures of smokeless powder when the old order changed, requiring no modification other than a barrel of increased tensile strength. Listed in the Winchester line as the Model 71 until 1957, it was chambered for the powerful .348 cartridge, which throws a 210-grain bullet with an initial velocity of 2510 F.S.

John applied for a patent on the gun in late May 1884, and it was issued in October of the same year. The inventor did not spend the intervening months impatiently waiting. He designed another rifle of the same class and character, but with no similarity in mechanism. Why he did not turn to something entirely different remains unknown; the guess might be hazarded that he found the second rifle so nearly worked out in his mind when he finished the first that he could not resist the temptation to see it shooting. This was the beginning of a creative rampage unmatched in the history of firearms development. One might accept John's own explanation, that this was the reaction to years of vexing responsibilities, if the surge of exuberance had lasted a year or two. It was to last the better part of his life, however, with only the briefest interruptions. One of these occurred in October 1884, when John and Matt made their first trip East.

John had decided to take the 86 Model to the Winchester factory himself and to let Matt accompany him. He had promised Bennett first chance at the rifle and hoped they would reach an agreement. He had asked ten thousand for the Single Shot because that was as high as he could think in terms of money. But the model he now wrapped with brown paper and twine had matured him—he could think higher now. He was reasonably sure that Bennett would not let him get away to show the rifle to a competitor, but if it came to that, he and Matt would have much to consider. Besides, it was high time they had a look at the world beyond the mountains.

For the rest of their lives it amused the two brothers to recall

John M. Browning at about thirty. This photograph was probably taken about the time John and Matt made their first memorable trip East, in 1884. The rifle they brought along and hoped to sell became the famous Winchester Model 1886.

JOHN M. BROWNING ARMORY

incidents of that trip. They had spent so much of their time in the shop that they were unsophisticated even by Ogden standards, and an occasional thirty-five-mile train trip to Salt Lake City was something to talk about for days afterward. Now they were boldly boarding a trans-

Matt Browning in his mid-twenties. When it came to travel, the brothers were unsophisticated even by Ogden standards. Guns, however, were another matter.
JOHN M. BROWNING ARMORY

continental train bound for New York City, and thence to New Haven, a trip that excited deep anxiety in the families of the travelers and comment throughout the town. The only mishap was suffered by Matt. In those days the dining cars had one price, a dollar per meal, with no limit on the amount one ate. John said that Matt had probably been a little hungry all his life. Besides, the food was richer than any he'd known. He ate so much the first meal he had to skip the next two. "But," John added, "he kept it down, and at a dollar a meal, he was money ahead."

They spent a day and night in New York City, one of their first calls being on Schoverling, Daly and Gales, the jobbers from whom they had been buying most of their sporting goods. A salesman who had called on them several times in Ogden was in and was delegated by the manager to entertain the visitors. He took them first down to the Battery, giving them glimpses of the Hudson and of New York Harbor, busy with shipping. Toward evening, he guided them to an ornate bar in a large hotel, where they had a fancy drink that was so good all agreed to have a second. Matt watched in utter fascination as the bartender mixed it. Neither of the young Mormons had ever before seen or tasted anything quite like it. From the bar they went into the hotel dining room, where they had a meal that made the dining cars look like the summer kitchens back home. In the most pleasant state of mind imaginable, they went to the theater. Finally they returned to their hotel, where they sat in the lobby and chatted.

"Confound it," their guide said by and by, "I wish we could think of something else to do. The boss gave me ten dollars to blow on you boys, and I've got two dollars left."

'Well," John suggested, to Matt's surprise, "we can go upstairs and let you have a look at the rifle we're taking up to New Haven."

Instantly their host was on his feet. "I've been aching to see that gun since you first mentioned it."

John knew from talking with the man in Ogden that he had been selling guns for a long time and was familiar with all makes. He handled the rifle with the ease of long practice and especially pleased John by the way he put his finger on the locking mechanism, and his method of pivoting the lever. When he had finished his examination, but still held the rifle, reluctant to let it out of his hands, he said, "John Browning, you know so much about guns it isn't necessary for me to tell you that you have, right here in this hotel room, the best rifle in the world—by long odds." He passed the gun back to John respectfully. "And you probably are also aware that right now you're holding the future of the Winchester Company in your hands."

The day and night in New York City were recalled by the brothers long after the details of selling the rifle were mostly forgotten. There was much to laugh at. Matt, for example, as soon as the salesman had said good night, told John he had better go to bed and sleep off his liquor, or, next thing, he'd be going down and showing his rifle to the hotel clerk.

John grinned and admitted that he had even surprised himself a little when he heard himself asking the salesman up to see the gun. "But, Matt," he said, his smile changing to a frown, "it's time we woke up

The Winchester Model 1886 Lever Action Repeating Rifle, production model. For its revolutionary mechanism the inventor received "more money than there was in Ogden"; Winchester in turn had a rifle which handled all the big cartridges and which remained in its line for seventy-one years.   WINCHESTER GUN MUSEUM

to the fact that quite a lot of the United States isn't covered with sagebrush. We've been blinded by the four walls of the shop for so long that we don't even know what's going on in Ogden, let alone what's happening back here. I'm not the only gunmaker in the world, and somebody may be ready to bring out a good repeater for the big cartridges. I don't want to hit Bennett for more money than there is in Ogden, and have him tell me that somebody else, maybe Winchester, is ahead of me. While we were talking down in the lobby, it struck me that Schoverling would get wind of anything going on back here among the gun people. That's why I brought him up, and I feel easier than I've felt for weeks."

That, by the way, is the only reference within the family to the price John received for the rifle—"more money than there is in Ogden." In his book *Winchester,* Harold F. Williamson, after examining all surviving Winchester and Browning records, concludes: "It should be noted that the Company always made an outright purchase, and never entered into a royalty agreement with Browning. An absence of records makes it impossible to state how much the latter received for his inventions sold to the Company. It is believed that he was paid $50,000 for the patent covering the 86 rifle. This was undoubtedly a top price and paid because of the importance of the repeating action involved."[7]

With the 86 safely tied up, Bennett asked John if he would make a repeating shotgun, lever-action, and submit it. He did not ask John if he thought he could make such an arm. Matt was present, as at all the early interviews with Bennett, and remembered some of the things that struck him most forcibly. He said that John, taking no time for thought, nodded his head, saying, "Yes, I've thought a good deal about a lever shotgun. I think it would sell. But a slide-action gun would be easier to operate and better-looking. I think I have one worked out now that's pretty good."

Bennett agreed that there was much to be said for the slide action, but Winchester had made only lever-action arms. The lever had become almost a Winchester trademark. How long would it take John to make the gun at a guess? Two years?

John guessed he could have one ready a wee bit before that. The interview took place in October 1884. The patent on the lever-action repeating shotgun was filed the following June.

This became the Winchester Model 1887. Of it Mr. Williamson says: "While the most widely used shotguns of the time were single-barrel and double-barrel models, it is not astonishing that Winchester should be interested in producing a lever-action repeating shotgun. Browning showed his versatility by inventing such an action . . . This was not the first repeating shotgun made," but, "it was the first successful one. The action was simple and rugged, and held up well in the hands of shooters."[8]

OGDEN MORNING HERALD

PUBLISHED IN THE JUNCTION CITY OF THE WEST.

OGDEN UTAH, TUESDAY SEPTEMBER 27, 1887.

MORE INDIAN FIGHTING.

Two Bands of the San Carlos Reservation

APACHE INDIANS UP IN ARMS.

Serious Trouble Anticipated—The Uprising is the Result of Very Little Provocation.

By West'n Associated Press to the HERALD.

SAN FRANCISCO, Sept. 26.—A special to the *Examiner* from Tucson, Arizona, says the most intense excitement prevails in this city over the reported outbreak of the San Carlos Apache Indians. A courier arrived at Santano at noon to-day, notifying all the settlers in the valley that two bands had left the reservation and were marching south. This is supposed to be the result of the killing of Horton. The post trader was murdered by the Indians yesterday, and intense excitement prevails along the valley. The outbreak bids fair to be of a very serious character. Already two bands are reported to be out, and if such is the case destruction of life and property will be great. Fa-

BROWNING BROS.,

168 Main Street, OGDEN, UTAH.

——WHOLESALE and RETAIL——

Firearms, Ammunition, Fishing Tackle, Tents, Hammocks and Base Ball Goods.

In fact we have the largest stock and variety of Shooting and Sporting Good to be found anywhere in the West at prices lower than any. We are also prepared to do all kinds of fine Gun or Machine work from an Engine or Threshing Machine down at

Reasonable Figures!

Illustrated Catalogues Free to Everybody!

THIS IS FOR YOU!

Where do you buy your groceries, fresh oysters and family

A Bloody Capture.

HOLBROOK, A. T., Sept. 26.—Sheriff William Mulvenon and posse met Charles Blevins and John Graham, outlaws, in Pleasant Valley last Thursday. The sheriff ordered them to surrender. Being refused, both were killed. The sheriff now has a posse of seventy-five men, and says that Tonto Basin must be righted. All the Tewksbury faction who were not killed have surrendered to the sheriff. Only one of Graham's men, Oliver Pike is wounded.

A Cowboy Rumpus.

Yesterday afternoon a couple of cowboys filled up on tarantula juice and then started to paint the town red. One of them ran his horse around on Fourth Street and ran against one or two buggies. Officer Brown called on him to desist, but the request was unheeded, and the uproarious fellow bolted off up Fourth Street hill, his companion following him. Sheriff Belnap happened along with his horse, and he started in pursuit. He chased the couple up to the top of Fourth Street, along the bench and down to Main Street by way of Sixth. The exuberant cowboys then headed southward, the sheriff still in hot pursuit. On reaching the end of the lane the officers

JOHN M. BROWNING ARMORY

In three successive years, 1885, 1886, and 1887 Winchester announced the Single Shot, the 86 rifle and the 87 shotgun. The Single Shot soon became the leader in its class. The 86 rifle and the 87 shotgun were revolutionary; they were able to do what no other arms at that time could do. All three came out of Ogden. John was thirty when he made the shotgun, having, he often complained, wasted three years before he started inventing, plus three more with his factory enterprise.

In retrospect, John's creativity seems unbelievable. *In a period of two years—between October 1884 and September 1886—Winchester bought eleven new guns from him.* Yet his success was mixed with a proportionate share of grief. His second son, Austin, born in October 1882, died in August of the following year. His third son, Hugh, born in November 1884, also died before he was a year old.

Yet both John and Rachel considered themselves "blessed."

As has already been noted, soon after his marriage John built a house for his bride, on the corner by his mother's adobe. Originally a brick house with four rooms, John added an additional room from time to time, and it served them until 1897, when he built a larger house on the same corner, on the land where the adobe and the shop had once stood.

One Sunday afternoon, in the course of a family chat on the porch of the large home, the small predecessor was mentioned. There were many memories attached to the first house, but John chose to recall a special favorite. "Mama," he said to Rachel, "remember when we were standing on the sidewalk, trying to decide what color to paint the new house, and old Brother Hall came along? He settled the question in a few words. 'Rachel,' he said, 'you and John should paint your new house white, as a sign of welcome, and someday an angel will visit you and bless you'."

"And he did," Rachel said quickly. "Oh," she added, "he didn't reveal himself to us, but you can't deny that we've been blessed."

John smiled at her and nodded. "Yes, Mama, as Pappy would have said, 'I reckon we've been blessed'."

At that moment Rachel was called into the house, and John laughed. "Did you notice how Mama hastened to defend Brother Hall and his angel? She was afraid I'd say something sacrilegious. All I was going to say," he grinned, "was that it looked like an easy way to fool an angel."

Little has been said thus far regarding John's own Mormonism. Family reminiscences lead to the conclusion that during his youth John was neither more nor less active in church activities than most of the other young people in the community. The Church of Jesus Christ of Latter-day Saints, since early in its history, has attempted to create and maintain for its members a complete world within its own framework, including diverse social activities. In part this was made necessary by the church's theological beliefs (to its members it is *the* Church); in part it was due to the fact that it was a frontier religion, existing, in Utah, in nearly complete isolation; and in part, too, it was a remedy for that great breeder of sin that so bothered Jonathan, idleness. Even today a Mormon youth, growing up in a predominantly Mormon community, can find a church activity open to him every night of the week, if he so desires. It is imagined that John and his brothers participated in church activities as often as their work would permit, and probably with enthusiasm.

On March 28, 1887, two months after his thirty-second birthday, John Moses Browning was "set apart" as a Mormon missionary to the southern states.

The Mormon Church remains to this day one of the most proselytizing churches in existence. Most young men, active in the church, spend at least two years preaching the doctrine of Mormonism. Though today only single men are chosen, in John's time married men were also set apart for missionary work, and John spent two years as a Mormon missionary in Georgia.

In later years, he rarely referred to this period; typically, the only incidents that survive have their touch of humor. It would be easy to imagine John's feelings at the time. He and Rachel now had a son and a daughter—John, seven years old, and Louie, who was two. In his four year association with Winchester John had sold them some twenty separate firearms, with ideas for others probably firmly in mind. It would be simple but presumptuous, since we lack evidence, to suppose that John, already a man of set habits, impatient at even the briefest interruption, looked upon these years as wasted time. Whatever his feelings, he kept them to himself. In later years he occasionally accompanied Rachel to church, and his family grew up in the church, but, because of the press of his inventions, he never again took an active part in church activities.

These missionary years, however, were not inactive ones. If John had, as Matt claimed, a proclivity for preaching, he now had occasion to utilize his oratorical gifts. Mormon missionaries then traveled "without purse or script," totally dependent on the charity of their audiences. John, who had reason to believe the lean years were behind him, went through two of the hungriest of his life. The Mormon Church has succeeded in establishing stakes or wards in almost every part of the world; it has had the least success, and some of its most violent resistance, in the southern portion of the United States. It was little consolation to John that his ancestors had been one of the first families of Virginia. Often, John recalled, he and his companion had to sing for their supper. Singing contests were one of the best ways to draw an audience. But at times even this was not effective. The people of Georgia were, on the whole, unreceptive to new doctrine. On one occasion John and his companion were driven from a town by a mob. John was fortunate in that his long legs made him a fast runner; his companion, less fleet of foot, later joined him covered with tar and feathers.

John's favorite incident, however, told in later years, always brought forth gales of laughter.

After several days on the road the two missionaries entered a large southern town. They had been unshaven for days, their hair was hanging long, and their clothes were worn and covered with dust. As they walked down the town's principal street John suddenly stopped and pointed toward the window of a sporting-goods shop. There, on display, was the Winchester Model 1887, the lever-action repeating shotgun. The finished gun had been released in June of that year; John hadn't seen it, having left on his mission in March.

Despite their appearances, John felt compelled to have a look at the gun. They seem to have overwhelmed the storekeeper, and before he had time to refuse, John had the shotgun in his hands. He opened and closed it several times, scrutinizing the movement of the parts. Then, suddenly, as though a covey had flushed, he threw the gun to his shoulder and operated it so rapidly that hand and lever were a blur. The exhibition and John's appearance were too dissimilar to be readily reconciled, although for a moment the storekeeper seemed swayed in the direction of admiration.

"Well," he said wonderingly, "you seem to know how to handle that gun."

"He ought to," John's companion remarked. "He invented it."

The remark relieved the storekeeper of any doubt and indecision. Without a word he reached over and took the gun from John's hand, and, with ostentatious care, set it safely back in the window.

8

JOHN RETURNED from his mission in March 1889. From the large number of patents soon issued to him—20 in a little over three years—it is apparent that he was determined to make up for the two-year break in his routine. It was undoubtedly a relief to be back at the bench; he could set aside a gun and forget it, once he had made it work, but that initial step was vital to him, and many of the guns that appeared during this period he had carried in his mind for some time.

His working routine was well established. Before undertaking the making of a model, he had to have the mechanism well assembled in his

Original and production models of over ninety Browning-designed arms were at one time on display in the John M. Browning Armory, Ogden, Utah. In addition to the rifles, shotguns, machine guns and aircraft cannon shown in this view and in those on the following three pages, various historical materials and twenty-six automatic pistol models are now in the John M. Browning Firearms Museum in Ogden's Union Station. ALL PHOTOS JOHN M. BROWNING ARMORY mind. He perceived nothing unusual in his ability to visualize in distinct outline. He had always done so, supposing that he was merely exercising a common attribute of mind. When he had a problem that demanded some ingenuity, he would tilt his head slightly, stare through squinted eyes for a moment, and envision a procedure. Ed stood alongside him at the bench, saying nothing, working at whatever John had set him to, waiting for John to come back to earth with his picture developed.

Aided by sketches and templates, he proved to himself that the parts and movements were sound mechanical concepts. The templates were one of his most dependable methods of checking parts, their movements and relationships. He always had a scattering of them on the bench when he was making a gun.

He drew no blueprints. Occasionally he would pick up a scrap of paper, usually a letter or an empty cartridge box, and make a little sketch. It would be crude, meaningless to anyone except himself and Ed. Only the measurements would be carefully noted. Then he would return to the templates and the image in his mind. Always his own most severe critic, he never helped a mechanism through a doubtful phase with a mental nudge. It had to be smooth, and it had to be safe. Perhaps nothing that John said is more often quoted than his statement, "Any-

thing that can happen with a gun probably *will* happen, sooner or later." When the work was going well John often whistled or sang, usually snatches from old familiar songs. He never finished a whole song, and he never seemed to be aware that he was giving expression to his feelings. He once said that the sounds of the machines and tools were an orchestra to his ear. Whenever he was stumped, for an hour, or a day or two, or occasionally for a week, the music stopped.

At times he might spend several days on a single part, fingering it

over and over. Ed would remain silent until John would finally say, "It's no good, Ed." After John had explained the problem, Ed might protest that the part worked perfectly. John would reply, "Oh, it will work, but not exactly like I want it to." Then, his mind having been at work while he talked, he would interrupt himself to say, "See how much better it would be if we did it this way!" grabbing the nearest paper at hand and quickly sketching a possible alternative.

The next step followed immediately. He would remind Ed of a small piece of steel he had tossed on the junk pile a day or two ago, "about this size and shaped like this." Together the two men would root through the litter of odds and ends. John would watch as Ed set the piece of steel in

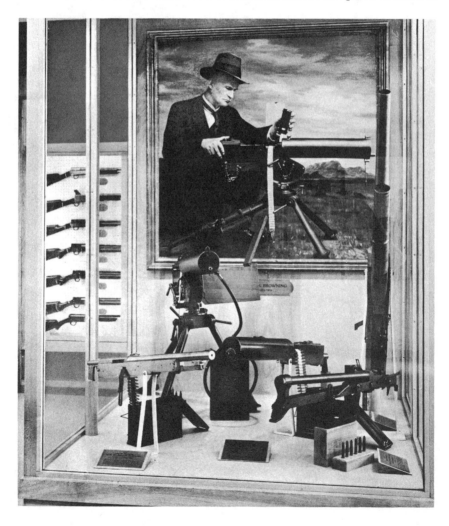

the miller or lathe, make a suggestion or two, then return to the rough drawing. Or he might notice the discarded part on the bench and without thought toss it onto the junk pile; always he would then give two quick, brushing slaps, as though dusting his hands, and the incident would be closed. When he bent over the machine with Ed, the discarded part would be forgotten and his entire interest centered on the new part.

He would stand by the miller or lathe with a ruler or caliper. "Hold on a second, Ed," he would say, and make a measurement. After staring a moment at the blueprint in his mind he might note, "That slot ought to be a little deeper. A thirty-second, I think, will be about right." Now and then he would use a micrometer, but not often. A shop foreman once told one of John's sons, "It's fun working with your Dad. Some of these inventors are always talking in thousandths. John talks in inches."

If we picture the pieces of steel as characters, struggling to become smoothly working parts of a gun mechanism, and the laws of mechanics as inherently malicious villains, it is not hard to imagine the intense dramas that were sometimes staged on the littered workbench, with only John and Ed to see and understand.

Now and then John got mad, not boisterously, but scowlingly and intensely. The madder he got, the harder he worked, as though his anger generated a heat that consumed all obstacles. Occasionally the tension would be too much for Ed; he would wander through the store and finally out into the office where George was busy at his desk.

"Why aren't you working upstairs?" George would ask.

"Oh," Ed would grumble, "John's stuck. He's swearing every little while. He doesn't know whether I'm there or not."

"That's too bad. I thought it was coming along fine."

"Don't worry," Ed would reassure him. "It won't be long now. John's so hot that something's got to give pretty soon—and it won't be John."

Part by part, a step at a time, the model would take form. Asked how he managed to determine the size, the exact location, and the precise movement of every part of a weapon, in relationship to every other part and movement; how he figured so accurately that every sliding part found its groove, that every hole for screw or pin lined up with its mate; how, in short, he created a gun of numerous parts and functions with no other instruments of precision than an inside and outside caliper, a compass, which also served as scriber, a foot rule graduated down to sixty-fourths, and a little spirit level picked up someplace years before by Jonathan—when John was asked that long question, he smiled as it unwound, and, when breath ran out, reduced the whole episode of the model to the commonplace with a shrug, saying, "Why, I went at that job about the way I've gone at every job. I found a good starting place, a fixed point—like the North Star, for example—from which I could make exact calculations, and then," he grinned, "I calculated."

Once a model was completed, he would spend considerable time testing it in the hills beyond Ogden. He would return home quiet and thoughtful. After supper, he would sit with the model in his hands. Often he called Rachel in to operate it, to see if she could easily work the mechanism. Gradually he would begin to withdraw from the room, lines of thought deepening on his face. He wouldn't hear the children romping around him. He would fill a magazine, run the dummies through slowly, tracing the full course of each one, watching it while it was visible, listening, after it disappeared, to every moving part, feeling every movement with his sensitive fingers.

The following morning he would be up early, as usual. Ed, who lived across the street, would see him leave the house, then run to join him on the way to the shop, all eagerness to learn how the gun had worked. By the time they reached the shop, usually about eight, Ed would have the first operations of the day's work clearly in mind. Then might follow several days of changes and modifications, broken occasionally by an afternoon's hunting if the season was right and the gun going well. Before long the model and a list of claims would be shipped off to the patent attorney. After that, as far as John was concerned, the gun was largely forgotten until his next trip East.

Inevitably the cycle would repeat itself. As it often happened, John might drop in on Matt in the office. For an hour or two they would discuss the business end of the operation. Gradually Matt would become aware that although John nodded and replied to questions, at some point his attention had been lost. Suddenly John would jump up, slap on his hat, and say, "I've got to go to the shop. Think I'll whack out another pistol," or rifle, or shotgun, or whatever was forming in his mind.

It went on like this all his life, model after model. If he had invented

The Four B's. During the 1890s these four Ogdenites were Utah's premier live-bird team. Later they made national history at the traps as a squad of four. Left to right: G. L. Becker, John M. Browning, A. P. Bigelow, and Matthew S. Browning. (Top), Winchester Model 1897 Pump Action Repeating Shotgun, production model. (Bottom), Winchester Model 1887 Lever Action Repeating Shotgun, production model. Both arms were invented by John M. Browning.
JOHN M. BROWNING ARMORY

an average of one gun, say, every three years, each new model would have made a wave, instead of a ripple, in his household and shop, and his average would still have far exceeded that of any other gun inventor. As it was, he often made several guns a year. It is not surprising that a new model became somewhat commonplace to members of his immediate family. His speed and productivity made his accomplishments blur like spokes in a fast-moving wheel.

As the years passed he seemed to try to cut more and more of the excess and friction out of his life, to concentrate ever more fixedly on the job at hand. He wanted little, except to work in the loose comfortable routine he had formed around himself. Though he made millions during his lifetime he never spent as much as one hundred dollars a month for his own purely personal needs. Birthdays and holidays always brought consternation to the Browning household; there was so little John ever wanted. Christmas morning he would appear at the head of the stairs and call down, "Bring on the suspenders, ties, and socks."

One of his sons once told John of an article he had read concerning the life of the dramatic poet Edmond Rostand. In an interview, the poet had confessed that he could only write indifferently well unless he wore a certain dressing gown, ragged with long wear, and reclined on a certain couch that also showed the ravages of time. John, instead of ridiculing the poet's idiosyncrasy, nodded thoughtfully and said, "Yes, I can understand that."

He thought about it for a minute and then admitted that while a couch and robe would hardly be practical for a mechanic, he could see why Rostand felt that way. Perhaps, John surmised, he had hurt his foot and had had to lie about the house for a week or two. And during that time, lying on the couch, wearing the robe, he might have had one of his best writing periods. Before long, it became a habit.

Yes, he understood. Creative concentration, he remarked, needs the help of habit. He could work best in his shop, where the sights and sounds were so familiar he couldn't see or hear them. They formed a screen around him. Maybe Rostand, he decided, was one man who could understand why he kept the old lathe and milling machine.

The conversation took place late in John's life, after his break with Winchester, and he recalled that at Colt's he had a desk in the corner to himself, he always stayed in the same hotel, and always walked the long distance between the hotel and factory. It was the same at Remington. In Liege, Belgium, at the Fabrique Nationale plant, there was another set of habits, old and pleasant. He admitted that he didn't like to have any part of any of those habits upset. "But if I have to," he added, "I can work anyplace. And I'd bet that, in a pinch, Rostand could do some pretty fair writing on a streetcar."

9

JOHN'S ASSOCIATION with the Winchester Repeating Arms Company, which began with the purchase of the Single Shot in 1883, lasted nineteen years, until 1902. During that period things could not have been arranged more to John's satisfaction. Relieved of the burdens of the factory, he was able to devote nearly all of his time to inventing.

The sales to Winchester had supplied ample capital. A newly erected two-story building in the middle of the busiest block on Main Street was acquired, and a complete stock of sporting goods put in. Browning Bros. soon became known throughout the mountain states. It was not only a retail store; it was also a jobbing and mail-order business, sending out thousands of catalogues yearly. The railroad junction of Ogden was a natural jobbing center for the rapidly growing region.

Shelves and showcases were installed and a gun rack built, which at the time was said to be the longest in the country. John left the construction (and the management) to his brothers but often dropped in to see how work was progressing on his new shop in the rear. That shop took little time in the building. It was very much like the old one, except that Matt, choosing a time when he knew John was particularly busy in the old place, had the interior plastered and whitewashed. John was not pleased. "How long," he asked, "do you suppose all this is going to stay white, with the engine puffing out smoke every time we throw in a shovel of coal? It hurts the eyes. It doesn't look like a shop." And it didn't, not by the time-honored family tradition.

But by the time the shafting and pulleys were up and the machines in place, the walls and ceilings were looking more homelike, and John made no further complaint. Within a year or two the once white ceiling was thickly smudged. And not long thereafter, occurred one of those absurdities that seemed attracted to each of the Browning shops. The incident was recalled by the brothers as The Passing of Tom Emmett.

The Brownings depended on Tom Emmett for all odd jobs, either at the store or in their homes. He professed no specialized skill but would tackle any job and get it done. On this day he was up on a stepladder near the ceiling of the shop, by the line shaft, taking measurements. His job kept him near the shaft for so short a time that he did not ask to have the power shut off. Nobody paid any attention to what he was doing, except John. He remarked to Ed, "Tom shouldn't be working up there with the power on." Ed looked over his shoulder and said, "Oh, he'll be through in a minute, and I need the lathe." It happened just then, while John was looking straight at Tom.

Emmett had his coat off and his vest unbuttoned. Intent on his work, trying to reach too far with his ruler, he draped an edge of his vest on the whirling shaft. There was a space of only about eighteen inches between shaft and ceiling, and he went whirling through head-first, in a horrible blur of sound and motion. John yelled at the top of his voice, "Shut off the power!" and started running toward Tom, from whom he was separated by the length of the room. One of the brothers ran for the nearest doctor.

The shaft stopped. Tom, no longer in the grip of centrifugal force, unwound toward the floor and landed with a jolt on his feet. Since he had gone through head-first, his heavy felt hat was rammed down over his eyes. That, a suit of red underwear, and shoes completed his attire. His shredded apparel flapped on the shaft. He staggered to and fro. Every hand in the place reached out to help, but he bumped into a bench, clutched a vise, and remained upright. He had to hold on with both hands; even so, his tendency to stagger nearly pulled him loose. Someone thoughtfully pulled his hat off for him.

The doctor arrived in a matter of minutes, and a space was cleared on a workbench. Everybody contributed a coat to be spread for cover, and Tom was lifted up bodily and stretched out for the doctor's examination. As that man, having heard the tale quickly told, went over Tom inch by inch, he grew more and more incredulous. Now and then, he glanced up at the clean spot on the ceiling, shook his head, and muttered. He prodded and twisted muscles and joints, asking from time to time, "That hurt, Tom?" And Tom would say, "No, nothing to speak of." "And that?" "Well, maybe a little, not much." Up and down, and round the ribs, and up again to the neck. The doctor gave particular attention to Tom's back. "That hurt?" after a series of prods. "Well," Tom said, "that's kinda funny. Had a little backache when I got up this morning. Did a lot of lifting yesterday. But it seems to be gone now."

Finally the doctor said, mystified, with almost a trace of disgust, "Not even a skinned knuckle." He glanced again at the clean spot on the ceiling. "How many times did Tom spin through there?"

"Must have been at least fifty times," someone guessed.

"I don't believe it!"

"Oh, yes I did, Doc!" Tom protested. "Yes, I did."

Smoke as it would, the little engine never succeeded in covering the trace of Tom's passing. The spot gradually darkened with the years, but as long as the shop stood, it was distinct against the black that surrounded it. Tom had given the spot such a high polish that grime did not easily adhere to it.

The work went on, but no more manufacturing. "Never again!" was written high among John's resolutions. He and Ed had the west end of the shop to themselves. A workbench extended the width of the room, with vises and tools, and the miller and lathe were in easy reach. John worked as zealously as Jeremiah preached, but he laughed easily. He liked the hot summer days, with the afternoon sun flooding in on him. The windows were not even shielded with awnings. On a particularly hot day, the brothers might pin up a newspaper with a compass and scriber. John never wore coveralls or apron. When he was ready to start a job, he simply took off his coat and vest. "All right, Ed! I got an idee— as Pappy used to say."

Bennett had had a good opportunity to take John's measure in Ogden when he bought the Single Shot. Later, when John came to New Haven with the 86, he was probably uneasy from fear of losing him to a competitor. Such a fear was not without solid foundation. A year or so after the 86 came on the market, one of Winchester's most aggressive competitors met John and found opportunity for a few private words. "Mr. Browning," he said, "it's none of my business what Bennett paid you for the 86, but if you had brought it to me, I'd have bought it if it had taken half the capital stock of my factory."

But John had had a factory.

Bennett was a most determined man. He was in complete control of the Winchester Company by reason of his marriage to one of the daughters of Oliver Winchester, founder of the business. Two daughters, only children, had inherited their father's factory and fortune, and the stock of both sisters was voted by Bennett. He was in a position to do much as he pleased, and he seems to have decided early that the company could not afford to lose Browning. There was never a serious argument over price. The Brownings frequently made one concession that saved Winchester considerable money. The jobbing business grew rapidly, and a number of times Winchester merchandise was accepted as part payment in a deal. There is one letter extant in which John agrees to take a certain sum in cash, and eighteen thousand dollars in Winchester products. The merchandise was valued at regular jobbing prices, and Winchester made its normal profit.[9]

Bennett's dependence on John is emphasized by the fact that for nearly twenty years Winchester did not bring out an arm designed by their own engineers. The new guns were all Brownings, although never known as such, and a large supply was left over. In the space of seventeen years, Winchester bought forty-four Browning guns. Ten of these were manufactured, with numerous reissues and modifications.

It should be emphasized that these forty-four guns were not variations on a few themes, as, for instance, a rifle and shotgun with highly similar actions. In several of the patent applications, John makes the statement that the mechanism described can, with only minor changes, be adapted to either a rifle or shotgun. But he rarely made both. The group comprised repeating rifles and shotguns, both pump and lever action, hammer and hammerless. A study of the mechanical tricks he performed makes one dizzy. Thirty-four of the guns purchased by Winchester were never made. Bennett could have had no intention of making even half the guns he bought from John. His line would not have absorbed them. But they had to be kept out of the hands of competitors. In effect, he was employing John to work exclusively for Winchester; instead of paying him a fixed salary, he was giving him his asking price for every gun he submitted.

Under this arrangement, which must have been tacitly understood by the two men early in their dealings, John came high, but Winchester became the world's leading manufacturer of sporting arms. During this period few, outside the arms factories, had ever heard of John M. Browning. John had never asked to have "Browning's Patent" stamped on Winchester arms, and it was to the interest of the Winchester Company to have it assumed that their arms developments were carried on in their own engineering department.

John liked the arrangement because of its simplicity. All he had to do was make up a bundle or two of guns once or twice a year and take them to New Haven. Sometimes he settled his business in one day. More often, his advice would be wanted in the drafting room, the model shop, or the production line. He enjoyed working with experts. He found the trips East interesting and relaxing. Arriving in New Haven, he would call at the factory with a bundle of guns on his shoulder. Sometimes his load weighed from thirty to fifty pounds and had to be

"The most popular hunting rifle ever built—bar none!" The Winchester Model 1894 Lever Action Repeating Rifle. Winchester's claim that "probably more deer have fallen to this old favorite in the past six decades than to all other rifles combined" is no idle boast; over two and one half million of these guns had been manufactured by 1961. This Browning-designed arm was America's first smokeless-powder sporting rifle. (Right) inventor's original model. (Left) Winchester production model. BROWNING ARMS COMPANY

wrapped in two packages. He enjoyed the little show he put on for Bennett, cutting the string with his pocketknife, removing the paper, exposing one gun after another. The one or two trips a year to New Haven became a habit.

Some of the older members of John's family looked on these trips with misgiving. His Aunt America, whose early experiences in Illinois and Missouri still disturbed her sleep and made her fearful of the thought of venturing beyond the high walls of her mountain valley, would caution him—"John Mose, I wish you'd give up these trips back East. Do you suppose the men you meet back there want to give you all this money you bring home—thousands and thousands of dollars? No, sir, John Mose! They'll poison you sooner or later—mark my word!"

John's brothers kidded him now and then after a successful "raid" on New Haven; he was, they said, in effect blackmailing Winchester, compelling the company to buy in self-defense more guns than all the factories in the country could manufacture.

John just laughed and said, "Bennett knows what he's doing. I sell him a gun—the 86, for instance. He pays a lot of money for it, and has a big investment in plant and materials. It would be a serious blow to him if somebody should come out with a pretty good gun of the same general type as the 86. I'm just building some protective fences for Bennett. That's what these guns are that he buys and never expects to make— fences." He grinned. "And he pays me pretty well for the fences too."

Bennett knew what he was doing. With every claim granted to John, the designing of a good gun became more difficult. Bennett had found in the young man from the West a firearms monopoly; and in buying gun after gun, he was buying stumbling blocks to harass and impede his competitors. As patent after patent was issued to Browning and assigned to Winchester, he felt more and more secure. He was cornering the market.

It was an astonishing array of guns, representing more arms than were patented by all other American inventors combined in that seventeen-year period. As a matter of fact, John's were the only repeating arms of lasting success put on the market during that time. Each of the forty-four was a mechanically distinct and original creation, although there were, of course, duplications of types, as, for example, several rifles for cartridges of comparable size and power, with both lever and pump action represented.[10] All the later shotguns were pump action, a system John had recommended when Bennett first requested the lever action. In a few years, Bennett had come around to John's way of thinking and put into production a pump action, first called the Model 93. Later, after a few changes, notably a simple takedown system, it became the famous Model 97, which was almost alone in the field of successful repeating shotguns for many years. It was not discontinued until 1957.

Bennett's conservatism is clearly shown by his decision to market a lever shotgun, even though John had proposed a pump-action gun. The Model 90 .22 rifle was the first pump action to invade the sacred precincts of the lever. It was followed by the 93-97 models. Evidences of conservatism still persisted in these guns. Each had the conventional hammer, although John had already made both rifles and shotguns in hammerless models. If Bennett, however, made a mistake in choosing the hammer, the fact did not become evident for many years; the 90 and 97 must be ranked high on the list of Winchester arms in popularity and sales.

Williamson calls the Model 90 "the most popular .22-caliber pump-action rifle ever made." After citing its wide use for small-game and target shooting, he adds that "its most extensive demand came from shooting galleries in the United States and foreign countries, becoming so popular in Great Britain, for example, that the shooting galleries in that country are generally called 'Winchester Rifle Ranges'."[11]

The success of the Model 90 must have caused a few red faces in the Winchester factory. John had been busy when Winchester asked him to make this gun and, contrary to his usual practice, to save time sent detailed drawings of the proposed model rather than making and sending the model itself. He received, in reply, a letter from one of the Winchester officials, suggesting that he discontinue his work on the gun; examination of the drawings by Winchester engineers had convinced them that it could not possibly work.

John made the model, boxed it up, and shipped it to New Haven, with a brief but appropriate rejoinder: "You said it wouldn't work, but it seems to shoot pretty fair for me."

Of the Model 97, Williamson says: "Made in various styles, the Model 97 became the most popular shotgun on the American market and established a standard of performance by which other kinds and makes of shotguns were judged, including the most expensive. The gun became known for its simple, rugged construction and unfailing reliability. According to one enthusiast, 'It would stand any kind of minor abuse, such as being run over by the old farm wagon, or being dropped in the creek and rescued a few days later, and never even stutter when called upon to speak'."[12]

"During World War I," Mr. Williamson writes, "a considerable number of 97 models were used as trench guns. A group of American soldiers especially skilled at trap shooting were armed with these guns and stationed where they could fire at enemy hand grenades in midair and deflect them from falling into the American trenches. The gun was especially effective on night patrols, and in protecting outposts against attack by superior numbers. Paul Jenkins tells of their devastating effect on a German infantry attack on an American position. The Germans were allowed to come on until within range of the shotguns: '. . . and when those shotguns got going—with nine .34 caliber buck shot per load, six loads in a gun, 200 men firing, plenty more shells at hand—the front ranks of the assault simply piled up one on top of the other. . .'"[13]

About 1890, on one of John's trips to the factory, Bennett brought up the subject of a rifle as nearly like the 86 as possible but reduced in size and weight for proper handling of the .44/40 cartridge, for which the old Model 73 Winchester was still being made. Bennett admitted that the 73 ("The gun that won the West") was falling behind in the race with competition and wanted to replace it with an arm of the quality of the 86. He said that they had been doing some work on the modification, but one thing and another had delayed them and he was in a hurry. He offered John ten thousand for such a gun, delivered in three months. If it could be delivered in two months, he would pay fifteen thousand.

Matt, who was present, has left us an account of the interview. John stared a moment at a calendar on the wall and said, "Let's see. It takes five or six days between here and Ogden. Say we call it twelve days for me to get home and for the rifle to get to you by express. I'll have the rifle in your hands in thirty days for twenty thousand or give it to you."

The offer was so preposterous that both Bennett and Matt stared at John in amazement. Bennett, after resettling himself in his chair and clearing his throat, suggested that John's amendment be added to his original proposal, with the gift clause omitted. Later, when John and Matt were alone, Matt asked why John had offered such a one-sided bet. John scowled. "I felt all at once that it would be worth ten or fifteen thousand to change the expression on Bennett's face. In all the years I've known him, since he came out to Ogden, he has hidden behind that heavy beard, and you can never guess what he's thinking. But I made him jump that time."

"You sure as hell did—and me too!" Matt exclaimed.

On the way back to Ogden, John planned the new rifle. He told Matt that the "delays" of which Bennett had spoken were snags that required some figuring. While the essentials of the 86, such as the locking mechanism, could be followed closely, some radical changes would be required to make a first-class job. They arrived in Ogden early one morning; that afternoon John and Ed were shaping a receiver on the miller. In a week, the parts were beginning to go together. In two weeks, the rifle was being fired. Well within the thirty-day period it was in Bennett's hands. He seems to have satisfied himself in short order that it was just what he wanted, for the check for twenty thousand dollars came through immediately. Matt said, "All right, you won. But what if Bennett had taken your bet and you or Ed had got sick, just a toothache, maybe—what then?"

"Oh," John said, "Ed and I don't get sick, or have toothaches. Besides, we could have worked a lot faster, if we'd had to—couldn't we Ed?"

Ed stretched his powerful muscles and groaned, "I'm damned if I know how!"

If twenty thousand dollars seems high pay for a month's work, especially back in 1890, consider the other end of the bargain: in December 1932, Winchester presented a beautifully engraved Model 92 rifle bearing the serial number 1,000,000 to then Secretary of War Patrick J. Hurley. It is also noteworthy that Admiral Peary carried a .44-caliber Model 92 on his final dash to the North Pole, and that it was a favorite of Annie Oakley. Though now discontinued, it is still a beautiful little rifle, its relationship to the 86 showing in the double-locking block which engages a slot in each side of the receiver. Many believe that a more ingenious and wholly admirable mechanism was never embodied in a firearm than that lever-and-lock combination in the 86 and 92 models.

10

A SMALL PINCH of powder, 30 grains to be exact, and 170 grains of lead molded to .30 caliber, shook the year 1894 by breaching the wall of the giants—the black-powder cartridge, long considered the "ultimate" in ammunition development.

The old, time-tested cartridge, entrenched behind its dense cloud of smoke and proclaiming its power with a mountain-shaking boom, offered some resistance to the new smokeless-powder cartridge. A hunter, beard streaked with gray, might stand a .30/30 and a .50/110 side by side on a showcase and say, "If you're going after grizzly, which would you rather have, this little popgun load, or this man-sized cartridge?" But the argument, though hot while it raged, did not last long. The muzzle velocity of the .30/30 was 2200 feet per second, against about 1600 feet for the .50/110, even with its lightest bullet. The flat trajectory of the .30/30, the amazing penetration, the light weight of both rifle and cartridge, a matter of importance on a long climb, soon left just a scattering of the old cartridges on the shelves.

It was particularly fortunate that there was a rifle, exactly right, ready and waiting for the .30/30. John had made a rifle for the .32/40 and .38/55, excellent black-powder cartridges for game up to and including deer. The rifle came on the market as the Model 94 Winchester. A year later, it startled the gun world by stepping out as the first smokeless powder sporting rifle. Like so many of John's inventions, it led a long procession. Its wide popularity, and the rapidity with which it gained that popularity, have never been equaled by a sporting rifle. By 1914, over one and one half million had been sold; in early 1961 the total exceeded two and a half million. It is still in the Winchester line.

Noteworthy is the fact that John's rifle, though designed for black powder, while smokeless powder was, at best, a distant and indistinct rumor, withstood the greatly increased pressure with no change whatever, beyond a steel of higher tensile strength for the barrel. Pressures of the black-powder cartridges for which the rifle was designed were about 25,000 pounds per square inch, while the .30/30 ran up to nearly forty.

Surprisingly, all of John's rifles that were manufactured by Winchester were designed for black powder, and later, without exception, adapted to smokeless and its increased pressures, with only a change of barrel steel. This includes even his first rifle, the Single Shot. Acting upon his dictum, "If anything can happen in a gun it probably will sooner or later," John figured his margins of safety far in excess of reasonable requirements. His philosophy was make it strong enough, then double it.

There has never been so sudden and complete a change in the gun world as was occasioned by the advent of the Model 94 .30/30. Few, if any, rifles made specifically for black powder appeared after the 94 came on the market. For years, if you met a rider in the mountains with a rifle in his saddle scabbard, you could lay long odds on its being a .30/30. That model, especially the carbine, was a favorite arm of Mexican rebels, in the days when uprisings were frequent in Mexico. Older jobbers can remember bonuses above retail for the carbines and cartridges, coming from points along the border. The .30/30 is still widely used, preferred by many as a deer gun, and a special favorite of ranchers and sheepmen. With them it is an old habit, hard to break. Winchester's 1958 advertisements represented it as "the most popular hunting rifle ever built—bar none!" and their catalogue of the same year states that "probably more deer have fallen to this old favorite in the past six decades than to all other rifles combined."

Winchester was quick to follow up its advantage and soon brought out the Model 95, also a Browning gun, which Sharpe calls "the first successful box magazine lever-action repeater." Sales of this rifle were limited by its specialized uses; it was a big-game rifle and as such gained a following that was notable but by no means as wide as that enjoyed by the Model 94. It was more expensive than the 94, heavier, and was chambered for the most powerful cartridges, including the .30/40 Krag, the Government .30/02, .30/06, and the tremendously powerful .405, with its striking energy of 3077 foot-pounds.

It has seen a wide variety of uses: in this country it was a favorite of President Theodore Roosevelt, Colonel Townsend Whelan, Edward M. House, and other famed hunters of that era, and was used for bear, elk, moose, and caribou; thousands were manufactured for use in the Spanish-American War; it was popular with the Texas Rangers; and some 300,000 were sold to Russia in 1915-16. "Even in Africa, against elephants, rhinos, lions, and buffalo, the 95 had its advocates," Mr. Williamson notes. He quotes author and big-game hunter Stewart Edward White, who in his book *Camp and Trail*, published in 1915, wrote: "This I have heard is not a particularly accurate gun . . . This may be. I only know that my own rifle today, after ten years' service, will still shoot as closely as I can hold it, although it has sixty-four notches on its stock and has probably been fired first and last—at big game, small game, and targets—upwards of a thousand times."[14]

Winchester's last new Browning gun was, like the first, a single-shot rifle. It was a .22 caliber, weighing less than four pounds, a boy's gun manufactured for the deliberate purpose of putting another rifle out of business.

John's Model 90 .22 repeater had given Winchester a highly profitable monopoly in its class. Mr. Bennett liked that. But there was a little Belgian single-shot .22 which was selling at about half the price of the Model 90. Many a man will remember the Flobert as his first gun. It was producing a large volume of sales on a level that Winchester did not

The Winchester Model 1895 Lever Action Repeating Rifle—another of the forty-four guns John M. Browning sold to Winchester. A big-game rifle, chambered for the most powerful cartridges, the 95 was a special favorite of President Theodore Roosevelt, who called it his "Big Medicine." Winchester production model.

BROWNING ARMS COMPANY

reach. Mr. Bennett did not like that. In a letter to John, he asked for a rifle that would, to quote him, "put the Flobert out of business."

John just happened to have such a rifle, in fact he had five of them, four of which he'd made one after the other in five or six weeks in 1892, and one he'd invented not long before Bennett's letter arrived. The latter gun was obviously the answer to Bennett's request, but John sent them all, and all were purchased by Winchester. The last gun was selected to attack the well-entrenched Flobert; a little bolt-action .22, it came out as the Winchester Model 1900, retailed for $5.00, and so effectually fulfilled its mission that within a year the Flobert disappeared from commercial gun racks. It was the sire of such a large family of .22 rifles, both single-shot and repeater, that it is almost lost amid its progeny. Over the years Winchester brought out nine versions of this gun (including a single-shot shotgun model) and sold close to a million and a half.

Winchester enjoyed another monopoly; the Browning Brothers enjoyed another laugh, one that was no less full the second time around. It concerned those four other models Winchester had purchased but would never manufacture, guns John had designed way back in 1892, solely for amusement purposes and with no thought of sale. Basically these were one rifle—one of the simplest firearms ever designed, even rivaling Jonathan's efforts—and three variations on the same theme.

One morning John had come into the shop with the first rifle complete in his mind, and in two days he and his brothers were firing and laughing. The gun employed such conventional parts as barrel, stock, trigger guard, etc., but of moving parts, parts which could be called the mechanism of the arm, there were only two. The hammer and trigger were in one easily made piece, and one coil spring served both as mainspring and trigger spring.

"It was a mechanical joke," John later recalled, "and Bennett would never have considered making it. I wouldn't, in his place. It was laughable, and Bennett would never let the Winchester name go on anything that would be laughed at. But he bought it, because he saw right off that it would be worse than the Flobert if somebody should hit on the same idea and retail a rifle for a dollar and a half."

11

THE FORTY-FOUR guns John M. Browning sold to Winchester during the seventeen years between 1883 and 1900 were by no means his total output during this period.[15] In 1889 he made a discovery which opened his eyes to an entirely new world, that of automatic arms: by 1895 his gas-operated machine gun had been developed to such a high degree of efficiency that it was officially adopted by the United States Navy; his first automatic shotgun patent was filed in 1900; and by that year both Fabrique Nationale d'Armes de Guerre and Colt's Patent Fire Arms Manufacturing Company had Browning automatic pistols in production. All this with no curtailment of his production of rifles and shotguns, plus various miscellaneous inventions, such as a machine for the loading of machine-gun belts, invented in 1899 at the request of the Ordnance Board.

To present a life of such varied accomplishments in a strictly chronological narrative poses numerous problems, not the least of which is the fact that many of the inventions of John M. Browning outlived their inventor, making their own history after his death. One aspect of Browning's genius was his ability to move with ease from one arm to another, however dissimilar they might be—rifle, pistol, shotgun, machine gun, or aircraft cannon. Yet merely cataloguing his inventions as they occurred causes one to lose sight of his over-all contributions to the various firearms fields. For these reasons, it seems best to bring the story of Browning's association with Winchester to its conclusion before treating separately the development of his machine guns, automatic pistols, and other arms.

John M. Browning's famous break with Winchester occurred in 1902, nineteen years after T. G. Bennett's purchase of the Single Shot. This period was unique because one man, solely through his inventive aid, gave one company a monopoly on the field of sporting arms. Not only was Winchester the only company in the world with a complete line of sporting arms, not a single model in that line had a competitor that was even remotely dangerous. It is safe to say that in 1900 at least 75 per cent of the repeating sporting arms on the American market—both lever and pump action—were of John M. Browning's invention.

Winchester's monopoly ended when T. G. Bennett lost the automatic shotgun.

That gun has been called Browning's most daring innovation. In bringing it to completion—through countless obstacles and with the expenditure of more time and effort than he gave to any arm before or after it—he mastered the basic principles of automatic arms, as he had

One of John M. Browning's miscellaneous inventions—a machine-gun-belt loading device, designed in 1899 at the request of Army Ordnance and adopted by the United States Armed Forces. Browning also invented numerous specialized pieces of equipment for use in arms factories. ROCK ISLAND ARSENAL

long ago mastered the basic principles of repeating arms. Fortunately he was in his prime, forty-three years old when he began work on the gun. The gun rewarded him by proving to be the most profitable of his sporting arms.

He could hardly have chosen a worse time for the development of an automatic shotgun. Shotgun loads were in the transition period between black and smokeless powder; some black-powder loads were listed in manufacturers' catalogues as late as 1914, surviving because they were cheaper and because many people were afraid of the new powders. The long prized Damascus barrels frequently blew up when subjected to the increased pressures of smokeless powders. The first smokeless loads put out by the big companies were far from perfect, and John was doing so much test-firing, thousands and thousands of rounds, that every defect sooner or later came to his attention. In one of his letters to Bennett, patience worn thin, he makes some very pointed comments, complaining especially about the frequent "cutting-off" between paper and brass. Without going into the history of shotgun loads, let it be simply said that those loads were the cause of many vexations in manually operated guns, and John was trying to make them behave in an automatic.

John's greatest difficulty was finding a method of adapting the automatic to the use of shells of widely different pressures. A model might operate perfectly with one load, then fail to eject with a lighter one, or with a heavier show signs of battering. He knew, of course, that it would be useless to prescribe a specific load for the gun. The gun had to handle all the loads.

The trick that solved the problem is a friction device called the shock absorber, so simple that its components can be made for a dime. One could paraphrase Sir Winston and say of the shock-absorber that never in modern shotgun design has so much been done by so little. It was the sort of thing that put and kept John in a merry mood for days, an idea amazingly effective and absurdly inexpensive. The blow of the recoil, the kick, was softened throughout the mechanism and on the shooter's shoulder. This simple device gave John a monopoly on the automatic shotgun market until its patent expired.

A fact of importance which has been largely forgotten in the course of time is that this automatic shotgun was also the first multi-shot shotgun with a solid breech. The conventional and time-honored hammer disappeared forever from multi-shot shotguns. John had made hammerless, solid-breech arms for Winchester, both rifles and shotguns, but Bennett was slow to change.

No widely popular gun was ever left so long without direct competition; and there never was a sporting arm that gave rival manufacturers a greater incentive to copy it. No sporting arm ever made a more sensational entry into the market. Few guns of any kind have equaled it in popularity. Few have been so profitable. *Fifty-four years* were to pass after its introduction before another successful functioning autoloading shotgun was developed.

John actually made three automatic shotguns. Though the whole gun world was baffled for years by the difficulties of finding a way around his automatic shotgun patents, even with the highly popular gun serving as incentive and guide, he, starting with only the bare idea of a shotgun that would operate automatically, made three such guns almost concurrently, employing two entirely different systems. He inter-rupted the test firing of the first model to finish the second and third.

John gave more time to their testing than to any other arm. He and his brothers fired thousands of rounds in the long room above the shop, using the three guns alternately. They were frequently fired in a speed competition, twenty-five rounds for a bet of two bits. The brothers took them hunting and to the traps, where everyone present was invited to try them. John, on untraveled ground, was making sure it was solid underfoot. All three guns operated well; with some reluctance he laid the first two aside, convinced that the third was the wiser choice.

John had Matt write Bennett; the letter, dated March 6, 1899, stated that he had an automatic shotgun ready to show and that he would be in New Haven about the last of the month. He arrived in early April, and the interview with Bennett was much like its predecessors, differing principally in the length of time John took to explain every detail of the mechanism. He was the only man on earth who knew what an automatic shotgun had to do, and he not only explained the various functions, part by part, he wrote detailed instructions.

Bennett was reserved in his attitude toward the gun, but John had learned to expect that. Mr. Williamson says of him: "He took matters seriously, and there was little joking in his presence. While he was frequently referred to as 'T.G.,' everyone called him 'Mr. Bennett,' except a cousin, who called him 'Tom'."[16]

He was only ten years older than John, yet neither man ever addressed the other by his first name, even after a long association that involved a fair-sized fortune. They developed, it would seem, an admiration and respect for each other, but their relationship never sprouted those intimacies that bloom into friendship. In that conference, nothing was said about price, which was a departure from custom, though it seemed perfectly natural to John that Bennett should ask for time to have his engineers make a study of the arm. Accordingly, he left his models at the factory. For some time Winchester had been taking out John's patents, in John's name, thereby relieving him of work he disliked. He had only to dictate a list of such features as he thought of first importance and leave the details to the patent attorney, who would consult him from time to time. Thus far neither party had any reason to question the wisdom of this practice; Winchester, however, was soon to regret it, and for a number of years.

Over the next several months considerable correspondence passed between Bennett and John regarding the gun. Only part of this correspondence is still extant; it seems evident from all accounts that it concerned routine changes of design, testing malfunctions, etc. On October 11, 1899, Bennett wrote John that the patent attorney had found a prior patent relating to the link-lifting arrangement in the gun; John devised a new arrangement. In July of 1900 Bennett returned the model to John for additional changes. John made them and returned the model on August 1. There had still been no mention of price, and John was growing impatient with what he considered an unjustified delay. His mood is apparent in the following letter, which was sent at the same time as the model:

WINCHESTER REPEATING ARMS CO.

NEW HAVEN, CONNECTICUT

Gentlemen:

We are in receipt of yours of the 23rd, and the gun which I have put in good order and return today by express. Have made a few changes which experiments in auto. guns since that was made, have shown to be for the better. I see the gun has been worked with considerably by parties who did not understand the system. The reason it jarred off was on account of the sear having been bent. You will see I have made an easier and shorter pull than it was before, yet, it will not jar off. We have had no misfires and think this fault is with the cartridges. By the way, this is a fault that bobs up with the Winchester cartridge more frequent than with any other cartridge we have had any experience with. The changes I have made are in the carrier latch, the ejector and ejector lever and at the end of the sear. Have also straightened the trigger which was bent. Think the way the trigger and sear got bent was by jerking the trigger plate out, unhooking the trigger from the sear; before pulling the trigger plate out, the links should be drawn back. Our experience has been that a gun gets worse treatment in a draughtsman's office than in a duck hunter's camp. Another thing the gun requires no oil at all and if you should oil it, it is not necessary to fill it full. Did you ever put oil on the end of a Winchester breech block and snap it; if not just try it. We have fired a lot of cartridges in the shop and in the field at doves and have no failures whatever and we hope you will have better luck with it. We have always considered the standard load for the gun is 31 grs. of du Pont, 1 oz. shot, 2⁹⁄₁₆ in. shell which is what we generally use, but the gun will work alright with 31 grs. 7⅛ oz. 34 grs. ⅞ or 1 oz., 3½ or 2¾ drs. black powder, ⅞ or 1 oz. shot. The gun will operate with smaller loads than above if held reasonably firm against the shoulder, but 31 grs. du Pont smokeless, 1 oz. in Repeater or Leader shells is a good load in our regular 16 gauge cartridge.

Speaking of cartridges will here say, that we got some .303 British cartridges from your San Francisco house which were loaded with Laflin and Rand powder and primed with black powder primers and in taking them out of a case that had never been opened, we found a .30 Government cartridge mixed with them. This would be a nice thing in a machine gun and a hot corner.

Yours very truly,
JOHN M. BROWNING

Bennett acknowledged receipt of the gun (also answering at some length John's criticism of Winchester ammunition) and John turned his attention back to his other work. Winchester's patent department had already begun taking out patents on the gun; the first was filed February 8, 1900.[17] Winchester had an exceptionally fine patent department; they were so thorough in their patenting of the gun that it was a number of years before any arms company, including Winchester, was able to devise a similar arm that did not infringe upon the patents they had taken out in John's name.

As early as April 19, 1900, John had written to Bennett, asking for a final decision on the gun, but Bennett had evaded committing himself. John waited. Years later, when he described his feelings at this time to his eldest son, he became angry just talking about it:[18]

"Whenever I thought of the matter, I wondered why Bennett didn't write that he was ready to talk business. And then, for a time, I would get busy and forget it again. Finally I woke up to the fact that I was boiling mad and had been too busy for some time to notice it. Something like one of those Yellowstone geysers that take a while to get hot enough to blow. So one day I grabbed my hat and told Matt I was going to New Haven. 'I want to get some action on those automatic shotguns,' I said. 'Those fellows down there are stalling, and we're letting the best thing I ever made die in its sleep.'

"Matt suggested that he come along. I replied that what had to be done would only take five minutes, either way, and there wasn't any sense in both of us making the trip."[19]

The interview, John recalled, lasted about as long as he had thought it would. Both men were mad. John, because he felt Bennett had marked time for almost two years, afraid to say yes or no; Bennett, because of John's terms.

John asked for what he himself termed "a whopping price, one so high there wasn't much chance he'd accept, but, if he had, it would have left me feeling satisfied." No one now recalls what the price was; the important thing, as far as Bennett was concerned, was that John demanded it be a down payment on royalties.

All of John's previous negotiations with Winchester had been straight sales. However, he had an unusual gun and knew it, and his dealings with the other arms companies were now all conducted on a royalty basis, leading him to feel that he could demand no less of Bennett. Winchester employee Edwin Pugsley, who knew both Bennett and John, summarized the conflict pointedly when he stated: "The word *royalty* was to T. G. Bennett what a red flag is to a bull."[20] Winchester had never paid royalties to anyone; Bennett had no intention of instituting what might become a costly precedent.

"I've often thought that neither Bennett nor I was much of a prophet," John told his son. "A lot of prophesying was done in Utah in the early days, but I never seemed to get the knack. Bennett could have bought that gun for less than it has produced most years since. But he was afraid of it.

"When I told him my terms his reply was certainly not diplomatic. We were both hot, for that matter.

"'Mr. Browning,' he said, just as though we were meeting for the first time, 'a royalty is a good deal to ask of the Winchester Company, which has a fixed policy against the payment of royalties.'

"'Mr. Bennett,' I said, 'for nineteen years you have had no occasion to consider the question of a royalty, and this policy you speak of must have been adopted for the present interview. It so happens that I have a policy of about the same age, which requires a royalty contract hereafter for each and every one of my arms. Doubtless our policies are equally inflexible. I suppose the guns are in the drafting room?' He nodded, without a word. 'Then I will pick them up,' I said. Still he just nodded, and out I went.

"It was not a very dignified parting, I admit," John added. "But I was younger then."

Hadn't Bennett seen the potential of the gun, his son asked. John's answer, as the son remembers it, follows. At the time the conversation took place, Bennett was still active in the management of the Winchester Company.

"Bennett," John said, "is the most conservative of men, and admittedly the automatic was something of an innovation. To put it simply, he was afraid of it, and so were the few men in his confidence. They were afraid that it would take ten years to develop such a gun to the point where it would be a profitable manufacturing article. It doesn't take many weak spots to eat up all the profit. Don't think of him as a coward. He enlisted at sixteen and fought through the Civil War, coming out a captain. Cowards don't do things like that. But he didn't replace the old 73 and 76 models until competition forced him to it. The 86 pulled him out of that hole. Winchester had a fine record. It was their boast at one time that the company had not borrowed a cent for forty years. The factory was a temple, and Bennett sure-pop was the high priest. He never had an official of the company present at any of our confabs. His conservativeness worked pretty well. He is a big man, and he looked so solid in his chair that I had the feeling I could come back year after year, find him there, make a deal without any wasted words, and get back to work. It was a comfortable feeling . . .

"The automatic shotgun," John continued, "put Bennett in a tough position. I'll bet he'd have shelled out a hundred thousand dollars just to have had it banished forever from the earth, leaving him with his levers and pumps. If he made the gun and it proved a failure, as he and his advisors seemed to have half suspected, it would leave a blot on the Winchester name. Even if he made it and it proved a big success, it would seriously hurt one of the best-paying arms in his line—the 97 shotgun. If a competitor got it, and it caught the popular fancy, he'd be left a long jump behind in an important branch of the business. That's why he marked time for two years, and why, once I'd forced a showdown, I got so mad."

John had two alternatives, both of which were undoubtedly in mind before he saw Bennett: he could find another American arms company to manufacture the gun, or he could take it to Europe, possibly to

Fabrique Nationale in Belgium, who had already produced the first of his automatic pistols. Neither course was sure. He decided to try Remington, who he had good reason to believe might be interested. On the morning of January 8, 1902, he called Marcellus Hartley, president of Remington Arms. Hartley's response was immediate and enthusiastic; he told John to come over first thing that afternoon.

John had time to spare. He spent it walking the streets. While walking he came upon a shooting gallery, managed by a pretty girl in a fringed buckskin shirt and a big Buffalo Bill hat. He went in. As he put it, "I never could resist a .22."

There were four Model 90s on the counter. John picked up one. There were no prizes, but for a perfect score the girl awarded an equal number of free shots. John began firing and kept firing, without a miss. He was having the time of his life, pretending surprise that his luck should last so long, and watching the expression on the girl's face. Twenty-two shorts were at that time fifteen cents a box. John went through two boxes before the girl refused to fill another magazine.

"Mister," she said, "do you think that's fair? I'm trying to make a living here."

John laughed so heartily that the girl broke into laughter too. He complemented her on the condition of her establishment and her care of the rifles, laid a dollar on the counter, and started out, tipping his hat. As he passed through the door the girl yelled, "Good-by, Mister Oakley. When you get home give my best regards to Annie."

John returned to his hotel to pick up his models and went to Hartley's office in a whistling mood. He was treated cordially by Mr. Hartley's secretary, George Bingham, who said that Mr. Hartley was expected momentarily. John had been waiting nearly an hour when he heard the telephone ring in the inner office. Mr. Bingham came out to the reception room, his face white. "I have sad news for you, Mr. Browning. Mr. Hartley died of a heart attack a few minutes ago."

John's choice was made for him. The automatic shotgun, one of the most revolutionary sporting arms ever invented in America, went to Europe, along with its hopeful but not overly optimistic inventor.

12

THE AUTOMATIC SHOTGUN, machine guns, and pistols of John M. Browning owed their birth to a commonplace event in the fall of 1889. Commonplace, that is, to all but John, who used it as a key to the truly fantastic.

John was thirty-four. He had returned from his mission that spring and on this particular fall day was attending the weekly shoot of the Ogden Rifle Club with his brothers on the range he'd helped lay out along the river bed east of town.

Will Wright was up, a man for whom John had a particular affection. Will was honest, quiet of speech, and an excellent marksman; that pretty much covered the ground with John. As Will fired, using his Browning-made rifle, a clump of weeds some distance ahead of him bent with the muzzle blast.

The men, waiting their turn, were intent on the target, watching for the results of the shot. All probably saw the movement in the weed-tops; possibly even one or two thought about it, for a moment considering the desirability of widening the aisle to permit an unobstructed view of the target. This they had done in the early spring, with a scythe, but the weeds had since grown. The bending of the weeds and foliage before a muzzle blast was, of course, as commonplace as the report of the shot and the powder smoke. It had been commonplace to John.

The creative spark is often nothing more than the faintest glimpse of an idea. Many of John's inventions were born in this way; that they grew to maturity was the result of the days and nights of exhausting and wholly unspectacular concentration which followed—the logical progression of steps, one after the other, some wasted, some having to be repeated, until finally the objective was reached, a workable firearm. But sometimes it is otherwise. This was such a moment—as John noticed the swaying of the weeds there occurred one of those brilliant, intuitive flashes which cut across time, effort, and preconceptions. He saw utilizable energy going to waste. And while the black-powder smoke was still curling in the air, his mind was considering methods of applying that energy.

His interest in the shoot ended abruptly. He had driven to the range with Matt and Ed. Now he rounded up his brothers, told them to sack their rifles and come along. It did not occur to him that he was interrupting the shoot, drawing the attention of the shooters. Ed answered the curious stares that were turned on the departing brothers by saying, "We've got to go back to the shop. Looks like John's just thought of something." One of the group said, "John's always thinking of something." Shooting was resumed.

The rigs had been left some distance away so the horses wouldn't be made restless by the shooting. As the three tall men strode rapidly toward their one-seater, Ed, approaching by indirection, asked, "Now, what the hell's struck him, Matt?" And Matt, relaying the question, said, "Yes, John, what the hell's struck you now?"

"An idea hit me," John answered, hurrying to the head of the horse to untie, handing the lines to Matt, who always drove. They settled themselves with much wiggling, three big men in the single seat. "Yes, sir!" John exclaimed, the thought still expanding in his mind, "An idee, as Pappy used to say—biggest one I ever had. Get that damn horse going, Matt." And then he began to explain.

He had been standing nearby when Will fired his last shot. He always liked to watch Will shoot; he was so short that his gun seemed too big and heavy for him, and he always seemed to lean back for balance. It was then he had noticed that a clump of sweet clover, ten feet ahead of him and to the left, had shaken with the blast. Why hadn't it occurred to him long ago that something could be done with that gas, that it might even be harnessed to perform some of the operative functions of a gun? "Why, it might even be possible to make a *fully automatic* gun," he surmised aloud, "one that would keep firing as long as you had ammunition." It was fortunate that Will was so short, he commented. Had a tall man been up the movement might not have been noticeable.

John explained the plan he had in mind. As soon as they reached the shop, they put it into operation. John took an old .44-caliber 73 Model and wired it to an inch board, with the rifle lying flat on its side. The board was then nailed to the floor. John chose the 73 because it was old, valueless, and handy.

A foot length of two-by-four was then found, and John had one of the brothers drill a hole through it just a little larger than .44 caliber. The block of wood was then placed on the floor about a quarter inch from the barrel, with the hole lined up with the bore. "What happens to that block of wood is what we want to see," John explained.

After a few safety precautions had been arranged—a block some distance away to stop the bullet, so it wouldn't go wild through the shop, and a four-foot length of wire, bent into a hook at the end, with which to pull the trigger—they were ready to begin.

The shop was low and long, with sufficient litter on the floor to mark it as a direct descendant of one of Jonathan's. The three sons of the old gunmaker were tense as John reached for the trigger with the wire. Had Jonathan been there even he would have let John's next remark go unnoticed: "That block will go hell-winding."

It did, coming to rest only when its momentum had been spent in a ricocheting course of leaps from one obstacle to another. It was a simple experiment, but for John it breached the wall of the future, giving him a glimpse of a vast region of wavering shadows to which in the coming years he would give shapes and substance. Turning to his brothers he said, "You know, we may not be more than ten years away from a pretty good automatic machine gun."

Matt, more impulsive than John, could never quite adjust to his brother's mixture of hot enthusiasm and cool, logical thought. Speaking of that moment later he said, "John had Ed and me as excited as a couple of kids at a circus. And then he tells us that we may have a pretty good machine gun, in ten years."

John was really arguing with himself aloud. He admitted that it did look as though they had stumbled onto something new, the possibility of an automatic gun, operated by the gas that had been wasted ever since the first shot was fired through a barrel. But, he cautioned, they shouldn't get too excited. Their Winchester business was certain and profitable. He could foresee several more guns that they needed to complete their line. And while he admitted that a gas gun might be a big thing, *eventually,* in the meantime it would mean a lot of work, learning a lot of new tricks. "But, damnation," he concluded, "it ought to be interesting. Anyhow, Ed, in the morning we'll make a gas-operated gun."

"Figure doing it by noon?" Ed asked without a smile.

"Hardly," John replied. "About four o'clock, I'd guess."

The laughter broke the tension.

It is not likely that John slept much that night. By the time he and Ed reached the shop early the following morning John had the gun planned in detail, and it stripped down to this: a modified lever and trigger in an old gun, and the addition of three pieces, one a rod that required only threading, the other two pieces so simple they could be hammered out on the anvil. With a few quick sketches he outlined the general scheme to Ed, and work on the gas-operated gun started. Taking the old 73 Model they had used the previous afternoon, they cut off part of the lever and lengthened and strengthened the trigger. Around the barrel, near the muzzle, they fitted a band with a descending arm, between four and five inches long. To the lower end of the arm they hinged a piece that ran back up to the muzzle, where it widened to a disk a little larger in diameter than the barrel. In this disk, they drilled a hole slightly larger than .44 caliber. John called this piece the

Artist's sketch of John M. Browning's first gas-operated experimental model. The "flapper" on the end of the barrel, pushed forward by the escaping gas on firing, actuated the mechanism of the rifle. Designed to test the inventor's basic ideas, the gun was disassembled as another model was being made and does not survive. The fate of a model once it proved workable was of no interest to the inventor. JOHN M. BROWNING ARMORY

"flapper," because of its rapid movement forward and back. As the bullet passed through the hole in the disk, the gas impelled the disk forward, and a spring snapped it back. The rod attached to the flapper, just under the hole, extended back to the modified lever, and the to-and-fro movement of the flapper actuated the mechanism of the rifle. The descending piece, attached firmly to the barrel, was slotted to permit the long rod to move up and down with the flapper's forward and backward movement.

The gun was being fired by four o'clock that afternoon. It was not the best-looking gun John had made, but it was the result that mattered. John reached his destination by the shortest possible route. The idea worked. Now the job could begin.

The Winchester 73 was not satisfactory for the high rate of fire to which John was subjecting it. He soon put it aside and made another rifle, also a shoulder type. Another gun followed, and another. The intervals between them could not have been long. Once the rat-tat-tat of the .44 began with the first experiment, the bursts seemed, in the memory of those present, to have gone on with only occasional interruptions. Several models preceded the filing of John's first patent embodying the gas-operating principle, on January 6, 1890. And many came after it. Some of these models no longer survive, except in the drawings and descriptions of the patent applications. Yet the route there is clearly marked. The ideas follow so logically that one almost forgets that there was no map for him to follow, no books for him to read, no experts to consult, that each step he took was at the time a lonely step into the unknown.

Over a year and a half passed before he filed his next two patent applications, on August 3, 1891. These covered two separate automatic gas-operated guns, both tapping the energy of the expanding gases at the muzzle but in completely different ways. One, instead of using the single flapper at the muzzle, used a small turbine. The other patent covered the entire mechanism of his first automatic machine gun.

On July 11, 1892, a patent was filed covering another completely new idea—drilling a hole through the barrel, in order to tap the high-pressure gases directly behind the bullet before the bullet had left the barrel. Many inventors would be content to spend their lives exploring the vistas this opened; in fact, new mechanisms are still being designed using this same concept.

That same year, on November 7, another application was filed, covering John's second machine gun. The first had proven highly successful for testing purposes; this, however, was his first full-scale attempt at a practical piece of machine-gun hardware. It employed a hole drilled through the barrel near the muzzle, which worked on a piston, which, through a swinging lever, worked the mechanism of the gun. Four additional patents were filed on this gun, between March 1893 and July 1895, covering additional modifications.

Toward the end of this development, on December 8, 1894, an application was filed on a purely experimental, shoulder-type automatic gun. The main purpose of this invention was to improve the gas port, which had undergone little change in his prior machine guns. Several ideas were embodied in the patent. One to be very important was shown in the drawings as an alternate method of constructing the gas port; this was the very simple idea of putting an elbow on the gas vent, so the forces of the gas would be applied along the axis of the barrel, making it possible to use a piston, rather than a swinging arm, to operate the mechanism. The possibilities were thus conceived at this time but not yet used.

From our perspective, John's automatic shotgun would appear to be only a few steps away. It seems almost inevitable that he would before long apply his gas-operating principle to a shoulder arm. However, he now took a different route—it was not a detour but rather the discovery of a huge new world. On September 14, 1895, he filed a patent application on his first semi-automatic pistol. The gas-operating principle had led him this far; this pistol was designed to see if the gas piston would also work on a hand gun. It did. However, the pistol did something else—it suggested the possibility of recoil operation, an operating principle which would be as greatly important as gas operation.

On October 31, 1896, John filed three patent applications. These contained systems as original and creative as anything he had ever invented: the first was blowback action; the second was the locked-recoil system with a turning lock; the third, the locked-recoil system with a pivoting lock. These three pistol patents were to have tremendous import on later automatic firearms.

And, before long, he came back to gas operation and the remaining steps to the automatic shotgun.

This was the course John M. Browning pioneered in one of the most significant decades in firearms development. Yet the patents tell only one part of the story. For history surrounded the making of each of these guns, and history would be made by them after they left their inventor's hands.

Following the experiment with the board, gun, and block, John had told his brothers that they might be able to develop a workable machine gun in ten years or so. It didn't take quite that long. It took less than a year. On November 22, 1890, Matt Browning sat down and wrote a letter which in time would have tremendous military significance. Written in longhand, on Browning Bros. stationery, it was addressed to Colt's Patent Fire Arms Manufacturing Company, Hartford, Connecticut. It read:

Dear Sirs:
We have just completed our new Automatic Machine Gun & thought we would write to you to see if you are interested in that kind of a gun. We have been at work on this gun for some time & have got it in good shape. We made a small one first which shot a 44 W.C.F. chge at the rate of about 16 times per second & weighed about 8#. The one we have just completed shoots the 45 Gov't chge about 6 times per second & with the mount weighs about 40#. It is entirely automatic and can be made as cheaply as a common sporting rifle. If you are interested in this kind of gun we would be pleased to show you what it is & how it works as we are intending to take it down your way before long. Kindly let us hear from you in relation to it at once.

Yours very truly,
BROWNING BROS.

If John was aware of the letter's historic import, he didn't indicate it.

2461 Washington Ave., Ogden ← ---→ 155 Main Street, Salt Lake City. JOHN M. BROWNING, MATT S. BROWNING

Browning Bros. Armory
WHOLESALE & RETAIL
Arms Sporting Goods
ETC·ETC·

Ogden Utah 22ᴿᴰ Nov. '90

Colts Pat. F. A. Mfg. Co.
        Hartford Conn.

Dear Sirs:

        We have just completed our new
Automatic Machine gun & thought we would
write to you to see if you are interested
in that kind of a gun. We have been at work
on this gun for some time & have got it in
good shape. We made a small one first which
shot a 44 W.C.F. Chge at the rate of about 16 times
per second & weighed about 8#. The one we have
just completed shoots the 45 Gov't Chge about 6
times per second & with the mount weighs about
40#. It is entirely automatic & can be made
as cheaply as a common sporting rifle. If
you are interested in this kind of guns we
would be pleased to show you what it is &
how it works as we are intending to take it
down your way before long. Kindly let
us hear from you in relation to it at once.

                Yours very truly
                Browning Bros

BROWNING ARMS COMPANY AND COLT'S PATENT FIRE ARMS MANUFACTURING COMPANY

"Damnation, Matt," he swore after reading the letter. "You make it sound like a finished gun, and it's just a crude first model!"

John's exasperation was directed more at himself than Matt. A month or two earlier he had come face to face with a disagreeable fact. For nearly a year he had abandoned his profitable and comparatively easy work with sporting arms; the result was a machine gun all right; it was also, he finally admitted to himself, a purely military weapon, of interest to no one except the government, and maybe not even to them. Moreover, the model was only a crude first step. The gun he had pretty well worked out in his mind would take most of his time for another year and might be no good when he finished it. Even if it turned out to be a good practical arm, what could he do with it? One thing sure: he was not going to Washington to try and peddle it. He might cool his heels in government offices here or in Europe for ten years. Then, to the surprise of the brothers, the firing ceased. The gun went into an out-of-the-way corner. The shop became unusually quiet and neat. For the better part of a year there had been empty shells underfoot and a roar in the ears, as John fastened one model after another in his vise and test-fired them into a sandbox down the bench. The shells were gone, and in place of the periodic bursts of fire there was contented whistling and now and then snatches of song. John had returned to a repeating shotgun he'd started earlier. His contentment didn't last long. Once he had finished the shotgun John had to again face the problem of the machine gun. This time he reached a decision. They would be going East with the new shotgun in a month or two, he told Matt. "You might write the Colt Company a short note saying that we have a fully automatic gun far enough along to show promise, and asking if they'd like to see it. They made the Gatling, which is quite a gun, from all accounts, and may not be interested. But they are the only people I know who have had experience with Government business. And they'd know what the government is doing—if anything—about machine guns. It may be a mistake to show this contraption we have here, but it shoots, and it shows that we have two essentials worked out—gas operation and belt feed. If I get enough encouragement I'll make a better model." That was John's real reason for writing; it was also the reason once he'd read Matt's letter his irritation was short-lived.

"Go ahead and send it," he decided. "What we want is to get in. The gun can talk pretty fast, and that will mean more than anything we might say." After a moment's pause he added, "Do you suppose they'll know who we are? And that brings up the question, 'Who are we'?"

But Matt was ready to lay long odds that Colt had learned where Winchester was getting the new guns that had been coming out in recent years. Hartford and New Haven were not that far apart.

The reply from Colt stated that the company's experience with machine guns was limited to the hand-cranked Gatling, and that more of the guns were sold abroad than to the United States Government. The sales effort had been very expensive and not altogether satisfying. If, however, the Browning Bros. were coming East on other business, and could make a visit to the Colt factory incidental to that business, the Colt management would enjoy having them call. The letter referred to the 86 Model Winchester as a masterpiece of the gunmaking art, and complimented the inventor. It was a cordial letter, somewhat sugared, John cynically suspected, because the Browning store was selling a good many Colt revolvers.

But it offered what John wanted—an opportunity to learn something about machine-gun possibilities. And so, a few weeks later, in early 1891, John and Matt arrived at the Colt factory, one carrying the machine gun, the other the mount wrapped in canvas covers that had been stitched by an Ogden tentmaker named John Hoxer. They were not so green as at the time of their first visit to the Winchester factory; but there was a vast difference between showing a sporting arm of an established type and demonstrating a gas-operated machine gun such as had never been seen before. It was not in the wildest dream of either young man that the sprawling factory they were entering, known the world over for its revolvers, would in a few years be as familiar to John as his own shop. There were periods in the future, when, under the stress of war, the bulk of the output of that great factory was made up of John's inventions.

After a short wait, they were taken to the office of the president of the company, John Hall. It was then that John fully realized how brash he was to come boldly into the Colt factory with his half-finished gun. He knew now that he had been so interested in watching every movement of the mechanism when he was firing it in Ogden that he was blind to its rough spots. But they had been registering in his subconscious mind, and for a minute or two he wished he could take his gun and go home. Fortunately, Hall was a genial man and did his best to put the brothers at ease, a kindness that John never forgot. It was John who finally suggested that they do some shooting, if there was a place handy.

In the firing room, as the brothers opened the sacks, cut string, and

Original model of John M. Browning's first gas-operated machine gun, circa 1890-91. Browning made this hammer-dented, heat-blackened model solely for experimental use, setting the rate of fire at 600 rounds per minute, not anticipating the remarkable testing it would soon undergo, first before Colt officials and later U. S. Naval personnel.　　　　　　JOHN M. BROWNING ARMORY

peeled off paper, exposing more and more heat-blackened and hammer-dented metal to Hall, his works manager, and a handy man, John's doubts increased.

"But," he said later, "the worst thing you can do when you have a weak case is make excuses. I saw we were at a place where we had to shoot, and shoot fast. I quit wishing that Matt and I had changed our shirts that morning, and before anybody had time to say much, we had the gun on its mount, banging away into one of the firing tunnels. We had brought along four loaded belts, fifty capacity, and I ran the two hundred through so fast nobody could think. We smoked up the Colt factory with those .45/70s, and waked echoes clear back to the colonel himself. When the last empty shell spanged on the floor, with not a hitch in two hundred, Hall and his men were too bug-eyed to see the hammer marks on the gun. They didn't look so deep to me, for that matter. It was comical. You know how it is in a circus, when a clown stumbles over everything and then suddenly turns into the star acrobat of the show. It was that way with the gun. It looked like a clown at first, but not any more. The changed expressions on the faces of Hall and his men put a pound of fat on my ribs."

After the demonstration, John felt free to explain the unfinished condition of the gun without the appearance of making excuses. Most of what he said was in the form of answers to questions put to him by Hall. The story went back to the bending weeds, described briefly the two small experimental guns which led to the "hammering out" of the gun whose thunder was still ringing in their ears. Matt, for good measure, added that John had taken time after that to make a repeating shotgun, which they had sold to Winchester the previous day. The story would not have been credible without the perfect performance of the machine gun. Hall insisted the Brownings stay a day or so in Hartford and talk things over. The brothers agreed.

13

THE TALKS BETWEEN Hall and the Brownings, which continued through two days, were, by the nature of things, limited to generalities. Neither the gun nor the market for such an arm was sufficiently developed to warrant definite promotional planning. John mentioned that he had a gun in mind that looked promising, but only a model would tell whether or not there were hidden snags, and the model would take months, maybe a year to perfect. He told Hall, as he had told Matt and Ed, that it looked like poor business to put aside his profitable work with sporting arms to tackle a job in which sweat seemed to be the only certainty.

Hall agreed but kept talking. He showed the Gatling gun to his visitors and was surprised to learn that it was the first machine gun they had ever seen, other than their own. The young man from the mountains had made a machine gun out of bending weeds. By degrees, enough of John's history came to light—revealed principally by Matt, who was a good salesman and not shackled by John's reticence—to convince Hall that a great future lay ahead of the inventor, and that his company should, if possible, share in that future. The pleasant and profitable connection between Colt and the Brownings that began that day endured for seventy years.

Hall suggested John leave the gun with him. He was sure that some of his acquaintances among officers of the Army or Navy would be glad to see an unofficial trial of the gun. He had become acquainted with a number of officers in the course of negotiating sales of Gatling guns and revolvers to the government. John could instruct the works manager in the operation of the gun. That should not be difficult, for the gun was obviously very simple in construction. "As a matter of fact," Hall said, "it looks as though there may be as many parts in one of our revolvers as in your gun." This statement, half jocular, was not far from the truth. It is hardly likely that another machine gun with so few parts has ever made such records of sustained fire.

John decided against leaving the gun but offered to come back with it any time a showing could be arranged. He did want to learn something of the government's attitude toward machine guns. He made it clear that he was not expecting to land an order. He was probably making a mistake in showing the half-finished gun. But he did not like the thought of working a year on a new model only to find that the armed services had no interest whatever in the type, which might very well be the case. There was no war in sight, and all was quiet along the old Indian warpaths. If he did show the gun, however, he insisted on showing it in the best possible light, and that meant handling it himself. Another thing; if he took the gun home, he might find time to smooth off a few of the roughest spots.

"Don't do it!" Hall protested. "When you set up the gun in the firing room, I nearly laughed out loud, but at the end of two hundred rounds, I felt like giving three cheers. If we get some officers in, put on the same kind of show for them. It's a great show!"

John laughed and said they might as well get some fun out of the gun. He would put on the show. He would not have agreed so readily if he had known the kind of show he would have to put on.

One day, several months later, Matt came out to the shop, flourishing a letter. It was from Hall and stated that he had found an opportunity to talk with two of his acquaintances in Naval Ordnance. They had expressed considerable interest in the gun, especially in its light weight, which was forty pounds with mount, as contrasted with the ninety-pound weight of the ten-barrel Gatling. They made it clear, however, that they would come only as interested spectators, without authority to speak for the department. It would be an unofficial test. That was more than John had expected, and he nodded approval as Matt read aloud. But the next paragraph brought a scowl to his face. The officers wanted continuous fire for a period of three minutes. John had adjusted the gun to fire at the rate of 600 per minute, and that meant 1800 rounds without a rest.

The year was 1891. It should be remembered that the United States Navy at this time had not advanced very far beyond where the Civil War had left it. The first of the modern-type battleships, the British *Dreadnaught,* was not commissioned until 1907. There had been no serious sea fighting for a good many years. The officers whom Hall quoted were thinking in terms of practice maneuvers with ships that would be obsolete in ten years. It was their theory that one of their ships, in combat, might find itself near enough to an enemy vessel to reach it with the machine gun, using the .45/70-caliber cartridges, in which case it would be highly desirable to rake the enemy's deck for at least three minutes. It was hardly likely that two ships would remain in range of the cartridge for a longer period.

At that point, John interrupted with, "Damnation! That's preposterous."

"The gun'll do it," Ed said with complete conviction.

"Sure it will" Matt exploded.

"Now, hold on," John said. "Let's say that the gun keeps on shooting till the barrel melts and runs into a puddle on the floor. There are a few other little things to consider. Who's going to stitch 1800 loops in half a mile of canvas strips? And who's going to stuff 1800 cartridges in those new stiff loops—with his thumb?" He held up a thumb for emphasis; so far, he had made all of the belts and loaded them. "But maybe I can figure out something. Read the rest of the letter."

Hall said he had taken pains to explain to the officers that the gun was an experimental model, hastily thrown together by the inventor to test certain of his basic ideas. The officers said they would not condemn the gun because of an occasional stoppage. It was a long and persuasive letter, in which Hall frankly disclosed his desire to have John put on his show, which, if reasonably successful, would serve as the best possible introduction for the new model John had in mind. The demonstration at the factory had given him the utmost confidence in the gun.

"Hall's pretty smooth," John admitted, with an admiring grin. "He doesn't actually promise anything, but he makes some mighty attractive suggestions. If he showed any cocksureness at this stage of the game, I'd drop him cold. Anyhow, I think I've figured out a scheme to dodge most of the belt-making trouble. I can make a pattern out of very thin tin. Hoxer can use it to mark the stitch-lines on the strips of canvas with a sharp pencil. He's a good man and ought to do a better job than I can when he gets on to it. I'll spend a day getting him started, and then I can drop in every day for an hour or so and keep him on the right track. As for loading the belts, we three are the only men who know just how the cartridges should be positioned, and I've got to save my thumb for the demonstration." He grinned at his brothers. "Looks like you two are elected. But," and he scowled again, "1800 rounds!"

"The gun will do it," Ed again asserted.

"Of course it will," Matt said positively.

"I'd agree with you," John said, "if I didn't know any more about the gun than you fellows."

John spent hours with the tentmaker, seeing that every stitch was in the right place. Ten belts were finally made to his satisfaction, each with a capacity of two hundred cartridges. As each belt was loaded by Ed or Matt, John went over it inch by inch, making sure that every cartridge was properly positioned.

John decided to go East alone. As he put it, "In three minutes the show will be over, or the gun will be melted, and there's no use in anyone else going just for that. A good diver can stay under water nearly that long." He planned to take the gun on the train with him but to ship the mount and cartridges by express. He made duplicates of a few small parts, those he considered most breakable.

Most of the time during the days of preparation he sat with the gun before him on the bench. Hour after hour he operated it, watching the movements of every part. Once, when Ed stopped a moment to watch, John said, "I wish I could talk things over with these parts and find out if any of them got pretty tired when we fired the two hundred back at the factory. It can very well be that one part is ready to break in ten or twenty rounds. Maybe the first shot."

In an exchange of telegrams, Hall and John fixed the date for the show, and John arranged a train schedule that would get him to Hartford a day early, permitting him time to set his stage. This was his first big show, excepting the two hundred rounds fired for Hall, and he was trying to leave nothing undone to make it a good one. He knew that the best way to emphasize the simplicity of operation, a matter of first importance, was to prove that it was a one-man gun. Therefore he had to do everything himself, and the gun had to do most of the talking.

In Hartford he asked for a woodworker and had him make nine feedboxes, each of a size to hold one belt. The belts were folded in the boxes, ten or a dozen cartridges to a layer. For firing, a box was clipped to the side of the gun, just under the feedway, and the belt, provided with a brass thumb and finger piece riveted to its end, was drawn through until the first cartridge clicked into place. The breechblock was then manually retracted and let speed forward under the impulse of its spring. These two movements drew a cartridge from the belt and drove it into the chamber. The gun was ready for firing.

John had fastened a bicycle seat on one of the tripod legs of the mount, to sit on while he operated the gun. He examined it carefully, knowing nothing could turn his show into a real comedy faster than to have the saddle slip and drop his long body on the floor. He had a large packing case brought in and placed within easy reach of the gun, arranging his ammunition boxes on it. In pantomime, he practiced detaching an empty box from the gun, reaching for a full box, and clipping it on. When the boxes were arranged to his satisfaction, there was nothing more to do. He went to the office and told Hall that he was going for a long walk and asked what sights were worth seeing. Hall thought he would enjoy a visit to the Connecticut State House, which contained a particularly fine collection of Civil War relics. John liked the suggestion and went swinging off on the first of many walks he made to that remarkably impressive building.[21]

The next day John was with his gun, trying to think of anything he might have overlooked, when Hall and his works manager came in with the two officers. Hall had wanted to have his directors present, but John had objected, saying that if anything went wrong, they did not want a crowd to see and talk about it.

After introductions and the usual amenities, John gave each man a small wad of cotton to stuff in his ears and warned them that there would be a lot of noise and smoke. One of the officers had a stop watch in readiness. John adjusted himself on the saddle, inserted the thumbpiece in the feedway, and drew the belt through until it clicked, saying, "This is how she works. Now you draw the breechblock back, let it slam forward like that, and she's loaded. And here she goes."

Twenty seconds of roar and smoke and he flipped an empty feedbox to the floor, kicking it out of the way as he clipped on a full box. Another twenty seconds, another empty box dropped to the floor. When he figured he had fired seven or eight hundred rounds, he tried to feel good about it, tried to think the gun had put on a pretty good show, whatever happened. But the thought of 1800 and a perfect score was still there. All his thoughts pounded to the rhythm of the gun. He seemed to think faster than ever before in his life. He had to think fast, he later said, in order to keep up with the gun and get his thinking done in three minutes. Out of the pounding emerged the realization that the hardest thing a man ever goes after is 100 per cent. Yet here he was, trying for it.

The barrel turned blue, and fine, mist-like shot filled the air at the muzzle, formed of lead melted from the bullets in the brief interval of their passing through the barrel. The tireless flapper fanned some of the molten mist back to him. Most of the particles were so minute that they instantly cooled below the burning point, but many were hot enough when they peppered his hands to make him swear. Then the barrel turned red. He had heated metal often enough to know what was happening. He thought of the extractor coming in contact with the barrel ten times a second, which was almost like maintaining uninterrupted contact. It would soften, and sure as hell it would break. And then the gun stopped.

"That's it," John thought to himself. "The extractor broke."

But his thought was interrupted by hand-clapping and a loud hurrah. He squinted around through the smoke, half-blinded, dizzy with the three minutes' uproar, looking for his audience, and noted to his utter amazement that there was not a feedbox on the packing case. The gun had fired the 1800 without a single stoppage. Blessing the smoke that half concealed him and whatever expression of strain or excitement might be showing in his face, he stood and shook his long legs. They were as cramped, he said, as though he had been sitting there for hours.

The four men were all trying to shake John's hand and slap him on the back. The officers were almost hysterical. No one can be a close observer of a machine gun through three minutes of continuous fire without getting excited.

Back in his hotel room a little later, John pulled a short screw driver and a couple of small wrenches out of a back pocket and fished his stock of spare parts out of his coat. "I hid those things," he later explained, "so there would be nothing in sight to suggest that I had any fear whatever of breakage. But," he laughed, "if anything had gone wrong, I'd have had to throw a couple buckets of water on the gun before I could touch it." As it was, he had blisters on his hands when he got home.

John and the officers were entertained at dinner that night by Hall. John said he made his second 100 per cent of the day by eating everything served to him and drinking his first glass of champagne. The dinner was held in the Heublein Hotel, for many years one of the best-known hostelries in New England, especially famed for its kitchen and soon to be John's headquarters in Hartford.

John later said that it was just as well that he ate heartily, for the meal was all he got out of the machine gun for several years. There was no bitterness in the remark; rather, he was smiling at the unsophisticated enthusiasm with which he had plunged into making the gun. He had not considered the fact that the United States Army was little more than a police force to patrol the regions where an occasional band of Indians tried to stage a little uprising. There was no war in sight. Army Ordnance had adopted the Gatling some years before and had a few of them scattered around at various army posts, but beyond that showed no interest in machine guns. Colonel George M. Chinn, in his comprehensive work *The Machine Gun*, notes: "The old line military men were still not inclined to accept anything as revolutionary as the Gatling . . . nothing can be found to show their use in the Indian warfare of the Western plains. For the purpose of conjecture and discussion, it should be noted that when General George Custer's entire troop was annihilated at Little Big Horn in 1876, his headquarters had on hand four of the 90-pound Gatlings, having a rate of fire of 1000 rounds a minute . . . They were chambered for the Army standard caliber .45-70-405 infantry centerfire cartridge. Had General Custer taken only one of the four that were available, the phrase 'Custer massacre,' so well known to every school child, would have had a reverse meaning—as one can hardly visualize a more perfect target for a machine gun than a band of Indians galloping in a circle. Conditions remained about the same until the war with Spain in 1898."[22]

The two officers who witnessed the demonstration told John that there was some talk in the Navy Bureau of Ordnance about the need for a lightweight machine gun, especially for landing parties. The Gatling, though a remarkable gun, was handicapped by its weight, ninety pounds, and was usually mounted on a wheeled carriage, like artillery. The officers were of the opinion that the bureau would, within a few years, call for trials of light machine guns; and it might be worth while for John to continue his development. They admitted, however, that the Navy would never have use for a great many machine guns, which, obviously, were better suited to the uses of the Army.

Hall offered John a generous royalty contract, suggesting that he go ahead and make a model of the improved gun he had been considering. When it was finished the Colt factory would make a model that would stand up for presentation before any board. Hall believed the Army would "wake up one of these days"; in the meantime there was all of South America, where Colt was selling gratifying quantities of revolvers and some Gatlings.

John declined signing a contract, simply giving Hall the assurance that he would have first chance at the new gun, if it were made. And so he again took his gun and went home.

He was not through with the machine gun. He continued to make arms for Winchester at about his usual pace and still had the new model firing within the year.

This gun, which became the Colt Model 1895 Automatic Machine Gun, was, like its forerunner, a gas-operated automatic type, firing over 400 rounds per minute. It had a very heavy barrel to prevent rapid heating, and was adapted to the .30/40 Krag and 6-mm. Lee cartridges.

It should be noted that smokeless powder was just coming into use and with it the rimless cartridge. These innovations required considerable redesigning of John's gun and extra work for him.

The model was officially tested by the United States Navy as early as 1893. It was first manufactured by Colt in 1895, and known officially as the "Colt." John saw no reason to put his own name on the gun; on the contrary, he argued, the Colt name would have great weight with an examining board, whereas his own name would be unknown. He did insist on conducting all trials of the gun himself, a job Colt was pleased to turn over to him. During the course of these trials he became acquainted with many officers of the armed services; as far as government business was concerned, this was the best advertising John could have.

Military thinking, in a large part because of these demonstrations, began to shift from the manually operated machine gun (like the Gatling) to the automatic. Rarely can one pinpoint such changes of thought, but in this case the year was 1895. The Inspector of Ordnance, in his report to the Secretary of the Navy covering the activities of this year, wrote:

"This year has been an eventful one in machine gun matters, and though at this date a final decision has not been made as to which one of several competing guns is the most desirable for adoption as the standard naval gun, much has been done toward that end, and it seems probable that a few weeks at most will see the problem settled.

"In the last annual report from this office three machine guns were named as being in course of development in this district for submittal to the naval board on machine guns; shortly afterwards, and before the August session of the board, the Pratt & Whitney Company suspended work on their gun, a two-barreled, crank-operated gun, on the Gardner system, having become convinced after long experiments that no crank gun could be made to handle successfully and safely the modern smokeless powder ammunition, owing to the danger from hang-fires. Repeated instances occurred of cartridges exploding after being entirely drawn from the gun, in rapid fire, and in one case a cartridge was discharged when partially out of the chamber, damaging the mechanism.

"The Gatling Gun Company, still having faith in the crank principle, and having met with gratifying success in handling .30-caliber ammunition, completed a gun of 6-millimeter caliber and submitted it in competitive trial to the Navy Board.

"The Colt automatic gun [Browning's Model 1895] was also completed and was tested by the board. Other guns submitted were the Accles Improved Gatling, the Maxim automatic, and an automatic weapon produced by a French arms company.

"The board held several sessions, at which all these guns were tested, and in January, 1896, all tests having been completed, a report

John M. Browning with his Colt Model 1895 "Peacemaker," the first automatic machine gun purchased by the United States Government. The gun saw naval action in the Spanish-American War, in the hands of U. S. Marines saved the foreign legations in Peking during the Boxer Rebellion, and was used in France in World War I until Browning's new model came off the production lines.

JOHN M. BROWNING ARMORY

was submitted. Shortly after, 50 guns of the Colt automatic type were ordered from the Colt's Patent Fire Arms Manufacturing Company . . .

"The Colt Company accepted the order for 50 guns, guaranteeing perfect operation with rimless cases (all competitive tests were with flanged cartridges) and a minimum uninterrupted speed of 400 shots per minute for one minute. Work was at once begun, and a model gun made, which has been tested and found to work in an eminently satisfactory manner, justifying the board's conclusion that a successful automatic gun could be produced . . .

"The Colt gun is exceedingly simple in construction, and has not more than one hundred parts, a surprisingly small number, considering the type. It has been designed with great care and with due attention to the often conflicting requirements of lightness and strength, so that with a maximum weight of 40 pounds, no part, with the single exception of the extractor, has broken in the course of a number of very severe tests . ,"[23]

Colonel Chinn summarizes the importance of the foregoing: "The Navy's order of 50 Colt weapons, which were delivered in 1897, represents the first purchase of an automatic machine gun by the United States Government. It is a matter of history that their use in the hands of the Marines saved the foreign legations in Pekin during the Boxer uprising. In 1898 an additional 150 Colts were procured. The machine gun field, as far as the Navy was concerned, had been cleared of crank operated guns. Browning had proven that the gas-operated automatic weapon was not only a possibility, but an accomplished fact. The Army, however, thought otherwise and kept the Gatling as standard equipment for another decade."[24]

The Model 95 was also produced by Colt for sale in South America and Europe and saw use in the Spanish-American War of 1898, where it was nicknamed "The Peacemaker."

In 1900, John began a new machine gun, recoil-operated and watercooled. There was no immediate prospect of profit in this undertaking. But there was a matter of pride involved. As he told his brothers, "One of these days, the Government is going to call for gun trials— maybe in a hell of a hurry; and all we have to show is the old Colt, a back number. They have been doing a lot of work on machine guns in Europe, and there isn't a thing in this country that would have a chance in competition. It would make me pretty hot to have a foreign gun come over here and steal a big order while I was taking a nap. Besides," he admitted, as if his brothers hadn't already suspected as much, "I have

one figured out to the point where we've got to do some shooting with it."
He had it finished and firing in about three months.

This was more than just another model, however. Chinn, in examining John's description of the gun's cycle of operation, written in 1900,
notes that in most essential details this was the father of all the
Browning machine guns that followed. "Browning's description," Chinn
observes, ". . . was written when there were only 45 states in the Union,
and three years before the Wright Brothers made their first flight in an
airplane. This serves as a yardstick by which to measure how far this
remarkable man was ahead of his time with his basic machine gun
principles."[25]

Another measurement is the fact that through World War I, World
War II, and the Korean War, all the automatic machine guns used by
United States troops, in the field, or mounted on U.S. planes, tanks, and
naval vessels, were Brownings.

John did not have this knowledge to comfort him when he returned
to Ogden after taking the gun back East to show to the Army Ordnance
Board. Although the gun had functioned perfectly and had been highly
praised, the matter rested there. In order to purchase arms, the board
had first to persuade Congress to appropriate money for this purpose,
and Congress was apathetic toward arms in general and machine guns
in particular. John never in his life wasted a minute lobbying. He took
the gun home, screening it in a corner of the little office where he hid
away from time to time to study and sketch. The period between 1900
and 1917 was, like every other period in John's life, a busy one. Instead
of inventing sporting arms for a single company, he was making them
for four. But the gun held an unusual fascination for him, and he spent
hour after hour with it drawn up to his chair, completely absorbed in its
mechanism, turning to his desk occasionally to make a note or rough
drawing. Those who worked with him during this period are sure the
gun never got "cold" in his mind.

In 1910 he made a new model; this, too, he kept perfecting. With the
outbreak of the war in Europe, John, certain that the United States
would be drawn into the conflict, began work on a military machine
rifle, designed expressly to provide the individual trench soldier with
the "walking fire" so often requested by Ordnance. When the military
belatedly called for arms tests in February 1917, less than two months
before the United States entered the war, the two weapons were ready.
Both were chambered for the standard Springfield rifle cartridge, the
.30/06, and both also bore their inventor's name. The machine gun was

first designated the "Browning Heavy Water Cooled Machine Gun." The "Browning Machine Rifle" went through several changes in name before it became known as the "Browning Automatic Rifle" or, far more popularly by the men who used it, the "B.A.R."

14

ON APRIL 6, 1917, millions of Americans read the headlines announcing that a state of war now existed between the United States and Germany. Only a few key military leaders read the secret memo distributed that same day, which stated that our requirements for this "machine-gun war" were by the most conservative estimates at least 100,000 modern machine guns—but that our preparedness consisted of exactly 1100 guns, all outdated: 670 Benet Mercies, 282 Model 1904 Maxims, and 158 Model 1895 Colts. Germany, upon entering the war three years earlier, had 12,500 improved Maxims and 50,000 more under construction.

"The fact remains, regardless of how unpleasant it may be," Colonel Chinn remarks, "that the country which originated and showed the world how to produce this deadly instrument, actually entered the war with a most obsolete assortment of machine guns. They would have been more in keeping with the armament of revolutionists in a banana republic than as weapons of soldiers representing one of the richest and most progressive nations on earth."[26]

Even though obsolete, the Colt Model 95 was the only machine gun which could be manufactured with any speed. Colt was tooled up for it and a few other companies were making rechambered versions for Russia. The gun was manufactured and used until a sufficient number of John's improved model were in production, whereupon it was relegated to training purposes.

John had taken his two new models East months before the United States entered the war, and had conducted a number of semi-official showings. The first official public exhibition of the guns took place February 27, 1917, at Congress Heights, just outside Washington, D.C. Some three hundred people witnessed the demonstration—senators, congressmen, military officials from Great Britain, France, Belgium, and Italy, as well as the United States, and members of the press. Chinn notes that the latter wrote much about the exhibition. "They gave a glowing account of the reliability and tremendous firepower of both weapons and painted verbal pictures . . . of how a hundred men advancing with these weapons firing full automatic would literally sweep an enemy out of the way. The only feature they seemed to forget was that though war, at this point, was practically inevitable, the superb weapons demonstrated were the only ones in existence and were a long way from mass production."

The B.A.R., obviously the answer to their request for "walking fire," made an immediate impression on the military officials. It could be carried by the individual soldier and fired from the shoulder or the hip, single shot or, with instant conversion, fully automatic, emptying its 20-shot magazine in 2½ seconds (*480 rounds per minute*). It was also so simply constructed that its 70 pieces could be disassembled and reassembled in 55 seconds. As a result of the exhibition, the rifle was officially adopted by the United States Government. (This was the second Browning gun to he adopted for use by all branches of the service. In 1911 the Colt .45 Caliber Automatic Pistol, invented by John in 1905, was made the official U.S. military side arm. This will be discussed in greater detail with John's other pistol developments.)

Despite its excellent performance, ordnance officials postponed decision on the machine gun, stating that they believed it should he given more extensive endurance tests. John took the gun hack to the Colt factory in Hartford, where the trial models had been built, and continued to make changes and modifications, probably silently cursing those who still acted as if the war was ten years away. He was quite familiar with apathy toward machine guns; he had not imagined that after watching Germany using these weapons for nearly two years, with horribly effective results, anyone could still he blind to their importance.

April 6, 1917, brought the war home. Additional tests were scheduled. In May John took the .30-caliber machine gun to the government proving ground at Springfield Armory. What happened there was so amazing that it had the curious effect of making some of the gun's strongest advocates suddenly turn skeptical.

"A total of 20,000 rounds was fired without a malfunction or broken part, at a cyclic rate of 600 rounds a minute," Colonel Chinn reports. "After the splendid performance of the weapon, Browning decided to test it further, and fired an additional 20,000 rounds. All 40,000 cartridges were expended without the failure of a single component part. This was such an unusual performance for a new gun that it aroused great interest and some skepticism among its most ardent backers."[27]

John had set a new machine-gun record, one so remarkable that

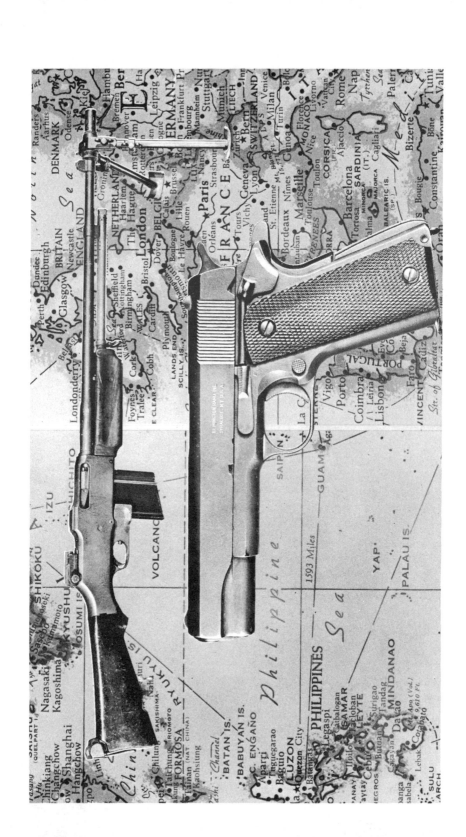

some refused to believe what they had just seen. They chose as alternative the possibility that the gun had in some means or manner been rigged for the test. Probably no one came right out and said this; the implication came across, however. John's reply and its effect are described by Chinn: "In order to show that the gun was not especially prepared for the test, a second weapon was used that not only duplicated the original trial, but bettered it by operating continuously for 48 minutes and 12 seconds. This was accomplished by having available sufficient belted ammunition for this phenomenal burst.

"Following this excellent demonstration, the board of five Army officers and two civilians appointed by the Secretary of War to study the problem of machine gun supply recommended for immediate adoption the water-cooled Browning, pronouncing it and the previously accepted B.A.R. 'the most effective guns of their type known to the members.'"

Both guns had that virtue which Jonathan so admired in a firearm, simplicity. Like the B.A.R., the .30-caliber machine gun was easily disassembled and reassembled. To demonstrate this dramatically, its operators accomplished it while blindfolded. Like many another of John's little dramas, this too had its long-range effect—the blindfold test became a permanent part of the machine-gun training program, as gunners of three wars well remember.

John had gone East before the Congress Heights tests; he was still there when the government gave out the first contracts for production of his arms, in August and September 1917. Shortly after this, an officer called on him at the Colt factory to discuss the terms of his compensation. Matt was also present at the interview.

The officer was authorized to make John an offer which granted the government full rights to manufacture the machine gun, machine rifle, and the .45 automatic pistol for the duration of the war. An additional condition, insisted upon by ordnance officials, was that John M. Browning personally supervise the production of these arms in all factories where orders were placed. "The offer, we know," Matt recalled the officer saying, "is only a fraction of what you would receive from

Two of the world's best known military arms: the B.A.R. (Browning Automatic Rifle), officially adopted by the United States in 1917; and the Government .45 Caliber Automatic Pistol, the official U.S. military side arm since 1911. World War II production models. The Browning Automatic Rifle was one of the first guns to bear its inventor's name. Even today many are unaware that not only the Colt .45 shown but all the automatic pistols produced by Colt's Patent Fire Arms Manufacturing Company have been of basic Browning design.
GUNS: JOHN M. BROWNING ARMORY. MAPS: RAND MCNALLY & COMPANY

After long insistence by ordnance officials, John M. Browning finally consented to pose for a formal portrait. His wife was equally insistent that he buy a new hat for the picture. However, when he arrived at the studio, the officers urged him to wear the same crumpled hat to which they had become accustomed during the various government tests. This may account for the faint traces of a smile in this photograph. Usually the inventor's fine sense of humor went into hiding when confronted with a camera lens. The gun is the infantry model of Browning's Model 1917 .30 Caliber Water Cooled Machine Gun.

royalties on orders already booked, and it may not be acceptable. In that event, negotiations will be necessary." He then made the offer.

"I supposed that John would ask for a little time to think things over and get my opinion," Matt noted. "But without hesitating a second, he said, 'Major, if that suits Uncle Sam, it's all right with me.'"

After the officer's departure, Matt told John that they could have received much more than John had settled for without the slightest argument. John's reply was, "Yes, and if we were fifteen or twenty years younger we'd be over there in the mud!"

The Secretary of War, upon hearing of John's agreement, wrote him as follows:

WAR DEPARTMENT
WASHINGTON

November 13, 1917

My dear Mr. Browning:

I have learned from Major Little of the patriotic and generous attitude taken by you in the negotiations for the use of your patents of light and heavy machine guns in this emergency, and beg leave to express my appreciation of it.

You have performed, as you must realize, a very distinct service to this country in inventions, and contributed to the strength and effectiveness of our armies. You have added to that service by the attitude you have taken in the financial arrangements necessary to have your inventions available to the Government.

Cordially yours,

(signed) NEWTON D. BAKER
Secretary of War

Several years after the war, the Associated Press disclosed that John had accepted $750,000 for his inventions and time, and that had he been paid standard royalties for use of the weapons he would have received $12,704,350.

John stayed in the East. Taking an apartment in Hartford, he had his wife and two youngest children join him. His "short trip" lasted nearly two years. During that time he returned to Ogden only once, drawn back by important business. This business he finished in three days, then hurried back to his job.

It was a job, indeed. He had to exercise supervision over the making of drawings and pilot models of the .30-caliber water-cooled machine gun, the B.A.R., and the .45-caliber automatic, then, once they were being made, check production in each factory. Fortunately, five of the six factories with contracts were closely grouped in New England: Colt in Hartford, with a subsidiary plant in Meriden, Connecticut; New England Westinghouse Company in Springfield, Massachusetts; and Marlin-Rockwell Corporation and Winchester Repeating Arms Company in New Haven. The Remington Arms Company plant in Ilion, New York was the longest trip from John's headquarters in Hartford.

John immediately found himself entangled in red tape, which stretched from his office in the Colt factory to Army Ordnance in Washington, D.C. One of his first acts was to cut it. The department had officers detailed to each factory on inspection duty. "They are some of the nicest young men I have ever met," John explained in a telephone call to the Chief of Ordnance, whom he had come to know well through the various government tests. "They are capable, courteous, and cooperative as far as their orders permit. But this is the way it works out. I decide upon a small change to simplify things, for example, and they all say, 'Yes, Mr. Browning; we'll hurry out a blueprint of the change and send it to Washington for approval, Mr. Browning.' And it's two weeks before the approval comes back. Now, General, I know I don't have to tell you there's a war going on and we're losing time. If there's anybody down there who understands these guns better than I do, send him up, and I'll go home."

The situation was so manifestly absurd that the general was laughing at the end of the speech. An order was immediately issued making John's instructions final in all matters pertaining to arms of his invention. This change was welcomed eagerly by all concerned with speeding up production.

This was only one of many problems, and the others were not so easily solved. Tooling up for production in some cases took months, and production itself, once begun, did not reach maximum efficiency immediately. Of the three companies given contracts for the .30-caliber machine gun, Westinghouse led in total production and also set a production record by having its first gun off the assembly line in sixty-three days. But Westinghouse was not given its contract until January 1, 1918. Remington was second in production, delayed by a prior Russian contract. That Colt was last seems curious, but Colt was not only delayed by fulfilling a British contract for the Maxim-Vickers machine guns, that company also had to prepare the drawings and precision gages for all the Browning arms manufactured in the other plants.

Even before John was called in, many were crying, *"Where are the machine guns?"* John probably observed that among them were congressmen who had voted against every arms appropriation in the past. Others were men who had preached preparedness long before America's entry into the war. One of these was former President Theodore Roosevelt. John soon learned what he had always suspected, that fame brought complications. Before the war the Browning name had appeared on few American arms of John's invention; it is probable that even Roosevelt, hunter that he was, was unaware that the Winchester 95, one of his favorite guns, was a Browning design. From one end of the country to the other and back again, Roosevelt swung his big stick, and one of his targets was the Light Browning (the B.A.R.), which he called a "paper gun," a "fiction," a "myth." John gave no interviews, took no part in the controversy, did not attend the second public showing of the gun at Congress Heights which followed first production and which silenced all criticism of the gun. He was far too busy. Teddy was wrong about the Light Browning, but much else he said John had said too. But this wasn't the time for talk. He worked days and nights and soon found this wasn't enough. Unable to make the rounds of the factories as frequently as the job required, he brought his brother Ed East to lend a hand. Ed, having made the models of the arms in question in the Ogden shop, could be sent to one factory after another, looking for slips that required John's attention.

Fame also brought questions. With these John was remarkably patient, as long as the question showed some prior thought. He was not a man who made conversation for the sake of "passing the time of day," but with the workmen in the factories he was completely at ease. One man, on the Colt assembly line, caught in the familiar pattern of endlessly making the same part and never understanding its place in the whole, once remarked this, in passing, to John. John talked to him for a quarter of an hour. When he was finished, the man not only knew the part's importance but understood the basic principles of the machine gun well enough to explain them to those around him. There probably were many men like him. Splendid engineering staffs had been assigned to aid in production; often John acted as teacher to them too. Where did he pick up his wealth of technical knowledge? When a young officer asked him the name of his college, John laughed and said, "My father's shop. He was a gunsmith." Then, to ease the young man's evident embarrassment, he added, "But I've been taking courses ever since, in colleges like this." Most of the major questions regarding firearms came to his office sooner or later.

One such incident occurred in March 1918, on the day the Germans startled the world by shelling Paris from the fantastic distance of sixty miles. Their mysterious gun caused speculation in all quarters. The Colt factory that day was humming, not only with acres of machines, but with multi-tongued curiosity. John was in his office when six or eight men, officers and civilian engineers, crowded in the doorway and asked permission to enter. Their spokesman came directly to the point.

"Mr. Browning," he said, "we've all been quarreling about that damn gun the Germans have cooked up, and we wish you'd give us your opinion. What's it like, and how did they do it?"

"Officers and gentlemen," John said, with his soft chuckle, "I'd ask you to sit down if there were seats enough, but my opinion won't keep you standing long. Like most mysteries, that gun, I'd say, is no mystery at all. It would be too expensive to make machines to bore and rifle a barrel as long as that one would have to be, so they just made two barrels and joined them together. We could do it at any of the shops where we turn out the big guns for the Navy.

"The projectile will be long, to give weight, but not over eight inches in diameter, to cut down air resistance. The trajectory," and John laughed, "will be somewhere under the moon." Then he frowned. "It's too expensive to make, too heavy to handle, too big to hide—in short, gentlemen, it's no good and just designed to scare us."

Time proved him right in every particular. In a month the Big Berthas were silent.

One of the companies which contracted to manufacture the B.A.R. was Winchester. John was in Hartford at the time Winchester was given the contract, and former Winchester employee Edwin Pugsley recalls that he went to see him with more than a little trepidation. Over sixteen years had passed since John's break with the firm, the event itself so well known by now in the various arms factories that it had reached the status of the "historic." But Pugsley, to his surprise and pleasure, found: "Browning was delighted to see me. We talked at some length. He recalled his years with Winchester and asked a number of questions about the personnel and the factory. He asked specially about T. G. Bennett and spoke of him with some nostalgia. He said that often, over the years, he had been lonesome for Winchester."[28]

Though John went to New Haven on numerous occasions and spent considerable time in the Winchester factory, apparently neither he nor Bennett felt nostalgic enough to bring about a meeting.

More than sixty different models of Browning automatic machine guns have been adapted to land, sea, and air use. (Upper left), A .30-caliber air-cooled machine gun on tripod mount. (Upper right), A .30-caliber air-cooled machine gun with shoulder stock and bipod arrangement. (Lower left), A .50-caliber air-cooled model with tripod mount. (Lower right), Another .50 caliber, this one water cooled, with an anti-aircraft mount. (Center), The first Model 1917 .30 Caliber Water Cooled Machine Gun to reach the American Expeditionary Forces in France during World War I. First used in action by the inventor's son, Val Browning. Tripod mount with water can. Its type is still in use by the United States Army. JOHN M. BROWNING ARMORY

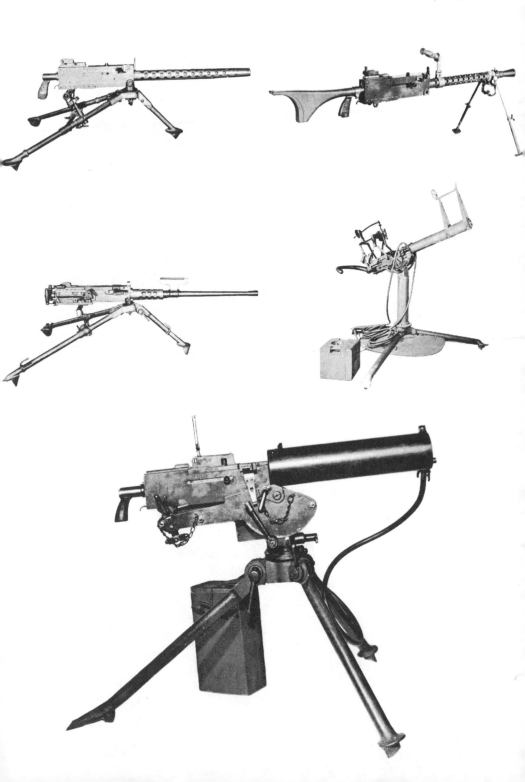

Browning Automatic Machine Guns—an essential part of United States military power from World War I. (Upper left), An Air Force waist gunner firing a .50 caliber air-cooled machine gun from a B-17 over Europe, 1943. OFFICIAL U. S. AIR FORCE PHOTO (Upper right) A 1st Marine Division squad firing a .30-caliber aircooled infantry model in combat. Korea, May 1951. DEFENSE DEPT. PHOTO: MARINE CORPS (Lower left), A tank crew manning a .50-caliber air-cooled, turret-mounted machine gun. Korea, September 1950. DEFENSE DEPT. PHOTO: MARINE CORPS (Lower right), Quartering view of a coast-guard Picket boat with a .50-caliber water-cooled machine gun on the bow. On World War II convoy escort duty. U.S. COAST GUARD OFFICIAL PHOTO.

In July 1918 the first B.A.R.s arrived in France, in the hands of the 79th Division. First Lieutenant Val A. Browning, son of the inventor, was the first to use the gun against the enemy. Val had been withdrawn from Cornell by his father to help with production in the various factories and was so familiar with the arms that the Ordnance Board sent him to France to serve as instructor. Again, in September 1918, when the first Browning .30-caliber machine guns arrived, Val inaugurated their use.[29]

On September 26, a small detachment of the 79th Division took the gun into combat. The following report was sent to General Pershing by the commanding officer of this detail: "During the five days that my four guns were in action, they fired approximately 13,000 rounds of ammunition. They had very rough handling due to the fact that infantry made constant halts, causing the guns to be placed in the mud. The condition of the ground on these five days was very muddy, and considerable grit, etc., got into the working parts of the guns. Guns became rusty on the outside due to the rain and wet weather, but in every instance when the guns were called upon to fire, they fired perfectly. During all this time I had only one stoppage, and this was due to a broken ejector."

Even before the Browning .30-caliber machine gun saw action overseas, General John J. Pershing, Commander of the American Expeditionary Forces, demanded a weapon of larger caliber. The Germans had begun using a heavy armor on their vehicles that was impenetrable to the .30 caliber. Both the British and the French were at work enlarging the caliber of their machine guns.

American Army engineers first attempted to adapt the regular .30 caliber Browning to the French 11-mm. cartridge, but the two were so different in ballistics that the attempt was not satisfactory. Besides, after a French gun had been procured for experimental purposes, it was found that the velocity was too low and the bullet weight too light to meet the specifications sent over by General Pershing, which called for a bullet of not less than 670 grains with a muzzle velocity of at least 2700 feet per second.

These attempts having failed, with loss of considerable time, officers from Army Ordnance brought the problem to John. Ed was with him in his Hartford office when the officers called. Would he make a .50-caliber machine gun? The matter was urgent; it was also becoming increasingly embarrassing to report the continuing delay to General Pershing. Could Mr. Browning find time to make the gun?

John then began to ask questions, principally about the cartridge.

"Well," he finally said, "the cartridge sounds pretty good, to start. As for the gun—you make up some cartridges, and we'll do some shooting."

"That was a little of John's sarcasm," Ed recalled, "as much as saying that he could make the gun before the government could make the ammunition. The funny part is, we had to wait for cartridges."

On September 12, 1918, Colt completed the parts for the first official model. John assembled the gun, and it was test-fired successfully in Colt's pasture. Six additional models were made by Winchester in record time. The government tests were scheduled for November 11, 1918, at the Aberdeen proving ground, but, when the Armistice was signed on that date, were postponed until the fifteenth. John handled the gun himself during the tests, firing 877 rounds in bursts of 100 to 150 rounds, with no malfunctions of any kind.

Following the completion of the tests, John was interviewed by an enthusiastic press. To what did the firearms genius attribute this

John M. Browning testing his .50-caliber machine gun in Colt's pasture, Hartford, Connecticut, September 1918. The gun was completed too late to be of use in World War I but was ready for the wars that followed. JOHN M. BROWNING ARMORY.

miracle, they asked. "One drop of genius in a barrel of sweat wrought this miracle," John replied.

It amused him several years later to read in a newspaper interview that his inventive contemporary, Thomas Alva Edison, had defined genius as "one per cent inspiration and ninety-nine per cent perspiration." Edison, he decided, had put it better. But it was still plain, old-fashioned sweat.

The Browning .50 Caliber Water-Cooled Machine Gun had the same basic operational features as the .30 caliber, but through the use of a unique oil buffer the necessary strengthening of the gun was accomplished without a proportional increase in weight, an important factor. The oil buffer absorbed the excess energy of recoil, thereby effectively reducing undue strain on the parts. In addition, the buffer provided a means of controlling the rate of fire. Instead of the pistol grip used on the .30 caliber, John incorporated double spade grips on the gun.

Though the war ended before this gun could be produced, it has since become one of America's most prominent weapons, and was used extensively in both World War II and the Korean War.

Prior to the completion of the .50 caliber, John made an air-cooled model of his .30 caliber that weighed only 22 pounds and had a rate of fire of approximately 700 rounds per minute. The weapon was the first in this country to be successfully affixed to pursuit planes so that it enabled the pilot to look along his sights and aim the gun by maneuvering his ship. To do this the firing mechanism of the gun was synchronized with the motor of the plane in such a way that the stream of bullets could pass through the revolving propeller without hitting the blades.

Later the .50-caliber Browning was also converted to an air-cooled model. Much lightened in weight, it fired an 800-grain bullet at a muzzle velocity of 2700 feet per second—sufficient to penetrate a 1⅛ inch piece of armor plate at 25 yards.

Both models, known as the Browning .30M2 and .50M2, were used as aircraft machine guns by the United States Army Air Force during World War II and are still in limited use at the present time.

A report from the commanding officer of the Army Air Force, dated November 1943, specifically pointed out the performance of the .50 caliber, calling it "the most outstanding aircraft gun of the Second World War." The report further stated: "This weapon, together with its ammunition, is the backbone of offensive and defensive guns for American aircraft and was brought to such a state of perfection by the Ordnance Department during the years of peace prior to the present conflict that it has enabled the Army Air Forces, the U. S. Navy and Marine Corps to show a definite superiority in aircraft gun power throughout this global war."[30]

Similar reports were received during the Tunisian campaign when 72 enemy aircraft were destroyed by 35 fighter planes with less than 200 rounds of ammunition expended per gun.

Colonel Chinn writes: "Students of warfare are generally in agreement that the most far-reaching single military decision made in the 20th Century was when a small group of British officers, shortly before World War II, decided to mount ten caliber .303 Brownings on their Hurricane Fighters. This single act undoubtedly brought about the turning point of the War."[31]

Axis reaction to the Browning machine guns was equally strong. Among the official German papers seized at the end of World War II was a congratulatory message from Field Marshal Goering to General Rommel. Rommel, in one of his most brilliant maneuvers during the African campaign, had captured Tobruk, at the same time seizing thousands of Browning .50-caliber machine guns just unloaded from an Allied convoy. Goering congratulated Rommel on his success and noted: "If the German Air Force had had the Browning .50 Caliber, the Battle of Britain would have turned out differently."[32]

The Japanese were no less impressed. Colonel Chinn makes the following interesting observation: "After their successful conquest of the Philippines, the Japanese captured thousands of our Browning machine guns, and upon this reliable mechanism they based practically all wartime cannon development . . . While the Japanese simply copied our Brownings in detail, and showed no originality, they did deserve great credit for furnishing an answer to one question that was asked all through World War II. If the Browning .50 caliber machine gun was the best of its kind in the world, then why did not American engineers scale it up to the 20-mm we needed so desperately at the time? While we advanced theories as to why it could not be done, they not only did it, but succeeded remarkably well. It had a rate of fire of 960 rounds per minute and weighed only 84 pounds. Even with the use of inferior metals the components had a life expectancy of 3,000 rounds."[33]

To date, no fewer than 66 different known models of the Browning recoil machine gun have been made. Latest aircraft models were stepped up to a cyclic rate of fire of 1300 rounds per minute in the .30 caliber and 1200 per minute in the .50 caliber.

The Browning automatic rifle has also proven its durability. Lieutenant General Levin H. Campbell, Jr., Chief of Ordnance, U. S. Army, 1942-46, notes: "Since acceptance by Ordnance in 1917, only a few modifications and improvements have been necessary in this 'old reliable' infantry weapon . . . Thousands of BAR's were shipped overseas in the Saint-Mihiel and Argonne offensives. They were used again in the bitter street fighting that took place in Aachen and other German cities in the Second World War. Their principal employment, however, was in the Pacific Theatre. The weapon had high jungle mobility and provided excellent firepower for short-range jungle targets frequently encountered." In November 1939, there were approximately 87,000 BARs in our war reserve, according to General Campbell; however, shipments to England immediately after Dunkirk greatly reduced this stock. During World War II, from the beginning of production to July 1945, 177,000 of these rifles were produced.[34] A separate chapter could be written on their use in the Korean War.

15

THERE IS NO direct evidence that John knew one of his pistols triggered World War I. No recollections, no remembered conversations. But at that time he was working closely with Fabrique Nationale, where the pistol had been manufactured, and both European and American newspapers reported the event in great detail. He knew. The gun with which the youth Princip assassinated the Archduke Franz Ferdinand and his wife Sophie on June 28, 1914, in Sarajevo, the capital of Bosnia, was the F.N. .32-caliber Model 1900, the first Browning pistol to be commercially produced.

John had begun work on his first automatic pistol in 1894. By that time several semi-automatics had already appeared on the European market. Very heavy and cumbersome, however, they had not proven popular, and as a result few were produced. John's first model—a .38 caliber gas-operated type with an exposed hammer—was finished in 1895, and on July 3 of that year John and the officials of Colt's Patent Fire Arms Manufacturing Company test-fired it in Hartford, Connecticut. On July 24, 1896, John signed an agreement that permitted the Colt company to manufacture his automatic pistols in the United States on a royalty basis. Four pistols were specified in this agreement, the above mentioned and three others John had invented in the intervening year; one of the latter, also .38 caliber, was chosen for production and appeared in 1900 as the first automatic pistol to be manufactured in the United States. *From that date to the present, every automatic pistol produced by Colt has been based on John M. Browning's designs.*

In his contract with Colt, John had limited their sale to the United States, as he planned to arrange his own contact in Europe. He had even gone so far as to make a very small and light .32 caliber, which he thought would have a stronger appeal in the European markets. He was partial to the lighter gun and at home in Ogden had taken to carrying it in a back pocket. Evenings, when he found time, he would slip a couple boxes of ammunition in his coat and walk up into the hills to fire it. He also practiced quick-drawing it, waiting until he had the trick perfected before he showed it to a surprised Matt.

In the spring of 1897 there occurred a meeting that John was later to look upon as one of the most fortuitous of his career. While at the Colt factory he met a man named Hart O. Berg. Berg had been born in Hartford but lived in Belgium, where he was employed as commercial director of a Liege firm, Fabrique Nationale d'Armes de Guerre. He was in the United States at this time, checking new developments in the manufacture of bicycles. Browning and Berg liked each other immediately. And what Berg told John about Fabrique Nationale filled the inventor with frustration and wonder.

Berg explained that the Belgian Government, a few years earlier, had given a mixed Belgian and German syndicate a large order for a military rifle but had imposed the condition that the arms should be manufactured, in their entirety, in Belgium.

Liege had been famous for its armorers since the middle ages, because of its easy access to iron and coal, some coal seams underlying parts of the city itself. Those natural advantages, together with a long heritage of gunmaking, marked Liege as an ideal location for an arms factory. The syndicate was convinced that with the Belgian order as a backlog, the factory, by the addition of other products from time to time, could be developed into a permanently profitable investment.

The hopes of the syndicate, however, were slow in materializing, and Berg had been brought in to head a new managerial organization to try to start the wheels again. He expressed the opinion that he had the

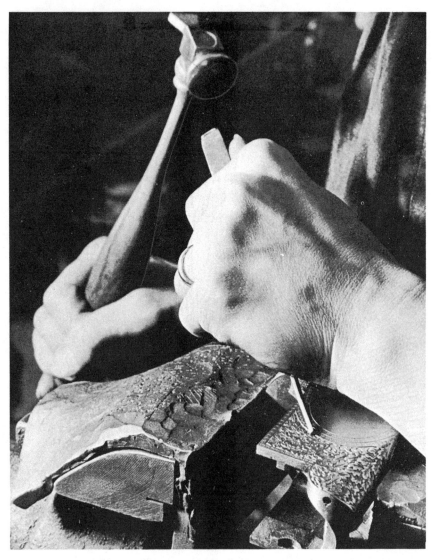

Since the middle ages, Liege, Belgium, has been famed for its armorers. A skilled artisan at Fabrique Nationale d'Armes de Guerre is shown engraving the receiver of one of the Browning arms. BROWNING ARMS COMPANY

most efficient arms factory in the world, because it was new, unencumbered by old equipment, and had skilled labor readily available, but thus far their manufacturing had mainly consisted of bicycles, motorcycles, and various munitions.

"Think of it—a new gun factory with nothing to make!" John later marveled to Matt, who was also in Hartford at this time. "I'll give them something that will set their wheels in motion!" When Berg left Hartford he carried with him the .32-caliber pistol model, a tentative agreement for its manufacture, and an unqualified belief in the genius of John M. Browning. His enthusiasm was soon shared by the officials and engineers of Fabrique Nationale (F.N.). Calling in various European arms experts, they subjected the pistol to careful scrutiny, then test-fired it 500 rounds without a single malfunction, a demonstration that approached the miraculous in those early days of automatic arms. All agreed on two important points: Browning's pistol was far superior to the cumbersome automatics then in use; and it was so simply constructed that their total manufacturing investment was estimated at only 12,000 francs. (When the gun finally went on sale it was priced at 30 francs; the cartridges sold for 55 francs a thousand.)

F.N. officials signed the contract on July 17, 1897, and the contract and initial advance against royalties were sent to the Brownings, who wrote on July 26, acknowledging their receipt. Production was not begun for several months. In January 1898, Berg was sent to the United States in an attempt to convince Browning that he should be present to supervise production. Matt's son Marriner recalls the arrival of the Europeanized Berg in Ogden and the interest of the residents. The Browning children liked him immediately; he came heavily laden with gifts. Though Berg was unable to convince John to make the trip, John apparently gave him detailed instructions regarding the pistol's manufacture.

A number of years later the head of the drafting department told John of an incident that had occurred during production. One of the draftsmen saw that a slight change in one of the parts would result in the simplification of a fixture. He went to the manager with his idea, asking permission to make the change. Instead of being commended, he was ordered to leave the pistol alone. "That's the way Browning made it," the manager said, "and that's the way it's going to be." "The funny part," John said, "was that the change wouldn't have hurt the pistol a bit, and *would* have simplified the fixture." But at least the manager's *faith* was sound, as results proved spectacularly.

The pistol appeared in January 1899, a year before the first Colt model, making it the first Browning-designed automatic pistol to be manufactured. It was immediately popular. Shortly after its appearance its merits were dramatically publicized: a band of French apaches, armed with the F.N. pistol, withstood for several days a siege by Parisian police armed with old-fashioned revolvers. (The pistol vs. revolver battle was to rage on long after this, however.) By 1909, 500,000 had been produced. Since F.N. had chosen to designate the pistol by the name Browning, very soon the Browning name was better-known in Europe than in the United States. Extensive advertising, together with the name stamped on every pistol, soon added a new word to the French language; *browning* appears in French dictionaries as a common noun, uncapitalized, defined as one of the pistols designed by the American inventor, John M. Browning. When F.N. at an early date began the manufacture of ammunition, John's signature was used on every box of pistol cartridges as a registered trade mark, much to his surprise. Long before he visited Liege for the first time, its residents were talking of Monsieur Browning, the American whose pistol had brought their city a new prosperity.

Despite the urgings of Hart O. Berg and others, John put off his first trip to Europe until forced into it by the break with Winchester.[35] This occurred in early January 1902. Late that month or early in February, he embarked on his first ocean voyage, his automatic shotgun carefully wrapped and under his arm.

Aboard ship he was soon aware that most of the passengers were quite at ease, himself excepted. Realizing that a "mountain man from Ogden" would appear "pretty green" in Europe, he spent most of the voyage in the ship's library, perusing histories and travel books. Impatient to get to Liege and settle the matter of the automatic shotgun, he was nevertheless anxious to see Paris; as long as he was passing through, he decided to stop over a week. His time was his own; he had not written anyone that he was coming.

After checking into a hotel, he hired a guide, one who had a sense of humor and a passable knowledge of English. John's first excursion was to a tailor, to be measured for a new wardrobe; he did not want to arrive in Liege in his Ogden ready-mades.

He wanted to "see Paris," and that was what he did, day and night, accompanied by the guide. They started with the Eiffel Tower; "from there," John recounted later, "we could see that we had a full week's work ahead of us." Then came the Louvre, Fontainebleau, Arc de Triomphe, and a night at the opera. John heard *Faust*, only to realize he had been whistling parts of it for years, without knowing their origin. He saw Paris, but his most lasting memory of that first visit was not the usual tourist sights but a brass breastplate that hung in the Hôtel des Invalides.

The plate was shaped to fit a man's chest. Just a little to the left of the center there was a dent that appeared to have been made by a ball about one inch in diameter. There was no identifying card or tag; probably its history had been long forgotten. John was intrigued. Even though the building also housed Napoleon's tomb and an interesting collection of old ordnance brought home by French armies through the centuries, John kept coming back to the breastplate.

The dent was deep enough to indicate a blow that certainly would have knocked the breath out of a man, especially considering that the thump would have been almost directly over the heart. The question was, did the warrior get his breath back? John stared and wondered, until he could see a big soldier with a plume on his hat swaggering along the street, proudly wearing the dent as a medal of valor.

John later described the event so seriously and intently that his family could also see the man, miraculously guarded by luck.

"It was a good ten-to-one bet," John then added, "that the big windbag had hung his breastplate on a tree, shot at it with his own musket, and so decorated himself with a permanent medal. In the days of armor, the temptation to put a valiant dent here and there would have been too strong for many men to resist. And by the same token, I'd bet that many a man very carefully tapped a dent out of a rear plate."

John arrived in Liege on a rainy evening in February. "A sadness seemed to hang over the city," he told one of his acquaintances at F.N. some years later. There are other clues to his state of mind. He was forty-seven years old. He carried with him one of his greatest inventions, the automatic shotgun. He had no assurance whatsoever that the European engineers would see its potentialities any more than had those at Winchester. He was not a superstitious man, yet the death of Marcellus Hartley, president of Remington, following almost immediately the end of his long relationship with Winchester, must have seemed, however vaguely, an uneasy omen.

According to the recollections of several F.N. officials, Browning's first call the following morning was not on Fabrique Nationale, but another Liege arms manufacturer, to whom he had a letter of introduction, supplied by "an important New York firm." This incident is at first glance perplexing. Since John's relations with F.N. were apparently highly satisfactory to all concerned, it seems unlikely that he would first offer the gun to another company. Possibly it was simply a social call, the fulfilling of a request to "look up so-and-so for me when you're in Liege," the kind of bothersome obligation John liked to get "over and done with." John, of course, would not have been unaware that such a call would provide an opening for later business discussions, if all did not go well at F.N. He may have had his doubts about this, as his friend Berg was no longer with the firm, having left it in 1898, shortly after his trip to Ogden. It is also possible that the Belgians, more protocol-minded than John, read into the incident more significance than it possessed.

Fabrique Nationale d'Armes de Guerre is located in Herstal, a suburb of Liege, and it was here John went on his second call of the day. The weather had now cleared, and with it John's spirits. From all accounts, John M. Browning was completely unprepared for his reception by Henri Frenay, F.N. director, and the other company officials. Always a little shy during first meetings, John was both surprised and embarrassed by what seemed to him an excess of exuberance. It is quite possible that he was unaware of the changes his pistol had wrought.

The automatic shotgun was received with no less excitement. F.N. had had little success in the field of hunting arms; the revolutionary new shotgun was more welcome than John could have anticipated.

Later John and Frenay continued their discussions in the director's office. A large window overlooked the inside of the factory. Through it John could see an acre or two of machines and workmen, busily attempting to keep up with the orders for his first automatic pistol. The director undoubtedly saw more, remembering the same scene five years previous—long rows of machines, like the Liege workmen, unemployed and brooding in silence. The .32-caliber pistol had set wheels in motion, thousands of them. As the sales of the pistol assumed the proportions of a flood, the number of F.N. employees increased accordingly. With the addition of each new Browning arm to the F.N. line the process would be repeated. Before long the original plant, which John now viewed, was lost in the vast expansion required to keep pace with his prodigious output. The wheels would stop only twice, with the German invasions of Belgium.

The new shotgun was submitted to detailed inspection and testing, John explaining painstakingly the function of each part of its mechanism but in return receiving spontaneous enthusiasm instead of Bennett's noncommittal caution. On March 24, 1902, a contract was signed, granting F.N. exclusive world rights to manufacture and sell the gun with a royalty arrangement for Browning. John stayed in Liege for

Fabrique Nationale d'Armes de Guerre, one of the world's largest manufacturers of sporting arms. The original factory which Browning saw during his first trip to Liege was soon lost in the vast expansion required to keep pace with his inventive output.
BROWNING ARMS COMPANY

three months, supervising the making of the pilot models. One of these was later fired 40,000 rounds, either by him or in his presence.

Shortly after his arrival John had been assigned an interpreter with a fair knowledge of technical English, through whom instructions were transmitted to draftsmen and modelmakers. He also bought a pocket-sized French-English, English-French dictionary, which bore many smudged fingerprints before he was ready to return to the United States. By that time, he knew the French name of every part in the pistol and the automatic shotgun, as well as the names of many of the machines and tools. He laughed at his fumblings with the language and encouraged the workmen to laugh with him. Greatly admiring those skilled men, he wanted none of them to feel constraint in his presence. He wore the same badge that identified them: grease on his hands and, occasionally, a smudge on his nose. He was still a gunsmith; he could pick up a tool, and, in pantomime, show a workman what he wanted done.

During his habitual long walks, M. Browning became well known to local residents. "By reputation and appearance he astonished the people of Liège," notes one of the F.N. accounts of John's first visit. "He was exceptionally tall and lean, and his head was extraordinarily shiny. The features of his face, as sharp and immovable as those of a medal, seemed animated only by the liveliness of his regard. He liked then to envelop himself in a somber cape and to wear on his head a broad-brimmed hat, which added not a little to his strangeness." From the first the residents seem to have felt a special affection for the American; though his way was quiet, John, over the years, often made it evident that the feeling was reciprocated. In time he attained a near legendary stature in the community. They called him "Le Maître," The Master.

John's faith in the automatic shotgun is measurable: in signing the contract with F.N., he ordered 10,000 guns, to be delivered as soon as they were manufactured, and placed a large deposit on the order.

The Browning shop in Ogden, Utah, shortly after the turn of the century.
JOHN M. BROWNING FIREARMS MUSEUM

Records and recollections are fragmentary on this point, but it appears probable that prior to sailing for Europe John reached a tentative agreement with Schoverling, Daly and Gales regarding American distribution of the gun, if it was manufactured abroad. For the 10,000 guns, stamped with the name of a nonexistent firm, Browning Automatic Arms Company, were upon completion sold to jobbers through the agency of Schoverling. The investment, however, was solely John M. Browning's.

Ten thousand guns was a large commitment for an untried article in a highly competitive market. An automatic shotgun? Hunters were unaware that such an object existed. John appeared to be stocking up for years to come. Yet he had fired the models thousands of times, tested them under every conceivable condition, and was convinced that the gun would sell itself. His supervision was close and strict; even after he returned to Ogden, he continued to perfect the gun, with the result that production did not commence until the fall of 1903.

Any worries about the success of the automatic shotgun were shortlived. Schoverling sold the 10,000 guns in one year.

John M. Browning's workbench. Among his tools were some made by Jonathan Browning in Tennessee during the 1830s.   JOHN M. BROWNING FIREARMS MUSEUM

From the late 1890s to the time of his death in 1926, John usually had two or more guns underway simultaneously. While he and Ed were making a new model, Colt might have one of his arms in the drafting room and F.N. another going into production. Though apparently absorbed by the work in the shop, John still followed the progress of the more distant developments. Any day he might go home to lunch and say, "Mama, I'm going to Hartford this afternoon." Or Ilion. Or Liége. He had postponed his first trip to Europe until it was made necessary in 1902; it is estimated that of his remaining years one and a half were spent on the Atlantic, traveling to and from Belgium.

Between 1900 and 1910 John made a new model of the machine gun; developed a well-balanced line of pistols for Colt, and another for Fabrique Nationale; designed numerous sporting arms (including the Stevens Hammerless Pump Action Model 1903, also known as the Model 520, and the Remington Semi-Automatic High Power Rifle, known as the Model 8); and put his automatic shotgun into production with F.N. and, not long after, Remington.

In his contract with F.N., John had given that firm world rights for the automatic shotgun. The year 1904 brought not only the immediate success of the new gun, but also restrictive tariffs on foreign products. Reluctantly, John decided it would not be practical to make his guns abroad under such a handicap. He negotiated with F.N. to cede to Remington the right to manufacture and sell the automatic shotgun in the United States; F.N.'s feeling for the inventor was such that they agreed. It was not an unwise gamble, as the number of new Browning arms produced by them in subsequent years, and their popularity, attest.

Remington brought out the automatic shotgun in 1905, as the Remington Model 11. As usual, John closely supervised production. Clarence Adney, one of John's Ogden hunting and trapshooting companions, remembers that when the Remington model was first announced he ordered one through the Browning Bros. store. Adney was no stranger to the gun; he had been one of the first men to use it, when John brought the original models to meetings of the Ogden Gun Club for test-firing. In ordering the gun he told John that, if possible, he would like one that made a very close pattern. John said that was no problem. He had just arranged with Remington to personally test-fire the first several hundred guns that came off the production line. He had noticed that occasionally one of the parts came out with a rough edge that could easily be hand finished with a file when it was discovered. With

John M. Browning's revolutionary automatic shotgun—which made firearms history even before it was manufactured, by causing a break between Browning and Winchester. First produced by Fabrique Nationale and later by Remington, it has proved to be one of the most popular sporting arms ever invented. Above is a current production model of the Browning Automatic-5; the scene is one that was a special favorite of the Browning Brothers—the duck marshes north of Ogden, Utah. BROWNING ARMS COMPANY

Remington's approval he was firing each gun five rounds as soon as it was manufactured, to look for this and any other possible defects. The following week, when he returned to Ilion to test the guns, he found one that made an unusually close pattern and had it shipped to the store, earmarked for Adney.

Over fifty years of growing popularity have proven the automatic shotgun one of the outstanding achievements in the history of sporting arms design. Total production figures to date cannot even be estimated. Since its appearance it has been copied by manufacturers in many countries and even today is being produced with little variance in basic design by Remington, Savage, Franchi, Breda, and others. The Browning Arms Company alone has sold well over a million of these guns.

16

THE SEVENTEEN original automatic pistol models shown in the photographs in Part Four are not all of the pistols made by John M. Browning in his Ogden shop. John himself was responsible for some of the gaps in the collection.

Shortly after John's death, his son Val called on those manufacturers who had made arms of John's invention, requesting all surviving models of arms that had gone into production, in order that they might be included in a single permanent collection (the John M. Browning Armory, Ogden, Utah). The models of many of the arms that had not been produced were, very reasonably, retained for reference. Whatever their age, they make instructive studies for arms engineers. This fact was confirmed more than once by Ed, who, examining an arm that had just come onto the market, put a finger on a part and said, "Look here John used this same idea thirty or forty years ago."

As for the missing models, some were lost, others were stolen, and John's working habits account for the absence of the rest. More than once, at the factory about the time a pistol was going into production, he would disassemble the model for some momentary reason, leaving the parts scattered on whatever workbench was handy. The contrast between his attitude toward a model to which he was giving the finishing touches at his bench and toward that same model when it was no longer needed for reference was extreme. The whole purpose of his life seemed to center on a model nearing completion; yet when the practical need ended, the romance died, and John had his eye on a new love.

Pistols of John M. Browning's design which were manufactured include: The Colt .38 Caliber Model 1900; the F.N. .32 Caliber Model 1900; the Colt Model 1903 "Pocket" .32 and .380; the F.N. Model 1903 9 mm. Military; the Colt Government .45 Caliber; the F.N., Colt and F.N./Browning .25 Caliber "Vest Pocket"; the F.N./Browning .32 Caliber Models 1910 and 1922; the Colt Woodsman .22 Caliber; the Browning 9 mm. Parabellum. Models based on these guns number in the dozens. Colt to date has introduced eight variations of the original Woodsman, ten commercial models based on the Model 1911 Government .45 Caliber. It is generally accepted that since the origin of the semi-automatic more pistols of Browning design have been manufactured than all others combined.

It is axiomatic that many of the best ideas in any of the arts and sciences are ridiculously obvious, once revealed. Until then, they seem to possess a protective covering, like wild creatures, to be discovered only by diligent search or lucky chance. The most common substitute for discovery, or invention, is the adaptation to a present need of something already in existence. Designers of the first pistols did exactly that. An example was the machine pistol, too long and heavy for a side arm, too short and light for a shoulder arm. John once said, "It's not so hard figuring out the essentials of a gun mechanism. The trouble is getting the essentials in the right place."

His method of distributing the essentials of the automatic pistol was absurdly simple, once he showed the way. One of his greatest contributions to pistol design was the operating slide, which, slotted to the frame, not only furnished the weight required to absorb the recoil, but completely enclosed the barrel and firing mechanism, permitting a pistol to be made of convenient pocket or holster length, smooth on both sides, and of a weight appropriate to its cartridge.

In his first pistol, John developed the principle of the slide; and he saw at once that the idea was adaptable to side arms of all calibers. That is not to say that he had only to scale the parts of a pistol up or down from one caliber to another. In all the illustrations the family resemblance is unmistakable, but each pistol embodies completely original ideas, clever mechanical tricks, not present in any of the others. As early as 1906, the revolutionary character of his contributions to the art of pistol design received notable recognition when the city of Philadelphia, acting on the recommendation of the Franklin Institute, awarded him, to his complete surprise, the John Scott Legacy Medal for his automatic pistols.

The operating slide is as commonplace on an automatic pistol today as is the cylinder in a revolver. Nobody remembers who invented the cylinder; almost as effectually obscured by time is John M. Browning's invention of the pistol operating slide, more than sixty years ago. This, like many of Browning's other pistol features, was soon widely copied. Once at Fabrique Nationale John met a man who had been employed in the engineering department of a major German arms factory when the first Browning began its historic invasion of world markets. The man, amused by the recollection, told John that he and two other engineers were called one day to the office of the general manager. They found him at his desk with three little Brownings in a row before him. Without the formality of asking the men to be seated, he handed each a pistol, saying, "Gentlemen, make me a pistol as nearly like this as the patents will permit, bearing in mind that our patent laws leave some convenient loopholes around patents applied for by foreigners. As nearly like this as possible," he repeated for emphasis. "This is the only pistol that is selling. Good day, and let me hear from you soon."

When it came to pistols, John was pioneering in an untraveled region, and there were no guides. He could not forecast the taste of the public with any certainty, since the public, in the matter of pistols, had had no opportunity to form opinions and preferences. He had not only to design automatic pistols, if he was to open a market for that new type of arm he had to constitute himself a kind of universal public, trying to determine all possible uses for these pistols, and then, for each use, to consider various combinations of shape, weight, and caliber. Many of his models never went into production; they were experiments. Both Colt and F.N. wanted a full line of automatic pistols. Theorizing, however, could not determine what pistols would constitute a full line. John showed them the arms; not just one every three or four years, but frequently three or four in a single year. He was so much the pioneer that he helped design the .25, .32, and .380 automatic-pistol cartridges, and was consulted by the Ordnance Board regarding the design of the .45 Government cartridge.

While John's first pistols were commercial models, his earliest experiments convinced him that the military side arm of the future would be an automatic pistol. He preached this doctrine so well that as early as 1902 Colt brought out a .38-caliber pistol which was called the Military Model, the caliber being the same as that of the army revolver then in use. John and the Colt company knew that the Ordnance Board had made some studies of the heavy foreign pistols, but, as far as they could ascertain, had shown little enthusiasm. It went without saying that the board, before considering the adoption of an automatic pistol, would conduct a long investigation. All that John and Colt hoped of the new pistol, in so far as government business was concerned, was that it might attract attention to the fact that a military side arm could be kept within reasonable limits of size and weight.

John, by reason of his versatility and the comfortable fortune he had already accumulated, could afford to be patient. The one-gun inventor cannot afford to wait ten years for a government board to make up its collective mind. And there have been many one-gun inventors. As a matter of fact, there is only one man in the history of firearms development known to have designed more than five original and profitable arms. When that man made an arm that was ten years ahead of its time, as happened more than once in the case of his military inventions, he simply put it aside and waited until the time was ripe, employing the waiting period to make, in his Ogden shop, more successful arms than any other man ever produced in a full lifetime.

The Colt Military Model did attract attention, as had been hoped, and John was called into consultation a number of times by the board. There was one point on which all the experts were in agreement. A more powerful cartridge than the Army .38 was needed. There were records of Moro insurrectionists in the Philippines who, shot two or even three times in the body with the .38, were still able in their frenzy to inflict serious injury with their bolos before dropping. Any discussion of a new side arm, therefore, had to begin with a new and more powerful cartridge.

It was decided early in the study that high velocity and long range were not required of a military side arm. Such an arm was for use only at short ranges. The first requisite was striking power, the sledge-hammer blow, a bullet that would stop the most deliriously berserk wild man in his tracks. As soon as it became evident that the .45 caliber would probably be the choice of the board, John designed a .45-caliber cartridge which he thought would do for initial experiments. To help the board toward a decision he made two shop models of the gun, one with a hammer, one hammerless. The relative merits of the two types of arms were being debated by members of the board, and John thought he could facilitate a decision by making both types available for study.

It was typical of the inventor that instead of letting himself become entangled in an argument over the relative merits of hammer and hammerless types, he made a model of each, leaving the military to settle the question while he busied himself with other work. The two arms were demonstrated by John at two army posts with such good results that Colt put the hammer model into production and had factory samples ready for the board by 1906. The hammer model was finally chosen. Though the board made a few minor changes during its four years of study, John's model and the Standard Service Pistol in use today are identical in all important details.

The .45 pistol was undoubtedly another of John's favorites. In the interim between the invention of the gun and the official tests, almost any afternoon, when John was in Ogden, he would leave the shop at four o'clock to wake echoes in the foothills with a couple hundred rounds.

When the date for the trials was finally set, John went at once to the Colt factory. Putting aside all other business, he gave his attention to making the model that was to be formally presented to the examining board. In this work he had the wholehearted assistance of Fred Moore, the production manager. John had found Fred in the model room of the factory early in his machine-gun development work there. Struck by the young man's intelligence, John gradually and tactfully had him advanced to the position of chief of the machine-gun division. That business increased in importance, and Fred shouldered his added responsibilities so well, that before many years he was made production manager of the entire factory, a position he held for the rest of his life. The two men worked together closely on all of the guns John made for Colt, but especially on the .45. It was John's way to watch every part of a model as though the slow, infinitely painstaking shaping endowed the part with life and consciousness. When he had two parts that fitted together, he began to educate them— or so it seemed—fingering them through their functional movements countless times. The lessons became more complicated as the number of finished parts increased. At times John seemed to be talking to each part. All this Fred understood; he geared himself to John's working habits in much the same way as did Ed in the shop in Ogden.

Colt museum curator Charles H. Coles (who in 1962 celebrated his *seventieth* year as an employee of Colt's Patent Fire Arms Manufacturing Company), recalls seeing John in the factory often during this period. "He was tall—six foot three, slim, straight as an arrow, nearly bald," Coles remembers. "He was a genuine gentleman, who spoke to and was interested in everyone in the shop. I can almost see him now, walking through, a pair of cheap iron spectacles in his hand, stopping and talking to a workman or watching the work in progress. He and Fred Moore were very close, always together."[36]

Coles was at this time working in the machine-gun division. He remembers, "Mr. Browning seemed to love peanuts. He always had a sack or two in his coat pockets. He would reach in and take out a couple occasionally, but if a gun wasn't going well, he would eat them furiously, one after the other." Coles also recalls frequently meeting John on the street at night. About seven each evening John would leave the Heublein Hotel, where he always stayed, and walk around Hartford for an hour or so for exercise. Sometimes Matt was along, but not often. During this period Matt usually came to Hartford only when John was in Liége, to check on operations for him, the brothers and half brothers working as a well-trained team.

Competitive trials for the .45 were finally scheduled for March 3, 1911. The Ordnance Command made the following stipulations: 6000 rounds were to be fired through each pistol under consideration. Firing was to take place in series of 100, after which the arm was to be permitted to cool for five minutes before the next series commenced. After each 1000 rounds each pistol was to be cleaned and oiled. The 6000 rounds of standard ammunition were to be followed by loads systematically deformed or made abnormal—some with bullets too deeply seated, some with bullets not seated deeply enough, and some cartridges with dented cases. Finally, the entries were to be given the rust and dust test, fired a number of rounds after being rusted with acid, and again after a sprinkling of dust through the working parts.

Colonel C. L. F. Robinson, managing president of Colt, and Fred Moore accompanied John to the trials. Fred later said that John was the coolest of the three. Upon arriving at the arsenal, both Robinson and Moore were jubilant on learning that two of the foreign pistols had been withdrawn after the requirements were published and that the only competing arm was a model none of them feared. (As things turned out, before the end of the test it had accumulated an impressively long list of malfunctions and broken parts.)

Fred happily predicted that it would be a walkover.

John disagreed, stating that they were up against the strongest competition in the world—tradition. All the weight of tradition was with the revolver, and the revolver, John was quick to admit, was a good arm. If a revolver should break a mainspring or sear, the board would say, "Oh, these things happen." But let the automatic pistol have a misfire —which wouldn't be surprising in 6000 rounds—and they would go over every part with a magnifying glass, in addition to having the ballistics experts dissect the cartridge. And they would feel less friendly toward the pistol from that time on. Being up against tradition, John reminded Fred, was pretty nearly like being up against 100 per cent.

Moore was not made any more comfortable by the fact the various generals were late arriving at the armory. But John, strolling around with his hands in his pockets, or sitting quietly on a nearby bench, showed no trace of nervousness.

Finally, in exasperation, Moore walked over to him and asked, "John, haven't you got a nerve in your body?"

"Fred," John replied, as Fred later told it, "I've got lots of nerves in my body, and they are all standing on end, like this." He held up both hands and wiggled his fingers. "But not a damned soul except you and me is ever going to know about it."

Eventually the test began. Several men had been trained in the simple routine of firing the seven rounds contained in a magazine, snapping out the empty magazine, and inserting a refill. Other men were loading magazines, keeping well ahead of the firing, so that there would be no interruption. The firing was done as rapidly as the trained operator could pull the trigger and replace the empty magazine; and the men were soon co-operating with such smooth precision that the changing of magazines caused only a slight hesitation in the rhythmic booming. When the arm became too hot to hold, it was dipped in a bucket of water.

The trials ran through two days of actual firing. John had acted as a consultant during the preparation, but once the firing started, he became an onlooker. He admitted that is was not easy to keep from crowding up close from time to time, in order to have an unobstructed view of the ejected shells as they arched out from the pistol, to study the way the different operators gripped the stock, and especially to get a magnifying glass in his hand whenever one came into play. He said that it was something of a strain to count from one to seven as each fresh magazine went into action and then not have time to breathe even a little sigh of relief before he was back to one again and another count of seven.

The strain grew worse as the count mounted. John swore that he'd never get into another government trial. When the booming came to a sudden end, he was not sure whether the pistol had finished the 6000 or whether there had been a malfunction. For a moment, the world was emptied of sound. Then one of the soldiers who had been filling magazines let out a hoarse ejaculation, "She made it, by God!" That caused an outburst of laughter, which led to three cheers for Browning, and then to the inevitable call for a speech.

John stepped up onto the bench where he had been sitting, took off his hat, and waited until the applause died down. "Gentlemen," he said, "the young man who spoke so eloquently a moment ago expressed my feelings precisely. There isn't a word I can add, except thank you all."

The eccentric loads which were still to be tried in the pistol did not worry John as much as might be expected. Permitted to examine them earlier, he had found nothing that had not been tried in his Ogden shop.

The purpose of the freak loads was to test the pistol with such deformities as might occur under battle conditions.

Nothing stopped the pistol, no part broke, and a long, painstaking examination under a magnifying glass failed to detect any sign of a crack or of battering. The pistol was the first automatic arm to make a perfect score in government trials; the record was not challenged until 1917, when John's recoil-operated machine gun was fired 40,000 rounds without a stoppage. Neither record has since been equaled, or even closely approached.

On March 20, 1911, the examining board submitted its official report, which read as follows: "The Board recommends that the Colt Caliber .45 Automatic Pistol of the design submitted to the Board for tests be adopted for use by foot and mounted troops in the military service in consequence of its marked superiority to the present service revolvers, and to any pistol, of its extreme reliability and endurance, of its ease of disassembly, of its accuracy and of its fulfillment of all essential requirements."

Orders from the Chief of Ordnance of the General Staff and Secretary of War dated March 29, 1911, made the adoption of the Model 1911 official. Today, after more than fifty years of continuous service, it remains the standard military side arm in all branches of the United States Armed Forces.

The award of the John Scott Legacy Medal by the city of Philadelphia for his achievements in automatic pistol development came as a surprise to John. His decoration by King Albert of Belgium as a Chevalier de l'Ordre de Leopold was less unexpected; for two years John had been trying to circumvent the occasion.

On January 31, 1914, Fabrique Nationale d'Armes de Guerre celebrated the completion of the millionth Browning pistol. *La Meuse,* the leading newspaper of Liege, carried an account of the function. The following is a translation of excerpts from the article, which covered the entire first page and part of the second page of the newspaper:

"The browning [long used as a common noun in French, a synonym for pistol] enjoys a universal celebrity. If one should submit to the desire to follow the subject, one would quickly fill a page with commentaries on the role of this remarkable arm, usually called the 'citizen browning,' possibly because, in this democratic age, it sometimes speaks freely, and with arguments to which there is no reply. More simply, one can

Acclaim embarrassed the inventor; besides, he argued, it took time away from his work. But it came, despite his attempts to avoid it. (Upper left), The Cross of Knighthood of the Order of Leopold, conferred on Browning by King Albert of Belgium in 1914. (Upper right), The John Scott Legacy Medal, awarded to John M. Browning in 1905 by recommendation of the Franklin Institute of Philadelphia for his automatic-pistol developments. (Below), The gold-inlaid 100,000th F.N. Model 1900 .32 Caliber Semi-Automatic Pistol, presented to its inventor in 1904. JOHN M. BROWNING FIREARMS MUSEUM say, with Minister Hubert, that the arm is reassuring or terrifying, depending on whether you stand behind it or in front of it.

"The success of the browning has been veritably prodigious from the commencement of its manufacture in 1898. Since then, production has reached the tremendous total of 1,300,000, a record which has never been equaled anywhere in the world. The millionth pistol was finished two years ago, and it had been planned to honor the occasion with a banquet, but the difficulty of arranging a date to suit the convenience both of the factory and the inventor necessitated postponement till the present.

"It is the happy alliance of factory and inventor that was celebrated Saturday with an extraordinary banquet, which took on the aspect of a grand industrial and patriotic demonstration. Two of the King's ministers were present, MM. Berryer and Hubert; the governor of the province of Liege; and a throng of military and industrial notables, representing Belgium and several foreign countries . . . to pay homage to Belgium's largest arms factory, and the world's greatest arms inventor. M. Browning, naturally, was the target of all eyes, and the principal subject of all the numerous discourses. Tall, smooth-shaven, keen-eyed, he seemed actually a little bewildered by all the encomiums that flooded him; and the smile that softened his dignified bearing seemed to say, 'Vraiment! Do they mean me? It is too much!'

"It was a fortunate day for all of us when this tall American came to our country. As M. Andri, Director General, told the assembly, it is largely to M. Browning that the factory owes its prosperity. Moreover, the community of Herstal has shared in that prosperity; and the

John M. Browning with a group of Belgian Government and Fabrique Nationale officials on the day of the banquet in his honor, January 31, 1914. The inventor is easily distinguished by his height.   JOHN M. BROWNING FIREARMS MUSEUM

extraordinary success of Browning arms has added notably to the fame of Belgian industry throughout the world.

"Following M. Andri's tribute, M. Hubert, Minister of Industry and Labor, made an impressive ceremony of bestowing upon M. Browning the Cross of Knighthood of the Order of Leopold. This happy gesture received a prolonged ovation. Then it was M. Browning's turn. He rose to his full height, a striking figure, and spoke slowly and distinctly, searching for words that could express his sentiments, the depth and earnestness of which were unmistakable in his voice and manner. He said that through all the years of his association with Fabrique Nationale, he had had the most generous co-operation from the management, the technicians, and the men at their machines and benches. He asked indulgence for his defective French, but, in truth, his brief discourse, simple and sincere, was more effective than a polished oration . . ."

Two pistols, each bearing the number 1,000,000, inlaid with gold, were made for the occasion; one was presented to King Albert, the other to John. The largest room of the cartridge division of the factory had been cleared of machines, the floor carpeted, the walls and ceilings decorated. A renowned Liege restaurant served a lavish banquet. There was also a Programme du Concert. During the banquet a bronze statue representing the spirit of genius, the work of the sculptor Rousseau, was unveiled to the strains of "The Star-Spangled Banner," rendered by a thirty piece orchestra. All in all, Fabrique Nationale spent about $10,000. It was a magnificent feast, a memorable tribute, even if the man at the head of the banquet table would have much rather been slicing watermelons in his Ogden shop.

John's homecoming must have been especially merry, at least for his brothers. It was not in their natures to let so fine a title as Sir John M. Browning pass unnoticed.

17

A T WORK in his shop, John lost consciousness of time. But outside the shop, hunting, talking with his brothers and a few close friends, attempting to relax, he was acutely conscious of its passage. While still in his twenties, he had bemoaned the years when he "could have been inventing, but wasn't." Now, in his later years, he became aware that there were in his mind guns he might never have time to make—and the awareness made him push himself all the harder.

One evening shortly after the end of World War I he was talked into attending the opera. A touring company had stopped in Ogden for three nights, and John's family insisted that he go. His interest lasted through the first act. By the middle of the second, he was mentally at work in his shop. He did not even notice when the second-act curtain fell, and when, during the third act, he suddenly became aware of his surroundings, it was with evident irritation that the opera was still in progress. As the family left the theater, John excused himself and returned to his shop, where he worked on through the night. When he grew tired, he lay down for a few minutes on a small cot near his bench, then returned refreshed to work. When morning came he had breakfast sent up from a nearby restaurant, so that he could work on without interruption.

This was not an isolated occurrence. It happened so often that it was almost habit.

Hunting provided some release, as did trapshooting. During the 1890s John and Matt Browning and two other Ogdenites, G. L. Becker and A. P. Bigelow, were Utah's premier live-bird team. Known as the "Four B's," they later made national history at the traps as a squad of four. But as the years passed John found increasingly less time for such activities. One of his close friends, Clarence Adney, remembers one year when a group of John's friends were planning a trip to a duck hunting camp some twenty-five miles north of Ogden. The marshes there drew all kinds of ducks. Of the fresh-water birds there were mallard, gadwall, pintail, and, late in the season, widgeon, as well as green-winged teal, some cinnamon teal, and now and then a few blue-winged teal. Of the saline-water or diving birds, there were canvasback, redheads, golden-eye, the greater and lesser bluebill scaup, the butterball, and some of the smaller divers, such as the blackjack. There were also geese— Canadian gray honkers, Hutchins's, and two varieties of white goose. The limit in those days was forty birds, and the men nearly always got their limits.

"I can't go hunting this fall, Clarence," John said, when Adney approached him regarding the trip. "I haven't the time any more." Adney, knowing how John loved hunting, attempted to argue with him, but in vain. There wasn't even enough time for work, John explained. He rarely talked of his private life, and even more rarely complained, but this time, when Adney suggested that perhaps he had one satisfaction the rest of them lacked, his inventing, John looked surprised and said: "Clarence—I don't have an arch enemy, but if I did, and I wanted

Browning devoted considerable time to testing each of his guns. In the case of the automatic shotgun, which he is shown carrying above, he not only fired thousands of rounds under varying conditions before its manufacture, he also tested many of the guns as they came off the production line and put the gun to practical use in the field as often as his work load permitted.

JOHN M. BROWNING FIREARMS MUSEUM

to invoke on him the worst calamity I could think of, the very worst, I'd make him an ardent inventor."

There just wasn't enough time.

John's last military invention, the 37-mm. cannon, like many of his arms was a special-request number; in the course of a few years, it was, in fact, requested many times. It was an arm he made in spite of a resolution not to make it; an arm brought so persistently to his attention by the solicitations of Army Ordnance that it was almost completely worked out in his mind before he consented to design it.

Prior to the end of World War I, the government assigned several experienced ordnance engineers to work on the development of this arm. Two models were finally made and exhaustive tests carried out in the government arsenals. One model proved totally unsatisfactory. The other was only slightly less disappointing; there is no record of its having been fired more than eight rounds without an interruption.

John M. Browning and Fred Moore were then called to examine the gun and give their opinions, in the hope that they might be able to devise some method of increasing its efficiency.

Colonel Julian S. Hatcher was present when the examination took place: ". . . when I showed this to Mr. Browning in 1917, he remarked with a dry smile, 'Where do you put the cheese?' We saw the point at once, for the resemblance to a rat-trap was rather marked."[37]

Colonel Chinn notes of the incident: "Needless to say, such an expression from America's greatest master of ordnance did not enhance the standing of the gun. Time proved the correctness of his evaluation, as attempts to convert it to a reliable mechanism met with one failure after another."[38]

The Bureau of Ordnance was still without a 37-mm. cannon but with a more urgent desire than ever to possess an arm of that type. John was asked to redesign the weapon, and it was shipped to the Colt factory for further study, but it was evident to all concerned that what was needed was a completely new gun. John was asked to make one; the Chief of Ordnance wrote to him several times. John begged off on the plea that he was too busy with sporting arms to undertake the job.

Late in 1920, he delivered in person to General C. C. Williams, Chief of Ordnance, what he intended to be his final answer. He and one of his sons were in Washington at the time, making a search in the Patent Office. When that business was finished early one afternoon, John suggested calling on the general. Since he was a good friend, John felt that he owed it to him to drop in and explain just how he felt about the 37-mm. cannon.

They called and were immediately received. It was as though the general had been waiting for John, primed and ready. After a warm welcome, he went straight to the subject of the cannon, presenting a long, eloquent, and persuasive dissertation.

"General," John finally said, with a good-natured smile, "if one gun would settle the matter, I might try to make it. But one gun would be just the start. You know that it would be impossible to make a gun your experts would unanimously approve. If I should come down to Aberdeen and put on a show for you with your present cartridge, the smoke wouldn't have time to settle before the clamor would start for a higher velocity and greater power. And that would go on till the law of diminishing returns stopped it; that is to say, until the cartridge got too big to be handled by an automatic mechanism. That could be an interesting development for a young man, but I'm too old for such a job. It's one thing to work for myself, making sporting arms. It's entirely different to work for the government, trying to please a lot of experts. Why don't the experts make the gun—just the way they want it?"

The general smiled wryly and shrugged. "We tried, as you know."

"Well," John said, "assume that I make the gun. Then what? You couldn't place an order without an appropriation from Congress; and Congress is tired of war and of buying implements of war. I couldn't possibly live to get ten cents out of the gun, whereas all my sporting arms are profitable. As a matter of fact, I'd much rather make them than military arms. To settle the matter, General, there is no war in sight, no emergency to call upon my patriotism."

As General Williams shook hands in parting, he said, "Mr. Browning, I haven't an answer to any of your arguments. They are all valid. But if you won't make the gun for us, I don't know where to turn."

In the street again, the son said, "That settles the 37-mm., I hope." He and the other members of the family knew that John's splendid physique had weakened under the tremendous strain of his war work. John was nearly sixty-six years old; they were trying to persuade him to take it easy. In reply to his son's remark, he said, "Yes, I guess that settles it." He walked on a few steps, and then, as though the words burst out before he could stop them, he said, "But, hell, son! I have a slick idea for a 37!"

He spoke half guiltily, as though caught at something he should not be doing. The son recognized the familiar ring of enthusiasm in his father's voice and knew what it portended; back in Ogden, he offered his associates in the office two-to-one odds that they would be hearing a 37-mm. cannon within six months. No one took him up on it.

John was embarrassed. He easily brushed off the half-hearted protests within the family, but writing to General Williams was not so simple. He might not have written until the gun was finished, except that he had to have ammunition, and the government was his only source of supply.

"Confound it!" he exclaimed, after he had been at work on the cannon for several days, figuring the dimensions of the barrel Colt would make for him, outlining the preliminary work for Ed. "I ought to have a 37 dummy right now, so that I can familiarize myself with all the details of the cartridge. I know the dimensions, but I like to handle the cartridge I'm working with. When I let my hands and fingers toy with a cartridge, simulating time after time some movement that is to be performed mechanically, the necessary parts begin to shape themselves in my mind."

"We could write General Williams to have half a dozen dummies sent by express," one of his sons suggested.

"That's easy enough," John growled, "but what will the general think? Not two weeks ago, you heard me tell him I positively would not make the gun, and now I've got to tell him that I'm at work on it. He'll think I've got so old I don't know my own mind."

"Why not try a little blarney?" the son suggested. "Tell him the 37 got to hurting your conscience, because it was the first job you ever refused for the government. Incidentally, it happens to be the truth."

John shook his head. "That sounds like the Fourth of July—blowing about my patriotism. No, just say that I hit on an idea that promises to simplify the job. Ask for a half-dozen dummies, and tell him I'll need five hundred live cartridges in three months."

General Williams, replying to John's letter, thanked him for the good news and wished him luck. The half-dozen dummies were being sent by express. The only 37s on hand were holdovers from the war, charged with TNT, and would hardly be safe for the forthcoming experiments. An order had been placed for a fresh supply, which would be ready well in advance of the time specified by John.

When the letter was brought up to the shop and read aloud, John said, "Ed, I'll bet you ten cents to a nickel that history is going to repeat itself. Remember how we finished the .50-caliber model back at Colts before the government had the ammunition ready for us? The delay will be longer this time—because the cartridge is larger."

Again John was venturing into a new region. Up to this time he had not worked with a cartridge larger than the .50 caliber, which was well within the category of small-arms ammunition. For convenience in designating various types of ordnance, a dividing line had to be established between small arms and artillery, and the 37 mm. was a logical marker. Its projectile weighed over a pound, and could be charged with a high explosive, such as TNT. It was obvious that an automatic arm, handling the 37 mm., would be highly useful against tanks, as well as for ground strafing by low-flying planes.

John began work on the gun in January 1921; it was finished in March of the same year. As he had predicted, the arm was ready before the ammunition. He had written to Army Ordnance twice, inquiring about progress, reiterating that he was almost ready for test-firing. Each time he had been assured that the cartridges would be ready. Lulled by these promises, and becoming each day more and more intent on his work as he saw the actual model approaching the smooth perfection of the model in his mind, he found himself with an assembled cannon but no means of testing it. He could run dummies through it by manual operation, but that was simply tantalization.

Then he chanced upon a small news item. There was a large government arsenal a few miles south of Ogden, started during World War I but not finished before the end of that conflict. It had remained unused until recently, when, according to the news item, two carloads of ammunition had been received for storage. It was unlikely that 37s would be included in the shipment, but John nevertheless phoned the officer in command. When the situation was explained to the offlcer, he laughed, saying, "I have two carloads of ammunition out here, all 37s." But, he explained regretfully, all the cartridges were charged with TNT, and Mr. Browning would probably not care to handle anything so ticklish in his experiments. The officer, however, did not know Mr. Browning. John immediately telegraphed General Williams for authorization to draw on the stock, adding that he knew of the TNT charges and was prepared to take precautions.

The cannon was taken up to the foot of a mountain just east of the city in a light pickup; John, Ed, Matt, and one of John's sons followed in a passenger car. The precautions promised by John consisted of four twelve-inch planks, cleated together to form a protective shield, with a prop to hold it upright. The plan was for John to insert a clip holding five cartridges, make the gun ready for firing, and pull the trigger with a wire lanyard, while all participants were bunched safely behind the screen. The occasion, however, was too much for mortal restraint, and each of the men craned his neck and got at least one look at the gun before John pulled the trigger.

The face of the mountain made a tremendous sounding board, and the cannon, firing at the rate of just under three shots per second, brought a thunder of jumbled echoes rolling down, a thunder in which the reports of the gun were blended and nearly lost. The mountain, which had endured so much of John's firing through the years with only mild complaint, seemed to rouse in wide-awake rage and roar. A long moment after the last shot from the clip of five, one of the party pointed and exclaimed, "Look!" High on the mountain, a small cloud of white blossomed, and then another, until five puffs of TNT had registered five points of impact. And still the show was not over. There was an interval following the last puff, and then the sound of the exploding TNT came down, in five distance-muffled pops.

Testing the 37-mm. cannon outside Ogden, March 1921. The mountain, which had endured so much of John's firing through the years with only mild complaint, seemed to rouse in wide-awake rage and roar. (Left to right), Matt Browning, Ed Browning, and John M. Browning.

Winter retreated as testing of the cannon continued, in preparation for the official government tests. (Left to right), Matt Browning, John M. Browning, John Browning, the inventor's eldest son, and Ed Browning.

JOHN M. BROWNING FIREARMS MUSEUM

The mount was a hurry-up makeshift of angle iron that served John's purpose in testing. It held the gun securely, and, with a monkey wrench, could be adjusted to any angle of fire. After a more businesslike mount was made, the cannon was shipped to the government proving ground at Aberdeen, Maryland. John went East for the test. It was his rule with first demonstrations to do the actual firing, and as clip after clip went through in hypnotic rhythm—with only intentional interruptions, as John took a moment to explain some detail of the operation to the assembled army and navy officers—it became evident that the master had done it again.

The officers were ordnance specialists, familiar with the Baldwin gun, on which the government had expended so much time and money. That model was a thing of beauty, if examined not as an example of design but of skilled workmanship; however, it would not shoot eight rounds without jam or breakage. On the other hand, here was Browning's gun, still bearing marks of hammer, anvil, and forge, but it

With the successful test-firing of his 37-mm. cannon at Aberdeen Proving Ground in the summer of 1921, John had made his 100 per cent—every arm entered by him in trials for government examining boards had won over all competition. (Left to right), General Ruggles, John M. Browning, Colonel Tchappett, Fred M. Moore, General Joyce, and Colt's President S. M. Stone.

JOHN M. BROWNING FIREARMS MUSEUM

would shoot and kept on shooting. The final shot was followed by instant and unreserved approval and congratulations. And John retained his status as a prophet. There, on the high emplacement where the gun was mounted, while the smell of powder smoke was still in the air, one of the group voiced the regret that the velocity of the cartridge was so low, only about 1400 feet per second, and wondered if Mr. Browning could adapt his system to a larger cartridge of higher velocity, say 2000 feet? The son who had been with John when he called on General Williams was with him now, and as their eyes met, each knew that the other was trying hard to suppress his laughter.

The party had a private car reserved for the short ride between Washington and Aberdeen. On the return trip, all attention was on a 37 mm. of greater power. Clustered around John, the officers pointed out that planes were flying faster and higher, that tanks were thickening their armor, changes which were making the present 37 mm. obsolete. John listened. He had no argument against the greater effectiveness of the higher velocity; the superiority was obvious. His occasional nods of agreement encouraged the group to find more facts to support their arguments.

Finally, he smiled and said, "Very well. Two thousand feet. That suit everybody?"

It suited everybody very much.

"Well," John said, turning to Fred Moore, "we'd better make this model at Colt. It's getting too big for my shop out West. I'll go up to Hartford with you from Washington, and we can start the drawings. There will be a good many changes. I've been giving the larger gun some thought."

John made the larger cannon, which was successful, and then, again under pressure from the Ordnance Board, he made a third. This last cannon was a far remove from the Ogden-made model, firing a cartridge approximately fourteen inches long, with a much heavier projectile, which attained a velocity of 3050 feet per second.

Colonel Chinn says that these three guns, produced in rapid succession, proved their reliability in several demonstrations, at which point interest in all military weapons in the United States became apathetic. "Development work entered a period of great lethargy. Not only was money lacking to carry on the work, but the public became actually hostile toward all who were connected with such a project . . . Even the Colt Company, one of the most outstanding automatic weapons factories in the world, turned its efforts to manufacturing electrical appliances, dishwashing machines and a variety of plastic articles in order to remain solvent. Mechanical drawings and the three successful working models of John M. Browning's 37-mm. automatic cannon were filed away against the day when perhaps there might be a need."[39]

Though a few of these weapons were produced in England in 1929, not until 1935 was American interest resurrected and first production of the largest model begun. This occurred nearly a decade after John's death, proving how truly he spoke when he told General Williams that he could not possibly live long enough to get ten cents out of the gun.

One wonders why he undertook the heavy task so near the end of his life. Possibly he felt fairly certain that his family would profit from royalties on the guns before the expiration of the patents and that his country might have need for the guns before they became obsolete. Probably, however, the simple truth is that he got hold of an idea and could not let it go.

John had made his 100 per cent. Every arm he had entered in trials for government examining boards had won over all competition.

18

THE DAY before his departure for Belgium on his sixty-first and last trip across the Atlantic, John sat on his broad porch with a few members of his family. It was Indian summer, a season of rare beauty in the Wasatch Mountains. Rachel, his wife, was to accompany him, and he had been bantering about the fun they would have. "Pretty Thing," he said, using one of his pet names, "when we board the ship, people in the crowd will whisper, 'That old chap must be rich to have such a young wife!' "

He was animated. There was no tremor of age in his voice. His enthusiasm was bubbling. He was at the end of a brief period of attempted relaxation. Rest was a kind of bitter medicine he now and then forced himself to take, in small doses. Not long before, he had turned over the pilot models of his latest and last arm, the Superposed Shotgun, to his son Val, who, since the war, had lived in Liege as engineering representative of the Browning company. Things were reported going well, but for weeks John had been worrying about little things that might slip. The fact was, his fingers were itching, those

John and Rachel Browning on the porch of their home in Ogden during the summer of 1926, shortly before the inventor made his sixty-first and last trip across the Atlantic.   JOHN M. BROWNING FIREARMS MUSEUM

fingers whose length revealed the artist, whose blunt tips and broad thumbs told of much handling of metal and tools. They were itching to feel every part of those models over and over. Now that he had decided to get back to the job, he was able to enjoy the sunny afternoon.

Long periods of silence replaced the bantering, as he looked out over shrubs and trees toward the mountains to which he had so many times walked. Through the foothills he had tramped countless miles with a variety of problems. Long walks, ending with sleep-compelling fatigue, were the only sedatives he ever took, though he was often tortured by insomnia. His gaze returned to the spreading locust that had shaded the old shop. And he began recalling Jonathan and the shop and the pattern of his own life.

"You know," he said, "the time and the place for a gunmaker just got together on this corner. And I happened along." He smiled and continued. "Of course, it was luck that dropped me here. And it didn't just walk off and leave me. It has stuck around pretty close ever since. My work has gone well, and I've enjoyed it. I've had good health, pleasant surroundings—and Mama to straighten my hat and tie and make me change my shirt as often as she could. I'd like to spend another lifetime just prettying up things. That would be pleasant work and easy. In the past half century," he smiled again, "I've become fairly handy with guns. In the next I'd not have to work so hard. More time for hunting. Still, I wonder how long I'd stick with an easy job. Anyhow, a man shouldn't be piggish. After he passes the allotted threescore and ten, he's just stealing from time, and can expect to get caught any day."

Those who listened that day remembered; they later felt that John, feet propped up on the stone coping, his quizzical humor seemingly at idle play, had been saying good-by to his mountains, to the locust that shaded the shop of many memories, to a rich and bountiful life, that he had been intuitively if not consciously informed.

He was again silent for a long interval. There was no telling what his thoughts were; he had a full life to choose from. Possibly he was thinking of Matt, who had died three years before and who was never long out of mind. He might have been thinking of Hartford, New Haven, Liége, or Ilion.

But probably his recollections extended back even farther, for when he spoke he seemed to be completing a long line of thought. "I'm glad Pappy kept coming until he got to these particular mountains. These big valleys and canyons with their bold streams. You know, one of the prettiest things in the world—maybe the prettiest—is a mountain

Inventing new guns didn't leave as much time for hunting with them as John would have liked. John and Matt Browning on one of their much enjoyed big-game trips, elk hunting in Montana. At seventy, a year before his death, the inventor shot 98 out of 100 birds at the traps. JOHN M. BROWNING FIREARMS MUSEUM spring, bubbling through colored pebbles, with moss and cress around it, and sometimes a fern and a flower or two. That's where the good Lord Himself sets up the drinks." He squinted slyly at Rachel, as though expecting reproof. But she knew John drank from a mountain spring with something like reverence.

The dusk of the long summer twilight was thickening. It had been a beautiful sunset; it reminded John of a story he had never before told his audience, about a hunting trip taken some years earlier with his old friend Split Barlow. He told it now, with great zest.

Split had talked John into going up to a camp he had pitched on a high mountain stream. He had managed to get a grubstake that would last him until snow and was pretending to prospect. Most of his prospecting, however, was done with fishpole and rifle. He had pecked a tunnel into the mountain fifteen or twenty feet where the digging was easy and was using it as a cellar. On it he had put a rough door, and inside were hung bear hams and bacon slabs and quarters of venison, all of which he had smoked or dried for winter meat.

John had shot a deer the first afternoon, early, not more than a quarter mile from the camp. Then he had had some bad luck. Leaning his rifle against a tree, where it seemed safe enough, they had set about dressing the deer. But when it came time to load the meat on the horse, the horse was skittish. Backing off to the end of the lead rope, he knocked the rifle over and stepped on it, breaking the stock off at the tang.

Split was upset and John was disappointed. He had been hoping for two deer. By the time one had been whacked up among the boys in the shop and some steaks set aside for Uncle Mose and a few others, there wouldn't be much left.

Split suggested that while he went back to the camp and hung the deer and caught some trout for supper, John borrow his rifle and go it alone. John needed little persuasion. They figured out landmarks that would keep him from straying too far, and Split agreed to come back with the horse if he heard a shot.

There was only one drawback. Split had a good rifle—John had sold it to him. But he was naturally careless and had let rust get into the barrel. The chamber was so badly pitted that nearly every shell stuck when it was fired. To remedy this, Split had made a little invention. He had sawed off the head of a bolt which was about six inches long and a little smaller in diameter than the bore and had sharpened one end like a screw driver. After a shot, he would drop the bolt down the barrel a few times and loosen the shell, then pry it out with the sharpened end of the bolt. He was proud of his invention. Besides, he said, the sticking didn't bother him much; he always got his game with one shot. John dropped the bolt into a pocket and struck out.

"The top of the ridge I was hunting was fairly flat and lightly timbered," John said. "I made good time and covered a lot of ground. But no deer. I'd been zigzagging along the east edge of the flat when the tints of sunset began to make me think of camp and trout for supper. I decided to make a quick circle back by way of the west edge. When I got to that edge I stopped suddenly. The ridge dropped sharply down a deep draw and on into Ogden Canyon; out there, filling the whole world, was a sunset that must have stopped the heavenly harps for awhile. I sat on a rock and forgot all about deer and Split and trout for supper. I seemed to be on the edge of the conflagration. The rocks and trees all around me had colors running over them, and I tried to take it all in—the big picture over the lake, and the small ones nearby.

"And then I saw him—a huge grizzly. Hunkered on a large outcrop, several feet higher than the surrounding ground, he was just staring into the sunset.

"The outcrop was like an altar, and a priest in robes never looked more worshipful. There was no reason for his climbing up on that outcrop except to get a clearer view of the stupendous picture. I watched till the colors began to fade and then tiptoed away. Two or three times, helped by a rise in the ground, I looked back, and Brother Grizzly was still on his altar. I thought that the Great Spirit of the mountains should be well pleased with his worshiper. I was about half ready to believe in the Great Spirit myself.

"I didn't tell Split about the bear," John admitted to his listeners. "I've never told anybody before. The incident was too complicated. There was the bear, not over a hundred yards away, sitting straight up, his left side toward me, offering me the choice of any part of his anatomy to shoot at, and I sat with a rifle on my knees just staring, wondering what he was seeing in the west, feeling that I had no right to interrupt his devotion with a shot. I'm a gunmaker and as much of a hunter as I've had time to be, and I had a most unusual chance at what is considered the prize big-game trophy of the Rocky Mountains. Yet I just walked away, under the influence of the sunset and twilight.

"Of course," John chuckled unexpectedly, breaking the spell he had cast, "there was the matter of the pitted chamber and the sticking shells. That bear was a hunk for one man with the best rifle in the land, and I, limited to one shot, had no business making him mad. I suppose that thought was in the back of my mind all the time, and if the bear had merely looked toward me, I'd probably have lit out pronto. But while I watched him he looked solemn and sad, and that's the way I felt. I hope he enjoyed the full hundred years they say a grizzly sometimes lives. I never went bear hunting again."

EPILOGUE

CAPTAIN Paul A. Curtis, well-known gun authority and author, wrote in 1931:

> It is difficult to find words to accurately describe John Browning's achievements. To say that he was a great gun designer is inadequate; to say that he was the Edison of the modem firearms industry does not quite cover the case either, for he was even greater than that. There are, and were, many great men working along the same lines as Edison, including Steinmetz, Westinghouse, Marconi and others too numerous to mention—but Browning was unique. He stood alone, and there never was in his time or before, one whose genius along those lines could remotely compare with his.

It is usually reckless to say of any man that in his field he was the greatest of all time, however imposing his life's work may have been. Fortunately, great men appear with some frequency. Yet in the case of John Moses Browning, Philip Sharpe's evaluation, that he was "the greatest figure in the history of firearms," seems to rest on a solid and unrivaled foundation—the inventor's accomplishments. "It is not because of personal bias that arms experts have declared John Browning the greatest firearms expert of all times," James E. Serven writes. "To Browning's credit are the greatest number of inventions in arms history—and many of the most important."

Both Sharpe and Serven give good reasons why this should be so.

"Browning developments all had one peculiar and very necessary feature," says Sharpe, *"they worked and kept on working."* Another persuasive reason, which could be applied to most of Browning's inventions, of whatever type, is supplied by Serven in discussing Colt's automatic pistols: "The success of the Colt-Browning automatic pistols inspired other manufacturers to enter this field. Among those who manufactured automatic pistols in America, Colt's most important early competitors were Savage, Smith & Wesson, Remington, Harrington & Richardson, and Reising. No automatic pistols are now made by these firms; that terse statement is significant and tells the story of Colt domination in the field of American automatic pistols."

Yet perhaps John himself gave the best reason, albeit unconsciously. His remark, "The time and the place for a gunmaker just got together on this corner. And I happened along" is especially apropos. John M. Browning appeared at a crucial moment in the history of firearms development. His genius found an opportunity which had not existed before his time, and which can not occur again, so long as developments in arms are limited to the present types of ammunition. In the forty-seven years between the patenting of his first gun and his death, he set the basic trends in repeating rifles and shotguns; automatic rifles and shotguns; automatic pistols; and military small arms, both gas- and recoil-operated—left so little undone, in short, that the industry no longer has a place for a genius of his rank. In the more than thirty-five years since his death no basically new practical small arm has appeared.

His accomplishments are remarkable whether they are measured by their innovations, their number, their duration, or their popularity. During those forty-seven inventive years, John M. Browning was issued 128 different patents, to cover a total of some eighty complete and distinct firearm models. They include practically every caliber from the .22-short cartridge through the 37-mm. projectile; they embrace automatic actions, semi-automatic actions, lever actions, and pump actions; they include guns that operate by gas pressure, by both the short and long recoil principle, and by the blowback principle; they include models utilizing sliding locks, rotating locks and vertical locks. Included among them are most of the successful sporting arms which appeared during this period, as well as many of the military arms. It is estimated that well over thirty million Browning-designed guns have been produced to date, by Winchester, Colt, Fabrique Nationale, Remington, Savage, and others.

Perhaps it is enough to say that the story of John M. Browning's life is the story of the evolution of modern firearms.

John and Rachel spent Thanksgiving 1926 in Liege with their son Val and his family. The following morning John and Val left the apartment early for the thirty-five-minute drive to the Fabrique Nationale plant. John seemed to be in good health, and he and Val chatted as usual during the drive.

Arriving at the factory at nine, they climbed the stairs to Val's office, where the inventor took off his coat and hat. John then went out into the factory to see how work was progressing on the new shotgun. Within a few minutes he returned to his son's office, pale and complaining of dizziness and a pain in his chest. Val summoned the factory physician.

Awaiting the doctor, John strode to and fro, swinging his arms back and forth in an attempt to rid himself of the chest pains. But after a few steps he faltered, and Val helped him to a nearby sofa.

Within a few minutes the doctor arrived. After listening to John's heart, he turned aside and explained to Val that he believed the situation serious. Stimulants were administered, and John's body was massaged in order to promote circulation. John then said to Val, "Son, I wouldn't be surprised if I am dying."

A few minutes later he was dead. Cause of death was attributed to heart failure. The great gunmaker had laid down his tools.

The War Department, as final tribute to the man who had served the armed forces so well, assigned a military escort to meet the ship carrying his body, drape the colors on the casket, and stand guard until all formalities were completed.

The following is an excerpt from a long eulogy delivered by the Honorable Dwight F. Davis, Secretary of War:

It is a fact to be recorded that no design of Mr. Browning's has ever proved a failure, nor has any model been discontinued. The War Department, through its agency, the Ordnance Department, will be greatly handicapped in its future development work on automatic firearms as a result of the loss of Mr. Browning's services. It is not thought that any other individual has contributed so much to the national security of this country as Mr. Browning in the development of our machine guns and our automatic weapons to a state of military efficiency surpassing that of all nations . . .

The great gunmaker had laid down his tools.   BROWNING ARMS COMPANY

PART FOUR

THE GUNS

"I wonder from time to time," John once confessed to one of his sons, "whether we are heading in the right direction. For instance, we are making guns that shoot farther, harder, faster, and calling it progress." He shrugged. "If just getting farther and farther from your starting place is progress, I suppose the meaning we usually give the word is correct. But if we limit the meaning to movement toward a destination where the most pleasure and satisfaction are to be found, then this progress we brag about is just a crazy, blind racing past the things we are looking for—and haven't the sense to recognize. And," he grinned, "in the matter of guns, that makes me crazier than most."

I. THE GUNS OF JONATHAN BROWNING (1805-79)

1. SLIDE REPEATING RIFLE (JONATHAN BROWNING)

History: One of the earliest known American repeating rifles, this arm was invented by Jonathan Browning sometime between 1834 and 1842, while he was residing in Quincy, Illinois. It was never patented but was manufactured by its inventor during his residences in Quincy; Nauvoo, Illinois (1842-46); and Kanesville, Iowa (1846-52). The total number manufactured is not known.

Description: This rifle has a number of particularly ingenious features. Its five-shot magazine is a rectangular iron bar with holes to accommodate the hand loads. The bar slides through an aperture at the breech and is manually operated. This permits loading in advance and results in five comparatively fast shots. The proximity of the forefinger to the hammer allows cocking without taking the rifle from the shoulder. A lever located on the right-hand side of the gun, thumb-operated, forces the slide against the barrel as each load moves into line with the bore, resulting in a positive gas-tight connection. It is not only one of the earliest repeating rifles made, it is also one of the simplest, both in its small number of parts and its operating ease.

Caliber: Approximately .45.

Magazine type and capacity: See Description. Though this magazine held five shots, others holding up to twenty-five were available.

Length: 58⅞".

Barrel length and style: 40⁵⁄₁₅" octagon.

Weight: 9 lbs., 14 oz.

Photo: Production model. *Barrel markings:* Browning Warranted. 1847. No serial number. Courtesy John M. Browning Firearms Museum.

2. CYLINDER REPEATING RIFLE (JONATHAN BROWNING)

History: This six-shot repeater was also invented by Jonathan Browning during his residence in Quincy, sometime between 1834 and 1842. It, too, was never patented and was not manufactured after Browning arrived in Utah in 1852. The total number manufactured is not known.

Description: The powder and ball are loaded into the cylinder and a cap placed on each nipple. The rifle is cocked by drawing back the hammer, but there is no mechanism for revolving the cylinder when the hammer is cocked. The cylinder must be rotated manually after each shot. The front edge of the cylinder has tapered cones around each chamber which fit into the breech of the barrel. It appears that at one time there was a conically shaped cam in the rear of the cylinder, which, when pushed in would jam the cylinder tight against the breech of the barrel. However, there is no cam on this surviving model of the gun, only a conically shaped hole traversing horizontally through the receiver immediately to the rear of the cylinder.

Caliber: Approximately .45.

Magazine type and capacity: Cylinder. 6 shots.

Length: 48¹⁵⁄₁₆″.

Barrel length and style: 29¹⁵⁄₁₆″ half octagon, half 16-sided.

Weight: 12 lbs., 2 oz.

Photo: Production model.

Barrel markings: Council Bluffs. J. Browning and Sons. No date or serial number. Courtesy John M. Browning Firearms Museum.

II. THE GUNS OF JOHN M. BROWNING (1855-1926)

A. RIFLES

1. SINGLE SHOT RIFLE (BROWNING BROTHERS AND WINCHESTER)

History: This was John M. Browning's first firearm model, invented in 1878 when he was twenty-three years old. Patent was filed May 12, 1879, and U. S. Patent No. 220,271 was granted October 7, 1879. Production by the Browning Brothers, Ogden, Utah Territory, began about 1880 and continued until 1883, with a total of approximately six hundred rifles manufactured. Manufacturing and sales rights were sold to the Winchester Repeating Arms Company in 1883 and the arm appeared in 1885 as the Winchester Single Shot Model 1885.

The following specifications refer to the Winchester Model:

Description: Lever-action, exposed-hammer, fixed-barrel single-shot rifle. The hammer drops down with the breechblock when the rifle is opened and is cocked by the closing movement. It can also be cocked by hand.

Caliber: The Single Shot has been adapted to over thirty-three different calibers, more than any other single-shot or repeating rifle known. Including both rim- and center-fire types, its loads ranged from the .22 Short to the .50/90 Sharps. It was the first Winchester rifle capable of handling the powerful metallic cartridges of the period.

Breechblock: Falling-block type.

Safety: Manual, half-cock notch on hammer. Mechanical, can only be fired when the action is closed.

Model style: Sporting and special sporting rifles, special target rifle, Schuetzen rifle, carbine, musket, shotgun.

Barrel length and style: Lengths vary, depending on the model, from the light carbine with a 15″ barrel to the 30″ Schuetzen. Round, octagon, or half octagon.

Weight 4½ to 13 lbs., depending on specifications.

Stock: Plain sporting rifle, rifle type, straight grip; special sporting rifle, rifle type, pistol grip; Schuetzen rifle, special Schuetzen type, pistol grip; carbine, carbine type, straight grip; musket, musket type, straight grip; shotgun, straight grip, rubber butt plate.

Modifications: Through the years the Single Shot was produced in a variety of models. The light carbine (called the "Baby Carbine") appeared in 1898. The takedown model was introduced in 1910. A special military target version was introduced in 1905; in 1914 it was revamped as the Winder Musket, named in honor of Colonel C. B. Winder, and was used for training troops in World War I. In 1914 the Single Shot was also made into a shotgun, chambered for the 3″, 20-gauge shell.

Date discontinued and production totals: Discontinued in all models in 1920. Total production of all models was approximately 140,325, which includes the 600-unit production by the Browning Brothers.

Photo: Browning Brothers production model. Courtesy John M. Browning Firearms Museum.

AUTHORS' NOTE: In many instances, serial numbers on manufactured models did not begin with the number "1" or even a relatively low number. As a result, guns will often be found bearing serial numbers which are higher than total unit production figures. This is applicable not only to the rifles but also to the shotguns and pistols.

2. TUBULAR MAGAZINE REPEATING RIFLE

History: The second arm invented by John M. Browning was a tubular-magazine repeating rifle. Patent was filed March 20, 1882, and U. S. Patent No. 261,667 was granted July 25, 1882. This gun was never manufactured, and no known models survive.

Description (from the patent application): This was a bolt-action gun having a rotating sleeve with locking lugs to engage locking shoulders in the receiver. The novel features of this gun were the arrangement of the tubular magazine under the barrel; the receiver, open at the top; and the carrier for elevating the cartridges from the magazine to the chamber. The cartridges were loaded into the magazine at the rear thereof, through the top of the receiver when the bolt was open. A system of grooves on each side of the inner walls of the receiver guided the cartridges as they were manually forced one by one into the rear opening of the magazine. The striker-type firing pin had a finger hook for manual cocking.

3. LEVER ACTION REPEATING RIFLE

History: This rifle was invented in 1882. Patent was filed September 13, 1882, and U. S. Patent No. 282,839 was granted August 7, 1883. It was never manufactured.

Description: This lever-action, exposed-hammer, tubular-magazine repeating rifle operates quite differently from most lever actions. It is of very simple construction, the breechblock and finger lever being essentially of one piece. The breech piece is hung to the receiver by the extractor in such a manner that the operating movement causes the rear end of the breech to drop, thereby unlocking the piece, while the forward end is guided longitudinally in the receiver by the extractor. The swinging movement of the combination breechblock and finger piece extracts and ejects the fired shell and pivots a one piece carrier upwardly with a fresh round ready to load when the action is closed. Cocking the hammer is not done automatically but must be effected manually for every round, thus constituting an automatic safety. When in closed position, the rear end of the breech rests squarely against the recoil-bearing surface in the receiver, holding the front end of the breechblock against the barrel. The purpose of this construction is to provide a lever-action rifle of extreme simplicity, with a minimum of parts.

Caliber: .45.

Magazine type: Tubular.

Barrel length and style: 26¾″ octagon.

Weight: 8¾″ lbs.

Photo: Inventor's original model. Courtesy John M. Browning Firearms Museum.

4. MODEL 1886 LEVER ACTION REPEATING RIFLE

History: Invented in 1882-83, this was the first Browning-designed repeating rifle to be manufactured. It was also the first repeating rifle to successfully employ sliding vertical locks which effectively sealed the breech and barrel of the gun; as such it was the forerunner of all later Browning lever-action-type rifles. It has been said that practically every improvement in lever-action repeating rifles has been taken from this basic patent. Patent was filed May 26, 1884, and U. S. Patent No. 306,577 was granted October 14, 1884. Purchased by Winchester in October 1884, it appeared in 1886 as the Model 1886.

Description: Lever-action, exposed-hammer, tubular-magazine, fixed-barrel repeating rifle.

Caliber: .45/70 U. S. Government, .40/82 W.C.F., .45/90 W.C.F., .40/65 W.C.F., .38/56 W.C.F., .50/110 Express, .40/70 W.C.F., .38/70 W.C.F., 50/100/450, .33 W.C.F.

Magazine type and capacity: Tubular, both full and half magazines, with varying capacities.

Breechblock: Lever-operated sliding vertical locks.

Safety: Manual, half-cock notch. Mechanical, sear contact only when action is closed.

Model style: Sporting and fancy sporting rifles, extra-lightweight rifle, half-magazine rifle, carbine, and musket.

Barrel length and style: Sporting rifle, 26″ round, octagon or half octagon. Fancy sporting rifle, 26″ round. Extra-lightweight rifle, 22″ round. Carbine, 22″ round. Special barrels and magazines furnished to specifications until 1908.

Weight: Varying widely depending on specifications and caliber.

Stock: Sporting rifle, rifle type, straight grip; fancy sporting rifle, rifle type, pistol grip; extra-lightweight rifle, rifle type, straight grip; half-magazine rifle, shotgun butt, straight grip; carbine, carbine type, straight grip; musket, musket type, straight grip.

Modifications: In 1894 it was converted to a takedown model. In 1936, the Model 1886, slightly modified to handle the .348 Winchester cartridge, became the Model 71.

Date discontinued and production totals: The Model 1886 was discontinued in 1935 with 159,994 produced; the Model 71 was discontinued in 1957 with 43,267 produced—making the total for this gun 203,261 and a life of seventy-one years.

Photo: Production model. Courtesy John M. Browning Firearms Museum.

5. MODEL 1890 .22 CALIBER PUMP ACTION REPEATING RIFLE (WINCHESTER)

History: Patent application on this gun was filed December 13, 1887, and U. S. Patent No. 385,238 was granted June 26, 1888. It appeared in 1890 as the Winchester .22 Caliber Repeating Rifle Model 1890, and was the first repeating pump or trombone-action gun manufactured by Winchester. It has been called "the most popular .22-caliber pump-action rifle ever made." The radical improvement in this rifle over previous .22-caliber repeaters was the carrier mechanism. Previously no positive method of handling the .22-caliber short cartridges had been developed. Browning accomplished this by installing a fingerlike cartridge stop on the front of the carrier, which metered one cartridge at a time onto the carrier from the magazine tube. At the correct instant, when the spent cartridge from the chamber had been ejected, the carrier raised and held the new cartridge in positive alignment with the chamber for loading.

Description: Pump-action, exposed-hammer, tubular-magazine, fixed-barrel repeating rifle.

Caliber: .22 long rifle, .22 long, .22 short, .22 W.R.F.; not originally interchangeable.

Magazine type and capacity: Tubular. .22 long rifle, 11; .22 long; .22 short, 15; .22 W.R.F., 12.

Breechblock: Sliding breechblock, operated by forearm slide.

Safety: Manual, half-cock notch. Mechanical, sear contact only when breechblock is locked down into receiver.

Model style: Sporting and fancy sporting rifles.

Barrel length and style: 24″ octagon.

Weight: 5¾″ to 6 lbs.

Stock: Rifle type, curved-steel butt plate, straight grip. Pistol-grip specials.

Modifications: First manufactured with barrel fixed to frame, it was converted to takedown in 1893. The Model 06, introduced in 1906, modified to accept any of the .22 cartridges except the .22 W.R.F. would hold 11 long rifle or 15 short. A 20″ round barrel replaced the 24″

octagon. In 1932 the Models 90 and 06 were renamed the Model 62, the primary difference being a slight change in barrel dimensions and sights.

Date discontinued and production totals: The Models 90 and 06 were discontinued in 1932 with 849,000 and 848,000 produced respectively; the Model 62 was discontinued in 1958 with 409,475 produced—making the total for this gun 2,106,475 and a life of sixty-nine years.

Photo: Inventor's original model. Courtesy John M. Browning Firearms Museum.

6. MODEL 1892 LEVER ACTION REPEATING RIFLE (WINCHESTER)

History: This model, first manufactured by Winchester in 1892 and known as the Winchester Model 92, was of the same basic design as the Model 1886, and incorporated many of its special features, including the double-locking system, covered under U. S. Patent No. 306,577. Two additional patents covered it—No. 465,339, filed August 3, 1891 and granted December 15, 1891, and No. 499,005, filed September 19, 1892 and granted June 6, 1893.

Description: Lever-action, exposed-hammer, tubular-magazine, fixed-barrel repeating rifle. The Model 92 was a simplified, lighter version of the Model 86, specifically designed for smaller-caliber cartridges.

Caliber: .44/40, .38/40, .32/20, .25/20.

Magazine type and capacity: Tubular. Sporting rifle, 13. Carbine, full magazine, 11; half magazine, 5. Musket, 17.

Breechblock: Lever-operated sliding vertical locks.

Safety: Manual, half-cock notch. Mechanical, sear contact only when action is closed.

Model style: Sporting rifle, fancy sporting rifle, carbine, and musket.

Barrel length and style: Rifles, 24″ round, octagon or half octagon. Carbine, 20″ round. Musket, 30″ round. Shorter barrels from 14 to 20″ and special lengths up to 36″ were also available.

Weight: 53½″ to 8 lbs. depending on model and caliber.

Stock: Sporting rifle, rifle type, straight grip; fancy sporting rifle, rifle type, pistol grip; carbine, carbine type, straight grip; musket,

musket type, straight grip.

Modifications: First made with barrel fixed to frame, it became available in a takedown model in 1893. A modified version with a decreased magazine capacity was introduced in 1924 as the Model 53. Its successor, the Model 65, was introduced in 1933.

Date discontinued and production totals: The Model 53 was discontinued in 1932 with a total of 24,916; the Model 65 was discontinued in 1947, with a total of 5704; the Model 92, though not produced except in the carbine model for several years after the introduction of the Model 53, was not officially discontinued until 1941, at which time 1,004,067 had been manufactured—for a complete total of 1,034,687.

Photo: Inventor's original model. Courtesy John M. Browning Firearms Museum.

7. MODEL 1894 LEVER ACTION REPEATING RIFLE
   (WINCHESTER)

History: Patent on this gun was filed January 19, 1894, and U. S. Patent No. 524,702 was granted August 21, 1894. It was first manufactured by Winchester in 1894 and known as the Winchester Model 1894. Often called "the most famous sporting rifle ever produced," the Model 94 is perhaps best-known as the "Winchester .30/30." It was revolutionary in that it was the first sporting repeating-action rifle to handle the smokeless-powder cartridges.

Description: Lever-action, exposed-hammer, tubular-magazine, fixed-barrel repeating rifle.

Caliber: Originally produced for black powder .32/40 and .38/55. In 1895 .25/35 and .30/30 were added, and .32 Special in 1902.

Magazine type and capacity: Tubular. Sporting rifles, full magazine, 8. Extra-lightweight rifle, half magazine, 3. Carbine, full magazine, 6; half magazine, 4.

Breechblock: Lever-operated sliding vertical locks.

Safety: Manual, half-cock notch on hammer. Mechanical, sear contact only when action is fully closed.

Model style: Sporting rifle, fancy sporting rifle, extra-lightweight rifle, carbine.

Barrel length and style: Sporting and fancy sporting rifles, 26″

round, octagon or half octagon. Extra-lightweight rifle, 22″ round. Carbine, 20″ round.

Weight: Carbine, 5¾ to 6¼ lbs. All others, 7 to 7¾ lbs.

Stock: Sporting rifle, rifle type, straight grip and pistol grip; fancy sporting rifle, rifle type, pistol grip; extra-lightweight rifle, shotgun butt, straight grip; carbine, carbine type, straight grip, changed to shotgun buttstock in 1937.

Modifications: First manufactured as a fixed barrel repeater, it became available in a takedown model in 1895. Modified versions include the Model 55, introduced in 1924 (principal differences being a shorter barrel, a redesigned stock and a switch to half magazine) and the Model 64, introduced in 1933 (the main difference being in the steel used). The Model 55 was discontinued in 1932 and the Model 64 in 1957.

Production totals: Still in production as the Model 94 carbine, this rifle has outsold any other manufactured by the Winchester Repeating Arms Company. Over two and a half million had been produced by 1962.

Photo: Inventor's original model. Courtesy John M. Browning Firearms Museum.

8. MODEL 1895 LEVER ACTION REPEATING RIFLE
    (WINCHESTER)

History: Patent application on this gun was filed November 19, 1894, and U. S. Patent No. 549,345 was granted November 5, 1895. It was first manufactured by Winchester in 1896 and known as the Winchester Model 95. This was the first non-detachable box-type magazine rifle designed to handle the jacketed sharp-nosed bullets.

Description: Lever-action, exposed-hammer, non-detachable box-magazine, fixed-barrel rifle.

Caliber: .30 U. S. Army (Krag), .38/72, .40/72 Winchester, .303 British, .35 Winchester, .405 Winchester, .30 Government 1903, .30 Government 1906, 7.62 mm. Russian.

Magazine type and capacity: Non-detachable box. Capacity varied from 4 to 6 rounds.

Breechblock: Lever-operated sliding vertical lock.

Safety: Manual, half-cock notch on hammer. Mechanical, sear contact only when action is locked.

Model style: Sporting and fancy sporting rifles, carbine, and muskets.

Barrel length and style: Varied. 22 to 36″, round, octagon or half octagon.

Weight: Varied, depending on barrel and caliber.

Stock: Sporting rifle, rifle type, straight grip; fancy sporting rifle, shotgun butt, straight grip; carbine, carbine type, straight grip; muskets, musket type, straight grip.

Modifications: Four slightly differing versions of the musket appeared between 1895 and 1908. One, the Musket .30 Army Model 1895 U. S. Army Pattern, was adopted by the U. S. Army in 1895. The same year some 10,000 muskets chambered for the .30/40 Krag cartridge were purchased by the U. S. Army for use in the Spanish-American War. Prior to America's entry into World War I, 293,816 of these guns, chambered for the 7.62 mm. Russian cartridge, were sold to Russia. A takedown version of the rifle appeared in 1910.

Date discontinued and production totals: Discontinued in all models in 1931 with a total production of 425,881.

Photo: Inventor's original model. Courtesy John M. Browning Firearms Museum.

9. MODEL 1900 BOLT ACTION SINGLE SHOT
    .22 CALIBER RIFLE (WINCHESTER)

History: Patent application on this gun was filed February 17, 1899, and U. S. Patent No. 632,094 was granted August 29, 1899. It was first listed in the Winchester 1899 catalogue as the Winchester Model 1900 Single Shot Rifle. Designed as a low-priced, single-shot "plinking" rifle, it was of especially simple construction and has been widely copied.

Description: Bolt action, single-shot, takedown rifle.

Caliber: .22 long and short, interchangeable.

Breechblock: Bolt handle locking into receiver.

Safety: Manual, cocking piece is pulled back after loading.

Model style: Sporting rifle.

Barrel length and style: 18″ round.

Weight: 2¾ lbs.

Stock: Sporting rifle, rifle type, straight grip.

Modifications and date discontinued: The Model 1900 was discontinued in 1902; the Model 1902, announced the same year, had a modified trigger-guard shape, a shorter trigger pull, a steel butt plate, a rear peep sight, and a slightly heavier barrel. In July of 1904 another slightly modified version appeared, the Model 1904, which had a longer, heavier barrel and a differently shaped stock. An interesting modification was the Model 99 Thumb Trigger Rifle, which also appeared in 1904. This rifle was void either of trigger or trigger guard. Just behind the cocking piece on the bolt was a button called the thumb trigger. When in shooting position, the shooter merely pressed downward on this button with the thumb to release the firing pin. In 1928 and the years following Winchester brought out other variations, the Models 58, 59, 60, and 68. In 1920 a shotgun version, similar to the Model 1902, was announced, the Winchester Model 36 Single Shot Shotgun. This was the only American made shotgun chambered for the 9-mm. paper shells; it was discontinued in 1927. The last model, the 68, introduced in 1934, was discontinued in 1946.

Production totals: Model 1900, 105,000; Model 02, 640,299; Model 04, 302,859; Model 99 Thumb Trigger, 75,433; Model 36 Shotgun, 20,306; Model 58, 38,992; Model 59, 9293; Model 60, 165,754; and Model 68, 100,730—for a total of 1,458,666.

Photo: Inventor's original model. Courtesy John M. Browning Firearms Museum.

10. SEMI-AUTOMATIC HIGH POWER RIFLE (REMINGTON AND FABRIQUE NATIONALE)

History: Patent application on this gun was filed June 6, 1900, and U. S. Patent No. 659,786 was granted October 16, 1900. U.S. manufacturing and sales rights were granted to the Remington Arms Company and the rifle first appeared in 1906 as the Remington Model 8 Autoloading Center Fire Rifle. This was the first successful autoloading, high-power rifle introduced in the United States. Fabrique Nationale introduced the gun in Belgium in 1910 as the F.N. Caliber .35 Automatic Rifle.

The following specifications refer to the Remington Model 8:

Description: Recoil-actuated, autoloading-type, takedown rifle.

Caliber: .25, .30, .32 or .35 Remington.

Magazine type and capacity: Non-detachable with clip. Five rounds. (Later replaced with detachable box.)

Breechblock: Rotating bolt head having double lug locks in barrel extension. Barrel recoils inside of jacket while locked to bolt. A stop-open latch holds the breechblock open after the last shell is fired.

Safety: Manual, thumb lever on right of receiver.

Model style: Sporting rifle, takedown. Sold in various grades.

Barrel length and style: 22″ round.

Weight: 7¾ lbs.

Stock: Rifle, rifle type, straight grip with shotgun style rubber butt plate or semi-pistol grip.

Modifications, date discontinued, and production totals: The Remington Model 8 was discontinued in 1936 and replaced by the Model 81 (Woodmaster) the same year. Modifications included an improved stock and forearm and a slight weight increase (to 8 lbs.). The Model 81 was discontinued in 1950. As a matter of company policy, production figures are not available on Remington arms. The F.N. model differed from the Remington models in that it had a solid-matted rib barrel; a bead-front sight and two-position-folding rear sight (the Models 8 and 81 had adjustable open rear sights); a checked forearm and buttstock; and a weight of 8¼ lbs. Like the Remington models, it was also takedown. The F.N. model was discontinued in 1931, with a total production of 4913 units.

Photo: Inventor's original model. Courtesy John M. Browning Firearms Museum.

11. SEMI-AUTOMATIC .22 CALIBER RIFLE
(FABRIQUE NATIONALE, REMINGTON AND BROWNING)

History: Patent applications on this gun were filed November 19, 1912, and March 20, 1913. U. S. Patents Nos. 1,065,341-2 and 1,083,384. were granted June 24, 1913 and January 6, 1914. It was first manufactured by Fabrique Nationale in 1914 as the F.N. .22 Caliber Automatic Rifle. Remington was later granted U.S. rights and their version, the Model 24, was brought out in 1924. The Browning Arms Company model, the Browning .22 Automatic, was introduced in 1956.

The following specifications refer to the F.N. .22 Caliber Automatic Rifle:

Description: Blowback, recoil-actuated, autoloading-type, takedown rifle.

Caliber: .22 long and short.

Magazine type and capacity: Tubular. Maximum capacity is 8 .22 long-rifle cartridges in the magazine and 1 in the chamber when the gun is loaded through the loading port. If the magazine tube is taken out of the buttstock and cartridges are loaded through the butt plate instead of the loading port, the capacity is 9 long-rifle cartridges in the magazine and 1 in the chamber. The capacity of the magazine with .22 short cartridges is 11 cartridges in the magazine and 1 in the chamber when loading through the port, and 13 cartridges in the magazine and 1 in the chamber when loading through the butt plate.

Safety: Cross bolt.

Model style: Sporting.

Barrel length and style: 19″ round.

Weight 4¼ lbs.

Stock: Rifle, rifle type, semi-pistol grip.

Modifications, date discontinued, and production totals: The F.N. model is still in production. The Remington Model 24 was first brought out for .22 short Lesmok only; the action was later modified to handle the .22 long rifle. While the magazine of the F.N. version loaded through an opening on top of the stock, the magazine of the Model 24 was loaded through a port on the side of the buttstock. Weight was 4¾ lbs.

Discontinued in 1935, it was replaced by the Remington Model 241 (Speedmaster) in 1938. While the two preceding models had 19" barrels, the length of the Model 241 barrel was 23½". It was chambered for .22 long and short, and weighed 6 lbs. Like the other versions, it was takedown. This model was discontinued in 1951. The Browning .22 Automatic is available in either .22 long rifle or .22 short models. Both are takedown, side loading, and have a bead-front sight and folding adjustable rear sight, semi-beavertail forearm and pistol grip. The long rifle has a 19¼" barrel, a magazine capacity of 11 rounds and weighs 3¾ lbs. The short model has a 22" barrel, a magazine capacity of 16 rounds, and weighs 5 lbs. Both are currently available in a variety of grades. Total production figures are not available on Remington models. By the end of 1961, F.N. had manufactured 199,160 units, and the Browning Arms Company 121,538 units.

Photo: Inventor's original model. Courtesy John M. Browning Firearms Museum.

12. PUMP ACTION .22 CALIBER REPEATING RIFLE (FABRIQUE NATIONALE)

History: This rifle was invented in 1919. Patent application was filed July 26, 1919, and U. S. Patent No. 1,424,553 was granted August 1, 1922. This is one of the few Browning designed guns never produced or sold in the United States. It was introduced by Fabrique Nationale in and is still in production.

Description: Pump-action, concealed-hammer, repeating rifle. The breech bolt of this rifle locks positively to the receiver. The locking surface on the receiver is the rear of the end of the ejection opening. The breech bolt is pivoted at its front end to the slide, and its rear end is free to swing sideways, in and out of locking engagement with the receiver.

Caliber: All .22 rifle cartridges, interchangeably.

Magazine type and capacity: .22 long rifle, 11; .22 long, 12; .22 short, 15.

Safety: Cross bolt.

Model style: Sporting only. (A few special engraved rifles have been produced.)

Barrel length and style: .22″ round.

Weight: 4¾ lbs.

Stock: Rifle, rifle type, semi-pistol grip.

Production totals: Still in production, a total of 126,907 units had been produced by the end of 1961.

Photo: Inventor's original model. Courtesy John M. Browning Firearms Museum.

13. THE BROWNING AUTOMATIC RIFLE (COLT, WINCHESTER, MARLIN-ROCKWELL, FABRIQUE NATIONALE AND OTHERS)

History: The Browning Automatic Rifle was invented prior to 1917. Patent application on this gun was filed August 1, 1917, and U. S. Patent No. 1,293,022 was granted February 4, 1919. Best known as the B.A.R., it is also known as the Browning Light Machine Rifle Model 1917, the Light Browning, the Colt Automatic Machine Rifle, and the Fusil Mitrailleur Browning. The B.A.R. was officially adopted by the United States Government in 1917 and first saw combat use in July 1918. (For the story of the tests which preceded its adoption and a summary of its use since that time, see Part Three, Chapter 14 of the text.)

The specifications below refer to the Colt Model 1917:

Description: Air-cooled, gas-actuated, detachable box magazine, automatic machine rifle. A lever on the receiver permits fully automatic or semi-automatic firing. Fully automatic it can be fired at a maximum rate of 480 rounds per minute, emptying a 20-round magazine in 2½ seconds.

This rifle has a bolt lock which is pivoted to the rear of the bolt and which rises in and out of locking engagement with a shoulder on the receiver. The rear of the bolt lock is attached to the slide by a link, which is a stirrup-shaped member encompassing the magazine, and which is free to reciprocate backward and forward. Attached to the forward part of the barrel is a gas piston which derives its energy from a gas port drilled through the barrel wall. In operation, the piston sends a slide to the rear, and, in turn, the slide, through its link connection with the bolt lock, pivots the bolt lock downwardly out of locking contact with the receiver.

Caliber: .30/06.

Magazine type and capacity: Detachable box magazine. Either 20 or 40 rounds. Staggered arrangement.

Safety: Fire-control change lever. When the change lever is in its forward position, marked with the letter "F," the rifle will shoot one shot with each pull of the trigger. In vertical position, marked with the letter "A," the rifle will fire full automatic. In the rearward position, marked by the letter "S," the rifle is safe. On some models, the "F" position, when the lever is all the way forward, merely reduces the rate of fire in such a way that single shots may be fired by quickly pulling and releasing the trigger.

Model style: Standard rifle only. Takedown. (Its 70 pieces can be completely disassembled and reassembled in 55 seconds.)

Barrel length and style: 24″ round.

Weight: 17 lbs., 6 oz. with full magazine.

Stock: Rifle, rifle type, pistol grip.

Modifications and production totals: During World War I approximately 52,000 were manufactured—by Colt, Winchester, and Marlin-Rockwell. After World War I production rights reverted to Colt and, by arrangement with John M. Browning, Fabrique Nationale began European production in 1920, calling their model the Fusil Mitrailleur Léger. Large quantities of the rifle have since been manufactured for various European countries. It was made in 6.5 mm., 7 mm., 7.62 mm., 7.9 mm., and .30/06 caliber. It has been widely copied; many nations now have the B.A.R. or a similar gun in reserve. In 1922 the U. S. Army brought out its Cavalry Model. In 1933 Colt produced the "Colt Monitor" for police and bank guard use. In November 1939, there were approximately 87,000 in our war reserve. Approximately 177,000 were produced in this country during World War II. In comparison with earlier models, the World War II B.A.R., the M1918A2, is slightly heavier and equipped with flash hider and bipod. It carries the conventional stock without pistol grip. A decelerating device permits either a high or low cyclic rate of fire, high at 550 rounds per minute, low at 350. No mechanical provision is made for semi-automatic fire, but, at low rate of fire, single shots can be discharged by pulling and quickly releasing the trigger. The F.N. version differed from the Colt model chiefly in having a quicker takedown mechanism which allowed the barrel to be removed easily for replacement. Total production by F.N. to the end of 1961 was 67,310 units.

Photos: Above, inventor's original model. Below, production model Fusil Mitrailleur Browning. Courtesy John M. Browning Firearms Museum.

Of the forty-four firearms John M. Browning sold to the Winchester Repeating Arms Company, thirty-one were rifles. Of this number only seven were manufactured. (Nos. 1, 4, 5, 6, 7, 8, 9.) The other twenty-four (Nos. 14-3) follow in the order of their patent filing date.

In addition John M. Browning submitted three other rifles to Winchester which were neither patented nor manufactured. These include a .44-caliber pump-action repeating rifle, a .22-caliber single-shot rifle, and a .45-caliber lever-action single-shot rifle. It is assumed that these guns were not patented because of previously existing patents and consequently were not purchased by Winchester, although the models remain in the Winchester Gun Museum. They are therefore not included in the totals of Browning-designed guns sold to Winchester or in the totals of original firearms invented by John M. Browning.

14. .38 CALIBER LEVER ACTION REPEATING RIFLE

History: Patent application on this gun was filed March 6, 1884, and U. S. Patent No. 312,183 was granted February 10, 1885. This gun was sold to Winchester but never manufactured.

Description: In this lever-action, tubular-magazine rifle the locking arrangement of the breechblock is greatly simplified, inasmuch as the lever itself, having a seat in the receiver, acts as the locking lug. The lever is spring loaded in such a way as to allow the lever to snap in and out of engagement with its socket or locking shoulder in the receiver.

Caliber: .38.

Magazine type: Tubular.

Barrel length and style: 28″ octagon.

Weight: 9¼″ lbs.

Photo: Inventor's original model. Courtesy Winchester Gun Museum.

15. .30 CALIBER GOVERNMENT LEVER ACTION REPEATING RIFLE

History: Patent application on this gun was filed March 5, 1885, and U. S. Patent No. 324,296 was granted August 11, 1885. This gun was sold to Winchester but never manufactured.

Description: The main novelty on this lever-action rifle is the locking lug, which is pivoted on the rear of the sliding breechblock in such a manner that the front end rises in and out of locking engagement with the receiver and breechblock. The locking lug also serves as the link between the rotary motion of the lever and the longitudinal motion of the breechblock.

Caliber: .30 Government.

Magazine type: Tubular.

Barrel length and style: 28″ octagon.

Weight: 9¼ lbs.

Photo: Inventor's original model. Courtesy Winchester Gun Museum.

16. .45 CALIBER LEVER ACTION REPEATING RIFLE

History: Patent application on this gun was filed May 26, 1885, and U. S. Patent No. 324,297 was granted August 11, 1885. This gun was sold to Winchester but never manufactured.

Description: This .45-caliber, lever-action, tubular-magazine gun features a toggle-locking system wherein the lever is the front part of the toggle bearing in a socket in the breechblock. The rear half of the toggle pivots at the rear against the receiver and houses the trigger. Opening the lever flexes the toggle joint and allows the bolt to slide to the rear. As in many of John M. Browning's designs, wherein one part has several functions, the links of the toggle joint serve to form a stout breech-locking system and act as the linkage necessary to reciprocate the breechblock. The action also features a firing-pin block which renders the gun safe until the lever piece is fully closed.

Caliber: .45.

Magazine type: Tubular.

Barrel length and style: 28″ octagon.

Weight: 9¼″ lbs.

Photo: Inventor's original model. Courtesy Winchester Gun Museum.

17. .44 CALIBER PUMP ACTION REPEATING RIFLE

History: Patent application on this gun was filed July 12, 1888, and U. S. Patent No. 367,336 was granted July 26, 1887. It was sold to Winchester but never manufactured.

Description: This is a pump-action or slide-action rifle, tubular-magazine type, with a pivoting breechblock, the rear end of which rises into locking engagement with the receiver. Instead of being placed to the rear of the breechblock, as is most common, the hammer works through a recess nearly in the middle of the breechblock, allowing for a very short receiver. The tail end of the hammer projects into the trigger guard forward of the trigger, allowing the hammer to be cocked or uncocked manually.

Caliber: .44.

Magazine type: Tubular.

Barrel length and style: 20″ round.

Weight: 5 lbs., 14 oz.

Photo: Inventor's original model. Courtesy Winchester Gun Museum.

18. .45 CALIBER LEVER ACTION REPEATING RIFLE

History: Patent application on this gun was filed November 21,

1887, and U. S. Patent No. 376,576 was granted January 17, 1888. It was sold to Winchester but never manufactured.

Description: This lever-action, tubular-magazine rifle loads through the bottom and ejects from the top of the receiver. The forward end of the operating lever contains the lock mechanism. The operating lever is hung to the receiver by a link, said link extending to the rear. The forward end of the lever is guided by cuts in the receiver. The sliding firing pin acts as a hammer and is cocked by the closing movement of the lever.

Caliber: .45.

Magazine type: Tubular.

Barrel length and style: 22″ round.

Weight: 7 lbs., 3 oz.

Photo: Inventor's original model. Courtesy Winchester Gun Museum.

19. .45/70 CALIBER LEVER ACTION REPEATING RIFLE

History: Patent application on this gun was filed November 18, 1889, and U. S. Patent No. 428,887 was granted May 27, 1890. This gun was sold to Winchester but never manufactured.

Description: In this unique firearm the breechblock, magazine, and lever are one unit. With the lever closed the assembly is in locking engagement with the receiver and comprises an effective breech closure. The cartridges ride in the magazine recess bullet down, with magazine-spring pressure urging them forward. Opening the lever turns this whole assembly and brings the cartridges in line with the bore. A selector lever on the side of the magazine portion urges the top cartridges out of the magazine into loading position. Closing the lever completes the loading cycle. Extraction is to the side and is effected by a combination extractor and pivot slide attached to the breech assembly. A further curious feature is the firing pin, which acts as its own pivot sear. The front of the firing pin is latched in cocked position by a hardened screw in the receiver. A lever attached to the trigger pushes the rear of the firing pin upward, pivoting the striker out of engagement with the hardened screw.

Caliber: .45/70.

Magazine type: Box.
Barrel length and style: 28″ round.
Weight: 8 lbs., 2 oz.
Photo: Inventor's original model. Courtesy Winchester Gun Museum.

20. .44 CALIBER LEVER ACTION REPEATING RIFLE

History and Description: This gun, covered by the same patent as No. 19, was sold to Winchester but never manufactured. A .44-caliber, lever-action, integral-revolving-magazine rifle, it is very similar to No. 19: the lever, magazine, and breechblock are essentially one piece; the cartridges ride bullet down in the magazine; the magazine is loaded from the bottom, the cartridges being inserted upwardly, rim first. The main variation is the arrangement of the firing pin and cartridge-feeding lever. Also, this gun operates as a five-shot repeater, while No. 19 operates either repeater or single shot.

Caliber: .44.
Magazine type: Revolving.
Barrel length and style: 24½″ octagon.
Weight: 6 lbs., 5 oz.
Photo: Inventor's original model. Courtesy Winchester Gun Museum.

21. .22 CALIBER PULL-APART REPEATING RIFLE

History: Patent application on this gun was filed August 3, 1891, and U. S. Patent No. 465,340 was granted December 15, 1891. It was sold to Winchester but never manufactured.

Description: This firearm, of the pull-apart variety, opens ⅞ of an inch, just far enough for the .22-caliber cartridge, which it feeds by carrier means from a tubular magazine. Ignition is by a striker, the rear end of which projects from the rear of the receiver. The two main parts are unlocked from each other by pulling the trigger.

Caliber: .22

Magazine type: Tubular.

Barrel length and style: 21½" octagon.

Weight: 5 lbs., 9 oz.

Photo: Inventor's original model. Courtesy Winchester Gun Museum.

22. .45 CALIBER LEVER ACTION REPEATING RIFLE

History: Patent application on this gun was filed August 3, 1891, and U. S. Patent No. 465,339 was granted December 15, 1891. It was sold to Winchester but never manufactured.

Description: This .45-caliber, lever-action, military-type rifle with detachable box magazine features a locking system with vertically rising locking lugs similar to the Winchester 86 and 94 models but utilizes a striker rather than a hammer. The novelty in this firearm is the magazine, which is positioned for the most part under the barrel forward of the breech face. The cartridges are pulled rearward out of the magazine onto a carrier by the breech bolt during its rearward movement. The carrier then lifts the cartridges into position for loading by the breech bolt during its forward movement.

Caliber: .45.

Magazine type: Detachable box.

Barrel length and style: 27¾" round.

Weight: 9 lbs., 2 oz.

Photo: Inventor's original model. Courtesy Winchester Gun Museum.

23. .30 CALIBER LEVER ACTION REPEATING RIFLE

History: Patent application on this gun was filed March 22, 1892, and U. S. Patent No. 492,459 was granted February 28, 1893. The gun was sold to Winchester but never manufactured.

Description: In this lever-action, box-magazine-type rifle, the locking block is pivoted to the receiver immediately to the rear of the hammer and encloses the hammer on both sides. Initial motion of the lever pivots the locking block downward, allowing the breechblock to slide to the rear. Ejection and loading of the magazine are through the top.

Caliber: .30.

Magazine type: Box.

Barrel length and style: 22¼″ round.

Weight: 8 lbs., 2 oz.

Photo: Inventor's original model. Courtesy Winchester Gun Museum.

24. .30 CALIBER LEVER ACTION REPEATING RIFLE

History: Patent application on this gun was filed June 6, 1892, and U. S. Patent No. 486,272 was granted November 15, 1892. It was sold to Winchester but never manufactured.

Description: This military-type, box-magazine, lever-action rifle features a novel hammer arrangement. The hammer does not pivot as is usual in exposed-hammer, lever-action rifles; it is essentially a striker which works in a recess in the upper tang of the receiver and has an exposed ear for manual cocking. As is the case in most of John M. Browning's lever actions, cocking is automatic with the operation of the lever. Loading is from the top by means of a cartridge clip.

Caliber: .30

Magazine type: Box.

Barrel length and style: 32½″ round.

Weight: 9 lbs., 2 oz.

Photo: Inventor's original model. Courtesy Winchester Gun Museum.

25. .30 CALIBER PULL-APART REPEATING RIFLE

History: Patent application on the gun was filed June 27, 1982, and U. S. Patent No. 486,273 was granted November 15, 1892. It was sold to Winchester but never manufactured.

Description: This pull-apart musket-type rifle with box magazine operates in an unusual manner; the receiver and barrel assembly and the breechblock, trigger guard, and stock assembly separate a predetermined distance, allowing the end of the breechblock to pick up rounds from the magazine. Connecting the two main separating components is a tube, inside of which the hammer works like a piston. The small finger piece at the front of the trigger guard is a sear-block safety. The breechblock locks at the rear on a shoulder in the receiver.

Caliber: .30.

Magazine type: Box.

Barrel length and style: 32¾" round.

Weight: 9 lbs.

Photo: Inventor's original model. Courtesy Winchester Gun Museum.

26. .30 CALIBER PULL-APART REPEATING RIFLE

History and Description: This gun is covered by the same patent as No. 25. The two rifles are alike in their basic principles and pull-apart operation, except in this model a safety lock is incorporated which locks the sear with the hammer cocked and also locks the gun against accidental pull-apart. It was also sold to Winchester but never manufactured.

Caliber: .30.

Magazine type: Box.

Barrel length and style: 22¼" round.

Weight: 8 lbs., 2 oz.

Photo: Inventor's original model. Courtesy Winchester Gun Museum.

27. .44 CALIBER LEVER ACTION REPEATING RIFLE

History: Patent application on this gun was filed September 19, 1892, and U. S. Patent No. 499,005 was granted June 6, 1893. Patent for the locking bolt was filed May 26, 1884 and U. S. Patent No. 308,577 was granted October 14, 1884. It was sold to Winchester but never manufactured.

. *Description:* This .44-caliber, lever-action, tubular-magazine repeating rifle contains the action on which was based the Winchester Model 92. It is identical in principle and differs only in minor detail.

Caliber: .44.

Magazine type: Tubular.

Barrel length and style: 23¼'' octagon.

Weight: 6 lbs., 14 oz.

Photo: Inventor's original model. Courtesy Winchester Gun Museum.

28. .30 CALIBER SWING GUARD REPEATING RIFLE

History: Patent application on this gun was filed October 15, 1892, and U. S. Patent No. 499,007 was granted June 6, 1893. This gun was sold to Winchester but never manufactured.

Description: This novel firearm works like a lever action with the lever mounted backward. The trigger is pivoted to the frame at its rear. The front of the guard is latched to the rear of the box magazine by a spring latch.

Caliber: .30.

Magazine type: Box.

Barrel length and style: 30¾'' round.

Weight: 8 lbs., 10 oz.

Photo: Inventor's original model. Courtesy Winchester Gun Museum.

29. .22 CALIBER RIM FIRE SINGLE SHOT RIFLE

History: Patent application on this gun was filed December 23, 1892, and U. S. Patent No. 511,677 was granted December 26, 1893. It was sold to Winchester but never manufactured.

Description: This .22-caliber, single-shot rifle, like the three models which follow, is of extremely simple design. The breechblock hammer and trigger are one piece and operate up and down at about 20 degrees from the vertical. In loading, the breech bolt is pushed down until the tail of the breechblock extends into the trigger guard and is latched there against the force of the mainspring, which tends to force the breechblock upward into a locked position with the barrel. The firing pin is a hardened pin installed rigidly on the face of the breechblock. A thumbpiece projects from the rear of the breechblock for the purpose of pushing it downward into locked position. The tail of the breechblock acts as a trigger. The gun is ready to fire the moment a fresh cartridge is placed in the chamber. Pulling the trigger allows the breechblock assembly to spring forcibly upward into locked position. The built-in firing pin ignites the cartridge simultaneously. Extraction is manual with two clearance cuts on the rear of the barrel to allow the fingers to pick out the cartridge.

Caliber: .22.

Barrel length and style: 18¼″ round.

Weight: 3 lbs., 3 oz.

Photo: Inventor's original model. Courtesy Winchester Gun Museum.

30. .22 CALIBER RIM FIRE SINGLE SHOT RIFLE

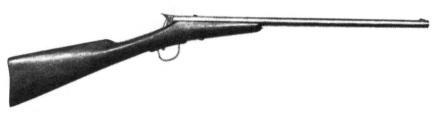

History and Description: This gun, covered by the same patent as

No. 29, was sold to Winchester but never manufactured. The operating principles of this model are identical to those of No. 29, except for a simple push-rod-type extractor and a different spring arrangement on the breechblock.

Caliber: .22.

Barrel length and style: 20¾" round.

Weight: 3½ lbs.

Photo: Inventor's original model. Courtesy Winchester Gun Museum.

31. .22 CALIBER RIM FIRE SINGLE SHOT RIFLE

History and Description: This gun, covered by the same patent as No. 29, was sold to Winchester but never manufactured. It is very similar to No. 29, except for a mainspring similar to that in No. 30, and various minor details.

Caliber: .22.

Barrel length and style: 24½" round.

Weight: 4 lbs., 10 oz.

Photo: Inventor's original model. Courtesy Winchester Gun Museum.

32. .22 CALIBER RIM FIRE SINGLE SHOT RIFLE

History and Description: This gun, covered by the same patent as No. 29, was sold to Winchester but never manufactured. It is very similar to No. 29, except for a replaceable firing pin screwed into the back of the breechblock.

Caliber: .22.

Barrel length and style: 23¾" round.

Weight: 3 lbs., 3 oz.

Photo: Inventor's original model. Courtesy Winchester Gun Museum.

33. .30 CALIBER PUMP ACTION REPEATING RIFLE

History: Patent application on this gun was filed April 29, 1895, and U. S. Patent No. 545,672 was granted September 3, 1895. It was sold to Winchester but never manufactured.

Description: This rifle is a pump-action repeater with box magazine which loads from the bottom. The breechblock is locked into a recess in the left side of the receiver, and is positively held in locking engagement with the receiver by a locking cam on the slide. The breechblock, instead of rising into a vertical position, moves laterally into a locking position with the receiver. Characteristically a Browning design, the gun cannot be fired until completely locked. The action is very smooth and suitable for relatively low-pressure cartridges.

Caliber: .30.

Magazine type: Box.

Barrel length and style: 28″ round.

Weight: 8 lbs., 10 oz.

Photo: Inventor's original model. Courtesy Winchester Gun Museum.

34. .40 CALIBER LEVER ACTION REPEATING RIFLE

History: Patent application on this gun was filed April 29, 1895, and U. S. Patent No. 545,671 was granted September 3, 1895. It was sold to Winchester but never manufactured.

Description: This .40-caliber, lever-action, tubular-magazine rifle features a one-piece locking block which lifts vertically on closing the lever into a recess at the rear of the bolt. The locking block is raised in and out of locking position by a link which also serves as a trigger housing. The arrangement disconnects the trigger from the sear until the action is fully closed.

Caliber: .40.

Magazine type: Tubular.
Barrel length and style: 25½" octagon.
Weight: 7 lbs., 6 oz.
Photo: Inventor's original model. Courtesy Winchester Gun Museum.

35. 236 CALIBER LEVER ACTION REPEATING RIFLE

History: Patent application on this gun was filed May 5, 1897, and U. S. Patent No. 599,595 was granted February 22, 1898. It was sold to Winchester but never manufactured.

Description: This .236-caliber, lever-action rifle with box magazine loads and ejects obliquely out the top of the receiver. The tilting breechblock is guided at the front only, the rear being left free to follow the lever through its downward arc, which allows a short receiver. The actuating lever carries the trigger and hammer as a unit. The piece is cocked on closing the lever. A projection on the rear of the mainspring guide latches the lever in closed position.

Caliber: .236.
Magazine type: Box.
Barrel length and style: 28" round.
Weight: 7 lbs., 9 oz.
Photo: Inventor's original model. Courtesy Winchester Gun Museum.

36. .30 CALIBER LEVER ACTION REPEATING RIFLE

History: Patent application on this gun was filed February 21, 1898, and U. S. Patent No. 619,132 was granted February 7, 1899. It was sold to Winchester but never manufactured.

Description: In this lever-action rifle the sear is part of the bolt assembly acting on a striker and allowing the trigger to pivot as a unit with the lever. The box magazine is attached with a screw to the gun and is not freely detachable. The receiver is cut away to conform to a one-piece stock. The safety on this hammer gun is on the top tang to the rear of the receiver.

Caliber: .30.

Magazine type: Box.

Barrel length and style: 28″ round.

Weight: 7 lbs., 13 oz.

Photo: Inventor's original model. Courtesy Winchester Gun Museum.

37. .30 CALIBER LEVER ACTION REPEATING RIFLE

History and Description: This gun, covered by the same patent as No. 36, was sold to Winchester but never manufactured. It is similar in principles to No. 36, except that it has a two-piece stock and the magazine is inside the receiver. It also differs in that it has a double row of cartridges in a staggered arrangement.

Caliber: .30.

Magazine type: Box.

Barrel length and style: 28″ round.

Weight: 7 lbs., 13 oz.

Photo: Inventor's original model. Courtesy Winchester Gun Museum.

B. SHOTGUNS

38. MODEL 1887 LEVER ACTION REPEATING SHOTGUN (WINCHESTER)

History: This was the first lever-action repeating shotgun made in the United States. It has been called "the first really successful repeating shotgun. Patent application on this gun was filed June 15, 1885, and U. S. Patent No. 336,287 was granted February 16, 1886. Manufacturing and sales rights were sold to the Winchester Repeating Arms Company in 1886, and it appeared in June 1887 as the Winchester Model 1887 Shotgun.

Description: Lever-action, exposed-hammer, tubular-magazine, fixed-barrel repeating shotgun.

Gauge: 10 and 12.

Chamber: 10 gauge, 2⅞" shell. 12 gauge, 2⅝" shell.

Magazine type and capacity: Tubular. Holds four shells in the magazine and one in the chamber.

Model style: Standard only. 10- and 12-gauge riot guns added in 1898.

Barrel length: 10 gauge, 30 and 32". 12 gauge, 30 and 32". 10-gauge riot, 20". 12-gauge riot, 20".

Choke: Standard, full choke. Riot, cylinder bore.

Weight: 10 gauge, about 9 lbs. 12 gauge, about 8 lbs.

Stock: Not checkered, pistol grip, hard-rubber butt plate.

Modifications, date discontinued, and production totals: The Model 1887 was discontinued in 1899. Redesigned to handle the smokeless powder loads it reappeared in 1901, in 10 gauge only, as the Model 1901. This model was discontinued in 1920. 64,855 of the Model 1887 were produced and 13,500 of the Model 1901—for a total of 78,355.

Photo: Inventor's original model. Courtesy John M. Browning Firearms Museum.

39. MODEL 1893 PUMP ACTION REPEATING SHOTGUN (WINCHESTER)

History: Patent application on this gun was filed June 30, 1890, and U. S. Patent No. 441,390 was granted November 25, 1890. Manufacturing and sales rights were sold to the Winchester Repeating Arms Company in 1890; the gun was announced in April 1894 as the Winchester Model 1893. This was the first shotgun with a sliding forearm or pump action manufactured by Winchester.

Description: Pump-action, exposed-hammer, tubular-magazine, fixed-barrel repeating shotgun.

Gauge: 12.

Chamber: 2⅝" shell.

Magazine type and capacity: Tubular. 5 shells.

Model style: Standard only.

Barrel length: 30 and 32″.

Choke: Full choke. Modified choke or cylinder-bore specials available.

Weight: About 7¾ lbs.

Stock: Not checkered, pistol grip, hard-rubber butt plate. Specials available.

Date discontinued and production totals: The Model 1893 was discontinued in 1897 when the Model 1897, a modified takedown version of the Model 1893, was introduced. Total production was 34,050.

Photo: Inventor's original model. Courtesy John M. Browning Firearms Museum.

40. MODEL 1897 PUMP ACTION REPEATING SHOTGUN (WINCHESTER)

History: The Model 1897 is a modified takedown version of the Model 1893, with a stronger frame and side ejection. Introduced in November 1897, it soon became one of the most popular shotguns in America. In addition to its great popularity as a sporting arm, the 97 saw other uses. A short-barrel version was widely used as a riot gun by law-enforcement agencies; also for a time the American Express Company armed its messengers with this firearm. During World War I the 97 was used by American troops as a trench gun, with considerable success.

Description: Pump-action, exposed-hammer, tubular-magazine repeating shotgun. (12 gauge in both fixed barrel and takedown, 16 gauge takedown only.)

Gauge: 12 and 16.

Chamber: 12 gauge, 2¾″ shell. 16 gauge, 2⅝″ shell (changed to 2¾″shell in 1931).

Magazine type and capacity: Tubular. 5 shells.

Model style: Standard (or field) gun, trap gun, pigeon, brush gun, riot gun, tournament, trench gun, standard trap, special trap.

Barrel length: 12 gauge, 26, 28, 30, and 32″. 16 gauge, 26 and 28″ (30″ added 1930). 12-gauge standard, 30″. 16-gauge standard, 22″. 12-gauge riot, 20″. 12-gauge trench, 20″. Barrel lengths on other models vary depending on year of manufacture.

Choke: Full choke, modified choke, cylinder bore. Intermediate chokes added 1931; Winchester Skeet chokes added 1940.

Weight: Varying, from 7 lbs., 2 oz. to 7 lbs., 14 oz.

Stock: Not checkered, pistol grip, hard-rubber or steel butt plate. Checkered stocks on special grades.

Modifications and dates discontinued: The standard, trap, pigeon, and brush guns were introduced in 1897, followed by the riot gun, 1898, the tournament, 1910, and the trench gun, 1920, (but previously manufactured for U. S. Army use in World War I). The trap was discontinued in 1931 and succeeded by the special trap, which was discontinued in 1939. The pigeon was discontinued in 1939, the brush gun in 1931, the riot gun in 1935, the trench gun in 1935. The tournament was discontinued in 1931 and succeeded by the standard trap, which was discontinued in 1939. The standard Model 1897 was discontinued in 1957.

Production totals: 1,240,700.

Photo: John M. Browning's personal trap gun. Courtesy John M. Browning Firearms Museum.

41. MODEL 520 PUMP ACTION SHOTGUN (STEVENS)

History: Patent application on this gun was filed July 10, 1903, and U. S. Patent No. 781,765 was granted February 7, 1905. Manufacturing and sales rights were acquired by the Stevens Arms Company in 1903 and the gun was placed on the market in early 1904 as the Stevens Model 520. A streamlined version, the Model 620, was introduced in 1927.

Description: Pump-action, concealed-hammer, solid-breech, tubular-magazine, takedown repeating shotgun.

The following specifications refer to the Model 520:

Gauge: 12.

Chamber: 2¾" shell.

Magazine type and capacity: Tubular. 5 shells.

Model style: Field, trap and deluxe.

Barrel length: 26, 28, 30, and 32".

Choke: Full choke, modified choke, and cylinder bore.

Weight: 7¾ lbs.

Stock: Field and deluxe, checkered, semi-pistol grip, rubber butt plate. Trap, checkered, straight grip, rubber butt plate.

The following specifications refer to the Model 620:

Gauge: 12, 16, and 20.

Chamber: 12 gauge, 2¾" shell. 16 gauge, 2⁹⁄₁₆" shell and 2¾" shell. 20 gauge, 2¾" shell.

Magazine type and capacity: Tubular. 5 shells.

Model style: Field and riot.

Barrel length: 12 gauge, 20, 26, 28, 30, and 32". 16 gauge, 26 and 28". 20 gauge, 26 and 28".

Choke: Full choke, modified choke, and cylinder bore.

Weight: 12 gauge, 7¾ lbs. 16 gauge, 7¼ lbs. 20 gauge, 6 lbs.

Stock: Checkered, pistol grip, corrugated butt plate.

Modifications, dates discontinued, and production totals: The streamlined Model 620 was designed to eliminate the rather abrupt angle at the rear of the receiver on the Model 520. The Model 520 was discontinued in 1932 and the Model 620 in 1955. No production figures are available.

Photo: Production model Stevens 520. Courtesy John M. Browning Firearms Museum.

42. MODEL 17 PUMP ACTION SHOTGUN (REMINGTON)

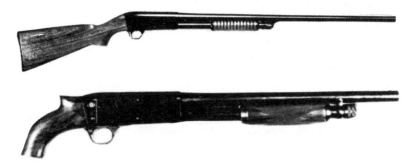

History: Patent on this gun was filed November 26, 1913, and U. S. Patent No. 1,143,170 was granted June 15, 1915. The Remington Arms Company was granted manufacturing and sales rights to this model, introducing it in 1921 as the Remington Model 17. It was John M. Browning's last repeater-type shotgun.

Description: Pump-action, concealed-hammer, underloading, tubular-magazine, takedown shotgun.

Gauge: 20.

Chamber: 2½″ and 2¾″ shells.

Magazine type and capacity: Tubular. 5 shells.

Model style: Standard, 5 grades, riot and police.

Barrel length: 26, 28, 30, and 32″. Riot, 20″. Police, 18½″.

Choke: Full choke.

Weight: Standard and riot, about 5¼″ lbs.

Stock: Standard and riot, checkered, straight grip, hard-rubber butt plate. Police, pistol grip only, no stock.

Modifications, date discontinued, and production totals: All production was discontinued in 1933. Since patent expiration, the design has been used with marked success by various manufacturers in all gauges. The Ithaca Model 37 Pump, still in production, is of the same basic design except that it is 12 gauge. No production figures are available.

Photos: Above, production model Remington Model 17. Below, Remington Police Model 17. Courtesy John M. Browning Firearms Museum and Remington Arms Company.

43. 44. 45. AUTOMATIC SHOTGUNS (FABRIQUE NATIONALE, BROWNING, REMINGTON AND OTHERS)

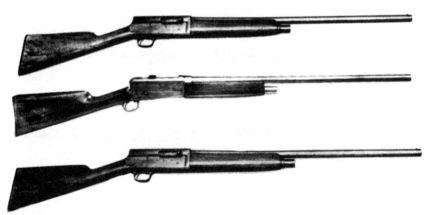

History: John M. Browning took out four patents on his revolutionary autoloading shotgun: U. S. Patent No. 659,507, filed February 8, 1900, was granted October 9, 1900; U. S. Patent No. 689,283, filed March 18, 1901, was granted December 17, 1901; U. S. Patent No. 710,094, filed January 11, 1902, was granted September 30, 1902; and U. S. Patent No. 812,326, filed June 30, 1904, was granted February 13 1906. The automatic shotgun was first manufactured by Fabrique

Nationale in 1903. In 1905 the Remington Arms Company was licensed to manufacture and sell the gun, bringing it out as the Remington Model 11 Automatic Shotgun. The Browning Arms Company model is known as the Browning Automatic-5.

(For the story of the development of this shotgun and John M. Browning's break with Winchester, see Part Three, Chapter 11 of the text. For the story of the manufacture and reception of the gun, see Part Three, Chapter 15.)

Of the three original models which appear in the photographs above, No. 43 is Browning's first version, a link-action model; No. 44 is the second version, closely resembling the first model, except the breech bolt has no operating handle, the device for opening the breech positioned on the underside of the stock; and No. 45 is the final prototype and is essentially the gun as it was first produced.

Description: Long-recoil-operated, takedown, automatic shotgun. The Automatic utilizes the forces generated by firing the cartridge to eject the empty case, reload, and cock the gun automatically. Through a simple but highly effective adjustable friction break and shock-absorber, Browning was able to make the gun adaptable to whatever loads were used.

The following specifications refer to the Browning Automatic-5:

Gauge: 12, 16, 20, and 3″ Magnum 12.

Chamber: All 2¾″ factory loads except in the 3″ Magnum 12, which is chambered for 3″ Magnum shells.

Magazine type and capacity: 5 shots except in 3″ Magnum, which has a 5-shot capacity with Folding Crimp 3″ shells and 4-shot capacity with Rolled Crimp 3″ shells.

Model style: Lightweight 12 gauge; Standard 12 gauge; 3″ Magnum 12 gauge; Sweet 16 gauge; Standard 16 gauge; Standard 12 gauge; Lightweight 20 gauge.

Barrel length: Lightweight 12 gauge, 26, 28, 30″. Standard 12 gauge, 26, 28, 30, 32″. 3″ Magnum 12 gauge, 28, 32″. Sweet 16 gauge, 26, 28″. Standard 16 gauge, 26, 28, 30″. Lightweight 20 gauge, 26, 28″.

Choke: All possible choke borings.

Weight: Lightweight 12 gauge, 7 lbs., 3 oz. to 7 lbs., 11oz. Standard 12 gauge, 7 lbs., 13 oz. to 8 lbs., 5 oz. 3″ Magnum 12 gauge, 8½ lbs. to 9 lbs. Sweet 16 gauge, 6 lbs., 9 oz. to 7 lbs., 2 oz. Standard 16 gauge, 7 lbs., 3 oz. to 7 lbs., 9 oz. Lightweight 20 gauge, 6¼ lbs. to 6 lbs., 7 oz.

Stock: Standard, hand checkered, French walnut, semi-pistol grip. Deluxe engraved specials available.

Modifications, dates discontinued, and production totals: The original F. N. Browning Automatic Shotgun was first offered in 12 gauge only; with 28" barrel, full choke, modified choke, or cylinder bore; and chambered for any cartridge up to 2¾". Weight was about 7¾ lbs., the stock English walnut with straight grip. It was available in three models, all takedown—regular, trap and messenger gun (20" barrel). While these models were of five-shot capacity, two-shot models were also available.

The Remington model was available in 12, 16, and 20 gauge. It was practically identical to the Browning Automatic-5, many of the parts being interchangeable. It differed in the following details:

The butt plate was of hard rubber. The stock had a full pistol grip. The safety was of the cross-bolt style but with no finger piece. There was no magazine cut-off. The forearm had a reinforcing dowel which the Automatic-5 does not have. The carrier was of the old style, without the quick-loading feature. The front trigger-plate screw was a pin, and the rear trigger-plate screw had no locking screw. On some of the models, the carrier-latch screw and cartridge-stop screw were pins with a transverse locking screw. There was a fiber cushion in the rear of the receiver to stop the breechblock and firing pin. On the early models, the firing pin was identical to the Automatic-5; on the later models the firing pin was changed to a straight cylinder which would not lock when the action was open. The Model 11 had no left-hand extractor. There were other very minor differences in detail, depending on the year of manufacture.

Two variations were offered in 1921—a Police Special, in 12 gauge, and a short-barrel Riot Gun, in all three gauges. The Model Sportsman, a 3-shot version of the Model 11, with semi-beavertail fore end, was introduced in 1931. All models of the Model 11 and the Model Sportsman were discontinued in 1948. The Remington Model 11-48 Autoloader was introduced in 1949 and is still in production. Except for changes designed to streamline the gun and make it easier to manufacture, it still has the same basic operation as its predecessor.

The Browning Automatic-5 is still in production and is offered in seventy-two different specifications. Combined production figures on this gun cannot even be estimated. It has been copied by manufacturers in many countries and even today is being produced with no variance in basic design by Remington, Savage, Franchi, Breda and others. F.N. alone had produced 1,377,785 of these guns by the end of 1961.

Photos: Inventor's original models. Courtesy John M. Browning Firearms Museum.

46. SUPERPOSED SHOTGUN (FABRIQUE NATIONALE AND BROWNING)

History: The Superposed Shotgun was John M. Browning's last invention. Patent applications on this "over-under" gun were filed October 15, 1923 and September 29, 1924, and U. S. Patents Nos. 1,578,638-39 were granted March 30, 1926. First produced by Fabrique Nationale in 1930, it appeared in the Browning Arms Company line in 1931.

Description: The Superposed is a two-barrel (over-under), standing-breech, pivoting-action, takedown repeating shotgun. The barrels are mounted one above the other, rather than side by side, to permit the improved accuracy of a single sighting plane.

The following specifications refer to currently produced models:

Gauge: 12, 20, 28, and .410.

Chamber: All 12-gauge models accept shells up to and including 2¾ in all factory loads. The Magnum 12 accepts shells up to and including the 12 gauge 3″ Magnum. All current 20-gauge models accept shells up to and including 20-gauge 3″ Magnum. The 28-gauge models have 2¾″ chambers. The .410 gauge accepts both 2½″ and 3″ shells.

Magazine type and capacity: Shells are placed directly in the two chambers. Automatic ejectors flip out the spent shells when the gun is opened. Unfired shells are retained in the chambers and merely elevated for easy removal by hand, if desired.

Model style: Standard, Magnum, Lightning, Lightning Trap, and Broadway Trap 12 gauge; Standard and Lightning 20 gauge; Standard 28 gauge; Standard .410 gauge.

Barrel length: Standard 12 gauge, 26½″ and 28″. Magnum 12 gauge, 30″. Lightning 12 gauge, 26½″ and 28″. Lightning Trap 12 gauge, 30″. Broadway Trap 12 gauge, 32″. Standard 20 gauge, 26½″ and 28″. Lightning 20 gauge, 26½″ and 28″. Standard 28 gauge, 26½″ and 28″. Standard .410 gauge, 26½″ and 28″. Extra barrel sets available.

Choke: All possible choke borings.

Weight: Standard 12 gauge, 7½ to 7¾ lbs. Magnum 12 gauge, 8 lbs., 2 oz. Lightning 12 gauge, 7 to 7¾ lbs. Lightning Trap 12 gauge, 7¾ lbs. Broadway Trap 12 gauge, 8 lbs. Standard 20 gauge, 6½ to 6¾ lbs.

Lightning 20 gauge, 6 to 6¼ lbs. Standard 28 gauge, 6 lbs., 3 oz. to 6 lbs., 6 oz. Standard .410 gauge, 6 lbs., 5 oz. to 6 lbs., 9 oz.

Stock: Hand-checkered, hand-rubbed walnut, semi-pistol grip. Deluxe engraved specials available.

Modifications: The first Superposed models had double triggers. Later John M. Browning's son, Val A. Browning, designed twin single triggers for the gun, and ultimately the single selective trigger. The twin single triggers differed from the double triggers in that after selecting and shooting one round in one barrel, a second pull on the same trigger would fire the remaining barrel, thus eliminating the necessity of moving the finger from one trigger to the other. In the final version, the single selective trigger fires both barrels, either barrel first, by moving a thumb selector. The Superposed was initially provided only in 12 gauge in this country. Val. A. Browning later designed the 20 gauge.

Production totals: The Browning Superposed is still in production and is currently available in a total of 269 specifications. Total production by Fabrique Nationale was 112,913 units as of the end of 1961.

Photo: No. 1 production model. Courtesy John M. Browning Firearms Museum.

John M. Browning sold thirteen shotguns to the Winchester Repeating Arms Company. Of these only three were manufactured (Nos. 38, 39 and 40). The other ten (Nos. 47-56) follow in the order of their patent filing dates.

One shotgun John M. Browning submitted to Winchester, a 12-gauge, pump-action shotgun, was neither patented nor manufactured. It is assumed that this gun was not patented because of previously existing patents and consequently was not purchased by Winchester, although the model remains in the Winchester Gun Museum. It is therefore not included in the totals of Browning-designed guns sold to Winchester or in the totals of original firearms invented by John M. Browning.

47. 12 GAUGE PUMP ACTION SHOTGUN

History: This 12-gauge, pump-action shotgun was sold to Winchester but never manufactured. It is apparently the same gun described in U. S. Patent No. 345,882, which was filed May 3, 1886 and granted July 20, 1886, though the model differs somewhat from the patent.

Description: This gun is locked by a turning breechblock which is actuated by a cam slot in the slide. The slot in the receiver to the rear of the ejection opening is the passage or clearance for the large locking lug on the bolt. The long, rail-type locking lug acts as a guide for the cylindrical breechblock as it reciprocates. A standard-type carrier elevates the cartridges from the tubular magazine into loading position. On the front of the carrier, however, is a simple dog which serves as a cartridge stop. The main difference between the patent and this model is the incorporation of a safety sear device which prevents the hammer from falling unless the bolt is locked fully forward.

Gauge: 12.

Magazine type: Tubular.

Barrel length: 30″.

Weight: 6 lbs., 7 oz.

Photo: Inventor's original model. Courtesy Winchester Gun Museum.

48. 12 GAUGE PUMP ACTION SHOTGUN

History and Description: This 12-gauge pump-action shotgun with tubular magazine was sold to Winchester but never manufactured. It is similar to the firearm described in U. S. Patent No. 345,882 and identical in function to No. 47.

Gauge: 12.

Magazine type: Tubular.

Barrel length: 30″.

Weight: 6 lbs., 13 oz.

Photo: Inventor's original model. Courtesy Winchester Gun Museum.

49. 10 GAUGE PUMP ACTION SHOTGUN

History: Patent application on this gun was filed September 6, 1886, and U. S. Patent No. 356,271 was granted January 18, 1887. It was sold to Winchester but never manufactured.

Description: The model, chambered for the 10-gauge shotgun cartridge, has a tilting breechblock which is pivotally mounted at the rear to the receiver. The front of the breechblock tilts downward far enough so the breechblock itself is used as a carrier, picking the cartridges up from the tubular magazine on a shaped tray on top of the breechblock. The breechblock pauses in its upward movement long enough for the extracting slide, which reciprocates longitudinally, to pick the cartridge off the top of the breechblock and force it into the chamber. The breechblock then tilts upward, ready for firing.

Gauge: 10.

Magazine type: Tubular.

Barrel length: 30″.

Weight: 8 lbs., 11 oz.

Photo: Inventor's original model. Courtesy Winchester Gun Museum.

50. 10 GAUGE PUMP ACTION SHOTGUN

History and Description: This 10-gauge, pump-action shotgun, covered by the same patent as No. 49, was sold to Winchester but never manufactured. It is very similar to No. 49, differing only in minor structural details.

Gauge: 10.

Magazine type: Tubular.

Barrel length: 30¼″.

Weight: 6 lbs., 15 oz.

Photo: Inventor's original model. Courtesy Winchester Gun Museum.

51. 10 GAUGE LEVER ACTION SHOTGUN

History: Patent application on this gun was filed November 21, 1887, and U. S. Patent No. 376,576 was granted January 17, 1888. It was sold to Winchester but never manufactured.

Description: This is a 10-gauge, repeating, lever-action shotgun with tubular magazine and pistol grip. The lock mechanism is arranged entirely within the forward position of the finger lever. The finger lever carrying the entire lock mechanism is hung to the receiver by a link on the left-hand side, the forward end of the link being hung upon a pivot in the finger lever. The rear of the link is hung upon a pivot in the frame. The upper portion of the finger lever is guided by the receiver.

Gauge: 10.

Magazine type: Tubular.

Barrel length: 32".

Weight: 9½ lbs.

Photo: Inventor's original model. Courtesy Winchester Gun Museum.

52. 12 GAUGE LEVER ACTION SHOTGUN

History: This gun, covered by the same patent as No. 51, was sold to Winchester but never manufactured.

Description: This 12-gauge, lever-action shotgun with tubular magazine has a one-piece breechblock, trigger guard, and lever combined. The breechblock works along its track on the side of the receiver by means of a round pin visible at the front of the breechblock. In working the lever, the greater part of the insides of the gun come out of the receiver with the lever. This, and the long lever throw, were two disadvantages of this extremely simple, rugged gun.

Gauge: 12.

Magazine type: Tubular.

Barrel length: 29½".

Weight: 7 lbs., 13 oz.

Photo: Inventor's original model. Courtesy Winchester Gun Museum.

53. 12 GAUGE PULL-APART SHOTGUN

History: Patent application on this gun was filed March 7, 1892, and U. S. Patent No. 487,659 was granted December 6, 1892. It was sold to Winchester but never manufactured.

Description: Another of John M. Browning's pull-apart firearms, only it handles the 12-gauge cartridge. A latch is positioned at the front of the trigger guard to prevent accidental pull-apart. The rear unit, which includes the trigger guard, has a lug projecting forward into the top of the receiver. The lug works on the rear of the breech bolt in such a way as to unlock it from the back of the frame. In this model the hammer and mainspring work inside a long tube attached to the receiver. The tube acts as a guide to keep the two essential parts—the stock and trigger assembly and the barrel and receiver assembly—in alignment when the gun is pulled apart.

Gauge: 12.

Magazine type: Tubular.

Barrel length: 32".

Weight: 8½ lbs.

Photo: Inventor's original model. Courtesy Winchester Gun Museum.

54. 12 GAUGE PUMP ACTION SHOTGUN

History: Patent application on this gun was filed November 19, 1894, and U. S. Patent No. 552,864 was granted January 7, 1896. It was sold to Winchester but never manufactured.

Description: This 12-gauge, pump-action shotgun with tubular magazine has a pivoting breechblock which locks at the rear to the side of the receiver. The slide which manipulates the breechblock is mounted on the opposite side of the receiver in such a way as to completely close the ejection opening when the gun is closed. In common with model No. 56, the magazine is pivoted at its front end to the barrel and attached to the receiver with a latching system. The rear end of the magazine can pivot downward free from the receiver, allowing the tube and handle to be used as a wrench for unscrewing the barrel from the receiver.

Gauge: 12.

Magazine type: Tubular.

Barrel length: 29½".

Weight: 7¾ lbs.

Photo: Inventor's original model. Courtesy Winchester Gun Museum.

55. 12 GAUGE PUMP ACTION SHOTGUN

History: Patent application on this gun was filed April 29, 1895, and U. S. Patent No. 550,778 was granted December 3, 1895. It was sold to Winchester but never manufactured.

Description: The locking system on the 12-gauge, pump-action shotgun is unusual but exceptionally strong. Instead of rotating or pivoting or being locked by a separate member, the whole breechblock raises vertically in and out of locking engagement with a series of locking lugs spaced along the top of the receiver. Both ends of the breechblock are raised by two links pivoted fore and aft on the slide. The extractor is pivoted to the breechblock to allow for its vertical movement.

Gauge: 12.

Magazine type: Tubular.

Barrel length: 30".

Weight: 7¼ lbs.

Photo: Inventor's original model. Courtesy Winchester Gun Museum.

56. 12 GAUGE PUMP ACTION SHOTGUN

History: Patent application on this gun was filed March 16, 1896, and U. S. Patent No. 577,281 was granted February 16, 1897. It was sold to Winchester but never manufactured.

Description: This 12-gauge, pump-action shotgun incorporates many of the features which were to later appear in John M. Browning's automatic shotguns and in many of the modern day shotgun designs. The locking block, assembled to and pivoting from the breechblock, is locked to the upper wall of the receiver. The hammer, sear, trigger, and carrier are maintained similarly to most modern shotguns as an assembly on a one-piece trigger guard, which in turn is fastened inside the opening at the bottom of the receiver. The double extractor system is similar to that later used in the Browning Automatic-5. The gun also has a barrel takedown using interrupted threads with a takeup ring very similar to that used in the Browning .22 Semi-Automatic rifle. The magazine tube pivots to the barrel. When the rear of the magazine is disengaged from the receiver, the tube swings down and is used as a handle to thread the barrel in and out of the receiver.

Gauge: 12.

Magazine type: Tubular.

Barrel length: 30″.

Weight: 7 lbs. 14 oz.

Photo: Inventor's original model. Courtesy Winchester Gun Museum.

C. AUTOMATIC MACHINE GUNS

(For the story of John M. Browning's discovery of the principle of gas operation, his initial experiments in testing his theory of a fully automatic gas-operated gun, and a summary of his inventive course through gas operation to his discovery of the recoil-operating principle and his first automatic pistols, see Part Three, Chapter 12 of the text.)

57. EARLY GAS-OPERATED FIREARMS
FIRST EXPERIMENTAL MODELS

History and Description: In the fall of 1889, John M. Browning made several experimental models which served as preliminary steps in his development of a gas-operated, fully automatic gun, one which would fire continuously as long as the trigger was depressed and a supply of cartridges fed through the action. The first of these was a crude affair, made in a single day. Using a .44-caliber Winchester Model 73, Browning hung a hinge on the muzzle end of the barrel and connected his gas flapper to the modified lever of the lever action gun. Though hastily constructed, the gun worked. There followed several other experimental models. None of these guns survives intact; it is probable that they were disassembled during the experiments; the remains of one model consist of the receiver and barrel of a lever-action gun, with a very crude, hand-forged flapper attached to the muzzle. Patent application was filed January 6, 1890, and U. S. Patent No. 417,782 was granted March 29, 1892. This was Browning's first patent embodying the gas-operation principle. Browning noted in the application, "This invention is applicable to machine-guns and also to firearms." The final model, shown in the patent drawings, and illustrated in the text, had a concave cap with a hole in the center which was fitted directly over the muzzle. A rod attached this cap to a spring-loaded operating lever attached to the action. When the bullet passed through the hole in the cap, the expanding gases following the explosion forced the cap forward. This in turn pulled the operating lever forward. Then the spring would return the lever rearward to its locked position and the cap to the front of the muzzle. The result was a mechanism successfully performing the identical functions of a hand-operated repeater automatically. It is referred to in the patent as an "Automatic Magazine-Gun." It fired .44/40 black powder cartridges at the rate of 960 shots per minute and weighed about 8 lbs.

LATER GAS-OPERATED GUNS

History and Description: Patent applications on two new gas-operated automatic guns were filed August 3, 1891 and granted March 29, 1892. Though both guns tapped the energy of the expanding gases at the muzzle, they did so in completely different ways. The gun covered in U. S. Patent No. 471,783 was Browning's first automatic machine gun and is discussed in No. 58, which follows. The gun covered in U. S. Patent No. 471,784 was probably first completed, however, as it is the clumsier of the two systems. On this particular model Browning used a small turbine at the muzzle, rather than a single flapper. The turbine allowed the bullet to pass through freely but tapped the energy of the expanding gases which followed, and through a system of gears operated the mechanism. This model does not survive.

58. FIRST BROWNING MACHINE GUN AND SUBSEQUENT MODELS

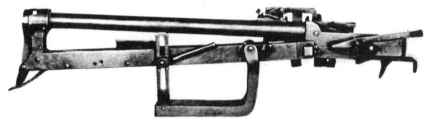

FIRST BROWNING GAS-OPERATED MACHINE GUN

History: This gun was invented in 1890-91. Patent application was filed on August 3, 1891 and U. S. Patent No. 471,783 was granted March 29, 1892. (For the story of the remarkable performance of this model before officials of Colt's Patent Fire Arms Manufacturing Company and the subsequent unofficial military tests, see Part Three, Chapters 12 and of the text.)

Description: Browning placed a bracket on the muzzle end of the barrel of this model. On it a lever was hung on a pivot, so that one end of the lever formed a cap over the front of the muzzle. This cap contained an aperture corresponding to the bore of the barrel, to allow passage of the bullet. The muzzle bracket acted as a spacer to keep the lever cap a short distance forward of the muzzle, thereby forming a small enclosed gas chamber between the end of the barrel and the cap. When a shot was fired, the expanding gases following the bullet pushed the cap forward. The cap lever was in turn connected to the action by a series of rods and levers. Thus, the forward action of the muzzle cap was the initial impetus which carried through the mechanism, permitting extraction, ejection, feeding, loading and firing of the cartridges automatically.

Caliber: .45/70.

Rate of fire: 600 rounds per minute.

Type of feed: Fabric belt.

Method of cooling: None.

Barrel length: 22½".

Weight: 40 lbs. with mount.

Photo: Inventor's original model. Courtesy John M. Browning Firearms Museum.

GAS-OPERATED BREECH-LOADING GUN

History and Description: Patent application on this gun was filed July 11, 1892, and U. S. Patent No. 502,549 was granted August 1,

1893. Another new idea appeared in this model: the energy was not taken from the muzzle; instead a hole was drilled through the barrel, tapping the high-pressure gases directly behind the bullet before the bullet had left the barrel. On this particular model, holes were drilled on both sides of the barrel. A pair of flappers was positioned on each side of the barrel and attached to the operating rod on the bottom of the barrel. The exploding gas caused both flappers to pivot rearward. This motion was transferred to the operating rod and subsequently to the operating mechanism. One of the reasons for this arrangement might have been to equalize the disturbance at the muzzle which occurred when there was only a single flapper. However, as soon as the holes were drilled through the barrel, Browning became aware of many possibilities for simpler mechanisms. This model does not survive.

EXPERIMENTAL GAS-OPERATED FIREARM

History: Chronologically, the above-described Breech-Loading Gun was followed by Browning's first manufactured machine gun, the Colt Model 1895. This gun in turn followed. However, as it was clearly an experimental model, designed solely to test the inventor's ideas, it is described here with Browning's other unmanufactured models. Patent application on this gun was filed December 8, 1894, and U. S. Patent No. 544,661 was granted August 20, 1895.

Description: Because of its hand-forged parts and unfinished appearance, this experimental model is often assumed to be a very early Browning gas-operated gun. Browning's main purpose in designing it, however, was to effect an improvement in the gas port, which, in all his prior machine guns (including the Colt Model 1895) had undergone little change. As stated in the patent: "The objects of the invention being to avoid the fouling and clogging of the mechanism by the gases and to prevent the escape of the gases until after the lever shall have commenced its opening movement and received its initial force, and to prevent the lateral spread of the gases and to generally improve and simplify the construction of the gas operated mechanism."

Several ideas tested in this model appear in later Browning mechanisms. One very important idea is illustrated in the patent drawings as an alternate method of constructing the gas port. This was putting an elbow on the gas vent so the force of the gases would be applied along the axis of the barrel, so a piston could be used to operate the mechanism rather than a swinging arm. The possibilities of this type of gas port were therefore conceived at this time but not yet used.

Caliber: .44.

Rate of fire: About 12 shots per second.

Type of feed: Box magazine, clipped in the top of the receiver. The original magazine has been lost but its capacity is believed to have been 20.

Method of cooling: None.

Barrel length:

Weight: 7¼ lbs.

Photo: Inventor's original model. Courtesy John M. Browning Firearms Museum.

59. MODEL 1895 AUTOMATIC MACHINE GUN (COLT)

History: The first patent application on this gun was filed November 7, 1892, and U. S. Patent No. 544,657 was granted August 20, 1895. Various modifications of the gun were covered by the following U. S. Patents: No. 544,658, filed March 15, 1893, granted August 20, 1895; No. 544,659, filed June 17, 1893, granted August 20, 1895; No. 544,660, filed September 11, 1893, granted August 20, 1895; and No. 543,567, filed April 16, 1895, granted July 30, 1895. Arrangements were made with Colt's Patent Fire Arms Manufacturing Company in 1895 for its manufacture the same year. In January 1896, the Model 95 was tested by the Navy in competitive trials. Its successful performance resulted in the Navy's placing an order for fifty of these guns with Colt. This was the first purchase of a fully automatic weapon by the United States Government. (For additional details, see Part Three, Chapter 13 of the text.) These guns, in the hands of U. S. Marines, saved the foreign legations in Peking during the Boxer Rebellion. After their use in the Spanish-American War the Model 95 acquired a nickname—the

"Browning Peacemaker." At the outbreak of World War I, the Model 95 comprised a large portion of the United States machine gun arsenal. Though the gun was outdated, a number were manufactured for military use in the interim before the Model 1917 Browning Heavy Water-Cooled Machine Gun, Caliber .30, went into production. This gun was then relegated to training use.

Description: Gas-operated automatic machine gun. This machine gun employed a hole drilled through the barrel near the muzzle, which worked on a piston that worked the mechanism of the gun through a swinging lever. When the mechanism was activated, it fed, fired, extracted, and ejected the cartridges automatically. The firing cycle was continuous as long as the trigger was depressed and ammunition supplied. The unusual movement of the piston, which swung in a half arc beneath the barrel, gave the gun an additional nickname—"The Potato Digger."

Caliber: .30/40 Krag, 6 mm. Lee.

Rate of fire: 400 rounds per minute.

Type of feed: Fabric belt.

Method of cooling: Air.

Barrel length: 21½". (A very heavy barrel was used to prevent rapid heating.)

Weight: 40 lbs.

Date discontinued and production totals: Discontinued 1917. Total production figures are not available. Some 1500 were produced during World War I.

Photo: Inventor's original model. Courtesy John M. Browning Firearms Museum.

60. MODEL 1917 .30 CALIBER MACHINE GUN
(COLT, REMINGTON, WESTINGHOUSE AND OTHERS)

History: In 1900 John M. Browning invented a machine gun to replace the outdated Model 95. Patent application was filed June 19, 1900, and U. S. Patent No. 678,934 was granted July 23, 1901. Although sometimes referred to as the Browning Model 1901, this gun was never manufactured, since the government lacked interest in military weapons at the time. Its basic operating features, however, are the same as those of all Browning machine guns since produced.

Browning continued working on the gun intermittently over the years, changing it to eject from the bottom rather than the right side, and increasing the rate of fire. Patent application covering these im-

provements was filed October 3, 1916, and U. S. Patent No. 1,293,021
was granted February 4, 1919. This model was first publicly demonstrated at Congress Heights, Washington, D.C., on February 27, 1917.
In May 1917, official tests were held at Springfield Firearms Museum.
(For the story of the gun's remarkable performance, see Part Three,
Chapter 14 of the text.) Following the tests, a board appointed by the
Secretary of War recommended the immediate adoption of the Browning .30 Caliber Heavy Machine Gun. The first combat use of the Model
1917 was by the 79th Division in France on September 26, 1918. This
model was water cooled, however Browning later made an air-cooled
model of the gun. The aircooled weapon was the first in this country to
be successfully affixed to pursuit planes so the pilot could look along his
sights and aim the gun by maneuvering his ship. To accomplish this the
firing mechanism of the gun was synchronized with the motor of the
plane so the stream of bullets passed through the revolving propeller
without hitting the blades.

Other versions of this gun made history in World War II and the
Korean War. The gun still occupies a prominent place in the military

arsenal of the United States. (For a summary of the development and military use of this gun, see Part Three, Chapter 14 of the text.)

The following specifications refer to the Model 1917:

Description: Short-recoil-operated, water-cooled, fully automatic machine gun. In the short-recoil system, the barrel and breechblock are locked together when the gun is fired and are allowed to recoil together for a short distance to permit the bullet to clear the barrel and the gas pressure to diminish. They are then unlocked, and the breechblock alone continues to recoil, during which time energy is stored in the springs, which return all parts to their normal or battery positions. During the recoil of the breechblock, the fired case is extracted from the barrel, ejected downward, and a fresh cartridge is fed into the chamber and fired when the breechblock has returned to battery. The firing cycle is continuous as long as the trigger is depressed and a supply of ammunition available.

Caliber: .30/06.

Rate of fire: 600 rounds per minute.

Type of feed: Link belt.

Method of cooling: Water.

Barrel length: 20″. Barrel is enclosed within a jacket, which is water filled to prevent overheating.

Weight: 37 lbs. with water jacket filled.

Modifications: Many modified versions of this gun have appeared since its invention. Browning's air-cooled model previously mentioned weighed only 22 lbs. and had an increased rate of fire of approximately 700 rounds per minute. The air-cooled Browning .30 in various models was one of America's most important military weapons in World War II. Aircraft models were stepped up to as high as 1300 rounds per minute.

Production totals: The U. S. Government contracted with three companies for World War I production of the Model 1917. Between its official adoption in 1917 and the Armistice, the following year, nearly 43,000 were produced: Westinghouse accounted for 30,150, Remington 12,000, and Colt 600. Over a million units of the World War II Browning .30M2 were manufactured. Most of the major countries now have similar weapons. Total production can only be estimated as well into the millions.

Photo: Inventor's original model. Courtesy John M. Browning Firearms Museum.

61. .50 CALIBER BROWNING WATER-COOLED MACHINE GUN (COLT AND OTHERS)

History: To meet the increased threat of armored combat vehicles, General John Pershing, Commander of the American Expeditionary Forces, requested a machine-gun cartridge heavier and more powerful than the .30 caliber. A .50-caliber cartridge was finally developed, which gave an 800-grain bullet a muzzle velocity of 2750 feet per second. To shoot this powerful load Browning developed the Browning .50 Caliber Water-Cooled Machine Gun. He began work in about July 1917; the gun was first test-fired in Colt's meadow in Hartford, Connecticut, a little over a year later. Patent application on the gun was filed July 31, 1923, and U. S. Patent No. 1,628,226 was granted May 10, 1927. Developed too late to see use in World War I, the Browning .50-caliber machine gun played a prominent role in World War II and the Korean War. (For a summary of the development and military use of this gun see Part Three, Chapters 13 and 14 of the text.)

Description: Short-recoil-operated, water-cooled, fully automatic machine gun. This gun has the same basic operating features as the .30 caliber, but through the use of a unique oil buffer the necessary strengthening of the gun is accomplished without a proportional increase in weight. The oil buffer absorbs the excess energy of recoil, thereby effectively reducing undue strain on the parts. In addition, the buffer provides a means of controlling the rate of fire. Browning also incorporated double spade grips on the .50 caliber, instead of the pistol grip used on the smaller .30 caliber.

The following specifications refer to the original .50-caliber proto-type model:

Caliber: .50.

Rate of fire: 750-850 rounds per minute.

Type of feed: Link belt.

Method of cooling: Water.

Barrel length: 39″. Barrel is encased in a water jacket.

Weight: 82 lbs. with water jacket filled.

Modifications: To date no less than sixty-six known models of the Browning recoil-operated machine gun have been manufactured by the U.S. and various Allied countries. The majority of these have been .50 caliber. Other highly effective models which followed the original proto-type were the Water-Cooled Infantry, the Water-Cooled Anti-Aircraft Single and Twin Mount, and the Air-Cooled Tank Gun. The latest aircraft model, the .50M3, was stepped up to a cyclic rate of fire of 1200 rounds per minute.

Production totals: During World War II the .50M2 was produced by the following companies: Colt's Patent Fire Arms Manufacturing Company, High Standard Company, Savage Arms Corporation, Buffalo Arms Corporation, Frigidaire, AC Spark Plug, Brown-Lipe-Chappin, Saginaw Division of General Motors Corporation, and Kelsey Hayes Wheel Company. Of the 3,283,837 Browning machine guns produced in this country during World War II, approximately two million were .50 calibers. Like the Browning .30 caliber, this gun has been widely copied by other countries, and again total production can only be estimated as well into the millions.

Photo: Inventor's original model. Courtesy Browning Arms Company.

AUTHORS' NOTE: Limitations of space have made it necessary for us to include here only the mechanical and production highlights of the many Browning automatic machine gun models. Nor has it been possible to acknowledge the work of Fred Moore, Colonel S. Gordon Green, and many others responsible for important later modifications in Browning's original machine-gun designs. For more detailed information the authors strongly recommend the reader consult Volume One of *The Machine Gun: History, Evolution and Development of Manual, Automatic and Airborne Repeating Weapons,* by George M. Chinn, Lieutenant Colonel, USMC, Ret., published by the Superintendent of Documents, Washington, D.C.

D. AIRCRAFT CANNONS

62. 63. 64. 37 MM. AIRCRAFT CANNONS (COLT, VICKERS AND OTHERS)

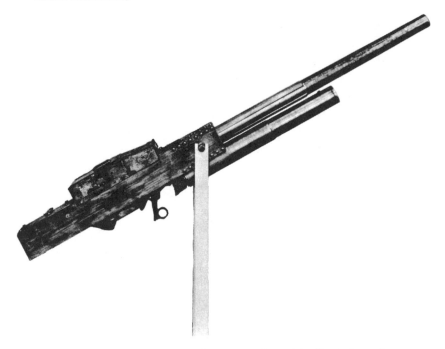

History: John M. Browning began work on his first aircraft cannon in early 1921; three months later it was successfully test-fired in the hills outside Ogden. Patent applications on this gun were filed December 15, 1923, April 11, 1924, and April 28, 1924, and U. S. Patents Nos. 1,525,065-67 were granted February 3, 1925. The cannon was successfully demonstrated to U. S. Army officials at the Aberdeen Proving Ground in mid-1921, firing a 1-pound projectile having a muzzle velocity of 1400 feet per second at the rate of 150 rounds per minute. Shortly after, Browning designed two additional models, each firing heavier projectiles, the first at 2000 feet per second, the second at approximately 3000 feet per second. (For a summary of the development and testing of these guns see Part Three, Chapter 17 of the text.) In 1929 a small number of these weapons were manufactured by the Vickers Arms Company in England for sale to Spain. The U. S. Government, for a time apathetic to the production of new military weapons, did not renew interest in the gun until 1935. In that year, the M4, the Army Air Corps model of Browning's cannon was produced. The World War II model, the M9, was used in rather limited quantities by the U. S. Army Air Corps, which eventually decided such heavy armament was neither practical nor essential. The cannon saw much use in the hands of the Russians, however, and, during their most critical defensive combat with Germany, was their primary aerial cannon. Several thousand of these guns were sent to Russia by the U. S. Government along with the P-39 Bell Aircobra planes on which they were mounted. The high-velocity, armor-piercing projectiles proved effective against the heavy German tanks.

Description: Operation is on the long-recoil principle. Both recoil and counter-recoil are controlled by a hydro-spring buffing mechanism. The breechblock is of the vertical, sliding-wedge type. When the projectile is fired and driven down the bore of the barrel, the barrel, breechblock, and locking frame, all locked together, recoil rearward ten inches before the breechblock cams downward. In turn, the hammer is cocked, the empty case ejected, a new shell loaded, the mechanism locked and again readied for firing.

The following specifications refer to the Browning M4:

Caliber: 37 mm.

Muzzle velocity: 2000 feet per second.

Rate of fire: 135 rounds per minute.

Type of feed: Magazine.

Method of cooling: Air.

Length: 65″.

Barrel length: 44″.

Weight: 313 lbs. without feeder. 406 lbs. with 15-shot magazine attached.

Modifications: The M9 was principally used for aircraft. It was either mounted to fire through the hub of the propeller or from the wings. With little change, it could be fed from either right or left. Its velocity was 3050 feet per second.

Production totals: Total production, including World War II, was under 100,000 units.

Photo: Inventor's original model. Courtesy John M. Browning Firearms Museum.

E. AUTOMATIC PISTOLS

65. .38 CALIBER SEMI-AUTOMATIC PISTOL

History: This was the first of John M. Browning's many semi-automatic pistol designs and was invented in 1894-95. It was a logical outgrowth of his development of the gas-operation principle, which during the preceding five years he had applied primarily to machine-gun models. Patent application was filed September 14, 1895, and U. S. Patent No. 580,923 was granted April 20, 1897. On July 3, 1895, the pistol was test fired by officials of Colt's Patent Fire Arms Manufacturing Company in Hartford, Connecticut. On July 24, 1896, American manufacturing and sales rights on this pistol (and three others) were assigned to the Colt Company—this agreement becoming the basis for all subsequent agreements between Browning and Colt. From that day to the present, Colt has produced no semi-automatic pistols except those of basic Browning design. This particular pistol was never commercially produced. (For a summary of John M. Browning's over-all contribution to automatic pistol development, see Part Three, Chapters 15 and 16 of the text.)

Description: Gas-operated, exposed-hammer, semi-automatic pistol. A gas vent is located on the top of the barrel a short distance from the muzzle, over which is positioned a piston lever, linked to the breech bolt. As the expanding powder gases pass through the vent, sufficient pressure is exerted on the lever to force it upward and rearward in an arc. The rearward movement opens the breech bolt, causing it to extract and eject the fired cartridge and cock the hammer. Then, as the lever and breech-block return to their forward position, a fresh cartridge is fed into the chamber, readying the pistol for the next round.

Caliber: .38.

Length: 8½".

Barrel length: 5¾".

Weight: 2 lbs., 2 oz.

Sights: Fixed.

Safety: Hammer type (no magazine safety).

Photo: Inventor's original model. Courtesy John M. Browning Firearms Museum.

66. .32 CALIBER SEMI-AUTOMATIC PISTOL

History: John M. Browning invented this pistol in the fall of 1895. It was test-fired by Colt officials on January 14, 1896, and American manufacturing and sales rights were assigned to Colt on July 24, 1896. Patent application was filed October 31, 1896, and U. S. Patent No. 580,926 was granted April 20, 1897. It was never commercially produced.

Description: This pistol differs from Browning's first hand gun in that operation is accomplished by the blowback principle. The expanding gases of the fired cartridge act directly on the breech bolt through the cartridge case, forcing both rearward, effecting extraction, ejection, and cocking during the movement. An action spring located above the barrel provides the energy to return the breech bolt to its forward position, and in the fractional interval during its forward motion, a fresh cartridge is picked from the magazine and chambered for immediate firing. The slide and breech bolt are integral, and, as with any blowback action, must provide sufficient inertia to delay rearward movement until the bullet leaves the barrel and gas pressures have partially diminished. This pistol is very similar in operation to the first Browning pistol manufactured by Fabrique Nationale, No. 71, which follows.

Caliber: .32.
Length: 9″.
Barrel length: 6″.
Weight: 2 lbs.
Sights: Fixed.
Safety: Hammer type (no magazine safety).
Photo: Inventor's original model. Courtesy John M. Browning Firearms Museum.

67. 68. .38 CALIBER SEMI-AUTOMATIC PISTOLS

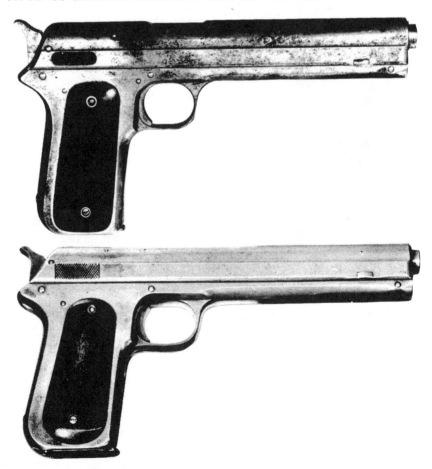

History: These two pistols were forerunners of the Colt Model 1900. They were invented in 1896 and manufacturing and sales rights were assigned to Colt on July 24 of that year. Patent application on No. 67 was filed October 31, 1896, and U. S. Patent No. 580,924 was granted April 20, 1897. Patent application on No. 68 was filed November 7, 1901, and U. S. Patent No. 708,794 was granted September 9, 1902. Neither was commercially produced.

Description: These are the first Browning pistols to employ a positively locked, recoiling barrel. The top of the barrel has transverse ribs and recesses which fit into corresponding ribs and recesses in the slide. Each end of the barrel is attached to a link which, when the barrel is in battery position, presses the barrel tightly upward against the slide and thereby interlocks these ribs and recesses. Thus, on firing, the barrel and slide are locked together with a secure seal at the breech.

Upon firing, the barrel and the slide recoil—locked together until the bullet has left the barrel and gas pressures diminish. Then barrel links draw the barrel downward out of the locking recesses, freeing the barrel. The slide alone continues to move rearward, accomplishing the extraction, ejection, and cocking functions in the process. The slide returns to its forward or firing position by spring tension, chambering a new cartridge from the magazine.

Both of these pistols were originally designed to eject from the top and were later modified to eject from the side.

Caliber: .38.

Length: 8⅞″.

Barrel length: 5¾″.

Weight: 2 lbs.

Sights: No. 67 none. No. 68 fixed.

Safety: Hammer type (no magazine safety).

Photo: Inventor's original model. Courtesy John M. Browning Firearms Museum.

69. .38 CALIBER SEMI-AUTOMATIC PISTOL

History: This pistol was also invented by John M. Browning in 1896. Patent application was filed October 31, 1896, and U. S. Patent No. 580,925 was granted on April 20, 1897. It was submitted to Colt in the spring of 1896, and American manufacturing and sales rights were obtained by the company on July 24, 1896. This was the first pistol to employ Browning's famous grip safety. The pistol was never commercially produced.

Description: This short-recoil-operated, semi-automatic pistol employs a rotating barrel which locks to the slide. It consists of a cylinder-shaped frame which contains a cylinder-shaped slide. The barrel, enclosed by the recoil spring, is wholly contained in the slide. Located near the breech end of the barrel are three pairs of locking lugs, which fit into corresponding grooves in the slide and lock the barrel and slide together.

When the gun is fired, the barrel and slide recoil together for a short distance. Upon recoil, two camming studs near the muzzle cause the barrel to rotate and disengage the locking lugs from their grooves. This allows the slide to separate from the barrel and continue to recoil alone, effecting the extraction and ejection of the fired cartridge, and cocking. The slide is then returned to its forward position by spring tension, picking up a fresh cartridge from the magazine and feeding it into the barrel chamber ready for firing.

Caliber: .38.

Length: 8¾".

Barrel length: 5⅞.

Weight: 2 lbs.

Sights: Fixed.

Safety: Hammer type (no magazine safety). Grip safety.

Photo: Inventor's original model. Courtesy John M. Browning Firearms Museum.

70. MODEL 1900 .38 CALIBER SEMI-AUTOMATIC PISTOL (COLT)

History: Patent application on this gun was filed October 31, 1896, and U. S. Patent No. 580,924 was granted April 20, 1897. The pistol was tested by Colt on June 29, 1896, selected for production in 1898, and

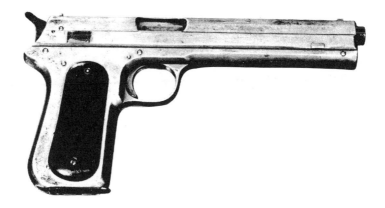

placed on the market in February 1900, becoming the first semi-automatic pistol to be commercially produced in the United States.

Description: Short-recoil-operated, locked-breech, exposed-hammer, semi-automatic pistol.

The following specifications refer to the Colt Model 1900:

Caliber: .38 A.C.P.

Magazine capacity: 7.

Model style: Sporting.

Length: 9″.

Barrel length: 6″.

Weight: 2 lbs., 3 oz.

Sights: Fixed.

Safety: Rear sight functions as a manual safety; when pushed down it keeps the hammer from striking the firing pin.

Grips: Plain walnut and, in very small quantities, checkered wood or rubber.

Modifications: Two modified versions appeared in 1902. In the 1902 Sporting Model the safety-sight was replaced with an adjustable rear sight, the hammer was changed from spur to stub round, and as a safety feature a shorter firing pin was used; this last feature soon became a Colt standard. In the 1902 Military Model capacity was increased one round, a slide stop added, and the grip made larger. In 1903 a short-barrel Pocket Model was introduced.

Date discontinued and production totals: The Sporting Models of 1900 and 1902 were discontinued in 1908, the Pocket Model in 1927, and the Military Model in 1928. Total production figures on this pistol are at best approximate. Not only were several numbering systems used for the serial numbers, but large blocks of numbers were set aside for pistols which were—as far as can be determined—never manufactured. Numbering on the military model started at a high figure, then receded, then started back up again. It is "estimated" that approximately 111,890 of the Sporting, Military, and Pocket Models were produced.

Photo: Inventor's original model. Courtesy John M. Browning Firearms Museum.

71. MODEL 1900 .32 CALIBER SEMI-AUTOMATIC PISTOL (FABRIQUE NATIONALE)

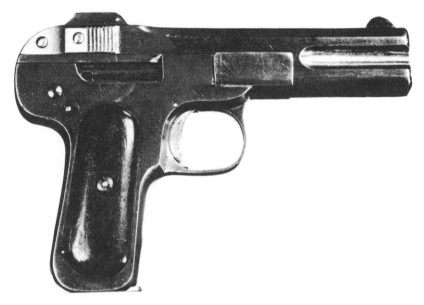

History: This gun was invented early in 1897. Patent application was filed December 28, 1897, and U. S. Patent No. 621,747 was granted March 21, 1899. It was shown both to Colt officials and a representative of Fabrique Nationale shortly after, and on July 17, 1897, a contract between Browning and Fabrique Nationale was signed, authorizing the Belgian firm to manufacture the pistol for all markets outside the United States. Actual production commenced in 1899, making this, the F.N. .32 Caliber Model 1900, the first Browning-designed automatic pistol to be manufactured. Its popularity was immediate and large—100,000 had been produced by F.N. by August 1904; 500,000 by 1909

Description: Blowback-operated, concealed-hammer, semi-automatic pistol. It utilizes the action described under No. 66 but contains numerous improvements particularly suited to a smaller-caliber hand gun.

Caliber: .32 A.C.P. (7.65 mm. Browning).

Magazine capacity: 7.

Model style: Sporting.

Length: About 6¾″.

Barrel length: 4″.

Weight: 1 Ib., 6 oz.

Sights: Fixed.

Safety: Thumbpiece on left side of receiver, positively blocks striker movement.

Grips: Walnut.

Date discontinued and production totals: The F.N. Model 1900 was discontinued in 1910, replaced by the F.N. Model 1910, after total production of 724,450 units.

Photo: Inventor's original model. Courtesy John M. Browning Firearms Museum.

72. MODEL 1903 POCKET .32 CALIBER SEMI-AUTOMATIC PISTOL (COLT)

History: The fantastic success of the F.N. Model 1900 caused Colt to reconsider manufacturing a pistol based on the blowback principle. Browning submitted this model on July 16, 1901, and it was immediately accepted to complement Colt's .38 Caliber Model 1900. The agreement between Browning and Colt on this particular pistol was unique, since, in addition to the usual clauses concerning royalties, etc., it stipulated certain standards in material and workmanship and further specified that Colt would endeavor to sell the pistol at a price low enough to compete with the revolvers of the period. Patent application on this gun was filed April 3, 1902, and U. S. Patent No. 747,585 was granted December 22, 1903. It was first manufactured in May 1903. Its reception in the United States was almost identical to that accorded its European counterpart, as one can see in comparing the total production figures on this model with the preceding, No. 71.

Description: Blowback-operated, concealed-hammer, semi-automatic pistol, very similar to the F.N. Model 1900 in basic operation but containing numerous improvements. Among them, simple disassembly features; Browning's manual thumb safety; and Browning's manual-grip safety, the latter appearing for the first time on a manufactured pistol. This was Colt's first concealed hammer (or "hammerless") pistol.

Caliber: .32 A.C.P.

Magazine capacity: 8.

Model style: Sporting.

Length: 6¾".

Barrel length: 4".

Weight: 1 lb., 7 oz.

Sights: Fixed.

Safety: Browning manual safety. Browning grip safety.

Grips: Black hard rubber.

Modifications, date discontinued, and production totals: The barrel on this model was later shortened to 3¾" and several other minor changes made. An identical model in the .380 A.C.P. caliber (magazine capacity 7) was introduced in March 1908 and remained in production until June 1945. The .32-caliber model was not discontinued until November 1946. There were 572,215 units of the .32-caliber model produced and 138,009 of the .380-caliber model—for a manufacturing total of 710,224.

Photo: Inventor's original model. Courtesy John M. Browning Firearms Museum.

73. MODEL 1903 9 MM. MILITARY SEMI-AUTOMATIC PISTOL (FABRIQUE NATIONALE)

History: From available records it is difficult to determine whether this model, produced by F.N., or the Colt Pocket 1903, just described, was developed first. The two are very similar, and both were submitted in 1901. The Belgian patent application on this gun was filed prior to

the filing of the U. S. Patent on the Colt model. This gun, like the Colt model, was a special-request number, submitted to F.N. by Browning in response to a request for a military-style pistol, and appeared on the market in 1903. F.N. technicians developed a new cartridge for this pistol, a 9-mm. rimless type called the 9 mm. Browning Long. Generally known in Europe as the Pistolet Automatique Browning Grand Modele, this pistol was adopted as the official Swedish military side arm and manufactured by Swedish Government arsenals as well as by Fabrique Nationale. Several thousand were supplied to Russia during the Russo-Japanese War.

Description: Blowback-operated, concealed-hammer, semi-automatic pistol. Like the 1903 Colt Pocket Model, the pistol has a quick disassembly feature, the mechanical safety and grip safety. A hammer is provided but is fully enclosed by the slide. The slide is made to stay at the rear after the last shot is fired through the action of a slide stop located on the right side of the frame. Other basic features are identical to those in the description of No. 72, the Colt Pocket Model 1903.

Caliber: 9 mm. Browning Long.

Magazine capacity: 7.

Model style: Sporting and military.

Length: 8".

Barrel length: 5". Weight: 2 lbs.

Sights: Fixed.

Safety: Browning manual safety. Browning grip safety.

Grips: Black hard rubber.

Date discontinued and production totals: The F.N. Model 1903 was discontinued in 1939 with total production of 58,442 units.

Photo: Inventor's original model. Courtesy John M. Browning Firearms Museum.

74. .45 CALIBER MILITARY MODEL SEMI-AUTOMATIC PISTOL

History: United States Ordnance began to show interest in a .45 caliber automatic pistol as early as 1905. This model, invented in that year, was one of a number of prototypes developed by John M. Browning, leading to the design finally accepted by the Army, Navy, and Marine Corps. It is covered by the same patent as No. 75, the actual prototype for the Government .45 Caliber Automatic. The two are of basically similar design, with the difference that this model was hammerless. Browning designed both hammer and hammerless models to help ordnance experts decide between them. At the insistence of the United States Cavalry, the exposed-hammer model was finally chosen as the offlcial U. S. Government side arm, and this pistol was never commercially manufactured. A small number of these pistols were produced by Colt for the tests, however.

Description: Short-recoil-operated, locked-breech, concealed-hammer, semi-automatic pistol.

Caliber: .45 A.C.P.

Length: 8″.

Barrel length: 3¾".
Weight: 2 lbs., 4 oz.
Sights: Fixed.
Safety: Grip safety. Manual safety. Thumb catch on rear of slide locks hammer and also prevents slide from being opened.
Photo: Inventor's original model. Courtesy John M. Browning Firearms Museum.

75. MODEL 1911 GOVERNMENT .45 CALIBER AUTOMATIC PISTOL (COLT, REMINGTON AND OTHERS)

History: Invented in 1905, this is the pilot model for what has, for over a half century, been the official United States military side arm. Patent application on the gun was filed February 17, 1910 and U. S. Patent No. 984,519 was granted February 14, 1911. A second patent application covering the details of the mechanical safety, was filed April 23, 1913 and U. S. Patent No. 1,070,582 was granted August 19, .

Colt commenced production in late 1905 with the first models reaching the market in the spring of 1906. The model was considered a commercial success and remained on the market in essentially its original design form until 1911, although it underwent various modifications in 1909 and 1910. The government automatic pistol trials, in March 1911, resulted in a recommendation for adoption. Official adoption occurred March 29, 1911, and the first Military Model was manufactured by Colt on December 31 of that year. (For the story of the tests which preceded the adoption of this weapon—the first official government trials in which a small arm achieved a perfect record—and a summary of its military use, see Part Three, Chapter 16 of the text.) A commercial model, identical with the military model except for markings, appeared March 9, 1912.

The following specifications refer to the Colt Government .45 Caliber Model 1910:

Description: Short-recoil-operated, locked-breech, exposed-hammer, semi-automatic pistol.

Caliber: .45 A.C.P.

Magazine capacity: 7.

Model style: Military and commercial.

Length: 8½".

Barrel length: 5". (On original model 3¾".)

Weight: 2 lbs., 7 oz.

Sights: Fixed.

Safety: Manual safety. Grip safety. Magazine safety.

Grips: Checked walnut, diamond pattern; later plain checked walnut; then Colt plastic.

Modifications: Slight changes in both of these models have been made over the years. The most important was traditionally Browning—redesigning parts so they served several functions, thereby reducing the total number of parts and simplifying the arm; these changes were covered in a Browning 1913 patent.

In 1929 Colt brought out the Super .38 Model, patterned after the .45 Model 1911 but chambered for the .38-caliber cartridge. In 1931 .22 caliber was added, with the .22 Ace Pistol. This was followed by two deluxe-grade models in 1933—the .45 National Match Pistol and the .38 Super Match. A lightweight model, the Commander, weighing 1 lb., 10½ oz., was made available in 1949 in .45, .38 Super, and 9-mm. calibers. In 1957 Colt brought out another deluxe .45-caliber target pistol, the Gold Cup National Match. A counterpart in .38 caliber, the .38 National Match, appeared in 1960.

Although these models cover a wide range of grades, all stick closely to the Model 1911 in basic specifications. One partial exception is the .22 Service Ace, introduced in 1937. Modeled on the Model 1911, it contained modifications by another designer which enabled the shooter to get the same recoil or "kick" with .22-caliber cartridges as with .45, effecting an economy in practice ammunition and paying an indirect compliment to the original inventor at the same time.

Dates discontinued and production totals: The two Ace models were discontinued in 1940, but because of parts on hand pistols were sold until 1947; 10,935 units of the Ace and 13,800 units of the Service Ace were manufactured. The .45 National Match and the .38 Super Match were discontinued in 1940; they were numbered with the regular commercial models as listed below.

Of those models still in production, estimated total production figures as of January 1963 were as follows: .38 Super (including discontinued .38 Super Match), 163,100 units; .45 Caliber Model 1911 Commercial (including discontinued National Match), 291,500 units; Gold Cup National Match, 10,950 units; .38 National Match, 4500 units; and Commander, 43,500 units. Estimated total production of all commercial models as of the same date was 538,285 units.

Between 1911 and the beginning of World War I, approximately 100,000 of the official government model were produced for the U. S. Armed Forces. In 1917 the Ordnance Department, in an attempt to step up production, contracted with nine companies to tool up for the pistol; only one, the Remington Arms Company, actually entered production before the war ended. During the duration Colt produced 488,450 and Remington 21,676—for a wartime total of 510,126.

During World War II an estimated 1,800,000 were made. Colt and Ithaca each produced about 400,000; Remington-Rand, Inc., about 900,000; and the Union Switch and Signal Company about 50,000. Martial arms authority Lieutenant Colonel R. C. Kuhn, after visiting all the factories which have produced this weapon and examining their records, has determined that by the end of 1945 total production of the military model was 2,695,212. No figures are available for subsequent years.

Photo: Inventor's original model. Courtesy John M. Browning Firearms Museum.

76. .25 CALIBER SEMI-AUTOMATIC PISTOL MODEL VEST POCKET (FABRIQUE NATIONALE, COLT, BROWNING AND OTHERS)

History: This pistol—the first .25-caliber semi-automatic—was invented by John M. Browning in 1905, and was patented in Belgium in that year. In the United States patent application on the gun was filed June 21, 1909, and U. S. Patent No. 947,478 was granted January 25, 1910. The pistol's size partially accounts for but is by no means proportionate to its sales. First manufactured by F.N. in 6.35-mm. caliber in 1905, approximately 100,000 were sold within the first five years. Colt

obtained license to manufacture the pistol in the United States and their version, chambered for the .25-caliber A.C.P. cartridge, functionally identical to the European caliber 6.35mm, was introduced in October 1908; sales by 1917 numbered 141,000. The current Browning Arms Company model, introduced in 1953, has also proven highly successful.

The following specifications refer to the Colt .25 Caliber Automatic Pistol:

Description: Blowback-operated, hammerless, semi-automatic pistol. This was the only Colt automatic pistol that was actually hammerless— it was discharged by a striker mechanism.

Caliber: .25 A.C.P.

Magazine capacity: 6.

Model style: Pocket.

Length: 4½″.

Barrel length: 2″.

Weight: 13 oz.

Sights: Fixed.

Safety: Thumb-lock safety on the rear left-hand side of the receiver. Grip safety. Also, on models after #141,000, there is in addition a magazine safety.

Grips: Black rubber with checked field; later, checked walnut.

Modifications, dates discontinued, and production totals: The F.N. and Colt models are almost identical, except for the safety. The F.N.

safety has a hook which latches into a notch forward of the regular safety notch in the slide and holds the slide to the rear in such a way that the barrel can be easily turned for takedown. The Colt model safety has no hook and has only one notch in the slide which locks the slide when the safety is on. The only modifications in the Colt model were the addition of a magazine safety in 1917 and a change in sights. The Colt model was discontinued February 1947, with total production of 420,753 units.

The first F.N. model was discontinued in 1940 after production of 1,080,408 units. The current Browning and F.N. Model .25 Caliber followed. The grip safety was eliminated and the weight of the pistol reduced to 10 ounces in the standard model and 7¾ oz. in the light-weight model; its length was reduced to 4″ in both. Still in production, 246,990 units of the pistol had been produced by the end of 1961. Even before the expiration of Browning's patents, numerous imitations of this gun had appeared on the market, particularly from Spain. Production figures on all models would number well into the millions.

Photo: Inventor's original model. Courtesy John M. Browning Firearms Museum.

77. MODELS 1910 AND 1922 SEMI-AUTOMATIC PISTOLS (FABRIQUE NATIONALE AND BROWNING)

History: John M. Browning completed this pistol design in 1910. It was patented in Belgium shortly thereafter and first manufactured by Fabrique Nationale in 1912.

Description: Blowback-operated, concealed-hammer, semi-automatic pistol. Basically the same functionally as the Model 1900, which it replaced, it contains as additional features both a magazine safety and a grip safety. Also, the action spring is placed around the barrel, rather than above it, resulting in a much more streamlined appearance.

Caliber: 9 mm. Browning Short (.380 A.C.P) in addition to .32 A.C.P.

Magazine capacity: 6.

Model style: Sporting and police.

Length: About 6¾″.

Barrel length: 4″.

Weight: 1 lb., 4 oz.

Sights: Fixed.

Safety: Magazine safety. Grip safety. Thumbpiece manual.

Grips: Black hard rubber.

Modifications, date discontinued, and production totals: The F.N. Model 1922, introduced in that year, is an enlarged version of the Model 1910. The barrel was lengthened to 4½″, magazine capacity was increased to 8 cartridges by lengthening the grip, and weight increased to 8 ounces. Both F.N. models are still in production. 572,590 units of the 1910 and 396,865 of the 1922 had been manufactured by the end of 1961, for a total of 969,455 units.

Photo: Inventor's original model. Courtesy John M. Browning Firearms Museum.

78. .22 CALIBER SEMI-AUTOMATIC PRACTICE PISTOL

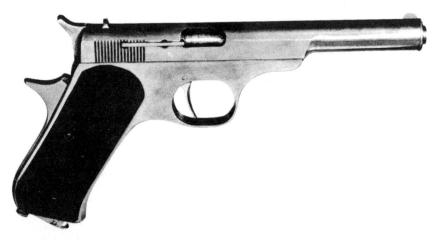

History: Shortly after the Ordnance Command adopted the .45 Caliber Model 1911 Service Pistol, they expressed interest in a similar design chambered for the .22 Long Rifle cartridge. Their objective was to have a pistol similar to the .45 in weight and handling characteristics for practice shooting. This model was one of three or four John M. Browning invented in 1915; the other models have been lost, either through theft or disassembly. This pistol was never manufactured as the project was dropped due to the war.

Description: This pistol has a full slide enclosing the barrel, an exposed hammer, and an overhang on the rear portion of the frame to give it the feel and balance of the Model 1911. Some of the features appearing on this pistol were employed on the Browning-designed Colt Woodsman Model, No. 79.

    Caliber: .22 L.R.
    Length: 9″.
    Barrel length: 4¼″.
    Weight: 1 lb., 7 oz.
    Sights: Fixed.
    Safety: Hammer type.
    Photo: Inventor's original model. Courtesy John M. Browning Firearms Museum.

79. WOODSMAN .22 CALIBER SEMI-AUTOMATIC PISTOL (COLT)

History: This pistol was invented by Browning in 1914. Patent application was filed March 30, 1917, and U. S. Patent No. 1,276,716 was granted August 27, 1918. Colt began production March 29, 1915, first calling it the Colt .22 Automatic Target Pistol. Not until 1927 was it given the name by which it is best known, the Woodsman.

Description: Blowback-operated, concealed-hammer, semi-automatic pistol. Unlike most pistols on the market at the time it appeared, it utilizes a half-length slide which completely separates from the breech end of the barrel.

The following specifications refer to the Colt .22 Caliber Target Model:

Caliber: .22 L.R. Originally Lesmok ammunition only; 1920 on, high speed.

Magazine capacity: 10.

Model style: Target, sport.

Length: 10½".

Barrel length: 6½" until 1933, then 4½".

Weight: 1¾ lb. with 6½" barrel; 1 lb., 10 oz. with 4½" barrel.

Sights: Bead type front sight; later "Partridge" type.

Safety: Manual thumb safety on left-hand side of the receiver. Automatic safety prevents firing until breechblock is in full forward position.

Grips: Checkered walnut.

Modifications, dates discontinued, and production totals: "Lesmok or semi-smokeless, lubricated cartridge only" was Colt's caution on ammunition for early models. About 1920 a change in magazine operation design made possible the use of high-speed ammunition. (Many owners converted their models before this; by replacing the original mainspring, housing, and recoil spring and employing a later-type magazine the pistol was made quite safe for higher-speed cartridges.) The 4½" barrel Sport Model was introduced in 1933, followed by the Match Target Woodsman in 1938, a deluxe model of the Target, with a 6½" heavy barrel, a larger grip, a new trigger, new sights, an added 7 ounces of weight and a radical change in design, the barrel flat-sided and the grips elongated and curved. All three models were discontinued in 1940; however, as a result of assembly of parts on hand they remained on the market until June 1947, with a total production of 187,423 units.

Two post-war Woodsman models were introduced in May 1947— the Target, with a 6" barrel, and the Sport, with a 4½" barrel. In December of the same year Match Target Pistols, with 6 or 4½" barrels, were introduced. In 1950 Colt brought out an economy model based on the Woodsman; the barrel was shortened to 4½" and various changes made in the sights, magazine, etc. First designated the Challenger, it was renamed the Huntsman in 1955. In 1959 Colt made a few minor changes in the Target Model and redesignated it the Targetsman.

The Woodsman Sport, Match Target, Targetsman, and Huntsman models remain in production. The Woodsman Sport, Target, and Match Target were numbered in the same series; as of January 1963 total production on these three models was estimated at 200,900 units. The Targetsman, Challenger, and Huntsman were numbered in the same series; total production on these three models as of January 1963 was estimated at 151,000. Estimated total production of all the Woodsman models as of the same date was 539,323 units.

Photo: Inventor's original model. Courtesy John M. Browning Firearms Museum.

81. 9 MM. PARABELLUM SEMI-AUTOMATIC PISTOL

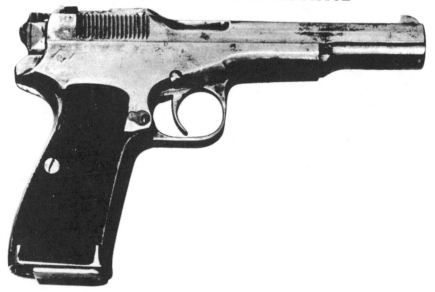

History: In early 1923 John M. Browning was informed that the French Ministry of War was interested in obtaining a semi-automatic pistol of large magazine capacity chambered for the 9 mm. Parabellum cartridge (the same as the 9 mm. Luger). Browning completed this model and No. 81 in a few months. This model, which was produced first, was never patented or commercially produced.

Description: Blowback-operated, concealed-hammer, semi-automatic pistol. The barrel is designed to move rearward a short distance in a line parallel with the movement of the breechblock and slide without being locked to the breechblock.

Caliber: 9 mm. Parabellum.

Length: 8¼″.

Barrel length: 5⅛″.

Weight: 2¼ lbs.

Sights: Rear adjustable for elevation, front fixed.

Safety: Positive-hammer and sear-block thumb safety. Also locks slide (no magazine safety).

Photo: Inventor's original model. Courtesy John M. Browning Firearms Museum.

81. 9 MM. PARABELLUM SEMI-AUTOMATIC PISTOL (FABRIQUE NATIONALE, BROWNING AND OTHERS)

History: This was John M. Browning's last pistol development. Patent application was filed June 28, 1923, and U. S. Patent No. 1,618,510 was granted February 22, 1927, three months after the inventor's death. It was first produced by Fabrique Nationale in 1935 as the Model 1935.

Description: Short-recoil-operated, locked-breech, exposed-hammer, semi-automatic pistol. The visible ribs on the breech end of the barrel are engaged by corresponding grooves in the slide which securely lock the two together upon firing. The breechblock is demountably fixed to the slide so the breechblock effectively seals the breech against the forces of the fired charge. Recoil continues in this locked position until the bullet leaves the bore. Then the rear of the barrel is tilted downward by a camming action which disengages it, freeing the slide and breechblock to continue rearward alone. The mechanics of ejection, cocking, and loading are closely similar to Browning's other breech-type pistols.

Caliber: 9 mm. Parabellum (9 mm. Luger).

Magazine capacity: 13.

Model style: Commercial and military.

Length: 7¾".

Barrel length: 4⅝".

Weight: 2 lbs., 3 oz.

Sights: Blade front. Fixed rear. Some military models have folding-leaf graduated rear sight.

Safety: Positive-hammer and sear-block thumb safety. Also locks slide. Magazine safety.

Grips: Checkered wood. Military models are supplied with a stock/holster, which can be quickly fastened to the rear face of the grip, permitting the pistol to be fired as a semi-automatic rifle.

Modifications and production totals: The Model 1935 was adopted as the official side arm of the Belgian Army and other European and colonial troops. Over 200,000 were manufactured in Canada for the Chinese Army during World War II.

This pistol is currently sold by the Browning Arms Company as a sporting and defense pistol and is variously called the Browning 9 mm. Parabellum and the 9 mm. Browning Hi-Power. It is also the standard military side arm of many of the NATO countries and is still in production at F.N. Total F.N. production as of 1961 was 327,402.

Photo: Inventor's original model. Courtesy John M. Browning Firearms Museum.

OTHER BROWNING GUNS

As previously noted, a number of John M. Browning's original models no longer survive. Some were lost, others stolen, and many were disassembled by the inventor in the course of later experiments and developments. Among the patents assigned John M. Browning not specifically mentioned in the foregoing sections are thirty-two covering entire firearms for which there are no known surviving models. In addition often several models were covered by the same patent; it is known, for example, that Browning designed several additional experimental models of both the .45-caliber Government and the .22-caliber L.R. practice pistols. The total of John M. Browning's original firearms models is therefore well over a hundred.

No mention has been made here of the Browning Double Automatic. This shotgun was invented not by John M. Browning but by his son Val A. Browning, while he was president of the Browning Arms Company.

While discussion of this arm falls outside the limits of this text, it should be noted as one of a number of fine examples of the continuing Browning family gunmaking tradition.

To clear up existing confusion, mention should also be made of the F.N.-Browning Light Automatic Rifle, Caliber .308, the standard infantry rifle of the NATO nations. Despite its name, this weapon was not a Browning invention. The following excerpt from the Fabrique Nationale descriptive brochure on this gun explains why it is so designated:

"The designer of this weapon was Mr. D. D. Saive, Chief of Weapon Design and Development at F.N., who, in the course of his career was able to gain an extensive experience in automatic weapons. For many years he collaborated with the great inventor, J. M. Browning. It is not surprising therefore that one finds in this rifle in several places features which first appeared in Browning mechanisms (gas intake and piston, wire-spring-actuated extractor, recoil spring housed in the buttstock) and thus it can be said that the weapon is of Browning inspiration—a natural consequence of more than fifty years of continuous collaboration between the F.N. and Browning companies."

BROWNING FIREARMS MUSEUM

Many original prototypes and early production models of nearly every firearm invented by John Moses Browning are on display at the new Browning Firearms Museum in Ogden, Utah. A recreation of what the inventor's early workshop may have looked like shows many of the tools he used along with significant artifacts. A slide presentation outlines the life and achievements of "the greatest gunmaker the world has ever known."

The new Browning Firearms Museum is located at the
Ogden Union Station
25th Street & Wall Ave.
Ogden, Utah 84401
(801) 399-8586

Open Monday through Saturday.
Hours: Summer, 10:00—6:00. Winter, 10:00—5:00.

NOTES

(1) More than a century later, some of these tools were still in use. In the shop in Ogden, John cut his templates from sheet metal using a pair of two-foot shears forged by his father in Tennessee.

(2) To the knowledge of the authors, none of the guns Jonathan Browning made during his years in Brushy Fork are still extant. It is assumed that at least some of them saw military service, in the Seminole War of 1836—when Sumner County sent a whole company of men—and in the Civil War, when many of the men on both sides carried their own firearms. The number of guns Jonathan made during this period is not known, nor is it known if any of them were stamped with their maker's name.

(3) Various works give the date as 1831, and at least one firearms authority calls this arm "the original repeating rifle." Browning family reminiscences place the inventing of the gun during Jonathan's residence in Quincy, Illinois, which was between 1834 and 1842. It would be presumptuous, from the evidence, to say that this was definitely the first American repeating rifle; it evidently was one of the earliest, however.

(4) One of these guns, in the Browning family collection, was fired fifteen rounds as recently as 1952; in tribute to the old gun, it should be added, without a malfunction of any kind.

(5) Living expenses in Quincy reflected its frontier location. The following is a list of prices for commodities in that city in 1835:

Bacon, hams, hog, round, per lb. .05	Furs, otter 3.50 to 4.50
Beef, on ft., per cwt. 3.00	Flour, superfine, per bbl. 4.50
Beef, fresh in market, per lb. .04	Flour, fine, per bbl. 3.50
Beeswax, per lb. . 15	Wheat, per bu. .50
Butter, fresh, per lb., scarce .16¾	Rye, per bu. .37
Butter, kegs, per lb. none	Oats, per bu. .25
Candles, sperm, per lb. .40	Corn in sacks, per bu. .30
Candles, mold, per lb. .20	Corn in ear, per bu. .25
Candles, dipped, per lb. .16¾	Hides, dried, per lb. .09
Coal, per bu. .20	Pork, mess, per bbl. 11.00
Hides, green, per Ib. .04½	Pork, prime, per bbl. 9.00
Iron, bar, per lb. .08	Pork, cargo, none

Iron, hoop, per lb. .12½

Lard, per lb. .05

Lead, pig, none

Leather, sole .28 to .33

Leather, upper .50

Nails, cut, asst, per lb. .10

Nails, wrought, per lb. .25

Coffee, per lb. .20

Deer skins, per lb. .10

Furs, muskrat skins .16¾

Furs, raccoon .12½

Potatoes, Irish, per bu. 7.00

Potatoes, sweet, per bu., none

Sugar, loaf, per lb. .20

Sugar, Havana white, per lb. .16¾

Sugar, brown .12½

Salt, Lib Bloom, per bu. 1.50

Salt, Alam ground, per bu. 1.00

Salt, Kanawha, per bu. 1.00

Shot, per lb. .12½

Tallow, per lb. .10

Whiskey, country, per gal. .30

(6) Orville H. Browning came to Illinois from Kentucky in 1831. In 1836 he was elected to the Illinois State Senate and served four years. In 1842 he was again elected to the state legislature, this time to the assembly. In 1843 he ran for Congress against Stephen A. Douglas, their debates being considered the most famous in Illinois history, until some fifteen years later, when Browning's friend Lincoln faced the same opponent. Browning also lost the first round to Douglas, by 409 votes. When Douglas died in 1861, while a United States senator, Browning filled out the remainder of his term. In 1866 President Johnson named him Secretary of the Interior.

In one of those strange twists of fate, Orville H. Browning was the lawyer who, in 1844, defended and won acquittal for the two men charged with the murder of Joseph and Hyrum Smith.

(7) Joseph Fielding Smith, *Essentials in Church History,* 400.

(8) Ibid., 404-5.

PART TWO: THE SON

(1) The birth dates of the boys in the third family were as follows: Jonathan Edmund, January 26, 1860; Thomas Samuel, April 15, 1861; William Wallace, February 28, 1862; George Emmett, August 1, 1866. Another boy, Benjamin Franklin, was born on October 18, 1868 and died on August 31, 1869.

Though the boys were actually John and Matt's half brothers, for purposes of simplicity they are collectively referred to throughout the narrative as their brothers. Polygamy results in some complicated relationships.

PART THREE: THE MAN

(1) The price of anonymity is often misunderstanding and confusion. In part because of the inventor's refusal to give interviews regarding his personal life, and certainly in part because no full biography of John M. Browning has previously appeared, a remarkable amount of misinformation has crept into many of the articles concerning him. Even his date of birth is incorrectly given

in all the standard references. One of the most recurrent but least factual stories relating to this period is that John set a manufacturing total of six hundred rifles, refusing to let any be sold until that number was reached. And that Winchester then bought them all.

The Browning Brothers Factory did produce approximately six hundred Single Shot rifles, but this is the only part of the story that is correct. Twenty-five guns were manufactured and held for the initial display; these were sold in less than a week. The rest were sold almost as soon as they were manufactured, over a period of three years. There were never more than a dozen new rifles on display in the shop at any one time, after the initial twenty-five, and usually only two or three.

(2) There are several variations in print regarding this first meeting between John and Bennett. One says that Bennett, upon his arrival, was told that the inventor was in the shop. He went back to the shop but in a few minutes returned to the counter. There were only two workmen back there, he complained. Matt then identified the "workmen" as his brothers John and Ed. Another account has it that Bennett on entering the shop found only a man he thought to be the janitor, who stood at a bench whittling and whistling and who paid him not the least bit of attention. (Similar incidents did occur in the inventor's later years, as is indicated in that portion of the biography dealing with his working habits.)

The account of the Browning-Bennett meeting in the text is based on Matt's recollections and Browning family conversations. The story was a favorite of the brothers, of course.

(3) It has been said that Bennett took a wooden model of the repeater back to New Haven with him. The authors have been unable to find any evidence supporting this statement. To our knowledge the inventor never made wooden models of any of his guns—excepting, of course, the play guns he whacked out for Matt. While Jonathan has been described as sometimes gullible, this was not one of John's particular traits. It is probable that, as in the recollections on which this version is based, John told Bennett only enough to get his reaction and indicate that his mechanism had solved the particular problems of such a gun. The Winchester-Browning relationship was soon one of complete mutual trust. In later years John let Winchester handle the patenting of all his arms.

(4) Philip B. Sharpe, *The Rifle in America*, 237-39.

(5) Kingsley P. Karnopp and Gerald Keogh, in their article "John Browning's First Rifle" in the August 1961 issue of *The American Rifleman,* state that the highest known serial number on a Browning Brothers Single Shot is 515. From this they conclude that the total number of guns produced by the brothers was probably closer to 525 than 600. They also note that a number of rifles have been found bearing no serial numbers. A possible explanation would be that none were placed on those guns manufactured after the sale of the Single Shot to Winchester. Many of the deluxe grades also lack serial numbers.

(6) Sharpe, *op. cit.*, 239.

(7) Harold F. Williamson, *Winchester: The Gun That Won the West,* 106.

(8) *Ibid.,* 104.

(9) Collectors are sometimes puzzled on discovering Winchester arms stamped BROWNING BROTHERS OGDEN UTAH or similarly. Winchester never stamped the Browning name on any of their firearms, other than those they manufactured under military contract; nor did the Browning Brothers at any time manufacture a portion of the Winchester arms in Ogden, as has at least once been suggested, quite seriously. These particular arms, like those of other arms companies, were thus stamped by the Brownings to advertise their sporting-goods business. Similar confusion has arisen over the occasional appearance of a Browning Brothers Single Shot with a Remington barrel. Apparently some of the barrels the brothers purchased from Schoverling were manufactured by Remington.

(10) The original models of those Browning-designed guns which were manufactured by Winchester are on display in the Browning Firearms Museum, Ogden, Utah. The arms which John M. Browning sold to Winchester but which were never manufactured are a part of the collection in the Winchester Gun Museum, Olin Mathieson Chemical Corporation, New Haven, Connecticut. Photographs of these guns and descriptions of their mechanisms appear for the first time in book form in Part Four.

Winchester museum curator and firearms expert Thomas E. Hall, in a conversation with co-author Curt Gentry, pointed out that nearly all of the models showed their crude gunshop heritage—most were roughly finished and some bore hammer marks. "But," Hall added, "the actions are as smooth as water going over rocks. They are tight where they should be tight, free where they should be free. There is no extra metal—everything works easily and perfectly."

(11) Williamson, *op. cit.,* 156.

(12) *Ibid.,* 158. Mr. Williamson attributes this quotation to Captain E. C. Crossman, "With Captain Crossman at the Big Winchester Factories," *The Sporting Goods Dealer,* January 1920.

(13) *Ibid.* The quotation is from Paul B. Jenkins, "The Trench Gun of the A.E.F.," *The American Rifleman,* November 1935. The balance of the quotation is of interest:

". . . Perhaps it was this fight that resulted in the historic cablegram of September 14, 1918, to Secretary of State Lansing:

"'The German Government protests against the use of shotguns by the American Army and calls attention to the fact that, according to the laws of war, every prisoner found to have in his possession such guns or ammunition belonging thereto forfeits his life.'

"The passage in the Hague decrees alluded to in the German protest reads: 'It is especially forbidden to employ arms, projections or materials calculated to cause unnecessary suffering.' The American reply, too long to be quoted here, remarked pointedly that shotguns did *not* come under the Hague ban, and that if the Germans carried out their death-threat 'in a single instance' the United States Government knew what to do in the way of reprisals, 'and notice is hereby given of the intention to make such reprisals!' Uncle Sam did not intend to have his trench-shotgunners massacred simply because he had given them a weapon which even the pick of the Prussian 'shock troops' dreaded more than anything that four years of war had called on them to face. The shotguns went right on at their business—so terrible a success that message after message from G.H.Q. to America begged: 'Give us more shotguns!' and by November 1918 two more models (the Winchester hammerless and the Remington) were about to be brought into production; when the Germans cried 'Enough'!"

(14) *Ibid.,* 162-63.

(15) Two points should be clarified here. First, the period of seventeen years referred to is the time between John's sale of the Single Shot to Winchester in 1883 and his submission of the automatic shotgun in 1900. John's actual break with Winchester did not occur until January 1902; he sold no arms to Winchester during the two years the shotgun was under consideration, however. Second, as a result of the absence of most Winchester and Browning records for this period, there is no documented evidence regarding the number of guns Browning sold to Winchester. Harold F. Williamson estimated the figure at 41. The authors, after examining the Browning patents assigned to Winchester and those models of unmanufactured Browning-designed guns in the Winchester Gun Museum, conclude that the figure was probably 44.

(16) Williamson, *op. cit.,* 131.

(17) A total of four patents were issued on the gun, all in the name of J. M. Browning. The first three were prosecuted by Seymour and Earl, acting for the Winchester Repeating Arms Company: #659,507, filed February 8, 1900, granted October 9, 1900; #689,283, filed March 18, 1901, granted December 17, 1901; and #710,094, filed January 11, 1902, granted September 30, 1902. The fourth patent, prosecuted by N. A. Bartlett, acting for J. M. Browning, was #812,326, filed June 30, 1904, and granted February 13, 1906, some time after John's break with Winchester.

(18) Harold F. Williamson devotes considerable space to the "break" in his book. His account is substantially correct and the authors are indebted to him for his extensive research. John's own account, however, appears here for the first time. Co-author John Browning, eldest son of the inventor, was not in Ogden at the time of Mr. Williamson's visit while researching his book; therefore the recollection of this conversation was not called to his attention.

(19) The interview occurred in early January 1902, probably on the sixth or seventh, as it preceded the death of Marcellus Hartley, President of Remington, which occurred on the eighth. Either Bennett did not consider the break final or he did not immediately notify his patent department, as Winchester filed their final patent on the gun, in Browning's name, on January 11, 1902.

(20) In an interview with co-author Curt Gentry November 10, 1961.

(21) Today this is also the location of the famed Colt's Fire Arms Collection, which contains a large number of Browning-designed guns.

(22) Lieutenant Colonel George M. Chinn, USMC, *The Machine Gun,* Vol. I, 58-59. The authors are indebted to Colonel Chinn for far more than reliance on this definitive multi-volume work. Over the years Colonel Chinn collected

hundreds of documents, newspaper clippings, etc., concerning John M. Browning's relations with the government and his military arms. He made available to the authors literally boxes of this material, much of which would have been lost had it not been for Colonel Chinn's strong belief in John M. Browning's genius.

(23) *Ibid.,* 163-64.

(24) *Ibid.,* 165.

(25) *Ibid.,* 172.

(26) *Ibid.,* 174.

(27) *Ibid.,* 174-79.

(28) In an interview with co-author Curt Gentry November 10, 1961.

(29) Following the war Val Browning was sent to Liege, Belgium, to take charge of production of Browning arms in the Fabrique Nationale plant. A noted inventor in his own right (the Browning Double Automatic is one of his designs), Val Browning made Liege his home for nearly twenty years. For many years one of his sons, John Val Browning, now president of the Browning Arms Company, held the same position. Another of Val's sons, Bruce Browning, is active in the design department of the company.

(30) Lieutenant General Levin H. Campbell, Jr., *The Industry-Ordnance Team,* 246.

(31) Colonel Chinn in a letter to the Browning Arms Company.

(32) *Ibid.*

(33) Chinn, *op. cit.,* 614-15.

(34) Campbell, *op. cit.,* 195-96.

(35) As a result of conflicting recollections and the unavailability of pertinent records, there has been disagreement as to whether John M. Browning first went to Europe in 1896 with his automatic pistol or in 1902 with his automatic shotgun. Wording on the Browning Memorial Plaque at F.N.— quoted in the preface—supports the earlier date. However, it is F.N. which has finally settled the controversy, establishing the latter date as correct, in *Les relations de la F.N. avec la famille Browning de 1897 à 1914,* in the April, May, and June 1962 issues of the Fabrique Nationale house organ, *F. N. Revue.*

(36) Interview with co-author Curt Gentry November 14, 1961.

(37) Julian S. Hatcher, Major General, U. S . Army, Retired, *Hatcher's Notebook,* 141.

(38) Chinn, *op. cit.,* 527.

(39) *Ibid.,* 532.

BIBLIOGRAPHY

Of the many periodicals consulted in researching this volume the following proved most helpful: *The American Rifleman, F. N. Revue, The Gun Digest, The Gun Report, Outdoor Life, The Shooter's Bible, Sports Afield,* and *True Magazine.*

The following books and pamphlets contained information relative to the subject of this volume:

Arnold, Richard. *Automatic and Repeating Shotguns.* New York: A. S. Barnes, 1958.

Bady, Donald B. *Colt Automatic Pistols 1896-1955.* Beverly Hills, Calif.: FADCO, 1956.

Browning, Orville Hickman. *The Diary of Orville Hickman Browning, Vol. I, 1850-1864.* Lincoln Series. Springfield, Ill.: Illinois State Historical Library, 1925.

Campbell, Lieutenant General Levin H., Jr. *The Industry-Ordnance Team.* New York: McGraw-Hill, 1946.

Chapel, Charles Edward. *The Boy's Book of Rifles.* New York: Coward-McCann, 1949.

—. *The Complete Book of Gun Collecting.* New York: Coward-McCann, 1961.

Chinn, Lieutenant Colonel George M., USMC. *The Machine Gun: History, Evolution, and Development of Manual, Automatic and Airborne Repeating Weapons,* Vol. 1. Washington, D.C.: Superintendent of Documents, 1951.

Cisco, Jay Guy. *Historic Sumner County Tennessee.* Nashville, Tennessee: Folk-Keelin Printing Co., 1909.

Edwards, William B. *The Story of Colt's Revolver.* Harrisburg, Pa.: Stackpole, 1953.

Foster-Harris. *The Look of the Old West.* New York: Viking Press, 1955.

Hatch, Alden. *Remington Arms: An American History.* New York: Rinehart and Co., 1956.

Hatcher, Major General Julian S., U. S. Army, Ret. *Hatcher's Notebook.* Harrisburg, Pa.: Military Service Publishing Company, 1947.

Haven, Charles T., and Belden, Frank A. *A History of The Colt Revolver and the Other Arms Made by Colt's Patent Fire Arms Manufacturing Company from 1836 to 1940.* New York: William Morrow & Company, 1940.

The History of Adams County, Illinois. Chicago: Murray, Williamson and Phelps, 1879.

A History of Browning Guns from 1831. St. Louis, Missouri: Browning Arms Company, 1942.

John M. Browning Armory. Ogden, Utah: Browning Arms Company, 1959. Koller, Larry, editor. *The American Gun, Vol. I, Nos.* 1-3. New York: Madison Books, 1960 and 1961.

—. *The Fireside Book of Guns.* New York: Simon and Schuster, 1959.

O'Connor, Jack. *Complete Book of Rifles and Shotguns.* New York: Harper & Bros., 1961.

One Million Browning Machine Guns: A Chapter in the History of General Motors War Production. Privately printed, 1944.

Remak, Joachim. *Sarajevo.* New York: Criterion Books, 1959.

Russell, Carl P. *Guns on the Early Frontiers.* Berkeley, Calif.: University of California, 1957.

Sandburg, Carl. *Abraham Lincoln: The Prairie Years and the War Years.* New York: Harcourt, Brace & Co., 1954.

Serven, James E. *Colt Firearms.* Santa Ana, Calif.: Privately printed, 1960.

Sharpe, Philip B. *The Rifle in America, 4th* edition. New York: Funk and Wagnalls, 1958.

Smith, Joseph Fielding. *Essentials in Church History.* Salt Lake City, Utah: Deseret Book Co., 1928.

Smith, Walter H. B. *The Book of Rifles.* Harrisburg, Pa.: The Stackpole Company, 1962.

—. *The Book of Pistols and Revolvers.* Harrisburg, Pa.: The Stackpole Company, 1962.

Watrous, George R. *Winchester Rifles and Shotguns,* 2nd edition. New Haven, Conn.: Winchester Repeating Arms Company, 1950.

Wilcox, David F., editor. *Quincy and Adams County Illinois: History and Representative Men.* Chicago: Lewis Publishing Co., 1919.

Williamson, Harold F. *Winchester: The Gun That Won the West.* Washington, D.C.: Combat Forces Press, 1952.

Winant, Lewis. *Firearms Curiosa.* New York: Greenberg, 1955.

INDEX

For specific gun models, see type: Aircraft cannons; Machine guns; Pistols; Rifles; Shotguns.

Aberdeen Proving Ground, Maryland, 177, 210–11, 280
AC Spark Plug, 279
Adams County, Illinois, 9
Adney, Clarence, 190–91, 203–4
Aircraft cannons:
  Baldwin gun, 205
  Browning 37 mm., viii, 205–12, 280–81
Albert I, King of Belgium, 199–202
American Rifleman, 309–10
Ammunition, changes in, 10, 30, 54, 104, 129–30, 135–36, 233
Andri, M., 201–2
Arc de Triomphe, Paris, 184
Argonne offensive, 180
Army, United States, 153, 159, 172, 292
Army Air Force, United States, 178–79, 281
Associated Press, 169
Awards and decorations, 73, 193, 199–202

Baker, Newton D., 169
Barlow, Split ("Split Nose"), 79–81, 86, 216–17
Bartlett, N. A., 311
Becker, G. L., 119, 203
Belgium, vii, 29, 164, 181, 190, 199–202, 213, 295, 297, 303

Bennett, Thomas Gray ("T.G."), 97–103, 108–9, 123–42, 172, 186, 307, 309
Berg, Hart O., 181, 183–84, 186
Bigelow, A. P., 119, 203
Bingham, George, 142
Birch Creek (Ogden), 36
Bledsoe Creek, Tennessee, 3, 6, 7
Book of Mormon, 15
Boxer Rebellion, 161–62, 274–75
Breda Arms, 191, 262
Brewer, Alex, 37
Britain, Battle of, 179
Browning, Austin, 110
Browning, Benjamin Franklin, 306
Browning, Bruce, 312
Browning, Edmund, 3–4
Browning, Elizabeth Clark, 27, 29–35, 37–39, 44–46, 48, 50, 56, 58, 60
Browning, Elizabeth Stalcup, 7
Browning, Frank, 60, 61
Browning, George Emmett, viii, 27, 52, 75–101, 117, 197, 306
Browning, Hugh, 110
Browning, Captain John, 4
Browning, John (son of John M. Browning), 71, 111, 309
Browning, John Moses:
  birth, viii, 25, 27

childhood and youth, 29–57 passim, 111
makes first gun, 33–36
repairs freighter's gun, 40–44
makes a gun for Matt, 46–50
schooling, 29–30, 32, 43, 53, 94–95, 171
early gunshop training, 29–57 passim
reconditions old shop, 57
bequeathed shop, 63
nominal head of brothers, 27–29, 66, 93–94
hunting experiences, 34–35, 36–37, 45, 203, 215, 216–18
invents Single Shot Rifle, 57–62
invents second single-shot, 60–61
expands gunshop business, 66–68
patents Single Shot, 60–66
builds arms factory in Ogden, 68–70, 75–78
manufactures and sells Browning Bros. Single Shot, 75–103 passim, 307–9
marries, 62 first child born, 70–7i
children of, 70–71, 110, 111. See also Browning, John; Browning, Louie; Browning, Val A.
association with the doctor and the professor, 89–91
trapshooting, 91`, 118–19, 203, 205
sells Single Shot to Winchester, 97–103, 307–9
early experimental guns, 95–96, 104
invents Model 86, 96–97, 100–1, 103–4, 3o7
first trip East, 104–9
sells Model 86 to Winchester, 104–8
asked to design lever action shotgun, 108–9
invention and sale of Model 87 Shotgun, 109–10
sells Winchester eleven guns in two years, 110

Mormon missionary to Georgia, 3
working habits, 37, 59–60, 89, 113–21, 123, 143, 190, 202–5
mutual benefits of Winchester association, 100, 108, 121, 123–34 passim
total number guns sold to Winchester, viii, 110, 124–34 passim, 242, 264, 309. For specific firearms, see Rifles: Winchester; Shotguns: Winchester
miscellaneous inventions, 134, 135
invents automatic shotgun, 134–42
break with Winchester, 134–41, 309
discovery of principle of gas operation, 91, 142–44
initial experiments in development of a fully automatic gun, 91, 134, 142–46
first patent embodying gas-operation principle, 146
inventive course leading to development of machine guns, pistols, and other automatic and semiautomatic arms, 146–48
invents first automatic machine gun, 147, 148–50
discovery of recoil operation, 147
invents first pistol, 147
important pistol patents, 148
writes Colt regarding completed machine gun, 148–50
trip to Hartford and exhibition of the gun, 151–52
beginning of long association with Colt, 153
preparation for "unoffficial" military machine gun test, 153–57
personally conducts the test, 157–58
development of Colt Model 1895 Automatic Machine Gun, 160
participates in official tests, 160–62

model is first automatic machine gun purchased by U.S., 162

continues machine gun development (1900–17), 162–64

invents B.A.R., 163–64

first public exhibition of .30-caliber machine gun and B.A.R., 164–65

B.A.R. offlcially adopted, 165 sets new machine gun record, 165–67

.30-caliber machine gun officially adopted, 167

agreement regarding wartime production of models and services, 167–68

commended by the Secretary of War, 169

World War I service, 169–78

revisits Winchester, 172

asked to design .50-caliber machine gun, 176–77

completes successful .5o-caliber model, 177

"One drop of genius . . . ," 178

military use of inventions, 178–80

early pistol development, 180–81

grants Colt rights to manufacture pistols in U.S., 181

beginning of association with F.N., 181

first pistol manufactured by F.N., 183–85

takes automatic shotgun to Europe, 141–42, 184, 310

incidents of first trip abroad, 184–85

reception at F.N., 185–86

remains to supervise making and testing of automatic shotgun pilot models, 187–88

learns French, 91, 187 described, vii, 188, 196

"Le Maltre," 188

faith in automatic shotgun vindicated, 188–89 varied activities (1900–10), 190–91

attitude toward models, 192

manufactured pistols, 192

develops pistol operating slide, 192–94

development, testing, and offlcial adoption of .45-caliber automatic pistol, 165, 194–99

attitude toward workmen, 171, 187–88, 196

friendship with Fred Moore, 196–98

awards and decorations, 73, 193, 199–202

not enough time, 202–5

effect of wartime work on health, 206

opinion of the Baldwin gun, 205

designs and tests 37 mm. cannon, 205–12

every arm entered in government trials wins over all competition, 212 recollections prior to last Atlantic trip, 213–18

summary of inventive career, 218–19

death, 220–21

inventions (discussed singly), 227–304

total number firearm inventions, viii, 219, 303

total number patents, viii, 219

firearms authorities on accomplishments, vii—viii, 163, 218–19

Browning, John V., 310

Browning, Jonathan:

birth, 3

parents, 4, 5, 8

childhood, 4–5

repairs flintlock, 4

association with blacksmith, 4–5

apprentice to gunsmith, 5–7

makes first barrel, 6–7

first gunshop, 7

mechanical aptitudes, 7

marries first wife, 7

makes and repairs guns, 7–8, 305

children of first wife, 7, 8–9
moves to Quincy, Illinois, 8–9
residence in Quincy, 9–15 passim, 305–6
invents slide repeating rifle, 9–10, 307
makes and sells rifles, 1, 10, 11, 20
elected justice of the peace, 11
acquaintance with Lincoln, 11–14
converted to Mormon religion, 14–15
moves to Nauvoo, Illinois, 16
residence in Nauvoo, 16–17
flees Nauvoo, 17–18
settles near Kanesville (Council Bluffs), Iowa, 18
attempts to join Mormon battalion, 18
attempts to join first Mormon scouts, 18–20
chosen by Brigham Young to make guns for the exodus, 18–2
makes trek to Utah, 21, 26
change in character and habits, 26–44 passim, 69
marries second and third wives, 27
children of second wife, 27
children of third wife, 27, 306
moves gunshop, 29
builds and operates a tannery, 31–32
comments on John's first gun, 35
acknowledges John's development as a gunsmith, 40–44
preoccupation with ventures outside the shop, 44, 69
civic and church offlces, 44
assists John in invention of the Single Shot, 58–63
test-fires finished Single Shot model, 62–63
bequeaths shop to John, 63
death, 63
inventions discussed, 225–26
Browning, Jonathan Edmund (Ed), viii, 27, 45, 52, 61, 67–69, 75–101
passim, 114–18, 123, 129, 43–45, 153–56, 176–77, 190, 192, 196–97, 207–10, 306
Browning, Louie, lll
Browning, Marriner, 183
Browning, Matthew Sandifer (Matt), viii, 27–29, 33–35, 38–40, 46–52, 57, 59–60, 67, 70, 75–101, 104–8, 111, 118–19, 121, 129, 136, 39, 143–45, 148–51, 153–56, 67–68, 181, 183, 196–97, 208–10, 214, 306–7
Browning, Orville, 11–14, 306
Browning, Rachel Teresa Child, 61–62, 70, 76–77, 81, 86, 110, 118, 169, 213, 220
Browning, Sarah, 3
Browning, Sarah Emmett, 27
Browning, Thomas Samuel (Sam), viii, 27, 52, 75–101 passim, 197, 306
Browning, Val A., 172, 176, 213, 220, 264, 303, 310
Browning, William Wallace (Will), 27, 52, 306
Browning Arms Company, vii, viii, 125, 132, 149, 182, 187, 191, 221, 238, 260–61, 263, 279, 295–97, 302–3, 310. See also Pistols; Rifles; Shotguns
Browning Automatic Arms Company, 189
Browning Bros. (firm), 88–89, 94, 121, 148–49, 190, 227–28
Browning Brothers Factory, 68–70, 75–103 passim, 307. See also Rifles
Brown-Lipe-Chappin, 279
Brushy Fork, Tennessee, 3, 4, 6–9, 15, 305
Buffalo Arms Corporation, 279

Camp and Trail, 131
Campbell, General Levin H., Jr., 180, 310
Canada, 303

Carbine. *See* Rifles, specific model

Carthage, Illinois, 17

Central Pacific Railroad, 52

Chevalier de l'Ordre de Leopold. *See* Cross of Knighthood of the Order of Leopold

Child, Rachel Teresa. *See* Browning, Rachel Teresa Child

Child, Warren G., 62

China (in World War II), 303

Chinn, Colonel George M., 159, 162–65, 167, 179, 205, 212, 279, 309–10

Church of Jesus Christ of Latter-Day Saints. *See* Mormon Church

Civil War, 54, 141, 157, 305

Clark, Moses, 44–45, 57, 81–82

Coast Guard, United States, 175

Coles, Charles H., 196

Colt Firearms, 218–19

Colt's Patent Fire Arms Manufacturing Company, viii, 42, 120, 134, 148–81 passim, 183, 190, 194–99 passim, 207, 219, 240–41, 272–75, 277–91 passim, 293–97, 299–301, 309. *See also* Machine Guns; Pistols

Congress Heights Tests, 164–65, 167, 171, 276

Council Bluffs, Iowa. *See* Kanesville, Iowa

Cross of Knighthood of the Order of Leopold, 199–202

Crossman, E. C., 310

Culpeper County, Virginia, 4

Cumberland River, Tennessee, 3

Curtis, Captain Paul A., 218

Custer, General George, 159

Davis, Dwight F., 220

Douglas, Stephen A., 306

Douglas Blacksmith Shop, 67, 70

Dunkirk, France, 180

Edison, Thomas Alva, 178, 218

Eiffel Tower, 184

Emmett, Tom, 121–23

Ensign, Ed, 92–94, 100–1

Essentials in Church History, 17–18, 306

Fabrique Nationale d'Armes de Guerre (F.N.), viii, 42, 120, 132, 141, 180–91 passim, 199–202, 219–20, 238–42, 260, 262–63, 288–91, 295–98, 302–4, 310. *See also* Pistols; Rifles; Shotguns

Father of Waters. *See* Mississippi River

Ferguson, Major Patrick, 54

Fontainebleau, 184

Ford, Henry, vii

Ford, Thomas, 17

Four B's, 118, 203

France, 164, 176, 30

Franchi, 191, 262

Franklin Institute. *See* John Scott Legacy Medal

Franz Ferdinand, Archduke of Austria, 180

Frenay, Henri, 186

French language, 91, 184, 187, 199

Frigidaire Company, 279

Frontier Guardian, 1, 20

Gallatin, Tennessee, 3

Gatling Gun Company, 161. *See also* Machine Guns

General Motors Corporation, 279

Georgia, Mormon mission to, 111–13

Germany, 164, 165, 171–72, 176, 180, 281, 308–9

Goering, Field Marshal Hermann, 179

Great Britain, 127, 164, 170, 179, 280

Great Salt Lake, 20–21, 25

Green, Colonel S. Gordon, 279

Hague Decree, 308

Hall, Captain John Harris, 54

Hall, John (president of Colt), 151–59

Hall, Thomas E., 308

Harrington and Richardson, 219
Hartford, Connecticut, 148–49, 151,
    53, 156, 158, 165, 169, 172, 176,
    181, 183, 190, 196, 213, 278, 282
Hartley, Marcellus, 142, 309
Hatcher, General Julian S., 205, 310
Hatcher's Notebook, 205, 310
Henry, Tyler, 54
Herstal, Belgium, 186, 199–202
Heublein Hotel, 158, 196
High Standard Company, 279
Hotel des Invalides, 185
House, Edward M., 13
Hoxer, John, 151, 156
Hubert, M., 201–2
Hudson's Bay Company, 25
Hurley, Patrick J., 129
Hurricane Fighters, 179

Ilion, New York, 169, 190–91
Industry-Ordnance Team, The, 180,
    310
Italy, 164
Ithaca Gun Company, 260

Japan, 179
Jenkins, Paul B., 308
John M. Browning Armory (Ogden,
    Utah), 42, 55, 66, 87, 105, 109,
    113, 118, 146, 152, 161, 167–68,
    172, 177, 192, 204, 201–11, 215,
    225–26, 228, 230, 232–37, 239–
    41, 256–60, 262, 264, 272, 274–
    75, 277, 281, 283–86, 288–90,
    292–93, 295, 297–99, 301–3, 308
John Scott Legacy Medal, 199, 200

Kanesville, Iowa (later designated
    Council Bluffs), 1, 18, 20, 26, 42,
    49, 225, 226
Karnopp, Kingsley P., 307
Kelsey Hayes Wheel Company, 279
Kentucky, 11
Keogh, Gerald, 61, 307
Korean War, 163, 175, 178, 180, 276,
    278

Kuhn, Colonel R. C., 295

Laflin and Rand, 139
Lane, Charley, 90
Lansing, Robert, 308
Liberty, Missouri, 15
Liege, Belgium, vii, 120, 181–90,197,
    200–2, 213–14, 310
Lincoln, Abraham, viii, 11–14
Little Big Horn, battle of, 159
Louvre (Paris), 184

McAusland, Andrew, 97–98
Machine Gun, *The,* 159, 162–65, 167,
    179, 205, 212, 279, 309–10
Machine guns:
    Benet Mercies, 164
    Browning .50. *See* Machine guns:
    Browning .50 Caliber
    Browning .50 Caliber, vii, viii, 172,
        173, 174, 175, 176–80, 278–79
    Browning .50M3. *See* Machine
        guns: Browning .50 Caliber
    Browning .50M2. *See* Machine
        guns: Browning .50 Caliber
    Browning .30. *See* Machine Guns:
        Browning .30 Caliber
    Browning .30 Caliber, vii, viii, 163–
        64, 165–67, 168, 169, 170–71,
        172, 173, 174, 175, 178, 179–
        80, 275–77, 278, 279
    Browning's experimental proto-
        types, 91, 134, 142–47, 270–71
    Browning's first model, 147, 148–
        59, 271–72
    Colt:
        Model 1895 Automatic, 159–62,
            164, 273, 274–75
        Model 1917 .30 Caliber *See* Ma-
            chine guns: Browning .30
            Caliber
        .50-caliber models. *See* Machine
            guns: Browning .50 Caliber
    Gatling gun, 150, 151, 153, 159,
        160, 16
    Maxims, 164

Maxim-Vickers, 170

Missing Browning models, 146, 271, 303

Other Browning experimental models, 272–74

"Peacemaker." *See* Machine guns: Colt: Model 1895 Automatic

"Potato Digger." *See* Colt: Model 1895 Automatic

Preparedness, World War I, 164

Marine Corps, United States, 161–62, 175, 179, 274, 292

Marlin-Rockwell Corporation, 169, 240–41

Meriden, Connecticut, 169

Mexican War, 54

Mexico, 130

Missionaries, Mormon, 111–13

Mississippi River, 9, 17

Moore, Fred, 196–97, 211–12, 279

Mormon Church, 14–21, 26–27, 62, 82, 90, 111

Mosquito Creek, Iowa, 1, 18

Musket. *See* Rifles, specific model

Napoleon's Tomb, 185

Nashville, Tennessee, 3–5, 15

NATO, 304

Nauvoo, Illinois, 15–17, 26, 225

Navy, United States, 134, 153–54, 160 162, 179, 292

New Browning Gun Shop, 78

New Haven, Connecticut, 98–99, 106–9, 123–27, 151, 169, 172, 213, 307–8

New York City, 61, 106–7

Oakley, Annie, 129, 142

Ogden, Peter Skene, 25

Ogden, Utah, 21, 25–27, 32, 34, 42, 44–45, 47, 52–54, 60–61, 65–67, 75, 87, 89–90, 97, 101, 105, 108–9, 113, 118, 121, 123, 128–29, 48–49, 151, 169, 181, 183–84, 190–91, 195–96, 198, 202–3, 207–9, 227, 280, 307, 308

Ogden Morning Herald, log

Ogden Rifle Club, 90–91, 143

Olin Mathieson Chemical Corpora tion. *See* Winchester Repeating Arms Company

Omaha, Nebraska, 51, 66, 87, 90, 99

Ordnance, United States Army and Navy, 73, 132, 154, 159–63, 169, 176, 180, 194, 197–99, 205–9, 292, 295, 298

Overland Trail, 67

Paris, France, 171, 184–85

Peary, Admiral Robert Edwin, 129

Peking, China, 161–62, 274

Pershing, General John J., 176–77, 278

Philadelphia, Pennsylvania, 199–200

Pidcock, Sarah, 70

Pidcock, Tad, 46

Pistol vs. revolver, 183–84, 197

Pistols (Semi-automatic, popularly called "Automatic"):

Blowback-operated, 148, 219, 283–84. *See also* specific model

Browning Arms Company:

9 mm. Parabellum (Browning HiPower), 192, 302–3

.380 Caliber, 192, 297–98. *See also* Pistols: F.N.: Model 1910

.25 Caliber, viii, 192, 295–97. *See also* Pistols: F.N.: Model Vest Pocket

Browning's first experimental models, 180, 282–88

Browning's major contributions to development, 147–48, 193–95, 219

"Citizen Browning." *See* Pistols: F.N.: Model 1900

Colt:

agreements to manufacture Browning models, viii, 180–81, 282–99 passim

all manufactured models based

on Browning designs, viii, 181

Model 1900 .38 Caliber, 134, 181, 183, 192, 285, 286–88, 289

Model 1902 Military, 287–88

Model 1902 Sporting, 287–88

Pocket Model, 287–88

Model 1903 Pocket .32 and .380 Caliber, 192, 289–90, 291

Model 1911 Government .45 Caliber Military, vii, 165, 166, 167, 168, 192, 195–96, 19799, 292–95, 298–99, 303

Model 1912 Government .45 Caliber Commercial, 192, 294–95

Super .38, 294–95

.22 Ace, 294–95

.45 National Match, 294–95

.38 Super Match, 294–95

Commander, 294–95

Gold Cup National Match, 294–95

.38 National Match, 294–95

.22 Service Ace, 294–95

.25 Caliber, 192, 295–97. See also Pistols: F.N.: Model Vest Pocket

Woodsman .22 Target (1915), vii, 192, 299–301

Sport Woodsman (1933), 300–1

Match Target Woodsman (1938), 300–1

Target Woodsman (1947), 300–1

Sport Woodsman (1933), 300–1

Match Target Woodsman (1947), 300–1

Challenger, 300–1

Huntsman, 300–1

Targetsman, 300–1

F.N.:

Model 1900 .32 Caliber, 134, 141–42, 180, 181, 183–84, 186, 187, 192, 200, 284, 288–89, 290, 298

Model 1903 9 mm. Military, 192, 194, 290–92

Model 1903 Sporting, 291

Model Vest Pocket 6.35 mm., 192, 295–97

Model Vest Pocket .25 Caliber,

Model 1910 .380 Caliber, 192, 289, 297–98

Model 1922, 192, 297–98

Model 1935 9 mm. Parabellum, 192, 302–3

Gas-operated, 142–48, 219, 270–71, 282. See also specific model

Missing Brcwning models, 192, 292, 299, 303

Operating slide, 193

Other Browning experimental models, 192, 292–93, 298–99, 301–2, 303

Pistolet Automatique Browning Grand Modele. See Pistols: F.N.: Model 1903

Recoil-operated, 147–48, 219, 285. See also specific model

Polygamy, Mormon, 27, 308

Porter, Samuel, 5–7

Pottawattamie Indians, 18

Pratt & Whitney Company, 160

Promontory, Utah, 52

Pugsley, Edwin, 140, 172

Quincy, Illinois, 8–9, 11–15, 26, 225–26, 305–6

Rand McNally & Company, 167

Reising Arms, 219

Remington Arms Company, viii, 42, 123, 142, 169–70, 190–91, 219, 236–39, 259–62, 275, 277, 279, 293, 295, 308, 309. See also Rifles; Shotguns

Rifle in America, The, vii, 131, 218–19, 307

Rifles:

B.A.R. (Browning Automatic Rifle), vii, 163–65, 166, 167, 168, 171, 172, 176, 180, 240–42

Bolt-action. See specific model

Breechloading, 30, 54. *See* specific model

Browning Arms Company: .22 Automatic, 238–39, 270. See also Rifles: F.N.: .22 Caliber Automatic

Browning Bros.: Single Shot, 57–62, 60–66, 75–103 passim, 227–28, 307. See also Rifles: Winchester: Model 1885 Single Shot

Browning experimental models, 60–61, 95–96, 104, 228, 229

Browning, Jonathan:

Cylinder repeating, 1, 9, 10, 16, 19, 20, 226

Slide repeating, 1, 9–10, 16, 19, 20, 49–50, 225, 305

Colt Automatic Machine. *See* Rifles: B.A.R.

Colt Monitor. *See* Rifles: B.A.R.

F.N.:

Caliber .35 Automatic, 237. *See also* Rifles: Remington: Model 8

Fusil Mitrailleur Léger. *See* Rifles: B.A.R.

.22 Caliber Automatic, 238–39

.22 Caliber Pump Action, 239–40

F.N.-Browning Light Automatic, 304

Flobert, 131–33

Hall, 54

Lever-action, 124, 126, 134, 141, 219. *See also* specific model

Light Browning. *See* Rifles: B.A.R.

Missing Browning models, 89, 95–96, 228, 303

Model 1917 Browning Light Machine. *See* Rifles: B.A.R.

Muzzleloading, 54. *See also* specific model

Peabody, 54

Pull-apart. *See* specific model

Pump-action, 109, 124, 126, 134, 141, 219. *See also* specific model

Remington:

Model 8 Autoloading, viii, 190, 236–37

Model 81 Woodmaster, viii, 237

Model 24, viii, 238–39. *See also* Rifles: F.N.: .22 Caliber Automatic

Model 241 Speedmaster, viii, 239

Remington-Rider Rolling-Block, 54

Sharps, 54, 79, 80

Single-shot. *See* specific model

Slide-action. *See* Rifles: Pump-action

Swing-quard. *See* specific model

Trombone-action. *See* Pump-action

Winchester:

B.A.R. *See* Rifles: B.A.R.

Model 73, 88, 128, 141,144,145, 146, 271

Model 76, 88, 141

Model 1885 Single Shot, viii, 97–103 passim, 110, 123, 130, 134, 228, 307, 308, 309. *See also* Rifles: Browning Bros.: Single Shot

Model 1886 Lever Action, viii, 96–97, 100–1, 103–8, 110, 123, 128, 129, 151, 229–30, 232, 247, 307

Model 1890 Pump Action, viii, 127, 131, 142, 231–32, 308

Model 06, 231–32

Model 62, 231–32

Model 1892 Lever Action, viii, 128–29, 232–33, 250

Model 53, 233

Model 65, 233

Model 1894 Lever Action, viii, 125, 130–31, 233–34, 247

Model 55, 234

Model 64, 234

Model 1895 Lever Action, viii, 131, 132, 171, 234–35

Model 1900 Bolt Action Single Shot, viii, 131–33, 235–36
Model 02, 133, 236
Model 04, 133, 236
Model 58, 133, 236
Model 59, 133, 236
Model 60, 133, 236
Model 68, 133, 236
Model 99 Thumb Trigger, 133, 236
Models purchased from Browning but never produced, 124, 126, 133, 242–55, 308
.30/30. See Rifles: Winchester: Model 1894
Ring, H. W., 90–91
Robinson, Colonel C. L. F., 197
Rock Island Arsenal, 10, 135
Rommel, General Erwin, 179
Roosevelt, Theodore, 131, 170–71
Rostand, Edmond, 120
Rushton, Frank, 82–84, 87, 100–1
Russia, 131, 164, 170, 234–35,

Saint-Mihiel offensive, 180
Saive, D. D., 304
Salt Lake City, Utah, 21, 25, 52, 69, 82, 88, 91, 105
Sarajevo, Bosnia, 180
Savage Arms Corporation, viii, 42, 191, 219, 262, 279. See also Stevens Arms Company; Shotguns: Stevens
Schoverling, Daly and Gales, 61, 77, 89, 106–8, 189, 308
Seminole War, 305
Serven, James E., 218–19
79th Division, 176, 276
Seymour and Earl, 309
Sharpe, Philip B., vii, 131, 218–19, 307
Shotguns:
Browning Arms Company:
Automatic-5, viii, 190, 191, 260–62, 270. See also Shotguns: Browning automatic

Double automatic, 303–4. See also Browning, Val A.
Superposed, viii, 11, 220–21, 263–64
Browning automatic, viii, 134–42 passim, 147, 148, 184, 185–87, 188–89, 190, 204, 260–62, 309. See also specific model
F.N.:
Automatic, 190, 260–62. See also Shotguns: Browning automatic
Superposed, 220–21, 263–64. See also Shotguns: Browning Arms Company: Superposed
Ithaca:
Model 37, 260
Lever-action, 108–9, 124, 126–27, 134, 141, 219. See also specific model
Missing Browning models, 303
Over-under. See Shotguns: Browning Arms Company: Superposed
Pull-apart, 268
Pump-action, 109, 124, 126–27, 134, 141, 219. See also specific model
Remington:
Model 11 Automatic, viii, 190–91, 260–62. See also Shotguns: Browning automatic
Model 11-48, 262
Model Sportsman, viii, 262
Model 17 Pump Action, viii, 259–60
Savage. See Shotguns: Stevens
Single-shot. See specific model
Slide-action. See Shotguns: Pump-action
Stevens:
Model 520 Pump Action, 190, 258–59
Model 620, 258–59
Superposed. See Shotguns: Browning Arms Company: Superposed

Trombone-action. *See* Shotguns: Pump-action

Winchester:
Model 1887 Lever Action, viii, 108–10, 112, 118, 119, 255–56
Model 1901, 256
Model 1893 Pump Action, viii, 126–27, 256–57
Model 1897, viii, 118, 119, 127–28, 141, 257–58, 308
Model 36 Single Shot, 133, 236
Models purchased from Browning but never produced, 124, 126, 264–70, 308

Smith, Hyrum, 17, 306
Smith, Joseph, 14–17, 306
Smith, Joseph Fielding, 17–18, 306
Smith and Wesson, 219
Smithsonian Institution, 60–61
South America, 159, 162
Spanish-American War, 159, 161–62, 235, 274–75
Springfield Armory, Massachusetts, 165, 169, 276
Stanford, Leland, 52
Stevens Arms Company, 190, 258–59. *See also* Savage Arms Corporation: Shotguns
Stone, S. M., 211
Sugar Creek, Iowa, 17
Sumner County, Tennessee, 3, 4, 7–8, 305
Sweden, 291

Texas Rangers, 131
Tobruk, Libya, 179
Ukich, Dr. A. L., 89–91
Union Pacific Railroad, 52
Union Switch and Signal Company, 295
Utah Central Line Railroad, 52–53

Vickers Arms Company, 280

Wasatch Mountains, 23, 26, 212
Wayne County, Illinois, 8

Weber Canyon, 25
Weber County, Utah, 44
Westinghouse, 169–70, 275, 277
Whelan, Colonel Townsend, 131
White, Stewart Edward, 131
Williams, General C. C., 205–8
Williamson, Harold F., 108–9, 127–28, 137, 308, 309
Winchester, Oliver, 54, 123
Winchester Gun Museum, 98, 108, 242–55, 265–70, 309. *See also* Hall, Thomas E.
Winchester: The Gun That Won the West, 108–9, 127–28, 137, 308, 309
Winchester Repeating Arms Company (Winchester-Westem Division, Olin Mathieson Chemical Corporation), viii, 42, 54, 62, 77, 97-110, 120–21, 123–42,151, 153, 169, 172, 184–85, 191, 219, 227, 230–36, 240–58, 261, 264–71, 307, 308, 309. *See also* Rifles; Shotguns
"Winchester Rifle Ranges," 127
Winder, Colonel C. B., 228
World War I, 73, 128, 161, 163, 172, 175, 180, 228, 235, 241, 258, 275, 277–78, 295
World War II, 163, 167, 175, 178–79, 180, 241, 276–81, 295, 303
Wright, Will, 143–44

Yale Sheffield Scientific School, 98
Young, Brigham, viii, 17–21, 25–26, 52

JOHN M. BROWNING: AMERICAN GUNMAKER

A POSTSCRIPT

◆

by

Col. W. R. Betz

(Retired)

in collaboration with

Harmon G. Williams,

Browning Co., President (Retired)

and with the concurrence of

The Browning Company and Curt Gentry

coauthor of the First Edition

◆

1994

◆

DEDICATION

To the memory of Val Allen Browning, "Mr. Val,"
inventor, philanthropist, patron of the arts
and raconteur par excellence.

P O S T S C R I P T

CONTENTS

Illustrations — 327

Introduction — 329

More On The Early Automatics — 332

The Military Brownings — 346

Development of the 9mm HP Pistol — 348

Birth of the Superposed — 351

The John M. Browning Firearms Museum — 359

Bruce W. Browning's .22 Pistols and the New BAR — 375

Return to Sarajevo — 378

The 1,000,000th Browning Pistol — 380

A Pair of Unique Winchester Shotguns — 383

The Smithsonian's Browning Portrait — 384

The John M. Browning Bronze — 388

The American Gunmaker Movie — 389

Bibliography — 391

ILLUSTRATIONS

Cartoon by Belgian artist Jacques Ochs, 1914, Fabrique Nationale, *page 328*

Souvenir medallion, obverse and reverse, the author, *page 329*

Modele 1899 prototype automatic pistol, Ogden Union Station, *page 330*

Belgian firearms proof marks,* *page 333*

Auto-5 assembly line, FN plant, Herstal, Fabrique Nationale, *page 334*

Browning Brothers Armory, Ogden, Utah 1889, Ogden Union Station, *page 335*

Souvenir ashtray, Browning Brothers stores, the author, *page 336*

Butt plate, 2-shot Auto-5, the author, *page 337*

Superposed engraving by Felix Funken, the author, *page 338*

Typical Funken engraving on Auto-5, the author, *page 388*

One millionth Auto-5 in FN historical inventory, Fabrique Nationale, *page 339*

2,000,000th Auto-5 Commemorative model, Browning Arms Co., *page 340*

FN Grande Rendement 9mm pistol, Fabrique Nationale, *page 348*

Gus L. Becker, member of the Four-Bs trap team, Fabrique Nationale, *page 350*

Early open top BAR action, prototype, Ogden Union Station, *page 359*

Superposed cutaway, Liege Musée d'Armes, the author, *page 360*

Union Station, Ogden, Utah, Ogden Union Station, page 362

Seventh Browning prototype pistol sold to Colt, the author, page 364

Model 1878 rifle made by Jonathan Browning, the author, page 364

J. Browning's lathe and tools, Union Station, Ogden Union Station, *page 336*

"The Father" display, retitled by editor, examples of Jonathan Browning's most famous percussion rifles, the slide and cylinder models, displayed in the Browning Firearms Museum, Ogden Union Station, *page 367*

Side plate, Jonathan Browning rifle, the author, *page 368*

Action, Jonathan Browning cylinder rifle, the author, *page 368*

Slide rifle believed made by J. M. Browning,[1] *page 369*

Experimental trombone rifle donated to Museum, the author, *page 372*

Exposed action, experimental trombone rifle, the author, *page 372*

Special engraving, Medallion .22 pistol, Fabrique Nationale, *page 374*

"Un million" M1905 Vest Pocket pistol, 6.35mm, the author, *page 379*

"Spirit of Genius" statue presented to J.M.B., Fabrique Nationale, *page 380*

M93 Trap gun, right side, the author, *page 383*

M93 Trap gun, left side, the author, *page 383*

J. M. Browning portrait by Henry Taggart, ca. 1902, Ogden Union Station, *page 385*

Clay model for J. M. Browning bronze statuette, the author, *page 387*

Credit Notes: * from The Blue Book of Gun Values, S. P. Fjestad
[1] from private collection

INTRODUCTION

*POSTSCRIPT: Any addition or supplement, as one ap-
pended to a book to supply further information.*
Random House Unabridged Dictionary . . . 1967.

The biography of John M. Browning, the Utah Mormon gunmaker,
is the only biography of the great inventor that has ever been published.
It is also the only one that can ever be written. The book's coauthors,
John Browning, the inventor's eldest son, and Curt Gentry, were ideally
suited for the job. John Browning provided the intimate details of his
father's life that cannot now be written by any other family member,
and Curt Gentry, an experienced historian and professional writer,
performed the arduous task of research that has made the book the
single authoritative work on the life and works of the inventor.

Like his younger brother, Val A., John was proud of his father's
achievements and sought to compensate, in a way, for John M.'s reticence and inherent modesty by creating a record of his life. The resulting manuscript, completed by midsummer 1956, was in the style and
form to be expected of a businessman and sometime president of the
Browning Arms—perhaps a bit lacking in the detail and polish expected
in such literature, but rich in personal recollections.

Browning was in the process of expanding its interests in the field of
sporting goods, and the manuscript was not given very high priority on
the Board's agenda. John Val Browning, the company's Executive Vice
President, sent a copy to the San Francisco office of one of the country's
foremost publishers, Doubleday & Company for review. Their reaction
was to advise Browning to engage the services of a professional writer to
revise the manuscript and recommended Curt Gentry as having the
requisite literary experience. On July 10, 1961, an agreement between
the company and Mr. Gentry specified the terms under which the
manuscript was to be reworked, ". . . in a form acceptable to the company
. . . and no later than June 1st, 1962."

Three years later, Doubleday published the First Edition, dated 1964 and retitled, JOHN M. BROWNING, AMERICAN GUNMAKER. The author of the original manuscript did not live to see his work listed in the Library of Congress Catalog, having passed away in March of that year.

The Second Edition consists of the First Edition plus this Postscript written in collaboration with Harmon G. Williams, former President of the Browning Company and with the concurrence of Curt Gentry who lives in his beloved, foggy city on the shores of San Francisco Bay.

Since the first printing of the Browning/Gentry book, there have been many new developments in the world of Browning firearms. A new member of the line of Browning gun inventors, Val Browning's son Bruce W. Browning, has invented a superb .22 caliber automatic pistol and a centerfire rifle aptly named the "new BAR."

In 1978, the John M. Browning Firearms Museum was opened in Ogden, Utah. A year later a group of Utah gun collectors obtained a state charter to organize the Browning Collectors Association with the approval of the Browning Arms Company.

Interest in Browning guns and history has burgeoned. Research performed by a number of internationally known writers including

Cartoon by Jacques Ochs.

Geoffrey Boothroyd, Yves L. Cadiou, Claude Gaier, William H. D. Goddard, and R. Blake Stevens has revealed a great deal of information not known when the First Edition was published.

When John M. Browning died while at work in the FN factory, his passing was mourned by those who had known him in Herstal, the industrial suburb of Liege. He was a humble man, shy to the point of aloofness, more at ease amid the din and grease of the shop than in the corporate offices. FN management respected him for his genius; the workers revered him as The Master and loved him for his unassuming manner. The Liege newspaper "La Meuse" had dubbed him Citizen Browning (also the nickname for the Model 1900 Browning pistol), and praised him for his contributions to the world of firearms. An earlier edition of another paper, "Tatene" had carried a story accompanied by a cartoon depicting the tall American with his most famous pistol and the title "GENS D'ARMES," a play on French words referring to both men at arms and gendarmes, the police who were armed with the M1900 pistol at that time.

Visitors to the old FN headquarters in Herstal are taken to the Board Room where John M's body had lain in state. The likeness of the inventor on the bronze memorial plaque on the wall there as described in the First Edition, was duplicated in miniature in limited numbers for presentation to members of the Browning family and friends. Visitors are also shown the street near the FN factory with its sign, "Rue John Moses Browning." A few blocks away on another side street is a small building now used as a dwelling with an unusual corner stone bearing

Souvenier medallion, struck some years after John's death.

the simple inscription, "CETTE PIERRE A ETE POSEE A LA LOUANGE DE DIEU LE 6 JUIN 1926." (This stone was placed to the glory of God, 6 June 1926.) The guide from the FN Public Relations office explains that the stone commemorates the generosity of John M. Browning who had contributed to the building's construction as a Mormon Chapel, a gift to the people of Herstal from the gunmaker from Ogden, Utah.

The objective of this Postscript, or as our friends in Belgium would say, its "raison d'etre" is to present these new data to Browning fans in the one, single most appropriate place as a supplement to the original book.

The biography of John M. Browning ended with his death. The story of his guns lives on.

MORE ON THE EARLY AUTOMATICS

Although the Browning stores were born of John M's inventions, for many years after the Model 1878 rifles were all gone, they offered no Browning guns for sale. They catered to the needs and varied interests of the Western sporting public, and in addition to Winchesters, Marlins, and Colts, they stocked cameras, fishing tackle, boxing gloves, and bicycles, including an adventurous ladies' three wheeler.

A Browning Brothers Armory letterhead in the late 1890s displays an illustration of the first Browning automatic pistol to be produced

Prototype, .32 (7.65mm) invented 1895, sold to Colt 1896 but never made for commercial sale. Made by FN as the Modele 1899, tested in England and Belgium, but not sold.

commercially, the Modele 1899. This forerunner of the famed M1900 was described in articles by the well-known firearms authority, John Walter, which had appeared in Stoeger's Shooters' Bible, 1979 and 1980 editions.

Mr. Walter states that the larger, heavier .32 was patented in 1898 in Germany and 1899 in Great Britain, and that close to 4,000 of the heavy model, known as the Modele 1899, were manufactured in Liege. Samples were submitted for trials by the British and Belgian armed forces. The British rejected the M1899 because of its small caliber, a very valid objection. The Belgians conducted trials of both the "large and small Brownings," i.e., the M1899 and M1900, and adopted the smaller model for issue to army officers and later to all personnel armed with sidearms.

Here's a comparison of the size of the two models:

	M1899	M1900
Overall length	183mm (7.2″)	162mm (6.4″)
Barrel length	122mm (4.8″)	102mm (4″)
Weight	765 grams (27 oz)	625 grams (22 oz)

The Brownings may have envisioned adding the Modele 1899 to their line of pistols, but none were ever made for sale in the U.S.

It was not until 1903 that the Ogden store could show its customers a Browning gun, the Automatic-5 shotgun, Serial No. 1, which had left the Fabrique Nationale plant on September 17 of that year. Tradition has it that John M. had ordered the first 10,000 guns to be shipped to Schoverling, Daly, and Gales, a New York jobber with whom the Brownings had done business since their first contact with Winchester. Research at the FN plant in Herstal has failed to reveal any records to substantiate the story. It is known from FN records that an Auto-5 bearing Serial No. 206 was shipped to Parent 5. Leroy, Paris, France, on September 28, 1903.

A very few of the early models of the Auto-5 have shown up in recent years, some of them marked "BROWNING AUTOMATIC ARMS COMPANY, Ogden, Utah U.S.A.," a non-existent company whose name also appears in the Browning Brothers Catalog of 1903, the first time the new shotgun was advertised. No explanation for the name has ever been found. It is quite likely that John M. plucked it out of the air in response to an inquiry as to the markings to be placed on the guns to be shipped to the U. S., since the guns shipped to FN's European customers were marked with the FN name.

When John M. visited Herstal in 1902, he brought more to the FN plant than the prototype of his new shotgun. The success of his firearms designs is due in no small part to the inventor's perfectionism. Every part of every gun in a new model was checked and rechecked until it "felt" just right. And John M. insisted on test firing new guns himself, in some cases firing hundreds of rounds and making several changes before he was ready to take the gun to a buyer.

Over the years, Browning guns have become known for their purity of design, strength, ease of manufacture and utter reliability. These have not been accidental virtues originating altogether with the manufacturer, but stem from the inventor's perfectionism and a tight quality control policy still enforced by the Browning Company.

When he first visited Herstal in 1897, John M. found a factory making military rifles and ammunition—whose production was governed by delivery schedules and performance standards set by military inspectors. Quality control involving stringent inspections of every component of a product as well as its overall performance was not known at the turn of the century.

For literally hundreds of years, the villages along the Meuse and Vesdres Rivers, with their ready access to local coal and iron mines and almost limitless source of cheap labor, had been noted for their production of arms and armor. The City of Liege, capital of the principality of the same name, became the center of an industry whose products were shipped to customers world wide, sustained by large orders for military arms and patronized by the nobility and the wealthy for sporting, target, and self defense guns.

As arms technology advanced from the sword and spear to the pistol and long gun, the reputation of the Liegois as gunmakers spread. Very early in the development of firearms, Belgian armorers realized that it was not practical for one gunmaker to fabricate an entire gun; but if several artisans cooperated, each making only one part of a gun, both quality and production increased measurably. Rather than working together in a single installation, most gun makers worked at home, often using their family members as helpers, avoiding the restrictions of either trade unions or employers. With the evolution of firearms from the "fire tube" and arquebus to the flintlock, the cottage gunmaker system spread, and the sounds of hammer and forge rang out in hundreds of homes in dozens of small towns throughout the Leige area.

Gun barrels, being the most difficult part to make, were the first to be produced in collective "factories" where welders, borers, grinders, breech forgers, stampers, and filers were employed by an entrepreneur who solicited business, arranged deliveries, and provided the necessary machines—usually powered by waterwheels—that could not be accommodated in home workshops.

Trigger guards, butt plates, and lock mechanisms continued to be made by individual artisans at home until well into the 20th century. Runners, usually members of the gunmaker's family, were used to transport parts to an assembly point operated by the merchant who acted as distributor of the final product which might bear his name or that of a client.

D.

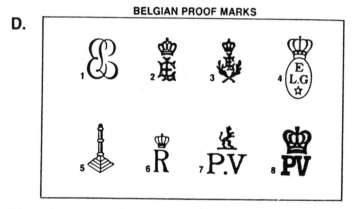

BELGIAN PROOF MARKS

D. Belgium liege proof marks – (1) Provisional proof. (2) Double proofed provisional marking. (3) Triple proofed provisional marking. (4) Definitive proofing. (5) View proof. (6) Rifled arms definitive proof. (7) Nitro proof. (8) Superior nitro proof.

Firearms proof marks required by Belgian law. No. 5 modeled after city of Liege logo.

Both parts and finished guns were, of course, inspected for obvious defects, both cosmetic and operational; but it was not until the middle of the 19th century that the proofing of barrels under government standards was made compulsory.

The ruralization of the gun industry in Belgium reached its peak in 1900 and was still the norm beyond World War I. The cut-and-fit, go-no-go inspection procedures that had sufficed for so many years became outdated with the introduction of automatic arms, especially in the case of the Auto-5 shotgun whose effectiveness depended upon the precise fit of its many parts.

John M. introduced what later became known as "quality control," a technique unknown to FN management. At the outset, he personally supervised the establishment of inspection and test procedures which

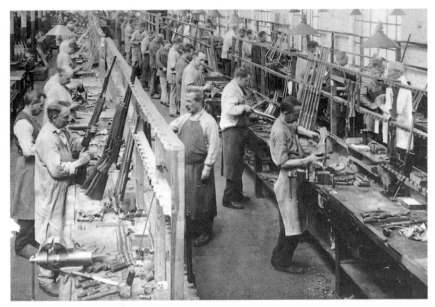

A-5 assembly line, FN Plant, Herstal, July 8, 1921.

would ensure the uniformly high quality of every Browning gun made by FN. In the case of the Auto-5, more than 2,000 separate inspections were eventually performed between some 650 machine operations. More than 1,500 precision gauges were used to check the dimensions of parts at various stages of production.

Each gun was proofed with a "blue pill" high pressure load at the Liege proof house, as required by Belgian law. Each gun was also fired five times at the FN plant for function testing and twice more to check the shot pattern. For many years pattern targets were included with each Auto-5 sold, but the practice was discontinued at the request of Browning's dealers whose customers insisted on unpacking all of the guns in stock in search of the one with the best pattern.

Some of the first guns produced prior to 1905 were sold in the Browning Brothers stores in Ogden and Salt Lake City, but no records can be found to show how many and when they were sold. John M. had licensed Remington to make his new shotgun in 1906, a decision brought about by the imposition of new U.S. import regulations that year, which included drastic increases in duty on firearms, making the continued importation of the FN Auto-5 unprofitable.

A faded copy of the 1914 Browning Brothers catalog No. 50 lists the "Remington Autoloading Shotgun, Browning's Patent" at $30, but does not advertise the FN model. By 1923, the restrictions on firearms

Browning Brothers "Armory" 2469 Washington Blvd. Ogden, Utah, in 1889.
Note wooden fish over the door, and the wooden Model 1878 rifle at the second
floor.

Bronze ashtray, souvenir of the Browning Bros. stores.

importation were lifted and the flow of Belgian Browning Auto-5s to the U.S. began.

The innovative autoloading shotgun had been accepted enthusiastically in the U.S., but the reception of the new gun among European shooters was lukewarm.

In America, even as late as 1900, hunting was almost as much an occupation as a sport. The typical American hunter was a pragmatist whose primary objective in the field was to put meat on the table. It was not difficult to convince him of the advantages of a fowling piece capable of firing five fast shots without reloading and one that could be depended upon to function without failure under the most adverse conditions.

But in Europe, the chase was still a royal sport indulged in only by the privileged few and conducted decorously with rigid rules of conduct, costume, and weaponry. The advent of the breech-loading double shotgun had been accepted by the gentry, but the American automatic raised eyebrows among shooters and beaters alike. The new gun was regarded as a shooting machine, not a proper fowling piece for a gentleman.

The FN salesmen, however, found a ready market for the new Browning shotgun in many other parts of the world. It became popular as a multipurpose arm capable of downing sizeable animals with buckshot or slugs, as well as being effective for water fowl and upland game.

Testimonials in the FN files from new Browning fans tell of leopards, gazelles, and wildfowl brought down by the Auto-5 in Africa; deer in Venezuela; geese in Austria; and hares and ducks in Italy. By the 1920s, the Auto-5 had also found favor on the target ranges. The 1921 Grand Prix de Monte Carlo live pigeon shoot was won by M. Lafite with a Browning Auto-5.

The world record in 1924 Paris Olympics was set by M. D'Heur of Herstal, shooting an Auto-5. The Italian champion, Guiseppe Cavaliere, used a Browning in his 1926 win over clay pigeons. On the other side of the world, the winning three-man team used Browning Auto-5s at the claybird shoot held by the Kobe Shooting Club, as did the Japanese claybird champion, M. Takahshi, in 1925.

The 1903 catalog described the "Browning Automatic Solid Breech Hammerless Repeating Shotgun" in several variations. The Regular Gun was offered with straight stock, matted receiver, and 28-inch barrel. The "Trap Gun" was identical except for checkering on buttstock and forearm. The "Messenger Gun" came with a 20-inch barrel,

Butt plate of the 2-Shot A-5 advertised in 1903 catalog.

cylinder bored. The "Two Shot Gun" was just that—a "Regular" model with a smaller magazine.

A deluxe version with select English walnut stock, pistol grip, and checkering was available on special order for an extra charge of $9. Full-choke guns were normally shipped unless the customer specified Modified or Cylinder, the only other two chokes made. Browning recommended the use of ¼ ounces of No. 8 shot, which the catalog said, ". . . will put better than 340 pellets in a 30-inch circle at 40 yards."

Although Continental shotgunners had at first snubbed Browning's "shooting machine," the engravers in the FN shops were fascinated by the expanse of uncluttered space offered to their chisels by the large Auto-5 receivers. The founder of the FN school of engraving, master engraver Felix Funken, used the Auto-5 to create some of his greatest masterpieces, many of which were displayed at the International Exposition of 1930 held in Liege. Funken's "Grand Deluxe" Brownings began

Variation of Funken's goat-head Chimera on Superposed shotgun for Val Browning.

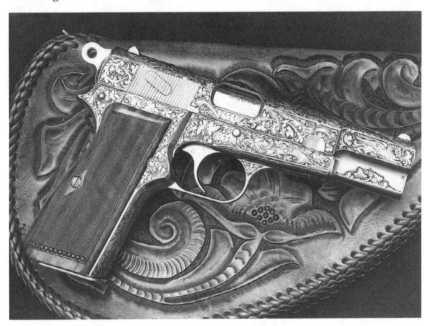

Right side, 9mm HP pistol engraved by Felix Funken for John V. Browning, grandson of John M. Browning, in 1950.

to find favor among European firearms connoisseurs and shooters, including M. Cotty, the President of France, and King Carol of Romania.

Some of what Funken called his "unique pieces" were made especially for Val Browning and his eldest son, John Val. A Superposed shotgun, exquisitely embellished by Funken with his favorite pattern of chimeras (dragons or gargoyles) for Val Browning is now on display in the Browning Firearms Museum. Another typical example of Funken's mastery of the burin, a Browning High Power pistol, decorated with nine different chimeras, was made for John Val Browning in 1950, and is now part of the Museum display. The artist must have chuckled as he worked on the central figure which graces the top of the slide. It is a "grand deluxe" chimera with the head and beard of a goat with wide spreading horns, a dragon's scaley neck and wings, human breasts above a pot belly, and a duck's webbed, taloned feet.

Along with the Winchester model 1894 rifle and Colt 1911 .45 automatic pistol, the Browning automatic shotgun has been a major contributor to the Browning reputation for longevity. For 90 years, beginning in 1903, interrupted only by two world wars, the Fabrique Nationale plant at Herstal has turned out literally millions of the shotguns.

To mark the production of the one millionth Auto-5 made from the cessation of hostilities in Belgium in 1944 to 1961, the plant was the scene of a celebration attended by Bruce W. Browning, grandson of the inventor, and local officials. The center of interest was the millionth shotgun inscribed "1944-1961 No. 1,000,000," which now rests in the

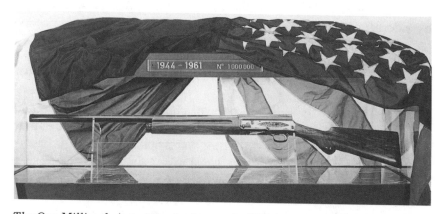

The One Millionth Auto-5 made since end of WWII, on display in the Fabrique Nationale Salle d'Exposition.   1961 FABRIQUE NATIONALE PHOTO

Browning Automatic shotgun No. 2,000,000, 1970, engraving after Funken's pattern of 1930.

company's display room at the factory. When the two millionth Auto-5 came off the line in 1970, Browning Arms Company ordered the preparation of a limited edition of 2,500 units of an especially deluxe model. Harmon G. Williams, who was the Company's president at the time, remembers the circumstances surrounding this special Auto-5 shotgun, as he wrote some years later.

"The actual, highly engraved and gold inlaid 2,000,000th Auto-5 shotgun was shipped from FN on June 26, 1970 via air and cleared through Customs in Salt Lake City.

"Its value of $8,350 was pretty much established by using the same calculations the Company used in setting the price for any routine production gun, strictly to establish a value for insurance purposes. No considerations were included relative to its significance value or collector value.

"The Company commenced to receive some of the 2,500 Commemorative Series in late 1970 and shipments continued through nearly all of 1971.

"To my knowledge only two of the original 2,000,000th were made; the original and an exact duplicate which was numbered 2,000,000X.

"It was decided at that time that the 2,000,000th should have a permanent place in an established museum and that an exact duplicate should always remain in the Company's archives, thus the reasoning behind the 2,000,000X model.

"It was not until 1978 that I learned that FN had manufactured some of the regular 2,000,000th edition for its own market. I happened to be at the factory early that year when some were found in some forgotten storage area. No one there at the time could tell me how many were made, but I recall the incident very well. I think at least two or three of this cache found their way into this country by or via Company personnel.

"The 2,500 models sold in the U.S. Market were handsomely made and finished. Each possessed a super polish and deep blue-black finish and the majority carried fine quality figured walnut with fine hand checkering and a high gloss lacquer finish. All 2,500 were made in the lightweight 12 gauge version with a 28" vent rib barrel, choked modified. Each had an ivory front sight rather than the typical steel sight.

"The black fitted luggage type gun case had a commemorative gold-looking (probably brass) medallion on the outside of the lid and the whole package included a somewhat historical black and gold collector's booklet.

"It is also my recollection that a few of these 2,500 (three or four) disappeared while in shipment to the dealers. A couple of the intended buyers wanting specific serial numbers were so insistent we finally satisfied them by having new guns with identical serial numbers made up but with the addition of an "X" behind the number.

"Being our first special edition, quite frankly, we were not very knowledgeable in the marketing techniques for such a product but had anticipated a quick sellout. Thus the gun was offered to our dealers through a special dealer letter on the assumption that only irritation and confusion would result were it illustrated and listed in Company literature.

"As it turned out, most of our dealers were about as uncertain as we about the market for a special issue Browning model and the Company was not overwhelmed with orders. Inventory was available through mid 1974. In 1971 and 1972, the shotgun was priced at $570. The 1973 price list carried the model at $675 and the 1974 list offered remaining inventory at $700. About the time all units were sold, consumer interest was at its highest which, of course, confirmed our ignorance in handling a collector-type gun.

"It was settled that Utah's distinguished Senator Bennett would present the 2,000,000th shotgun to President Nixon at a gathering at the White House. President Nixon would accept the gun and then present it to a high official of the Smithsonian Institution as a permanent part of the John M. Browning memorial there.

"President Nixon, however, backed out shortly before the presentation was to take place, on the advice of members of his staff, because it was their determination that the anti-gun climate then prevailing would have an adverse effect on his popularity.

"An interesting sidelight relates to the beautiful leather gun case which was part of the 2,000,000th package. On the lower right hand corner of the lid was a 14 karat gold medallion 1/16″ thick, 2½ x 1-½″ on which was engraved in Old English style the words, President Richard M. Nixon.

"On the inside of the lid, centered against the red velvet lining, was a larger plate, 3″ x 6″, with the following inscription:

Browning Automatic Shotgun
Commemorative 2,000,000th Model
Commemorating 90 years of gunmaking
Invented by John M. Browning
in the year 1900 at Ogden, Utah

Presented to President Richard M. Nixon
by
The State of Utah and Browning Arms Co.
Date

"NOTE: It was planned that the date was to be engraved in Washington, D.C. when the exact date of the presentation was settled. As I recall, the actual presentation was to take place in October of 1970."

This unique shotgun was donated to the National Shooting Sports Foundation by Browning, and was auctioned at the Shooting, Hunting and Outdoor Trade (SHOT) Show in Houston, Texas, in January 1986. The successful bidder, William H. Henkel, represented by Gary McDonald of the Old Dominion Sports Center, Winchester, Virginia, paid NSSF $50,001, to be used by the Foundation to further its educational programs. The other Auto-5, No. 2,000,000X is still in the Browning Company's vault.

Advanced gun collectors have always considered the high-grade Auto-5s as prime collectibles. There were four grades illustrated in the 1931 Browning Arms Company catalog. The Standard Grade No. 1 blued with no engraving, listed at $49.75. Grade Nos. 2 ($65.75), 3 ($175.50), and 4 ($277), engraved with patterns of increasing complexity and coverage, could be had on special order. The three high-grade models were discontinued in 1940. They occasionally turn up at gun shows, often in unfired condition, and command premium prices.

When FN reopened the Herstal plant after World War II, a few Auto-5 guns were assembled from parts on hand, but government orders for military hardware to rearm the Belgian Army kept the plant fully occupied. To satisfy the increasing demand created by the return of thousands of American soldiers to peacetime hunting, Browning Arms Company arranged to have the Auto-5 made by Remington, which was tooled to make its own Model 11 under Browning license.

Advertised as "The American Browning," about 45,000 were made in 12-gauge, 25,000 in 16-gauge, and 20,000 in 20-gauge from 1946 to 1951. The American Browning is seldom found in other than used condition, but is still considered a desirable piece for a complete Browning collection.

In 1985, the Browning Arms Company introduced two limited-edition deluxe Auto-5s, the "Classic" and the "Gold Classic." The Classic, made in Japan with silver-gray receiver tastefully engraved and signed in Belgium, was limited to 5,000 units. Only 500 of the Gold Classic model were made in Belgium from the few parts which remained in the sprawling FN warehouses. Both models were specially stocked in highgrade Claro walnut and were engraved with game scenes and heavy gold inlays on the grayed receiver.

In 1974, production of the Auto-5 was phased out in Belgium and begun at the Miroku plant in Japan where the gun is still being made with no major changes from the original design, an eloquent testimonial to the genius of its inventor.

Some time shortly before WWII, the FN designers came up with an Auto-5 in a super lightweight version in answer to objections to the standard model on account of its weight. The new gun had an aluminum alloy receiver and trigger guard assembly, and was produced in limited numbers for sale outside the U.S. An observer reports that the trigger guard assembly from one such gun had failed and was replaced by steel parts.

How many of these guns were made, their serial numbers and years of production and distribution are not known. The experiment failed for a number of reasons, including 1) some working parts in the trigger guard assembly did not wear well, 2) the anodized finish did not wear well and was difficult to replace, 3) in cold weather, the aluminum alloy parts contracted faster than the steel parts, causing malfunctions, and 4) the use of high brass (high pressure) shells caused the alloy parts to crack.

Although the super lightweight model was not a commercial success, it has become a highly desirable collector's item.

It will never be known how many automatic shotguns have been made on Browning's design. In addition to Remington, Savage also produced it as its Model 720 after Browning's patents had expired. Copies have also been produced by several firms in Europe and Kawaguchiya in Japan. It has been estimated that more than 3 million Auto-5s are in the hands of hunters and collectors—most of them still putting meat on the table.

THE MILITARY BROWNINGS

World War I brought the Browning name into the lives of thousands of American soldiers to whom it was synonymous with Machine Gun and "BAR." Trainees in hastily organized machine gun companies struggled to master the "2-mil tap" in order to qualify as expert gunners, a title that led to extra pay in the infantry. The Model 1917 Browning .30 caliber gun was equipped with an elevating screw to raise and lower the point of aim, but it had no traversing mechanism. The gun was prevented from swinging laterally by a simple hand screw. To shift point of aim left or right, the screw was loosened a trifle, allowing the gun to be turned in the desired direction by a smart tap on the flatside of the receiver. In range firing, the trainees were required to fire on a paper "landscape" target, resembling an imaginary battlefield, at a distance of 83.1 feet, or 1,000 inches.

Three-shot bursts were fired at one edge of the target, and the gun "tapped" just enough to move the next burst 2″ across the target. A mil is defined in this application as the angle subtended by an arc equal to 1 inch at 1,000 inches, so this firing technique became known as the "2-mil tap."

The Model 1917 .30 caliber gun was first used on the battlefield by the inventor's eldest son, Val A., who later wrote:

"On several instances, it has been reported that I was the first soldier to use the BAR or the Browning Machine Gun in combat. This is possibly true.

"When the several manufacturing companies designated to produce the machine gun and BAR started production, my father requested me to withdraw from my engineering studies at Cornell and assist in coordinating the manufacturing details, which I did. Later, in April 1918, I was commissioned a Second Lieutenant in the Ordnance Department and sent to France to instruct the instructors at the three United States machine gun schools for officers in France. My assignment was quite logical, for at that time I was probably more knowledgeable of these automatics than any other person save, of course, my father. My experience was gained from my own interest in gun making and working with him during the development period.

"The 79th Division, then stationed in France, was the first division to be fully equipped with the Browning Automatic Rifle and the 30-caliber water cooled machine gun. In early October 1918, the 79th Division was ordered to front line positions just west of Verdun, and I was assigned to the division as an automatic weapons instructor, observer and trouble shooter, which today might be called a "Tech Rep."

"About October 14th, the 79th Division launched an attack against the strong point of Montfaucon, which was taken after severe losses. I participated in this battle with the 79th, but as a United States Ordnance Department officer, not a member of the division. At the beginning of the attack, we laid down a machine gun barrage against German positions, and a gun I was handling quite possibly fired the first shot which, of course, is unimportant historically. More important, it was a critical time in our history and I was privileged to introduce the new weapons because of the knowledge and training which had been so generously given me by my illustrious father."

The popularity of the BAR in the trenches was not shared by No. 4, Rear Rank of the eight-man infantry squad of those times. The smallest man in the squad, which was sized from right front to left rear, the No. 4 Rear Rank was designated by some Army ouija board as the "BAR man." Not only did his primary armament weigh a hefty 17 pounds 6 ounces when loaded, but the little man was also expected to carry 4 extra magazines loaded with 20 rounds each, an absolute must in combat since the magazines were difficult to reload under the best of circumstances. Once the gun was put into action, it did its job well, but with a disturbing amount of jumping around, as the early models were not equipped with stabilizing bipods or shoulder braces.

After the war ended, Fabrique Nationale was licensed to make the BAR, which they proceeded to sell in Europe with some of their own improvements. One of the more significant improvements was a device invented by the famous weapons designer, Dieudonne Saive, which permitted the operator to regulate the gun's rate of fire. In 1931, when Prince Leopold (the future King Leopold III) in his Belgian Army uniform tried out the BAR, it had been fitted with a bipod, and was being produced for delivery to Poland.

Like the BAR, the Colt/Browning .45 semi-automatic pistol, highly effective on target and mechanically reliable under the worst of battle-field conditions, was decidedly unpopular with the troops in WWI. It is a mansized handgun, capable of excellent field accuracy, but in the unwilling hands of recruits, its shattering muzzle blast and boisterous recoil can be frightening. Dubbed the "GI 45," also known with less affection as "Old Hog Leg," it was often tossed in a ditch in favor of the 12-gauge Trench Gun. The U.S. Army's WWII logisticians recognized the need for a more effective personal sidearm for use by gun crews and other soldiers who had no need to carry the service rifle, and introduced the .30 caliber M1 carbine in its stead.

The Development of the High Power Pistol

The 1910 development of the Colt/Browning pistol in 9.0 mm (true .357) caliber for possible sales outside the U.S., as described by William H. D. Goddard in his exhaustive study, *"The Government Models,"* plus the adoption of the M1911 .45 by the U.S. Army spurred Fabrique Nationale to develop their own version of Browning's patent for sale in those areas of the world market which had been ceded to them under terms of the agreement with John M. Browning in 1897. The year before, Browning Brothers had granted Colt the right to make and sell all Browning pistols in the U.S., Great Britain, and Ireland. The 1897 agreement brought FN into the picture. Clarified and amplified by an agreement between Colt and FN signed in 1912, it divided the world firearms market, as seen at that time into the following three broad categories:

    A. Colt's territory was North America including Canada, Central America above and including the Panama Canal Zone, the West Indies, Great Britain, and Ireland.

    B. FN's territory was Continental Europe.

    C. All territory not specified above was to be open to sales by both parties without restriction.

FN's weapons technicians, at the urging of an anxious management, hastily produced a European counterpart of the M1911 Colt/Browning in caliber 9.65MM. Christened the "FN Grand Browning" it was intended for mass production as the flagship of the FN line, but WWI put an end to production which had not proceeded beyond a token number of pieces. The design and the idea would not surface again until some 25 years later.

John M. Browning invented the two pistols illustrated on pages

301-302 of the First Edition in response to an FN request for a 9mm, 15-shot pistol for entry in upcoming French Army trials. According to Val Browning, who was working with his father at the time, he took the prototypes to Colt under the agreement that allowed them to have rights to buy any new Browning automatic pistol. The New England firm which had a perfectly adequate line of Brownings from .25 to .45 caliber in production, declined Browning's offer of the 9mm guns, freeing Val to take them to Liege.

It has remained for a Canadian author, R. Blake Stevens, to tell the story of the birth of the new FN Browning pistol in his beautifully crafted and magnificently illustrated book *The Browning High Power Automatic Pistol* first published in 1984 and updated in 1990.

John M. had constructed two models to give FN the opportunity to decide which was best suited to their needs. The first was of the blowback type, adequate for low power cartridges; the second operated on the locked breech principle. But instead of using the type of lockup that he had invented for the Colt M1911, John M. designed a new, simpler method involving a barrel made with a lug which engaged a stud in the frame to cam the barrel down, disengaging it from the slide.

FN wisely chose the latter type, designated as their Model 1922, and hastily constructed two tool room models—one with a 131mm (5") barrel known as the "short" model, the other a "long" model with a 200mm (7.8") barrel for the French trials—the presumption being that the French Army might prefer a quasi-carbine weapon with detachable shoulder stock.

The first French trials were conducted in 1922. The Trials Commission appointed judges who complimented FN on the accuracy of their entries, but rejected them for several reasons, one being the complicated nature of the bolt assembly and its takedown procedure. The M1922 had a breech bolt containing the striker, striker spring, and an oddly designed, awkward safety slide which also acted as a lock to prevent the striker assembly from being blown back out of the frame.

Back at the drawing board, D. J. Saive, FN's chief weapons technician redesigned the short model using a slide with an external hammer similar to that used on the pre-WWI Grand Browning. Now tagged the Model 1923, the Belgian 9mm was entered in the French trials held in 1923. Once again, the Commission reported the FN entry as superior to all others including the German Parabellum, George Luger's famous design, but the French Government stalled and the Model 1923 was also rejected.

A less aggressive (or stubborn) competitor might have been so discouraged by its repeated failure as to abandon the attempt to win a French contract, but not the management of Fabrique Nationale or its equally persistent chief armorer, the ingenious D. J. Saive who proceeded to design, modify, redesign, and remodify one model after another for a total of 12 different pistols over a period of 14 years from 1922 to 1936. None of the first 11 models were ever manufactured in quantity for commercial sale, although the FN catalog of 1929 did list the Model 1926 "Grand Rendement" (high capacity). All were entered in French trials including the international "Concours" of 1935, and all were rejected. However, the frugal French purchased the units used in each trial and eventually lifted the best features of the Browning/Saive designs for incorporation in their own caliber 7.65mm models 1935A,

"Grand Rendement" 9mm predecessor of the M1935 High Power; very few made for commercial sale.

made by the Societe' Alsacienne de Constructions Mechanique, and 1935S, made by the Government Arsenal at St. Etienne and by several other arms makers.

After a brief hiatus when WWII ended, M. Saive's final design, which had been sold to the Belgian Army as the Model 1935, went back into production and has been accepted world wide as the finest military sidearm on the market. In a few years it had been adopted by the military and police forces of over 60 countries. This handsome, efficient pistol, borne of the genius of John M. Browning, nurtured by the mechanical expertise of Dieudonne J. Saive, and raised by the demands of the French military and the persistence of FN management, has become a legend in the lore of firearms, combining as it does the best features of the Colt/Browning M1911 with John M's tilting barrel and D. J. Saive's large capacity magazine and stream lined contour.

Today the M1911A1, basically the same gun as the 1918 GI .45, is by far the most popular handgun in the crowded field of competition shooting, whether it be the traditional NRA, one-hand type, the two-handed Combat match, or the more recent Practical Pistol match. The old reliable is still a mainstay in the Colt line, with several attractive (and cosmetic) variations. Copies of the M1911A1 and a host of lookalikes and offshoots (no pun intended) are being produced by a parade of manufacturers in this country and abroad. As an indication of its popularity, the articles and advertisements in a recent copy of a leading gun magazine contained illustrations of 171 handguns ranging all the way from single shot, black powder models to tiny pocket semi-automatics and derringers, and a host of conventional revolvers of all makes; 41% were Colt/Browning M1911s and their clones or lookalikes.

BIRTH OF THE SUPERPOSED SHOTGUN

Val Browning remembers his father's love of shooting, not only as a member of a championship trap team or as the final test of a new gun, but just for the fun of popping rocks with a pistol or hunting the wild game that was so plentiful in Utah in those days. Val tells of an evening in the early 1900s when he and his father were stalking through the brush in the hills east of town hunting rabbits. Quail were out of season at the time, but when a covey burst from cover with the thunder of dozens of wings, John M.'s Model 93 spoke sharply several times as though of its own volition, and several birds fell. Val said, "Father turned to me with an innocent expression on his face and said, 'Those were snow birds, weren't they, son?' "

Gus L. Becker, an Olympic class trap shooter and member of the famed Four B's trap team, like John M. and his brother Matthew S. Browning, used a Browning/Winchester Model 1893 12 gauge pump action shotgun for clay pigeon competition. We have Mr. Becker to

Gus L. Becker, member of U.S. 1924 Olympic team, with Auto-5

thank for a rare account of John M.'s approach to a new gun invention. Becker had kept a huge scrapbook of newspaper clippings which he also used as a diary. One yellowed clipping reports that, based on 40 years experience hunting game and shooting over the traps, he had suggested that John M. make an over-under shotgun which he believed would be superior to the classical, side-by-side double guns still popular among traditionalists. An entry in Becker's diary in the 1920s reads as follows:

"J. M. Browning called us together one day around the drafting table in the partitioned corner of his model-making shop. The table was covered with pencil sketches of details of arms mechanisms. Laid across one end of it were four shotguns of entirely different types, each of the latest word in its class. He spoke about as follows:

" 'The Great American Gun Rack is pretty well filled, but there is a conspicuous gap among the shotguns. I have had an eye on that gap for a long time, and now that there are no urgent military jobs on hand, I am going to have a try at filling it. As a matter of fact, I have the gun pretty well worked out in my mind and I have told the shop to get ready to start on the model at once. Probably there will be several models before the gun comes just as I want it, for this is not to be just a good gun. It must combine in a harmonious whole all the requirements I have in mind—and some others I'll think of as I go along.

" 'I have sensed the need for this gun by keeping my eyes and ears open whenever there has been shooting or talk of shooting. That's part of my job. If I hadn't figured out pretty well what sportsmen wanted for nearly half a century, they wouldn't have spent millions of dollars on my ideas.

" 'In order to get a glimpse of the possible market, just think over the men you know who have changed from one shotgun to another through all the varied types. When they aren't changing guns, they are changing stock dimensions, or otherwise tinkering—spending a lot of money and never quite satisfying themselves. And what are they looking for?

" 'They never find what they are looking for, because it doesn't exist. It is odd that the obvious is the hardest thing in the world to find, but everybody knows it is. I have worked a week to make several parts perform some function, and have suddenly seen the way to do it with one. The obvious seems to have a sort of protective coloring, like a grouse. At any rate, some very obvious laws of optics have been over-looked in shotgun designing; or, at any rate, they have never been harmoniously combined in one gun.

" 'As a single demonstration, hold the point of this pencil close to the eye, and note the fuzzy blur that gathers around it. Now move it away from the eye, and the blur gradually clears. If you get it too far away, however, the point begins to grow indistinct. There is, you observe, a range of a few inches within which the average eye can most accurately define a small object. The fact is demonstrated every time you read ordinary print.

" 'As a second demonstration, try those four shotguns—put them up in position for firing, and note the same fuzzy blur gather at the rear end of the sighting plane. Those guns are representative of the best that has been done to shotguns as an aid to sighting, and yet the blur gathers on every one of them. One of them has an ivory bead on the rib, but the bead is beyond the range of clearest vision. Besides, it nearly covers the front bead. And, moreover, it is seen through the blur that gathers where the eye first picks up the sighting plane. It isn't too much to say that every shotgun is aimed through a mist . . . and the bird gets away.

" 'All this may sound complicated, but, on the contrary, it is as simple as moving the point of the lead pencil from close to the eye into the range of clear vision—as simple as locating the rear sight of a rifle at a point where the notch is distinct and unblurred. Rifle sights, of course, cannot be used on a shotgun; there's no time for the eye to center the notch. But the same principle can be utilized. The sighting plane should not begin close to the eye, but should slope up to an apex, the pitch being pronounced, so that the angle where the slope and the level plane join will be abrupt enough to be well defined, but not abrupt enough to stop the eye.

" 'These ideas are obvious, but have you ever heard them analyzed before! And can you point me out a shotgun in which they are utilized? As a matter of fact, there is only one type in which they can be utilized.

" 'And now we have come to the Superposed. The barrels give the required side depth. Next, the frame must be smooth on both sides, and not so shallow that it will spread out like a double gun. The rib I have described, with the apex in the clearest range of vision, will fit on naturally.

"'But that's not all. The center of gravity must come just right, and the weight must be carefully distributed. These factors are of greatest importance, because of their influence on balance and swing. They also influence the whip of the recoil to a marked degree—and the gun must be easy on the shooter. In brief, the gun must fit and point like an integral part of the body.

" 'The next problem is manufacture and price. It must be borne in mind that present over/unders are made principally by hand. This is true of all high grade European shotguns. I know a very skilled gunmaker in Liege who can turn out four fine guns per year. Such a man has a set of chisels and files, peening hammers and a fiddle drill— possibly a small power drill. That's about his entire equipment. He starts with a block of steel, and in the course of time he turns out a finished gun. Such guns, however, would not lend themselves to quantity production with modern machinery. Their mechanical design requires endless fitting and tinkering. Naturally, they have to sell at prices that put them beyond the reach of most men.

" 'My plan is to design a mechanism so simple that it can go into regular quantity production. Of course, the barrels and frames will have to be fitted by hand, and some other hand work will be required, so that it will be a considerably more expensive job than the automatic shotgun, for example. But I figure that the retail price can certainly be brought below $150—the cheaper we can price it, the more people we can reach. To obtain these results, it will be necessary to lay down an expensive installation; and another fortune will have to be invested in the first lot of guns. In the first lot, we shall have to put through more guns than the total of all over/unders so far made-probably two or three times as many. But that's the only way it can be done. If we started with some chisels and files and fiddle drills, and turned out four guns per man per year, our price would have to be up with the others.

" 'That's about all. I have a lot of other ideas, but they are mechanical, and you can see them as they develop. If it all works out as I hoped, we shall be able to fill that gap in the Great American Gun Rack'."

It has been reported that the first Superposed shotgun delivered to an individual in the U.S. went to Gus Becker. With this gun he broke 401 clay targets straight without a miss. His likeness appears on the cover of the Browning 1935 catalog with a Superposed. According to Becker's notes, John M. had called the new gun the 'Superposed' from the start, but the 1935 catalog (No. 53) shows it as the BROWNING OVERUNDER in a Long Range Field Model and a Trap Model, both with 30″ or 32″ barrels, and a Lightning Model with 26″ or 28″ barrels. The Long Range gun carried a raised, matted, hollow rib, while the rib on the Trap Model was ventilated and the Lightning was offered with no rib, but a "Striped" barrel. Also featured on the Lightning was a new "Air-Plane" front sight, advertised to "aid the shooter to instantly line up sight with target," but without saying just how!

The newspaper clipping winds up by saying of the new Browning: "This shotgun is of the overunder type and authorities predict that it will supercede the present day double barrel shotgun."

The Superposed was conceived in the Browning Brothers shop on Hudson (now Grant) Avenue in Ogden, Utah, but John M. had no intention of "laying down an expensive installation" there. He had seen the problems attendant upon gun production and knew full well that there was more money to be made, and vastly more satisfaction to be realized in inventing rather than manufacturing guns. He had made himself known in Liege and that's where he took his most elegant invention. Like his pistols and the Auto-5 shotgun, the Superposed met with the welcome that always came as a surprise to the modest man from Utah.

The Superposed name may have stemmed from John M's familiarity with the French language gained during his sessions with the workers in the FN plant. It must have tickled the inventor's fancy to call his new gun by the past tense of the French verb "to place one atop another." The name stuck and has come to have new meaning distinct from "over-under" in today's shotgun world.

Work on the Superposed may have been delayed by the FN request for the 9mm military pistol, as the patent applications for the new shotgun were filed on October 15, 1923, and September 29, 1924, some time after the two models of the 9mm pistols had been delivered.

Production on the Superposed began in 1930. Val Browning, an engineer and inventor in his own right, had continued work on the gun after his father's death. It was introduced in the Browning line in the U.S. in 1931 with double triggers in 12 gauge only. Later Val improved the trigger system with his single selective trigger and modified the action to accommodate the 20 gauge which was coming into favor in the U.S. Oddly enough, the gun was never made in the popular 16 gauge, but in later years it came out in 28 and .410 gauges to satisfy the demands of American target shooters.

Sales of the new Browning shotgun, even at the modest price of $107.50, in 1931 were slow for the first few years in the U.S. market. In 1934, the Browning Arms Company dropped the price of the standard model to $99.50; again in 1936 the price was cut to $79.80 and held to that level through 1938. Twenty years later the company's "suggested retail" of the standard model Superposed was $280, and by 1970 it had risen to $440. One of the early standard grade guns in new condition would have brought over $1200 in 1991. The sturdiness of the Super-posed has become legendary. A Browning dealer in Ogden, Utah, who has kept track of the guns coming to him for work says, "Superposed Brownings just don't break down. All of those that have come to my shop have needed only cosmetic work such as refinishing or a new sight bead." However, increasing production costs and the soft market in 1976 influenced the company to discontinue the standard model. The former high grade guns designated Grades II, III, IV, V, and VI were also dropped from the line, being replaced by a new Presentation Series in 1977. Dozens of handsome patterns were available to the discriminat-ing purchaser who was not satisfied with anything less than top quality engraving. But by 1980, prices of these deluxe guns had escalated greatly, ranging from around $3,700 U.S. to $8,600 U.S. depending on the engraving coverage, with the Superlight Trap and Skeet models, and the 28 and .410 gauges available at added cost.

In an attempt to bolster sagging sales, Fabrique Nationale had introduced a modified version of the Superposed called the Liege, or B26, in 1973. In the next year's catalog, the gun was shown as the B27 with more minor changes to Browning's original design. Both guns sold for well under $1,000. Both were discontinued when a further modified version made in Japan, the Citori, appeared. The latter is today the mainstay of the Browning over/under line. It is offered in a host of specifications in 12, 20, 28, and .410 gauges, and in Lightning, Hunting,

Superlight, Upland Special, GTI, and Lightning Sporting models. The latter two were introduced in 1989 in response to the increased interest in the new Sporting Clays competition both in Europe and the United States. The Citori also comes in Grades I, III, and VI with engraving being done in Japan by a combination of hand artistry and machine embellishment.

In 1976, the year of the bicentennial of the United States, the Browning Arms Company brought out a special Bicentennial Edition of the Superposed. There were 51 of these commemorative guns made, one for each of the 50 states and the District of Columbia. On the right side of the receiver appeared a legend indicating the order in which that state had joined the Union, e.g. "36th State." The left side bore the name of the state and the date of its entry into the Union, e.g. "Nevada 1864." The engraving was inlaid in various colors of gold. The left face of the receiver carried a representation of the American eagle superimposed on the American flag and encompassed within a border of gold. A frontiersman and a wild turkey appeared on the opposite side. The guns were stocked with the finest grade walnut with deluxe checkering. The buttstocks were of the straight grip, "English" style, and the forearm had the "tulip tip" or schnabel used on the Superlight model. The guns were all chambered for 12 gauge with 28″ barrels choked full/full and with ventilated ribs. The receivers had false side plates to accommodate ornate engraving.

Fabrique Nationale made up two extra guns with the same embellishment except for the individual state identification. One of these rare pieces rests in the FN's own museum in the Herstal plant; the other was presented by the Belgian government to the Smithsonian Institution in Washington D.C. in September 1976, a memorial of the United States' 200th Anniversary. The presentation coincided with the arrival of the Belgian historical firearms exhibit which travelled throughout the U.S. in 1976 and 1977.

From 1966 through 1976, Browning offered limited numbers of supergrade Superposed guns known variously as "Exhibition" or "Exposition" models. These eminently collectible shotguns have puzzled gun collectors for many years.

Harmon G. Williams clarified the subject in a letter replying to an inquiry from a Browning collector.

"You requested some sort of clarification on Browning's 'Exposition' and 'Exhibition' model Superposed shotguns which is a reasonable request but, indeed, one with no easy explanation.

"In any event, let's start with terminology. Over the years, personnel within the company have used the words interchangeably to describe certain guns or series of guns. The same series by one person might have been called 'Exhibition' models and by another 'Exposition' models. I suspect the names originated at FN for some identification purposes and carried over into Browning, loosely to identify some specific gun or group of guns. Were Browning to acquire some models of a type of engraving or style, not considered a part of its regular cataloged line, for lack of a better name, they were called Exposition or Exhibition models depending on the inclination or propensities of the individual involved. I feel sure that generally both words were often used to describe the same gun or series of guns.

"Perhaps I can explain some of the reasons why such a unique gun appeared in the market place.

"Over the years I can recall a number of occasions when the Browning Company would want a new series of engraved models for its cataloged line. The FN engravers would receive general parameters and then were left to demonstrate their originality in concept and many samples would arrive, most of which would ultimately be rejected for adoption.

"Uniqueness or collector value never entered the company's mind in those days, and eventually most of these samples were disposed of at bargain prices.

"Only the word 'Exposition,' to my knowledge, was used in the 1966 through 1970 catalogs to describe the availability of specially engraved models. It was about then when Browning set up an engraving shop in Belgium somewhat separated from other FN engravers. It was in this shop that all of the finer Superposed shotguns destined for Browning U.S.A. were engraved. Browning accepted orders for almost any kind of special engraving a customer might want and all such orders were engraved and finished (stocks included) in this custom shop. To keep the engravers occupied, when custom orders were below capacity, these engravers were given a free hand to create original designs. These pieces seemed to sell just about as quickly as received, so there were rarely photographs or listings. Through dealer contacts in the marketplace, there always seemed to be a person ready to acquire one as soon as it was available. It is estimated that less than 100 of these unique designs were sold between 1970 and 1974 and there is no record or photo file of these particular guns.

"In 1974 and 1975, FN experienced a noticeable decline in European markets for highly engraved shotguns, perhaps a result of the economy during that period, and was encountering a heavy inventory situation. The Browning Company was made a rather attractive offer of a sizeable quantity of their guns and agreed to take quite a number, even though it recognized the shotguns were not, in the majority, of the styles generally preferred in the U.S. markets. This became the series most commonly referred to as the 'Exhibition' grades."

Although the inventor's original specifications called for a minimum of hand fitting, the Superposed was never a production line gun. Its assembly is done by skilled craftsmen in some 155 separate steps; some parts are delivered in the rough and must be totally finished by hand. The manufacture of its over 70 parts (in addition to barrels and wood), made of some 20 different kinds of steel, and using varying types of heat treatment, is extremely costly. Moreover, the Superposed design does not lend itself to modern technology and manufacturing methods such as electro-erosion and lost-wax processes.

Fabrique Nationale's introduction of the B26, B27, and Citori models was a successful attempt to cut costs, bolster a sagging Superposed market, and at the same time retain the original Browning gun for the discriminating buyer. In the process of redesigning the Superposed, some of its components were actually made more complicated, although cheaper. A prime example is the Superposed forearm, unique in that it is non-detachable, remaining fastened to the barrels when the gun is broken down. It contains 19 parts plus the wood. The Liege forearm is detachable, no great disadvantage, but takes 25 parts plus wood. The redesigned Citori, made in Japan since 1970, also has a detachable forearm taking 28 metal parts, some of which look like stampings.

The mechanical features of John M.'s original Superposed design which earned it top rank among discerning shotgunners have been retained in the Citori which is not to be confused with other overunder guns made in Japan.

THE JOHN M. BROWNING FIREARMS MUSEUM

For more than four decades, a strange compulsion drove John M. Browning to invent one gun after another, a process calling for tremendous imagination as well as great mechanical aptitude, remarkable in a relatively unschooled inhabitant of a pioneer village in the American wild west. Most of his ideas came to fruition in final form, were patented, manufactured and marketed successfully. It seems strange, therefore, that a man whose whole being was devoted to the creation of so many masterpieces would have so little regard for the end products of his genius. Once one of his guns was finished and tested to his satisfaction, the inventor seems to have lost all interest in it, possibly because ideas for a new gun had already crowded it out of his mind.

What became of some of the guns John M. made has been a question that has tantalized historians and gun buffs alike for many years. It is known that many were torn down for parts. A few of the rejected models have survived in complete form, including the M1882 lever action rifle and the first three models of the Auto-5 shotgun.

John M. was generous to a fault and gave many examples of his handiwork to friends and relatives. Some of his prototypes may also have been borrowed from the shop and never returned. Most of the models of the rifles and shotguns sold to Winchester were recovered but some are still missing, like that of his very first invention, the Model 1878 Single Shot Rifle.

There are several candidates for the honor of authentication as the prototype, Serial No. 1 Model 1878 rifle. As a matter of fact, there are probably several guns with that prestigious number in addition to the one John M. gave to his friend, Split-nose Barlow, and the model stolen from the shop in 1881. The unmarked patent model, with cutoff barrel and bob-tailed stock, reposes in the arms collection of the Smithsonian Institution. Another shortened, unblued Single Shot rifle bearing Serial No. 1 has stood for years in the basement arms racks of the Winchester Museum in Cody, Wyoming. It is believed to be the Winchester production prototype of the Model 1885. Another semifinished Model 1878 rifle bearing no serial number or other markings was in the Browning Collection. In order to comply with Federal regulations, it has been stamped with number "001."

Val Browning had realized the importance of his father's prototypes and, as he happened to be in the various factories that were making the guns and would see some of the old models in the shops, many in pieces, he would reassemble them and take them back to Ogden. At one time, several of them, including some of the machine guns, were stored on the third floor of the old family home on 27th Street in Ogden, a grand battlefield for the war games played there by Val Browning's sons and their friends.

Val had worked closely with his father for many years and recalls his participation in testing the prototypes of the BAR. The first model, which is in the Browning Collection, is of the top ejection type. Some 10

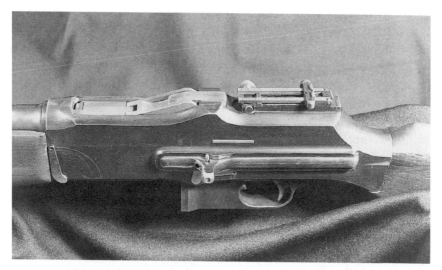

Top view of first prototype BAR with top ejection port and rear sight taken from US Springfield rifle, M1906

or 12 of them were made by Winchester before that design was abandoned.

"It's a good thing, too," said Mr. Val Browning. "While testing a solid-top model, I felt an extra heavy blow on my shoulder and something hitting my foot. I looked down and the receiver was swelled on both sides, the magazine had dropped out of the rifle, and the cartridge head was brazed to the bolt face. Apparently an extra heavy test load had been placed in the magazine, why or how we never did find out. Maybe it was loaded with Bullseye pistol powder by mistake, or it might even have been sabotage; we don't know. But my father said, 'It's a good thing that wasn't fired in the top ejection model. It would have blown up right in your face!'"

The first factory-produced Superposed shotgun bearing Serial No. 1 is in the Collection, but the prototype was never located. "It was probably all over the FN shop in pieces," said Val Browning. "We never did find it."

Among the more laudable characteristics that distinguish man from the other animals is his pride in his ancestors and their accomplishments. This most erudite nostalgia has filled libraries with words on all sorts of subjects and museums with all manner of artifacts. The urge to preserve the past continues to fill American pioneer museums with barbed wire, ruby crystal, steamer trunks, horse collars, and flintlock rifles. More sophisticated institutions vie for the rarest and

most costly examples of fine art, classic cars, aircraft, and railroad
memorabilia. In this latter group are some that specialize in firearms.
Perhaps the best known is the Liege Museum of Arms located on the
banks of the Meuse River in the heart of the ancient city famous for its
arms industry. An imposing structure recognized immediately by the
pair of mortars emplaced on either side of its carriage entrance, it was
built in 1775-76 as a private dwelling. Its many distinguished visitors
included Napoleon Bonaparte as First Consul in 1803 and later with his
second wife, Marie-Louise, as Emperor in 1811. Among its 11,000 items
of arms and armor, the museum displays a number of examples of John

*Cutaway model of the Superposed action, used to train gunsmiths at the FN
plant. On display in Liége Musée d'Armes.*

M. Browning's guns, including a cutaway model of the Superposed
shotgun showing details of the action.

Monsieur Claude Gaier, the museum's director, historian, and
coauthor of the Fabrique Nationale Centennial History, FN 100 YEARS,
has this to say of the museum's Browning collection.

"We have quite a few FN-made Browning rifles, pistols, and guns
(sic), but not all are on display. Practically all the models illustrated in
the last pages of the FN 1989 Centennial book are here. We also have
some other items designed by J. M. Browning but labelled under their
commercial brand names of, say Colt or Winchester. . . . I would like
very much to open an FN-Browning room in this museum. It does not
exist yet although we could easily set it up owing to the great amount of
undisplayed FN material we have gathered over the past decades, and
which is still being gathered. The problem is . . . budgets."

The U. S. Army operates a museum at its arsenal at Rock Island,

Illinois, containing examples of the items made there, a collection that is heavy on field stoves, ammunition, and insignia, as well as Civil War militaria. It was dedicated to the memory of John M. Browning in a ceremony on November 4, 1959, attended by Val A. Browning, at that time President of Browning Arms Company, and Harmon G. Williams, Vice President.

(Note: The announcement of the dedication bears across the bottom a typically GI footnote—"BAND TO PLAY UNTIL VISITORS HAVE LEFT DEDICATION SITE.")

Major Richard J. Keogh, in an Arms Gazette article on the museum, says, "There is a representative selection of his [John M. Browning's] inventions. Included are a couple of experimental rifles and pistols. Access to the display is somewhat restricted by the other displays that have crept in around it."

Much has been written about the collection of Browning firearms housed in the Winchester Museum at the Buffalo Bill Historical Center, Cody, Wyoming, including prototypes of the 27 models bought but never produced. Richard Rattenbury, curator of the Winchester Museum in 1982, published *THE BROWNING CONNECTION,* a treasure trove of information concerning the 27 orphans. His large format book, which he modestly calls a catalog, is beautifully illustrated with photographs and enlarged patent drawings of the 27 guns. He writes in his preface, "Unbeknown to most shooters who wielded the series of firearms introduced by the Winchester Repeating Arms Company in the late 19th century, all the classic rifles and shotguns were the original product of a fertile mind located not in New Haven, Connecticut, but in the former territory of Utah."

In the spring of 1958, Maj. Gen. Maxwell E. Rich, the Adjutant General of the Utah National Guard, announced plans for the construction of a new armory in Ogden, to be named in honor of John M. Browning. A year later, the building was occupied by Ogden Guard units. Provisions had been made for a secure display area for the Browning Collection, which was moved to its new location, along with a number of production firearms made available by the Browning Arms Company. Although Val Browning had been approached several times by national groups desiring to gain custody of the collection, he felt that the work of his father should not leave his Ogden home.

The collection was attractively displayed in the Armory, but its remote location on the outskirts of Ogden and the limited hours during which it was open to the public, tended to restrict its exposure to view. In 1976, when plans were laid for the Ogden City community center, Val

Browning decided to donate the collection to the city for the establishment of a firearms museum.

Once the busiest spot in Ogden, through which 50 passenger trains passed each day, the 55-year-old Union Station had become by 1968 a dreary, semi-deserted monument to the decline of rail traffic in the West. It was saved from the wrecker's ball by an informal coalition of the Utah Bicentennial Commission, Greater Ogden Chamber of Commerce, Golden Spike Centennial Commission, Ogden Junior League and the Ogden City Council. With funding provided by state and federal grants, as well as substantial private contributions, the building was renovated and became an active community center operated by the Union Station Development Corporation, a non-profit organization.

Built of Ogden-made buff brick in Italian Renaissance style, with Spanish tile roof and faced with Idaho white sandstone, the cosmopolitan structure now houses the John M. Browning Firearms Museum, a

The Ogden, Utah Union Station, home of the Browning Firearms Museum

Railroad Museum, a theater, conference rooms, banquet hall, gift shop, and the corporate offices.

The Browning Firearms Museum, opened in Ogden in October, 1978, is the only one of its kind in the world. It is dedicated to the memory and times of the Browning family of inventors and contains Browning-designed firearms only. Over 90 original prototype or production models, from the first to the last known example of John Browning's work, are on display there.

This unique museum has become a mecca for gun lovers and western history buffs. Over 700 visitors were logged in on one weekend, and the museum register contains names of visitors from every state in the Union and many foreign countries. To a gun collector, the fascination of the Browning Firearms Museum lies in its fabulous display of the inventor's original working models, still in the white, unpolished and still bearing the tool marks left by John M. Browning's hand. In this one-of-a-kind display are not only the prototypes of such well-known Browning arms as the Colt "GI .45" and the Winchester Model 1894 .30-30, but a number of those models which were never produced commercially. Among these are the .22 Practice Pistol ordered by the Army, a hammerless .45 auto pistol rejected by the U. S. Cavalry, the two Model 1922 9 mm High Power pistols purchased by FN and modified after the inventor's death, and six different .38 ACP cal. auto pistols sold to Colt prior to the production of the seventh model as the Colt Model 1900, the first auto pistol to be manufactured commercially in this country.

The forge-blackened but still functional .44 WCF semi-automatic "firearm," the forerunner of Browning's famous BAR automatic rifle, is another rare piece on display.

A collection of examples of all firearms produced on Browning designs can never be housed in any museum. A display of only the Browning automatic pistols and their variants used by military forces throughout the world would run into the hundreds of examples. Devoted as it is to original models and basic production types, the Browning Firearms Museum is not, however, merely a cemetery for dead guns. Planning calls for the future acquisition and display, as funding becomes available, of additional pieces, including several known prototypes and other historically significant Browning guns.

Other examples of museum quality Brownings in the hands of heirs or local collectors include the final model of the .38 ACP auto pistol which became the Colt Model 1900, but whose existence is not recorded in any text on the subject. A number of Jonathan Browning single shot, harmonica and cylinder rifles have appeared, as well as his last rifle, a Model 1878 Single Shot .38 Cal. Extra Long, inscribed on the receiver, "Made by Jonathan Browning on J. M. Browning's patent in 74 (sic) year of his age in 1879" (the year of his death). Jonathan gave the rifle to his son George, who, with John M., Matthew, Edmund and Samuel

John M. Browning's 7th pistol model sold to Colt, produced as their M1900. Prototype now in a private collection.

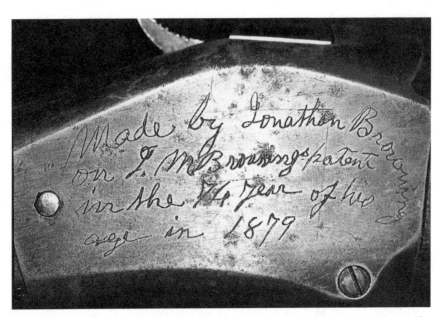

M1878 Single Shot Rifle made by Jonathon Browning in 1879, on display in the Browning Firearms Museum.

Browning, ran the Browning store in Ogden. It is now on loan to the museum by its present owner.

While the statement inscribed on the rifle has never been challenged, it is believed by family members to have been placed there by some one else, as Jonathan never learned how to read and write, signing business papers and other documents with his "sign," which looks like two script capital B's, back to back.

The museum is also unique in its decor and display techniques. The guns are housed in free-standing pylons providing all-around visibility of the contents. The pylons, lighted internally from above, are arranged by "time lines" on curving patterns of vari-colored carpet, leading the visitor through the chronology of Browning's inventions. Each pylon bears a rear-lighted glass header describing the contents and date of invention, with supplementary descriptions placed below each display.

At one end of the gun room is a section devoted to the Browning family history. Here are photographs of the Browning inventors, father and son, a near life-sized photo reproduction of the front of the first

Striking display of Browning firearms in lighted pylon cases. John M. Browning Firearms Museum, Ogden, Utah

Browning "gun factory," and a reconstruction of the workshop containing many of the tools and machine equipment used by Jonathan Browning and his sons.

Along one wall of the "Family Room" is a showcase above which is a poster headed "The Father" with a synopsis of the life of Jonathan

Jonathan Browning's lathe and many of his hand tools brought from Tennessee, now on display in the Browning Firearms Museum.

Browning, flanked by his portrait and a photograph with an unidenti-
fied woman thought to be one of his four wives.

The showcase contains examples of the two types of rifles that made
Jonathan famous, a beautifully stocked cylinder rifle resembling the
Colt Ring Lever rifle, and the only example of Jonathan's slide rifle that
can be authenticated as his work.

In recent years, there have been many cylinder rifles show up, all of
them bearing his name. Early models were marked "J. BROWNING" with
single letter stamps in a semi-circle above "& SONS," and below that,

*Examples of Jonathan Browning's most famed percussion rifles, the slide and
cylinder models, displayed in the Browning Firarms Museum, Ogden UT.*

"WARRANTED." Later models are marked with a single line stamped
simply "J. BROWNING."

Although the slide rifle may have attracted more attention because
of its unusual design, it appears that Jonathan preferred the more
sophisticated cylinder model. It is known that the rifle he carried on the
trek to Utah was a cylinder model which was sold in Ogden by his son
James Allen Browning, also a gunmaker, for the then astonishing price
of $125.

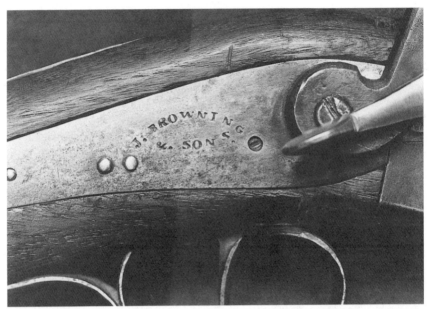

Side plate, Jonathan Browning percussion rifle. The lever forward of the hammer was used to cam the cylinder against the barrel cone. Made about 1834-1842 in Quincy, Illinois.

Cylinder on Jonathan Browning rifle was cammed forward to align with bore and provide tight gas seal. Engraved "Approved remedy for hunger." Made about 1834-1842 in Quincy Illinois.

Six of the cylinder rifles have been observed, all of them marked with Jonathan's name, but the only one of the seven slide rifles extant to bear his name is the one in the Ogden Museum. Some of the others are marked "J.M. Browning," and a few are unmarked. One of the latter has been displayed as having been made by Jonathan Edmund Browning, the expert tool maker who turned John M.'s patterns into working prototypes.

In the First Edition, John Browning recalls his Uncle Matt's story of his first real gun wheedled out of his older brother, John M., who used a new barrel found in the shop and old slide rifle parts brought out from Council Bluffs, Iowa, to make a rifle in time for Matthew's tenth birthday. But for whom the other rifles stamped with John M.'s name were made is not known. Perhaps they were made for his other half brothers, Sam and George, or were sold in the shop. And the question of

Top view of slide rifle action, believed to have been made by J.M. Browning from parts left from Council Bluffs shop. Note the top hammer, not seen on original models.

who made the unmarked slide rifles must go unanswered until another piece of early Browning history surfaces.

Stories of the existence of pistols or revolvers made by Jonathan Browning have circulated for years. Many of the pieces attributed to him have been identified positively as having been made by other gunsmiths. Only one pistol bearing Jonathan Browning's name is known to exist, although his ads in the Frontier Guardian, Kanesville, Iowa, promised to supply ". . . improved firearms, viz: revolving rifles and pistols . . ."

Sometime in 1901, an eleven-year-old boy found the remains of a percussion under-hammer "boot pistol" along the old trail from Ogden to Salt Lake City, near the present location of 46th Street in Ogden. All that remained was the rusty metal work. The oval-shaped grip panels had long since rotted away. The relic was tucked away on a shelf in a woodshed and forgotten for over 60 years until it was rediscovered by the finder's granddaughter. Careful cleaning uncovered the inscription on the right side of the receiver, "J. BROWNING, COUNCIL BLUFFS, IOWA" and the incomplete legend "G. Higl . . .," perhaps the original owner's name blurred by time.

The ancient 5″ barrel appears to be about 50 caliber. The lockwork is typically Browning; simple, sturdy, and with only four moving parts, hammer, spur trigger, and their two actuating springs. The bar hammer swings on a pin set in the frame. The trigger and sear are one piece, and with the replacement of the defunct springs, the lockwork would still function. As far as is known, nobody had checked the barrel to find out if it still held a charge. Assuming the pistol was indeed made in Council Bluffs, it can be dated between 1846 and 1852, a time when Jonathan was busily engaged as Brigham Young's armorer preparing weapons for the Mormon exodus to Utah. Whether Jonathan made the boot pistol for a customer or for his own use will probably never be known. However, one reason why other Jonathan Browning pistols have not surfaced may be the fact that Colt's revolvers were rapidly becoming the most popular sidearms in the West. With their much greater firepower, they may well have sounded the knell of the single shot pistol.

The Jonathan boot pistol eventually was sold to the Browning Arms Company and found its place in the company's historical inventory. When some of these pieces were moved to the John M. Browning Armory for display in the National Guard museum, the Jonathan pistol was left behind, probably by chance. Then in 1970, a request for the donation of Browning guns and artifacts was made to the company by representatives of the Mormon Church for the replication of the shop used by Jonathan Browning during his stay in Nauvoo, Illinois. The boot pistol and several others of Jonathan's guns and tools were given to the church and are now on public view in the restored Browning home and shop in Nauvoo, a fitting resting place for what is probably Jonathan's only surviving pistol.

In the fall of 1981, the Browning Arms Company decided to do a bit of housecleaning in their historical inventory room where a quantity of guns and gun parts had accumulated over the years.

The Museum staff was called on for assistance in selecting those items considered to be of museum quality and which the Company wished to donate to the Browning Collection in the museum. A team composed of museum staff members, Browning weapons technicians, and a local gun collector inspected scores of items, sorting them into three categories; 1) museum quality, 2) saleable merchandise, and 3) junk.

Among the most interesting items in the "museum" category were two prototype caliber .22 slide action rifles, the receivers unblued but liberally decked out in rust. At first glance, they appeared to be "Trombone" models invented in 1919 and sold to FN. A closer look reveals an ingenious takedown mechanism unlike any previously observed. At the front end of the trigger guard/floor plate assembly is a latch, flush with the floor plate and knurled at its front end. When this latch is raised against spring pressure to a position at right angles with the floor plate, the receiver and stock may be separated from the action by sliding them to the rear. The entire action is then exposed and the receiver is seen to be a thin housing only. The actions are entirely different on the two guns.

Both were intended to be loaded through a port at the base of the pistol grip, fed by a spring-loaded plunger like that used on John M.'s .22 semi-automatic rifle. One barrel is from a Winchester Model 62, indicating that the gun was assembled in its present form some time after 1932. The other bears only the marking ".22 short, long, or long rifle."

There are no records available at the Browning plant to identify these intriguing prototypes, but a member of the Browning family examined them carefully and was of the opinion that they were designed and partially completed by John M. during his development of the .22 semi-auto and Trombone rifles, and finished by someone else after his death in 1926.

Among the other prototype firearms in the lot donated to the Museum was a large, heavy machine gun without stand, which defied identification. It was intended to be a belt-fed weapon, air cooled, with an oversized barrel out to about 8″ from the muzzle, at which point it was tapered to almost rifle size. There were no documents of any kind to help in putting a tag on the gun, nor were any of the Browning staff able to contribute anything as to its origin.

Photos of the gun were sent to Colonel George C. Chinn, USMC, Retired, now deceased, who was known for his expertise in the machine gun world. According to Col. Chinn, it was made by Colt and tested at

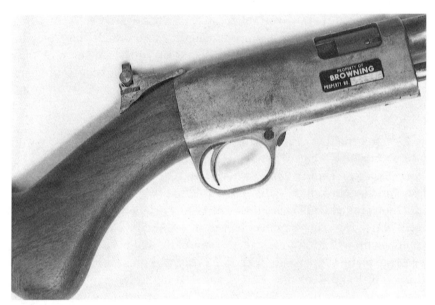

Experimental model of a "trombone" action .22 rifle, believed made by John M., but finished by another person.

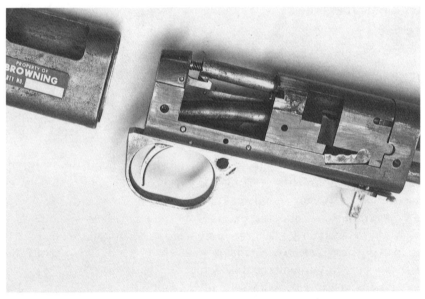

Action of experimental .22 rifle completed after the death of John M. Browning

Springfield Armory in 1934. It was essentially a modified, beefed up Browning Automatic Rifle (BAR) produced at the request of the U.S. Army to fill the need for a light machine gun. It was equipped with a spade grip assembly like that used on the early English Vickers and Lewis machine guns, and was given the Army name, "Gun, Machine, Light, Cal. .30, T10."

Extensive modifications ordered by the Army resulted in a lighter gun with shoulder stock, bipod and quick change barrel, called the "Browning Gas Operated Belt-fed Light Machine Gun, Cal. .30." Samples were made up by Springfield Armory in 1942, but were rejected with a request for still further modifications. The Auto Ordinance Company also made up other variations of the T10, but they were not successful. Remington Arms Co. was asked to bid on further development of the basic design, but declined. High Standard (then the Dixwell Corporation) undertook to produce ten models of another modification of the T10, to be known as the T10E3, but after testing four units, the Army concluded that the gun suffered so many malfunctions as to be unsatisfactory for standardization, and the project was abandoned.

BRUCE W. BROWNING'S .22 PISTOLS, AND THE NEW BAR

The treasure trove of Browning prototypes donated to the Museum included four prototype semi-automatic pistols. Two were invented and patented by Val A. Browning as experiments in the feasibility of one-hand operation to work the slide in loading or unloading the pistol by squeezing the grip. Parts of these interesting models, which were not put into production, were made by Bruce W. Browning, Val's youngest son, in the early 1950's.

The other two pistols, one in the white, were invented by Bruce, who inherited from his illustrious forebears the ability to convert dreams into live steel. Bruce is an accomplished machinist who was comfortable among the high tech machines in the Browning Arms Company's research laboratory. He began his career with Browning as an officer of the firm, but in the 1950's he spent most of his time in the shop. In 1959, he designed his first .22 caliber semi-automatic pistol, which he took to Belgium the following year.

He described his reception by FN as follows: "After examining the pistol, one of FN's engineers came to the Browning office at Herstal and gave me a fairly complete picture of the manufacturing process and the cost to perform each individual operation required by the gun's design.

He pointed out that, although my design was interesting, it would involve some 750 operations, which was way too many. . . . He gave me a lot to think about."

In May 1961, Bruce returned to FN with a new model .22 pistol, the blued prototype on display in the Ogden museum. Requiring a little over 400 manufacturing operations, it was produced by FN in 1962 as the Medalist. The barrel of this second prototype was a composite. The chamber and rifling came from a High Standard pistol, turned to a straight tube and force fit into a larger tube. From a bench rest, the gun would put ten rounds into a hole the size of a 50-cent piece at 50 yards.

The Medalist is a sophisticated target pistol with features especially appealing to participants in international competition. However, costs of production, transportation, and import duty made it too expensive to be a serious competitor with target pistols made in the U.S. The Medalist was dropped from the Browning catalog in 1975 after production reached 25,479 units. In a modified version, it is still listed in the FN catalog for sale outside the U.S. as the International Medalist.

Specially engraved Rennaissance style Medalist .22 caliber pistol invented by Bruce W. Browning, 1961.

At some time in 1963, Browning asked FN to design a semi-automatic sporting rifle along the lines of the Winchester Model 100. In the fall of 1964, a prototype designed by Ernst Vervier of FN was examined and tested at the Browning range in Utah. Vervier had carried

Browning's suggestion regarding the Winchester a bit too far. The gun even looked like the Model 100 with its rounded receiver and one piece stock. Moreover, the designer admitted the connection between the gas piston and the breech block was frail and had given trouble, and the gun had a further limitation in that it would handle only short cartridges such as the .308 and .243. On the plus side, it did have a swinging magazine, a feature which Browning liked.

In December 1964, Bruce Browning was given the project of designing the rifle which later became the new BAR. Most of the design work was done in the winter and spring of 1964-65 in the company's new facilities at Morgan, Utah, which had just been constructed. Bruce moved his drawing board from the old shop at 2450 Grant Avenue in Ogden while workmen were still finishing the building and there was still snow on the ground. After the shop was completed and the machines installed, Bruce and Willy Bertrand, a Belgian weapons technician, started building the prototype. It was finished in the first week of June. Bruce picks up the story as follows:

"Willy and I fired the first shot in the new outside rifle range. For the first shot we had left off drilling the gas hole in the barrel. The rifle fired OK, so we went back into the shop and drilled the hole. That same afternoon we went out again and the darned thing did just was it was supposed to do; it ejected the brass and loaded a round from the magazine ready to fire. We felt pretty good.

"On June 15, 1965, I took the rifle to Belgium. It had been fired only a few dozen times. I had a problem. M. Vervier was a very nice man, and we had asked him to do a design for us. Here I was with my own design. I told FN I had been strongly inspired by Vervier's prototype and had used much of his design in my prototype. This was true, especially as to the swinging magazine. The decision was made immediately to give my prototype an extensive firing test.

"The next day when I arrived at FN, shooting was well underway. I left the range and visited various parts of the factory with the head of the Browning staff in Belgium. Presently we were interrupted by a messenger who announced that there had been an accident with my prototype. I returned to the firing range and found everyone in shocked amazement. The barrel on my prototype had split lengthwise from near the muzzle and nearly to the receiver. The forearm had been shredded. The shooter had been stunned, but thanks to his protective gear, not otherwise hurt. It was not a pressure burst, but a structural failure. The receiver and breech were not damaged. Later FN did a laboratory analysis and found that there was a seam in the steel which ran the length of the barrel. The barrel blank I had used was one supplied to my father during the war when he was doing barrel cooling studies for the Army. As it happened, my gas port was drilled right through the seam.

"The design looked promising, so the work continued. I supplied FN with my drawings which they copied . . . with neatly pencilled millimeter dimensions written faintly under my inch dimensions.

"FN obtained a patent on the swinging magazine idea. I was granted four U.S. patents on the mechanism in my name only as the assignor to Browning. They are:

> # 3,395,613 on the trigger mechanism
> # 3,397,473 on the extractor and extractor spring
> # 3,368,298 on the breech bolt carrier and slide cover
> # 3,380,182 on the receiver stock assembly.

"Vervier replaced my solid locking lugs with an interrupted thread locking lug system as on his model, an improvement. He also did the conversion of the original model to take the magnum cartridges, a big advantage of my design."

Harmon G. Williams, former President of Browning Arms Company, recalls that much discussion took place early in the BAR project regarding the rifle's contour. It was finally decided that although the more modern, rounded receiver and one-piece stock of the FN design might be more esthetically appealing, the traditional Auto-5 "humpback" would give the new rifle a more easily recognizable identity. The result was a fortunate compromise, a good balance between the virtues of both contours with an added advantage that it allowed for shortening the overall length of the receiver.

According to Mr. Williams, the rifle underwent rigid and painstaking tests before and after actual production had commenced. The new BAR was introduced July 17, 1967, and has taken its place as a staple item in the Browning inventory.

RETURN TO SARAJEVO

By their very nature, museums have come to be considered as sources of irrefutable fact, available to the general public on demand. Many museums have established a permanent capability to respond to inquiries on subjects within their purview. Most provide this service for a modest fee, probably insufficient to support the operation.

The "Ogden Gun Museum" as it has become known locally, receives frequent calls for information. Some are spawned of idle curiosity (e.g. "How much is my Grandfather's shotgun worth?") But a number of serious requests for information have come from historians, collectors, and educators. The museum, an Ogden City agency, is not staffed to respond to such requests, but often enlists the assistance of members of the Browning Arms Company located in nearby Morgan, Utah, as well as members of local gun collectors organizations.

In the process of replying to many letters of inquiry about Browning firearms in recent years, the museum staff has recorded some new and very interesting Browning history.

In midsummer 1981, the museum staff was contacted by a German writer, Herr Paul W. Schwenke of Duisburg, requesting confirmation of the statement in the First Edition which he said also appeared in the Fabrique National archives, that the weapon used to assassinate Archduke Franz Ferdinand of Austria and his wife, Sophie, on June 28, 1914, was an FN Model 1900 automatic pistol.

Research of the newspaper files of the period revealed nothing about the weapons used in the assassination except to note that the Serbian Black Hand terrorists given the contract on the royal couple were armed with four Belgian pistols and some bombs. The account went on to say that a bomb attempt on the Archduke's car was a failure, but later another conspirator, one Gavrilo Princip, was able to get off two shots at close range fatally wounding the royal couple.

Johnson and Haven's 1941 book, *Automatic Arms*, says of the early FN/Browning pistols, ". . . The first model put out was the .32 pocket (sic), the model that gained fame as the pistol used in the assassination of Archduke Franz Ferdinand."

Fabrique Nationale's publication, "The American Gunmaker, John M. Browning, A complete comic strip album," brought out in 1978 to commemorate the 100th anniversary of the Browning company, says of the M1900 pistol, "This weapon finds unexpected fame in the assassination of the Crown Prince of Austria Hungary."

Dr. Joachim Remak's remarkably detailed account of the events of June 28, 1914, "Sarajevo, The Story of a Political Murder" published in 1959, states that four of the seven Serbian Black Hand terrorists were armed with "Belgian Army revolvers," then later describes the pistols as "Belgian automatics of the latest model." Only one of the young assassins ever fired his pistol that day. Police arrested all seven members of the hit team and were able to recover all four of the pistols which were introduced as evidence at the conspirator's trial.

Herr Schwenke wrote that his research indicates that the bullets used in the murders (only two were fired and both were recovered) were actually 9mm short, or .380 caliber. He listed the serial numbers of the four pistols taken from the Black Hand team by the police as Nos. 19074, 19075, 19120, and 19126, and forwarded copies of correspondence from the FN staff stating the Model 1910 pistols with those serial numbers had been shipped to a Belgian retail firm on December 3, 1913, but no record of their shipment to Serbia could be found.

Another German author, Karl Schaefer, associate editor of the Swiss magazine, Waffen Digest, who had done some research on the same subject, sent the museum staff a copy of a letter from the Direktor of the Heeresgeschichtliches (Army history) Museum in Vienna, which is quoted in part as follows:

". . . the Princip weapon in question was a Browning Model 1910, a caliber 9mm short, which was put on the market by FN in 1912. The handguns used by the assassins were located in Salzburg until the end of the war in 1945, but have since disappeared. Which of the four guns used to kill the successor to the throne and his wife, unfortunately, does not show in the records of the Austrian war archives in Vienna."

In all probability, the four pistols were "liberated" by the U.S. troops that made Salzburg their headquarters in Austria at war's end. The Sarajevo pistols may be languishing right now in some WWII veteran's footlocker in a dusty attic.

THE 1,000,000TH BROWNING PISTOL

At some time in 1912, nobody knows exactly when, the FN's Herstal works is believed to have produced the one millionth Browning automatic pistol. Something like 4,000 of the Modele 1899 were made, and by the time the Model 1900 had been discontinued in 1910-11, some 725,000 units of that model had come off the line. In the meantime, the 1903 "Large Model," the 1905/06 Vest Pocket Model, and the Model 1910 had been put into production. The upshot is that not only is the birthday of No. 1,000,000 unknown, but it cannot be identified by model.

However, this was a landmark not to be ignored. The FN management set up a grand celebration to commemorate the event and to honor the inventor. A lavish banquet was held in the plant according to the newspaper account of the day. Four Browning Vest Pocket 6.35mm pistols were prepared for the occasion, inlaid in gold on the left side of the frame, "Un million." On the evening of January 31, 1914, during the banquet, one of the little pistols was presented to John M. Browning and another was accepted by the Belgian Minister of War, M. Berryer, on behalf of King Albert who was unable to attend.

As a grand finale to the evening's celebration, the FN Master of Ceremonies unveiled a specially commissioned bronze female figure representing the Spirit of Genius, about ¾ life size with outstretched

M1905 in case, given to Val A. Browning.

arms and soaring wings, which was presented to the guest of honor. A likeness of the figure appeared on the evening's program with the legend, "La F.N. a M. Browning, En Commemoration de la fabrication du Millionieme Pistolet" which needs no translation. The lovely young lady now graces the formal garden at Val Browning's home in Ogden, Utah.

Val Browning remembers the evening well. He attended the affair,

"Spirit of Genius" statue, near life size, presented to John M. Browning by FN management, 31 Jan. 1914.

very proud of his father, but, as he put it, "I was a bit nervous because that was the first time I had ever worn a tuxedo." At 18, he was probably the youngest guest at the affair.

The next evening, Val was invited to a private dinner given by FN's Director General, M. Andri, who presented him with one of the "Un million" pistols. This piece became part of the Browning Collection along with its satin-lined presentation case. The fourth Vest Pocket pistol was retained by FN for display in the company museum at the Herstal plant.

In the spring of 1982, a Browning collector of Dover, New Hampshire, wrote to ask about a caliber .25 Belgian Vest Pocket pistol which he had seen for sale at a gun show. It was distinguished by the words

"Un million" inlaid in gold. Contact with the owner, a well known firearms dealer, revealed that the gun had been purchased in the mid 1950s from the English firm of Parker and Hale who reported it as having been bought from an English officer who admitted having "liberated" it in Liege during the Allied Occupation in WWII.

The purchaser stated that the English firm had contacted FN at the time of the sale and had been told that the pistol, Serial No. 456,602, was the one given to John M. Browning, adding that the firm was not interested in its return. A letter from the museum staff to the FN Chief of Customer Services produced the information that the pistols inlaid with gold had been released from production to the engravers in late January 1914 and had been presented at the commemorative banquet and at M. Andri's dinner, confirming Val Browning's recollection of the events. The FN letter also stated that the fourth inlaid pistol, "No. 456,188, which came out of production on January 31, 1914, is exhibited in the FN display room as it seems to have been from the beginning."

According to Val Browning, it had long been thought that the Vest Pocket pistol given to his father had been lost or stolen, as it had not showed up in his father's possessions at the time of his death.

By way of explaining the presence of the fourth "Un million" pistol in Liege during WWII, he said, "My father didn't think much of guns, per se. If he wanted one, he'd make one!"

While the wayward gold embellished Vest Pocket gun cannot be certified as the identical one presented to John M. on that night in Liege, the museum's contact at the FN plant wrote, "The history of unit S/N 456,602 will remain a riddle. All that can be said is that chances are that it is the one presented to J. M. Browning." Based on this admittedly sketchy provenance, a generous supporter purchased the pistol and donated it to the John M. Browning Museum where it is on display alongside its sibling, Val's No. 456,354.

A Pair of Unique Winchester Shotguns

John M. Browning was a Winchester fan. He could afford to be; he had invented all of the rifles and shotguns produced by Winchester from 1883 to 1900. In addition to being a mechanical genius with a flare for innovative repeating gun mechanisms, John M. loved to shoot.

One of John M. Browning's favorite pastimes, when he could bear to leave some unfinished job in the shop, was trap shooting. John M. with his brother Matthew S. Browning and two other Ogden shooters, G. L. Becker and A.P. Bigelow, made up the "Four Bs," a trap team that won national honors around 1900. Photographs of the team show John and Matt holding Winchester M1893 shotguns.

An article in the October 1983 issue of a national trade journal featured the Winchester M1897 shotgun and made some surprising remarks about the unreliability of its predecessor, the M1893; "Unfortunately, the '93 had a mechanical weakness that made rapid firing rather difficult. The trouble generally started when the shooter held backward pressure on the slide as the cartridge was fired. Firing the cartridges also fed the '93's action. Consequently, the shooter was opening the action as the shotgun was fired. Normally the speed of ignition minimized the safety hazard. However, the problem frequently caused jamming and misfires."

When this statement was called to the attention of Mr. Val Browning, he remarked, "Oh, no, that's not so, or my father would never have used the M1893 for trap shooting."

Among the most unique of the guns donated to the city of Ogden for display in the Browning Firearms Museum is the Model 1893 used by John M. with the Four Bs trap team. It's a 12 gauge, S/N 5168, with deluxe wood and engraved on both sides in game scenes, signed by the well-known American engraver, J. Ulrich. The gun shows plenty of signs of heavy use, but the action is still smooth as silk.

Recently, a member of Matthew S. Browning's family mentioned in a casual conversation that he had a gun "just like that one" at home. Inspection proved it to be the M1893 used by Matt, identically engraved and signed, and with the serial No. 5166. Through the courtesy of the present owner, Matt's '93 now hangs alongside his brother John's; they make an unusual and most interesting pair of rare Browning Winchesters.

THE SMITHSONIAN'S BROWNING PORTRAIT

One fall day in 1979, Thomas M. Harding of Birmingham, Michigan, a gun fancier and member of the Smithsonian Institution visited the famous National Portrait Gallery and noticed that the section devoted to outstanding American inventors did not include a portrait of John M. Browning. Mr. Harding wrote to the gallery curator suggesting that the Institution obtain such a portrait. The reply thanked Mr. Harding for his interest and promised that his suggestion would be taken under advisement.

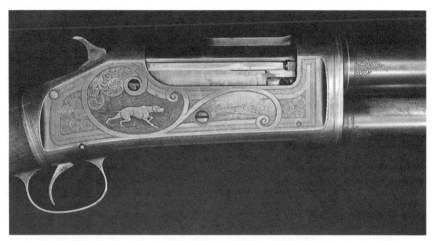

Right side, M1893 12 gauge Trap gun used by John M. as member of "4-Bs" team. Displayed in Browning Firearms Museum.

Left side of John M.'s M1893 Winchester trap gun. An identical model made for brother Matt is also on display in the Firearms Museum.

Not to be so easily put off, Mr. Harding wrote to the Browning Arms Company recommending the Company take action to make a portrait of the inventor available to the Smithsonian. The Company's Public Relations Manager passed the ball to the Browning Firearms Museum Executive Director, Mrs. K. E. Griffith, since the Company had expressed little interest in filling the gap in the National Portrait Gallery's collection of inventor's portraits.

In subsequent correspondence and telephone calls between Ogden and Washington, members of the Smithsonian staff made it clear that Institution policy dictated certain restrictions applicable to the acceptance of portraits to be hung in the National Portrait Gallery. To qualify, the portrait must have been painted from life, ruling out the Ogden suggestion that a British artist, professor of art at the University of Utah, Alvin Gittins, noted for his portraits of Emperor Haile Selasie, Utah Governor Calvin Rampton, and Utah Senators, Jake Garn and Frank Moss, be commissioned to paint a portrait from a photograph.

A member of the local Museum Board of Trustees mentioned the "Smithsonian Portrait Project" to Val Browning, who smiled and said, "I've got one you can have, but I'm not going to pay for sending it to Washington." The life-size portrait by George Henry Taggart had been hanging in the Browning Company Board Room until Val Browning's retirement as an officer of the Company.

According to Mormon Church archives, Taggart was a New York artist who came to Utah for his health. The artist's own diary records Browning's portrait as having been done in 1902, probably in Ogden. The inventor's innate modesty and his well-known dislike of being photographed made it difficult to understand John M.'s willingness to sit still long enough for the completion of a portrait. Val Browning believes that the painting was done in repayment of a loan at a time when Taggart was working on portraits of Mormon Church leaders, probably on a non-reimbursable basis.

Almost three years after Tom Harding's visit to the Smithsonian, a letter dated May 12, 1982, to Val Browning from the National Portrait Gallery read as follows:

> "Dear Mr. Browning: I am happy to inform you that at their meeting on May 11, the members of the National Portrait Gallery Commission accepted your gift of the portrait of your father, John Moses Browning, by George Henry Taggart. This portrait of one of the country's leading inventors will be a great addition to the collection.
>
> "The Commissioners have asked me to thank you for your generous gift on their behalf and on behalf of the Secretary and Regents of the Smithsonian Institution.
> Sincerely,
> /s/ Robert T. Stewart
> Curator"

Oil portrait of John M. by Henry Taggart, ca 1902, now hanging in the Smithsonian Institution, a gift from Val A. Browning, the inventor's son.

THE J. M. BROWNING BRONZE

An outstanding running back and member of the Brigham Young University football team that won two Holiday Bowl games, Blair Buswell, a soft spoken young man with a ready smile, taught sculpture in BYU's art department for two years, 1979-1981. At the same time, his bronzes depicting sports figures were earning national recognition, some of his football pieces having been displayed in a New York art gallery.

In addition to specializing in sports subject, Buswell excelled at portrait busts. One of his best works, a remarkably lifelike bust of Val A. Browning, was presented to the City of Ogden in 1983 for display in the Browning Firearms Museum.

That summer, Buswell accepted a commission from members of the Browning family, friends and the local members of the Browning Collectors Association to create a bust of John M. Browning for placement in the Museum. In discussing the project with reporters later, Buswell said that he had originally intended to make a bust similar to that of Val Browning. Then one day he had come across a photograph of John M. carrying a gun on an elk hunt in the Utah mountains, and decided that a full figure of the inventor showing him with a gun in the field as he might have looked in his prime would be more characteristic.

A few months later, Buswell had finished a ⅓ life-size clay model of a tall hunter carrying an Auto-5 shotgun, the Browning gun best known to the general public. When Val Browning was shown the model, he immediately pointed out a number of details that needed correction. "My father never wore a cowboy hat like that," he said, "and he didn't wear cowboy boots either. He wore full length, laced hunting boots with his pants tucked in."

That was the first of several sessions at Val's home during which he and Buswell spent hours detailing the model. Val showed the sculptor places on the gun's receiver that needed some screws, and pointed out that the gun's front sight was a bead, not a ramp type. Dimensions of the model gun were carefully checked with Buswell's calipers and an Auto-5 from the gun cabinet in Val's study, and John M's boots got their laces properly tied.

At the last of these pleasurable sessions, Val made a final inspection of the gun model and mused to himself. "That stock really ought to be checkered," then glanced up to see the sculptor's reaction. Unperturbed, Buswell reached for a small spatula when Val chuckled and said, "It's fine, Blair, just fine."

The completed bronze figure was delivered to the Museum in early 1985 where it was unveiled and presented to the City by Rodney A. Herrmann, President of the Browning Collectors Association at the time.

THE AMERICAN GUNMAKER MOVIE

The modest man from Ogden whose name was better known in Europe at one time than it was in Utah, had been knighted by the King of Belgium, honored by his own government, saluted by the Smithsonian, and immortalized in bronze. But he received the ultimate American accolade—a movie of his life and accomplishments—from an imaginative film maker from Bountiful, Utah. Lee Groberg, head of Groberg Communications, with the approval and support of Val Browning, wrote, directed and produced the 58-minute video entitled, "American Gunmaker; The John Moses Browning Story," which was previewed before a select audience in Ogden on April 30, 1991. Based in part on the First Edition of the Browning/Gentry book, the film has been aired on the Salt Lake City Public Broadcast System channel, and has received favorable reviews at the national level.

John P. Tartaro, former Executive Editor of Gun Week, wrote in the August 16, 1991, issue, "The American Gunmaker video is technically as good as any TV documentary you might see, and better than most. Hosted and narrated by Fess Parker of Davey Crockett fame, this film deals with the extraordinary contributions of one man to the development of sporting and military arms in the past century. Producer Lee Groberg has caught the essence of the inventive genius of the self-taught Browning."

Clay model of bronze statuette by Blair Buswell, on display in Browning Firearms Museum, Ogden, UT.

The author extends his grateful acknowledgment to Val A. Browning for his encouragement; to his sons, John V. and Bruce W. for their cooperation; and especially to Harmon G. Williams, retired president of Browning, whose recollection of events during his years with the company could not have been so ably presented by anyone else.

The author also wishes to thank Fred and Laura Selman, Browning history buffs and advanced collectors, and Mrs. K. E. Griffith, Executive Director of the Union Station Development Corporation, Ogden, Utah, for their invaluable assistance in the preparation of this work; and to the distinguished author of the First Edition, Curt Gentry, for his concurrence.

Portions of this manuscript have appeared previously in *The American Rifleman,* whose editor has granted permission for their republication.

POSTSCRIPT
BIBLIOGRAPHY

"Armes Browning," Fabrique Nationale, Herstal, Belgium, ca 1927.

Boothroyd, Geoffrey, *"The Handgun,"* Bonanza Books, NY, NY, 1970.

Browning Collectors Association Newsletters, 1979-1989.

John M. Browning Firearms Museum Archives, Ogden, Utah.

Cadiou, Yves L., *"La legende WINCHESTER,"* Le Hussard, France, 1991.

Funken, Felix, diary *"Souvenir of my Activities at Fabrique Nationale, 1 June, 1926 to 30 June, 1960,"* courtesy of M. Claude Gaier, Liege, Belgium.

Gaier, M. Claude *"Four Centuries of Liege Gun Making,"* Liege, Belgium, 1985.

"FN 100 YEARS," with Auguste Francotte, Liege, Belgium, 1989.

"The American Gunmaker, John M. Browning," with EMJY, Fabrique Nationale, Herstal, Belgium, 1978.

A History of Browning Guns from 1831. St. Louis, Missouri: Browning Arms Company, 1942.

Goddard, William H. D. *"The Government Models,"* Andrew Mowbray, Inc., 1988.

Johnson, Melvin M. Jr. and Haven, Charles T., *"Automatic Arms,"* William Morrow Co., NY, NY, 1941.

Rattenbury, Richard, *"The Browning Connection,"* Buffalo Bill Historical Center, Cody, WY, 1982.

Remak, Joachim. *Sarajevo.* New York: Criterion Books, 1959.

Smith, Walter H. B., *"The NRA Book of Small Arms, Vol. I,"* National Rifle Association, Washington DC, 1946.

Stevens, R. Blake, *"The Browning High Power Automatic Pistol,"* Collector Grade Publications, Toronto, Canada, 1982.

Tyler, Homer C., *"Browning .22 Caliber Rifles 1914-1991,"* Walsworth Publishing Co., Marceline, MO, 1992.